This collection brings together current research on morality in human development. Morality in its various forms is a dominant influence on the conduct and evaluation of day-to-day life. The pervasiveness of the moral domain can be detected in every aspect of social life; moral commitments shape the goals and aspirations of individuals, and moral judgments are apparent in discourse about most forms of human interaction. Two broad themes integrate this book: social context and development. Contexts include interpersonal as well as societal communities and cultures. This volume will appeal to scholars from many disciplines, including psychology, anthropology, education, sociology, law, linguistics, and ethics.

Cambridge Studies in Social and Emotional Development

General Editor: Martin L. Hoffman, New York University

Advisory Board: Robert N. Emde, Willard W. Hartup, Robert A. Hinde, Lois W. Hoffman, Carroll E. Izard, Nicholas Blurton Jones, Jerome Kagan, Franz J. Mönks, Paul Mussen, Ross D. Parke, and Michael Rutter

Morality in everyday life

Morality in everyday life

Developmental perspectives

Edited by

MELANIE KILLEN
University of Maryland, College Park

DANIEL HART
Rutgers University

CAMBRIDGE
UNIVERSITY PRESS

Published by the Press Syndicate of the University of Cambridge
The Pitt Building, Trumpington Street, Cambridge CB2 1RP
40 West 20th Street, New York, NY 10011-4211, USA
10 Stamford Road, Oakleigh, Melbourne 3166, Australia

First published 1995

Printed in the United States of America

Library of Congress Cataloging-in-Publication Data
Morality in everyday life: developmental perspectives / edited by
Melanie Killen, Daniel Hart.
p.   cm. – (Cambridge studies in social and emotional
development)
Includes indexes.
ISBN 0-521-45478-6 (hbk.)
1. Moral development.   2. Moral development – Social aspects.
I. Killen, Melanie.   II. Hart, Daniel.   III. Series.
BF723.M54M688   1995
155.2'5 – dc20   94-45499
                                                     ˙   CIP

A catalog record for this book is available from the British Library.

ISBN 0-521-45478-6 Hardback

For Rob and Sasha (M.K.)
For Matthew and Sarah (D.H.)

Contents

vii

Contributors

William Arsenio
Ferkauf Graduate School of
  Psychology
Albert Einstein College of
  Medicine Campus
Bronx, NY

Marvin W. Berkowitz
Department of Psychology
Marquette University
Milwaukee, WI

David M. Bersoff
Department of Psychology
Yale University
New Haven, CT

Jennifer Castle
MRC Child Psychiatry Unit
DeCrespigny Park
Denmark Hill
London

Anne Colby
The Henry Murray Research
  Center
Radcliffe College
Cambridge, MA

Philip A. Cowan
Department of Psychology
University of California, Berkeley
Berkeley, CA

William Damon
Department of Education
Brown University
Providence, RI

Lisa Davies
Section of Perinatal Psychiatry
Institute of Psychiatry
DeCrespigny Park
Denmark Hill
London

Suzanne Fegley
Department of Psychology
Temple University
Philadelphia, PA

Daniel Hart
Department of Psychology
Rutgers, The State University
Camden, NJ

Dale F. Hay
Faculty of Social and Political
  Sciences
Cambridge University
Cambridge, England

Charles C. Helwig
4/F Sidney Hall
100 St. George Street
Toronto, Ontario
Canada

ix

Karl H. Hennig
Department of Psychology
University of British Columbia
Vancouver, British Columbia
Canada

Jeffrey P. Kahn
Center for the Study of Bioethics
Medical College of Wisconsin
Milwaukee, WI

Melanie Killen
Department of Human
   Development
University of Maryland, College
   Park
College Park, MD

Marta Laupa
Department of Psychology
University of Nevada
Las Vegas, NV

Anthony Lover
Ferkauf Graduate School of
   Psychology
Albert Einstein College of
   Medicine Campus
Bronx, NY

M. Kyle Matsuba
Department of Psychology
University of British Columbia
Vancouver, British Columbia
Canada

Joan G. Miller
Department of Psychology
Yale University
New Haven, CT

Gregg Mulry
Center for AIDS Intervention
   Research
Department of Psychiatry and
   Mental Health Sciences
Medical College of Wisconsin
Milwaukee, WI

Larry P. Nucci
College of Education
University of Illinois, Chicago
Chicago, IL

Jeanne Piette
Loyola University of Chicago
Chicago, IL

Russell C. Pitts
Department of Psychology
University of British Columbia
Vancouver, British Columbia
Canada

Judith G. Smetana
Graduate School of Education and
   Human Development
University of Rochester
Rochester, NY

Carol A. Stimson
17 Ogleforth
York, England

Elliot Turiel
School of Education
Tolman Hall
University of California, Berkeley
Berkeley, CA

Cecilia Wainryb
Department of Psychology
University of Utah
Salt Lake City, UT

Lawrence J. Walker
Department of Psychology
University of British Columbia
Vancouver, British Columbia
Canada

Gerry Wilson
Department of Psychology
Rutgers, The State University
Camden, NJ

Miranda Yates
Department of Psychology
The Catholic University of
   America
Washington, DC

Preface

Although the psychological study of morality has many aims, ultimately its goal is to understand how moral regulation occurs in the daily lives of individuals. We believe, as do many of our colleagues, that this goal is now being realized in a range of new lines of investigation. The purpose of this book is to bring together discussions of some of the most original research in this area. For researchers and theorists of morality, the various chapters in the volume present the most current advances and consider as well the complex issues revolving around morality. These include fundamental developmental questions, such as: Where does morality come from and how is it acquired (origins)? How does morality change over time (sequence)? How does culture play a role in the acquisition of morality? What does morality look like throughout the lifespan (ontogenesis)? We asked our contributors to address these issues to the extent that they were relevant to their work, and we especially encouraged our authors to consider the two overall guiding themes for the book: everyday life (context) and development.

None of this work would have been conducted without the ground-breaking studies of morality by Jean Piaget in the 1930s (*The Moral Judgment of the Child*) or by Lawrence Kohlberg in the 1960s, 1970s, and 1980s (see Kohlberg's *Essays in Moral Development,* 1984, for a compilation of his writings). Piaget's and Kohlberg's works were important because, among other things, they sought to outline a structural developmental approach to moral judgment and reasoning. Their projects were vast and covered many aspects of moral development. One of the ways in which current research has moved beyond these foundational works is by providing new approaches for studying how morality is acquired and how moral judgments are constructed out of daily experiences. These are among the themes that pervade the research in this book and are, we believe, what make the current research significant and fundamental.

The idea for bringing together a book on the current psychological research in the field of morality began at a symposium (with the same title as this book) that we organized at the American Psychological Association conference in 1992. The reception to the symposium was very positive and it reminded us, as participants, that many psychologists outside of developmental psychology are still somewhat unfamiliar with the enormous output of exciting, original research that has been conducted on morality in various social contexts over the past few decades. Moreover, much of the psychological work on morality has been influenced by theories and research in the disciplines of anthropology, philosophy, and sociology. Thus, although the focus of this book is on psychological accounts of morality, most of the authors make references to theorists and researchers in other disciplines; this is part of what makes the topic of morality so compelling, enigmatic, and fascinating.

We wish to thank the contributing authors, all of whom submitted thoughtful, insightful chapters. Their conscientiousness in submitting drafts and revisions in a timely manner was greatly appreciated. Julia Hough at Cambridge University Press provided encouragement and thoughtful suggestions at many points in this project; her help was invaluable. Melanie Killen acknowledges support from the Spencer Foundation and the Ford Foundation for her research. Melanie Killen also thanks Bill Damon, Jonas Langer, Paul Mussen, Larry Nucci, Samuel Scheffler, Judith Smetana, and Elliot Turiel for meaningful and influential exchanges about morality and development, and the many undergraduates and Master's students at Wesleyan University who generously and enthusiastically participated in her various research projects. Dan Hart acknowledges the generous support of the Lilly Endowment's Program on Youth and Caring directed by Joan Lipsitz. Dan Hart also thanks Anne Colby, Bill Damon, Al Patterson, Mark Reinhalter, Larry Walker, and Jim Youniss for useful discussions on morality and everyday life.

Introduction: Perspectives on morality in everyday life

Daniel Hart and Melanie Killen

Morality in its various forms is a dominant influence on the conduct and evaluation of day-to-day life. The pervasiveness of the moral domain can be detected in nearly every aspect of life: Appeals to rights and responsibilities are found in the discourse occurring in every sphere of social life; moral commitments shape the goals and aspirations that give direction to individuals' lives; moral judgments are constituent elements in the determination of appropriate courses of action in situations involving opposing values; and the patterning of emotions (e.g., shame, guilt) within an individual often is influenced by engagement with moral issues. It is because of its centrality in understanding human affairs that morality has received such focused attention from scholars in a wide variety of disciplines (psychology, anthropology, sociology, education, government, and philosophy). Our goal for this volume was to bring together the best of the recent work by psychologists interested in morality.

Psychological research of the past decade has primed the field for a focused discussion of morality. The cumulation of findings has provided the foundation for a number of fruitful efforts to explain when, how, and why persons act morally. In our view, much of the psychological research on morality can be framed within three issues: (1) the role of judgment, (2) developmental acquisition and transformation, and (3) moral integration and character. Each of the chapters in this book addresses these issues in varying ways; there is broad consensus among authors concerning the role of judgment, substantial agreement concerning the importance of developmental acquisition and transformation, and a range of perspectives concerning moral character. In this chapter, the connection of these issues both to morality in everyday life and to the various chapters that follow is outlined.

1

Judgment in morality

A fundamental question for psychological and philosophical analysis of morality in everyday life is this: Do persons make reflective judgments about the real moral issues of daily life that in turn guide behavior? Many influential philosophers and psychologists believe that persons do make reflective judgments in the course of daily life. Kant (1785/1959), for instance, believed that when faced with a moral problem in daily life persons frequently judge whether a line of action is an appropriate response by asking themselves, What would be the consequence if *everyone* did this? with the result of this hypothetical reflective judgment influencing behavior. In psychology, Piaget (1932) and Kohlberg (1969, 1984) reached a similar conclusion and studied the ways in which reflective moral judgments are transformed over the course of development. Most of the major psychological accounts of morality of the past 20 years have expanded on these traditions and, in so doing, have accorded judgment a central role in human morality.

Whereas psychologists substantially agree that judgment is an essential component of a full account of moral life, nonpsychologists who are unfamiliar with current psychological research often reject such a conclusion. Frequently, these critics base their rejection of judgment on "behavioristic" interpretations of the role of emotion that have their roots in Hume (1739/1969) and contemporary advocates among Blum (1987) and Murdoch (1970). Emotivist philosophies are taken to demonstrate that moral emotions control behavior directly and are unmediated by judgment. From these positions critics, such as J. Q. Wilson (1993), conclude that moral reasoning is unimportant in real moral life:

When people act fairly or sympathetically it is rarely because they have engaged in much systematic reasoning. Much of the time our inclination toward fair play or our sympathy for the plight of others is immediate and instinctive, a reflex of our emotions more than an act of our intellect, and in those cases in which we do deliberate (for example, by struggling to decide what fair play entails or duty requires in a particular case), our deliberation begins, not with philosophical premises (much less with the justification for them), but with feelings – in short with a moral sense. The feelings on which people act are often superior to the arguments that they employ. (pp. 7–8)

What gives rise to this noncognitive (behavioristic) emphasis on the emotions as the key to morality? Biologically directed emotions are attractive because they appear to permit the construction of theories of human morality that derive directly from physiology and anatomy. Emotion-based theories offer naturalist and evolutionist views of human ethical conduct according to which morality is just one more quality of persons (such as the human thumb opposing the fingers, or widened feet to permit upright walking) offering an adaptational advantage that leads to its universal presence in the species. Morality could then be directly linked to sociobiology and the study of evolution, thereby gaining scientific credence for the topic as an area of study.

The rejection of reflective judgment in favor of emotions also reflects the deep distrust many psychologists have for persons' construals of self and the world. This distrust is the legacy of both past and current trends in the field: the individual's sense of the self and the world first came under scrutiny from Freud (1930/1961) and his colleagues, who suggested that the important forces driving a person were "unconscious" and not available to self-reflection. This same sort of bias continues in the current cognitive zeitgeist where the information processing constituting much of psychological functioning is thought to consist of "cognitively impenetrable" skills, which operate out of conscious awareness (see Hart, 1992, for a discussion). Psychologists come to view the essence of human nature as that which is outside of the limits of consciousness. Emotions, because they appear to be automatic reactions subject to intentional modulation but not elimination or redirection, become windows to the human soul (hence the fascination with polygraphs as measures of truthtelling, etc.).

We believe this to be a problematic trend for accounts of morality for several reasons. First, the demotion of reflective reasoning risks being imperialistic, restricting thoughtful consideration of moral judgments to Western philosophers and denying it to the "masses" who are judged to respond mindlessly to environmental stimuli (Putnam, 1990). Second, it may be true that persons lack awareness of their own Oedipal complexes (to give a Freudian example) or availability biases (for a cognitive example). But moral regulation is unusually public: Persons discuss and argue about which lines of action are morally correct, and how such judgments can be aligned with legal codes, religious obligations, and the expectations of particular relationships. These exchanges pervade human social life. Under such conditions reflective access to moral principles undoubtedly is widened.

Fundamentally, however, the banishment of judgment and the reification of emotions as the source of morality is incomplete: Both conceptually and empirically this route fails to arrive at a satisfactory account. Charles Taylor (1989) has described other reasons for efforts to dispense with judgment in accounts of morality:

An important strand of modern naturalist consciousness has tried to hive . . . [judgment] off and declare it dispensable or irrelevant to morality. The motives are multiple: partly distrust of all such ontological accounts because of the use to which some of them have been put, e.g., justifying restrictions or exclusions of heretics or allegedly lower beings. And this distrust is strengthened when a primitivist sense that unspoiled human nature respects life by instinct reigns. But it is partly also the great epistemological cloud under which all such accounts lie for those who have followed empiricist or rationalist theories of knowledge, inspired by the success of modern natural science. (p. 5)

The cynicism about human reason and the belief in innate human qualities to which Taylor points as reasons for the abandonment of judgment in discussions of human morality are, he believes, unfortunate because it is impossible to achieve a satisfactory account of ethical conduct with some attention to judgment. Taylor writes:

Our moral reactions . . . have two facets, as it were. On one side, they are almost like instincts, comparable to our love of sweet things, or our aversion to nauseous substances, or our fear of failing; on the other, they seem to involve claims, implicit or explicit, about the nature and status of human beings. From this second side, a moral reaction is an assent to, an affirmation of, a given ontology of the human.

Taylor argues that if it were the case that moral reactions were merely instincts, then there would be little interest in considering the nature of the objects that elicited these reactions. Nausea, for instance, is elicited by particular environmental stimuli: Taylor points out that persons do not ordinarily argue whether one should or ought to be nauseous in response to a particular stimulus. However, the commonness of moral discussion and argument (p. 6) about what objects in the world deserve a moral reaction demonstrates that moral reactions *are* significantly different; moral reactions, Taylor suggests, necessarily reflect judgments about the nature of humans. Further, pointing to the importance of judgment in moral development does not demote the essential role that moral emotions play in the developmental process. Many investigators have shown that children use moral emotions as significant information, which they use to make judgments about the impact that their actions have on others (see Arsenio and Lover, Chapter 3, this volume; Dunn, 1988; Nunner-Winkler & Sodian, 1988).

A full account of morality must therefore be centrally concerned with judgment. Many of the chapters in this volume discuss in detail the nature of moral and social judgments in the specific contexts of daily life. This analysis takes place at two interrelated levels: cultural and relational. Moral thought and behavior develops in persons living in social groups that have historically transmitted norms, beliefs, and traditions. One of the challenges taken on by researchers in the past 20 years is the specification of the ways in which such cultural traditions influence social and moral judgments so as to influence the types of social and moral judgments made from persons of different cultural backgrounds. Although there is as yet no final answer to this question, considerable progress is being made, as chapters by Miller and Bersoff (Chapter 8, this volume) and Wainryb and Turiel (Chapter 9, this volume) demonstrate.

Specific relationships also influence the ways in which persons judge moral and social issues. Persons are involved in a range of relationships, each of which has different expectations and responsibilities: Children, for instance, must be able to regulate interactions with peers, resolve conflicts with parents, negotiate their obligations to social institutions like school, and so on. Each relationship context poses moral and social problems that elicit judgments attuned to both the unique features of the particular relationship and the general features of prototypical relationships. The consequence is that from a young age humans make moral judgments that reflect the relational context in which they occur. Many of the chapters that follow examine the differentiation of judgment across relational contexts.

Acquisition and developmental transformations of morality

How is morality acquired? Originally, the predominant explanations of the acquisition of morality focused on the role of the parents as transmitters of values to children. For example, Freud's explanation was tied to the formation of the superego which was a result of identifying with, and incorporating, parental values. Learning theorists assumed that morality was acquired through conditioning; parental use of rewards and punishments served as the mechanism by which children adopted parental values. One of the important aspects of Piaget's (1932) moral judgment theory was to point out that parents are but one source of morality. Piaget postulated that peers play an important role because relations of equality (peers) are more central for constructing an understanding of equality than are relations of constraint (parent–child). Further, Piaget's theory of acquisition was social-cognitive; children construct categories of equality and fairness based on their active reflection of their own experiences – in particular, ones that are cooperative in nature.

Research over the past several decades has revealed the multitude of experiences that are important for the acquisition of morality. These include diverse peer experiences, adult–child interactions, and cultural influences. Most theorists investigate how children interpret their experiences, acknowledging that the child's assimilation of, and reflection upon, social experiences as central to understanding how the experience plays a role in the child's acquisition of moral judgment (see Turiel, Killen, & Helwig, 1987, for a review). Early peer experiences that are considered to be important include reactions to the distress of peers (Hoffman, 1982; Zahn-Waxler & Radke-Yarrow, 1990) and sympathetic and empathetic responses to others (Eisenberg, 1982). Rather than viewing the young child as passive, research has shown that the young child actively constructs social and moral categories based on these diverse experiences (Damon, 1983; Turiel, 1983; Youniss, 1980).

Yet, some theorists dismiss the role of cognition in the child's moral acquisition process. Again, Wilson (1993), to use his writings as an example of a current nonpsychological perspective, offers a behavioristic explanation for ethical development:

Children do not learn morality by learning maxims or clarifying values. They enhance their natural sentiments by being regularly induced by families, friends, and institutions to behave in accord with the most obvious standards of right conduct—fair dealing, reasonable self-control, and personal honesty. A moral life is perfected by practice more than by precept; children are not taught so much as habituated. (p. 249)

The implicit folk theory in Wilson's argument is that children can be trained to become moral citizens through rewards and punishments; reinforcement by parents, friends, and social institutions will be sufficient to establish ("habituate") the correct patterns of behavior in children. As our argument for the centrality of judgment in morality made clear, we believe that this view is in error. Children, like adults, interpret their worlds and make action-determining judgments based on their understanding. Strangely, Wilson ignores the voluminous body of research showing that children interpret, evaluate, and reflect on messages and directives communicated by parents and society in myriad ways.

For example, current research has shown that the acquisition of morality is not a straightforward, unidirectional transmission process (see Grusec & Goodnow, 1994; Maccoby & Martin, 1983) but a bidirectional one (children influence parents and vice versa). Training and habituation have not been shown to be mechanisms that facilitate moral behaviors. Parental use of reinforcement does not always promote moral behavior (e.g., parental attempts to encourage sharing in toddlers does little to facilitate their sharing behavior as reported by H. Ross & Lollis, 1989). Researchers have repeatedly demonstrated ways in which behavioristic accounts of the acquisition of prosocial and moral behaviors are inadequate, particularly because the role of judgment is disregarded (Hay, 1994; Turiel & Smetana, 1984).

In their extensive review of parental discipline methods in relation to the development of values, Grusec & Goodnow (1994) demonstrate how the model advocated by Wilson (parents controlling children through reinforcement) is fundamentally wrong; it is essential to understand the child's perception and interpretation of parental messages. The child's cognitive interpretation of the parental action, as appropriate, for example, influences the extent to which the child internalizes a given value. Research has revealed the different types of justifications children give when evaluating different types of transgressions (Grusec & Pederson, 1989; Smetana, 1985) and the way that the child's judgment of appropriateness influences the effectiveness of the parental message (Nucci, 1984; Killen, Breton, Ferguson, & Handler, 1994).

Grusec and Goodnow (1994) point out how parents vary their discipline practices as a function of the nature of the social or moral transgression and children must make sense of these various methods of discipline. For example, parents use a combination of power assertion and reasoning when responding to moral transgressions but use reasoning alone when responding to a failure to show concern for others (Grusec, Dix, & Mills, 1982). Further, research on family interactions has shown that when parents use Socratic styles of discourse children use more advanced levels of moral reasoning (Walker & Taylor, 1991). These findings lend support to our claim that children are not passively adopting parental values. The acquisition of morality is not accomplished by parental training; rather, it is based on a gradual developmental process in which children interpret, transform, and evaluate norms and values.

Because persons are active contributors to their own development – interpreting their world and making judgments that determine their actions in it – there is substantial change from infancy in their moral participation in everyday life. These developmental transformations have been most extensively studied in the domain of judgment, where a great deal has been learned about the ontogenesis of moral reasoning. This research has demonstrated that moral understanding is acquired through a process of reflection about social experiences and interaction. The individual constructs moral principles by participating in social interactions, encountering social problems with moral dimensions (e.g., sharing, harming others, turn taking), formulating solutions to these problems through the use of the child's current moral principle adapted for the situation through either symbolic social exchange (role taking) or genuine collaboration with others (co-construction), and finally observing the satisfactoriness of the solution once it is implemented. Change in moral reasoning occurs when an individual recognizes a shortcoming in his or her moral principle and gradually articulates a more adequate one. It is important to note that the process through which moral thought and behavior develop is quite general: All sorts of social interactions can provide the necessary ingredients for growth.

Moral integration and character

One of the most fundamental questions about morality is one that we know the least about: How are moral behavior and judgment related and integrated to form what is often referred to as moral character. This complex issue involves a number of interrelated questions: How is moral judgment related to moral behavior? How are moral principles applied in actual contexts? To what extent is moral functioning a product of the integration of different social and moral experiences? Numerous debates have arisen around these issues, sometimes collapsing and combining these various questions which, we believe, each call for separate in-depth analysis.

For example, Darley (1993), a social psychologist, in reviewing the recent *Handbook of Moral Behavior and Development* edited by Kurtines and Gewirtz (1991), claims that findings in cognitive psychology cast into doubt the possibility of broad principles of judgment:

Largely unnoticed by moral judgment researchers, modern cognitive psychology has developed an alternative to rule-based learning: instance-based learning, which Estes (1993) summarized as follows: "Rather than generating abstract . . . rules at an early stage of processing and retaining these for future use, the system simply retains a large array of information in a form that makes it accessible to computations when the test situation arises" (p. 144). The recognition of the implications of this modern cognitive view of reasoning is the most urgent agenda that researchers studying moral reasoning face. (1993, p. 354)

Darley's depiction of moral judgment, in which persons carry with them knowledge of many specific situations and the appropriate reactions for them, is consistent with the contextualist emphasis increasingly popular in psychology and philosophy (see Helwig, Chapter 5, this volume for critical consideration of this perspective). But it is not necessarily inconsistent with principled views of moral judgment (which, in Darley's terms, are dismissive of contextual considerations).

In our view there are at least three interrelated, but different, issues involved in Darley's claim: (1) the rejection of general, global structures that reflect moral principles, such as the ones proposed by Kohlberg; (2) the question of how principles, of any sort, are applied to actual contexts; and (3) the relationship between moral judgment and moral action. Regarding the first issue, there has been much work in the field that has empirically demonstrated domain-specific social and moral reasoning (Damon, 1977, 1983; Nucci, 1981; Smetana, 1985; Turiel, 1983; Youniss,

1980). This work has already challenged the view that there are general, global structures applicable in all settings. The research has shown that individuals make distinct judgments about the self, society, and morality that reflect different domains of social knowledge. Just as research in cognitive areas has shifted toward domain-specific reasoning models (Feldman, 1980; Keil, 1986; Siegler, 1984), so, too, have researchers in the social and moral area.

This does not mean that moral principles do not govern social judgment. We believe that knowledge of a person's moral principles is often crucial for understanding that person's thought, emotions, and behavior. This point is made both by developmental psychologists (e.g., Colby & Damon, Chapter 11, this volume; Wainryb & Turiel, Chapter 9, this volume), social psychologists (L. Ross & Nisbett, 1991), and philosophers (Dworkin, 1993). For example, Dworkin argues convincingly that many of the apparently conflicting judgments made by individuals concerning abortion and euthanasia can be understood by reference to principles. For instance, Dworkin points to former U.S. President George Bush's claims that (1) abortion is murder, and (2) he would comfort and assuage his daughter if she decided to have an abortion. The two claims apparently are inconsistent because Bush would not suggest that he would comfort his daughter if she murdered her two-year-old. But Dworkin suggests that there is no inconsistency if one posits that the principle underlying the abortion debate is that a fetus is not truly a human (therefore abortion is not really murder), but as a precursor possesses some of the sacredness of human life and therefore must be treated with great respect (and therefore its destruction in abortion is regrettable). Inferring such a principle, Dworkin demonstrates, explains the ways in which superficially inconsistent judgments in fact are generated by the same underlying principle.

Although we believe that there are good reasons to infer that persons do form principles that guide their moral and social judgments, the chapters in this book make clear that the number of moral principles and their relation to each other is not yet known. Clearly, persons make principled distinctions among different sorts of issues; those which are genuinely moral, for instance, are understood in different ways than those which concern arbitrary social conventions. But how judgments from different principles are reconciled and synthesized has only recently been studied.

Second, how principles are applied to actual contexts has not been ignored by philosophical and psychological advocates of principled moral reasoning. Despite frequent mischaracterizations to the contrary, Kant – the exemplar of advocates for principled reasoning – emphasized the importance of context in making moral judgments (Dietrichson, 1964, p. 169) and recognized as well that persons commonly made correct intuitive moral judgments without resorting to reflective use of the categorical imperative (Kant, 1785/1959), p. 72). Kant believed that both context and habitual responding could be accommodated within his theory. Psychologists like Piaget and Kohlberg have claimed that habit and reflexive action could be reconciled with reflective judgment. Although the details vary among psychological theories, the various paradigms generally agree that habit and reflective judgment can be imagined as part of a single dialectical process: Actions are emitted, the actor reflects upon the action and its consequences, with this reflection leading to broad principles or rules, which in turn result in modification of future actions. Both habit and principle characterize psychological functioning from this perspective. The difficulty for research in both areas of cognitive and moral psychology is how to document this process and how to investigate it empirically. In both realms of psychology, this work is warranted and, yet, difficult to undertake.

The third issue, that of the relationship between moral judgment and action, taps into deep and significant aspects of morality (How do our judgments inform our actions and vice versa?), and again, this aspect of what we have termed *moral integration* is enigmatic. The relationship between moral judgment and moral behavior has often been interpreted in terms of the variability that people exhibit in their moral behaviors across contexts. As Darley (1993) asserts (as have others, e.g., Brown & Hernstein, 1975):

There is an obvious and systematic tension between the developmental and social approaches; one emphasizes the inner determinants of morality, implying a consistency in an individual's behavior across situations, and the other finds the individual responsive to situational variation and therefore inconsistent in behavior. (p. 354)

While several generations of social psychological research have resulted in a long catalog of environmental factors that strongly influence the likelihood that persons will react prosocially in various experimental situations, other coexisting lines of social psychological research have interpreted contextual variation from cognitive viewpoints and have made links between individuals' attributions of situations and contextual variation (Asch, 1952/1987; Saltzstein, 1994; L. Ross & Nisbett, 1991). In his famous series of experiments, Milgram (1974) was able to show that the likelihood that a person would administer painful electrical shocks to an innocent other at the request of an authoritarian experimenter could be substantially altered by manipulating a number of factors, including the salience of the innocent other, the status of the authoritarian experimenter, and the social support the person received for refusing to provide the shock. Latane and Darley (1970) concluded that numerous factors influence the probability that a bystander will respond with aid to someone in need. The apparent ease with which behavior can be experimentally manipulated in social psychological investigations, combined with findings that apparently virtuous behavior in one context does not imply virtuous behavior in another (Hartshorne & May, 1928–1930) led many investigators to conclude that moral judgment and moral action are unrelated.

Yet, Asch (1952/1987) and more current social psychologists (L. Ross & Nisbett, 1991) have also provided evidence that what seems to be simple shifts in behavior alone is actually changes in subjects' attributions of situations; therefore, judgment influences behavior, rather than changes in behavior being merely a result of shifts in contextual variation. In other words, changing the stimulus that people respond to influences their interpretation of the situation and, thus, their new attribution of the situation changes their behavior rather than their behavior being influenced without such cognitive mediation.

We believe that those who dismiss the idea that judgment is integrally related to behavior have often rushed to do so without sufficient consideration of several key points. The first of these is that many of the behaviors that researchers have considered moral or nonmoral actions are not clearly so. It has been pointed out by Blasi (1980), Saltzstein (1994), and Turiel and Smetana (1984) that investigators frequently confuse moral and nonmoral social behaviors. As a consequence, research that demonstrates that a person emits two different behaviors (e.g., is honest with money in an experimental situation, but occasionally smokes marijuana, the latter not being clearly a moral issue in the United States) is wrongly interpreted as moral inconsistency.

Indeed, relations between different actions are likely to be detected *only* when the perspective of the subject is taken into consideration. Consistency cannot be expected to emerge from the researcher's personal cataloging of moral and nonmoral actions. This point is particularly clear in research by Krappmann and Oswald (1991), who studied in unusual detail the lives of children in the classrooms. In one of their analyses, Krappmann and Oswald examined acts of helping among children in the classroom. At first glance, their results suggest variability: Children frequently did, but often did not, aid their classmates.

However the detailed descriptions collected by Krappman and Oswald suggest that an accurate understanding of helping in the classroom is not to be found in the superficial conclusion that children sometimes do and sometimes do not assist their classmates. Rather, Krappmann and Oswald found that children made decisions about providing aid by weighing both the right of the person requesting the help to do so (friends have better grounds to expect assistance than other peers) and the goal toward which the help-requester was working (help was less frequently offered when the help-requester was attempting to achieve a competitive advantage of some sort over fellow classmates).

What appears at first glance to be inconsistency in the helping behavior of children in the classroom – and, through extension, evidence against the coherence of moral behavior – is actually much more complex when the behavior is studied more carefully. The consistency in a child's behavior is not to be found in the mindless emission of superficially similar behaviors, but in the judgments and principles that result in coherent decisions to help or not to help classmates. For instance, one might usually help friends, but refuse to do so when the friend is seeking to take advantage of others, or when the friend is known to reject the help that was solicited; the consistency of this pattern is to be found in the judgment process.

A fair reading of the research literature would indicate that the extent of consistency, and the means through which it is achieved, are mostly unknown. We know little about how the acute sensitivity of persons of all ages to context in making social and moral judgments is balanced by the coordination of these judgments with principles. Similarly, our understanding of how persons are able to synthesize moral principles with action to result in consistent moral action is quite limited. However, some light is shed on both issues in the chapters by Colby and Damon, Hart and his colleagues, and Walker et al.

Chapters in this volume

We now turn to an introduction of the chapters in this volume, which we believe provide further evidence for our claim that an impressive amount of studies and investigations has been conducted over the past decade revealing the importance of the role of judgment, and the ways in which morality is acquired and transformed in the context of familiar, everyday social interactions and social contexts.

We organized this volume into parts that reflect our view of the central issues in the field of moral development: (I) *The Acquisition of Morality* (Hay, Castle, Stimson, & Davies; Killen & Nucci; Arsenio & Lover); (II) *Social Judgment in Different Contexts* (Laupa, Turiel, & Cowan; Helwig; Berkowitz, Kahn, Mulry, & Piette; Smetana); (III) *Social Judgment in Different Cultures* (Miller & Bersoff; Wainryb & Turiel); and (IV) *Moral Integration and Character* (Hart, Yates, Fegley, & Wilson; Colby & Damon; Walker, Pitts, Hennig, & Matsuba). We created two sections for social judgment: context and culture. Although culture *is* a context, its study raises issues unique to the field of morality and these sets of issues warrant a section separate from the more general topic of context.

The acquisition of morality

The first three chapters address issues pertaining to the acquisition of morality and involve investigations of social interaction and judgment in early and middle childhood. Dale F. Hay, Jennifer Castle, Carol A. Stimson, and Lisa Davies describe their research on morality in the context of early social relationships. Their specific focus is on the construction of character in the second year of life. In their work, character is defined in terms of the orientation to demonstrate moral behaviors, particularly to behavior revolving around sharing toys and resources. Interestingly, their findings show that neither modeling nor reinforcement increase the likelihood of a toddler's sharing behavior. Rather, the playing of "give-and-take" with adults increases sharing behavior. Their review of the literature shows that virtually all normal infants offer and give toys to others. Yet, they also find that the tendency to share decreases after the second year of life; preschoolers become more possessive of their objects. Because children get more, rather than less, moral with age, this decline in sharing behavior suggests that objects take on a different meaning to children, particularly in different social contexts. Early moral behaviors, such as sharing toys, are not simply skills that are acquired in a unidirectional fashion. Hay and her colleagues consider the implications of interactions with peers for the development of moral principles that govern social interactions with parents and other adults.

Melanie Killen and Larry P. Nucci's chapter continues the examination of early social interaction and the development of morality in young children. The aim of Killen and Nucci's chapter is to argue for a reconceptualization of the relationship between morality and autonomy in early development. Killen and Nucci propose that viewing morality and autonomy as integral aspects of early development rather than as polar opposites of a single dimension helps to understand the dynamics of young children's conflicts and conflict resolutions as well as their emerging sense of self and personal agency. Killen and Nucci describe findings with preschool-age children and their peers in order to show that children's justifications for personal claims and entitlements to objects coexist with their emerging justifications of fairness. The authors assert that conflicts are not necessarily a "clash of blind desires" but are often disagreements about legitimate claims of the self and claims of others. This is also the case with Japanese children, as Killen reports, from a recent study conducted in Tokyo with her collaborator, Lina

Sueyoshi. The authors then report on children's developing understanding of personal agency and the ways in which these categories are constructed in mother–child interactions. Mothers and children together identify specific content areas that fall within the jurisdiction of personal choice and personal agency (e.g., choosing what to wear to school). Killen and Nucci review recent research conducted in Brazil (by Nucci and his collaborators) that supports their claim about the universality of the role of personal agency in social and moral development. The authors propose that reformulating conflicts as struggles between autonomy and morality rather than as between selfish, egoistic, desires will generate positive forms of intervention as well as recast the way social and moral development has been characterized.

William Arsenio and Anthony Lover provide a detailed analysis of the role of emotions and affect in the acquisition of moral judgment. Arsenio and Lover present a theoretical model in which children's conceptions of sociomoral affect–effects links allow them to anticipate the consequences of their actions, and therefore permit them to select appropriate behaviors. In a review of findings from their own studies and those of others, Arsenio and Lover demonstrate that children believe that moral and immoral behaviors elicit very different patterns of emotional response. This model is also used to examine conduct-disordered children. Research indicating that conduct-disordered children expect sociomoral acts to have distinctly different emotional consequences than their more typical peers is described, and it suggests a potential link between maladaptive social behavior and unusual emotional expectancies. In the conclusion, Arsenio and Lover examine both the value of considering moral emotions as the "raw material" for the construction of broad moral principles in adolescence and adulthood and the importance of variations in sociomoral contexts for understanding children's highly differentiated conceptions of moral emotions.

Social judgment in different contexts

The second section, which examines moral judgment, begins with a chapter by Marta Laupa, Elliot Turiel, and Philip A. Cowan exploring the difficult question of obedience to authority. They provide an alternative view to the classic cognitive-developmental one (which states that an authority orientation comprises a stage in children's social-cognitive development). Laupa and colleagues propose that children's concepts of authority are influenced by (1) the type of command, (2) the attributes of authority figures, and (3) the social context. The authors describe a collaborative study on authority in the family context; they cite protocols from children regarding their conceptualizations of rules in the home: those that do and do not fall under parental jurisdiction. In their conclusion, Laupa and her colleagues consider the ways in which children's thinking about the family rule system is related to an understanding of other authority relationships (e.g., school) and how this is related to the more general and fundamental issue of obedience to authority.

In the second chapter of this section, Charles C. Helwig provides an insightful analysis of social context and uses this examination as an introduction to his own work on conceptions of psychological harm and civil liberties. Helwig discusses how theorists have defined and studied social context, and he argues that an adequate account of social context must go beyond mere documentation of shifts in, or influences upon, social judgments as a function of changing environmental conditions. A differentiated view of social context is needed that accounts for how various aspects of situations are represented in and engage the individual's developing conceptual structures. Helwig proposes that variation in moral judgment and reasoning is a function of diverse social concepts that are implicated in situational contexts. This requires the joint consideration of two potential sources of variation: that due to (1) the types of social and moral issues brought to bear in making a decision or judgment, and (2) developmental level. Helwig reviews data that show how the intersection of these two sources of variation illuminate our understanding of context and development in two areas: judgments of psychological harm in the elementary school years, and judgments of civil liberties and rights in adolescence and adulthood. In his conclusion, Helwig considers how specific categories of social and moral concepts are coordinated at different periods in development.

In the third chapter in this section, Marvin W. Berkowitz, Jeffrey P. Kahn, Gregg Mulry, and Jeanne Piette discuss moral judgment in the context of concerns about self-harm and substance use. Berkowitz and his colleagues consider drug use to be a particularly valuable issue for considering adolescents' understanding of their obligations to (1) society (one ought to refrain from illegal activities), and (2) themselves (one ought to consider the self-harm that may result from drug use). The authors provide an illuminating discussion of the psychological and philosophical status of self-harm and prudence. This theoretical analysis leads into their empirical study called Project Decide, an ambitious undertaking designed to investigate relationships between social reasoning and substance use. Their findings are quite revealing about the complex ways in which adolescents' categorizations of acts as moral, conventional, or personal are related to adolescents' actual substance use. Their discussion of adolescents' understanding of self-harm and ethics provides empirical support for the influence of social judgment guiding behavior.

In the final chapter in this section, Judith G. Smetana discusses the influence of context and development on adolescents' (and parents') conceptions of adult authority and on their moral reasoning in adolescent–parent conflict. In this thorough analysis of adolescent–parent interactions, Smetana discusses the different ways context has been conceptualized in the research and she describes several studies in order to demonstrate how conceptions of adult authority are influenced by (1) the domain of the issue (moral, conventional, prudential, and personal), (2) the type of adult authority (teacher versus parent), (3) the type of family structure (married versus divorced), and (4) the style of parental authority (authoritative, authoritarian, and permissive). Smetana also describes studies that have examined adolescents' social reasoning in real-life adolescent–parent situations. Interestingly, she finds that the majority of conflicts in actual situations pertain to interpersonal relations rather than to moral issues specifically. Despite the low frequency of moral conflicts in parent–adolescent interactions, adolescents view adults as having authority over these issues in actual family conflicts. Smetana asserts that contextual factors primarily affect judgments regarding the boundaries of adolescents' personal jurisdiction but that moral reasoning appears to be stable across contexts.

Social judgment in different cultures

The two chapters in this section have analyzed morality in varying cultural contexts over the lifespan. In the first of these chapters, Joan G. Miller and David Bersoff examine the moral obligations of family life in two very different cultures: the United States and India. Miller and Bersoff review their own research, which indicates that what is perceived to be morally obligatory in the context of the family varies substantially between the cultures. For instance, Americans are found to emphasize the importance of relationship building and communicating emotions for family life. In contrast, Hindu Indians tend to stress the importance of individuals being able to subordinate their personal desires in responding to the requirements of the family as a whole. Additionally, Hindu Indians tend to maintain that acting out of duty is fundamental in family relationships and provides individuals with their own satisfaction. In their conclusion, Miller and Bersoff suggest that morality in the context of the family is best understood as an extension of the larger cultural context; the family magnifies cultural norms, but it does not create a context qualitatively different from that of the culture itself.

In the second chapter in this section, Cecilia Wainryb and Elliot Turiel analyze the concept of culture and make a compelling case for a critique of holistic approaches. In their view, theorists who postulate general and homogeneous cultural orientations (e.g., individualism, collectivism) actually produce limited views of social diversity, particularly within-culture diversity. They describe research they have conducted with the Druze communities in Israel in order to support their view that individualism and collectivism coexist within cultures rather than reflect general cultural orientations. The Druze is a small, old Arabic community that is hierarchically organized (collectivistic), and, at the same time oriented to rights and entitlements (individualism). Wainryb and Turiel forcefully assert that it is necessary to analyze the social context of everyday life in order to understand the complexities of cultures and social judgments.

Moral integration and character

In this final section, research on moral commitment and moral character is described. Daniel Hart, Miranda Yates, Suzanne Fegley, and Gerry Wilson consider both the developmental and contextual prerequisites for the emergence of the acceptance of community responsibilities in adolescence. They are interested in understanding what it is that motivates individuals to help others voluntarily, especially in situations in which their own state of being is fairly impoverished. Hart and his colleagues review some of their own research on inner-city adolescents who have worked hard to improve their communities. The sources of their commitments to their communities – as well as the psychological costs of them – are analyzed in order to elucidate the complex intertwining of development and social support in the emergence of moral character. Hart and colleagues examine the difficulties in sustaining these moral commitments over the threshold of adulthood.

Anne Colby and William Damon continue the discussion of the relation between societal and cultural influences on moral judgments in their chapter on moral commitments. Colby and Damon review their own research on individuals who have shown exceptional commitment to the social good over several decades of their lives. Building on this review, Colby and Damon describe their model called "transformation of goals through social influence." According to this model, development occurs as the result of the interaction of the goals, motives, values, and beliefs people bring to situations they encounter as they pursue their goals. The social influences they then engage with, in turn, transform their goals. One of the central organizing constructs in this approach, then, is the influence of the social context in the development of moral commitment. Colby and Damon discuss the various social contexts that sustained the moral commitments of their subjects (e.g., religious traditions and communities) and consider as well the continuities and transformations across the lifespan of moral commitment, including important moral changes at midlife and beyond.

In the final chapter in this section, Lawrence J. Walker, Russell C. Pitts, Karl H. Hennig, and M. Kyle Matsuba discuss their research on social influences on individuals, which uses a methodology similar to Colby and Damon's. In this chapter, as with Colby and Damon, the authors are interested in studying the societal influences that bear on how individuals construe morality over the lifespan. Walker and his colleagues review their own studies in which persons were intensively interviewed about their conceptions of morality (e.g., the nature of the moral domain, how moral problems should be handled, criteria for moral exemplars) and their reasoning about a variety of moral conflicts (recent real-life moral conflicts, most difficult moral conflicts). In addition, Walker and his colleagues report on research in which they analyzed the types of moral exemplars that individuals believe are important to them (family, friends, religious leaders, humanitarians) as well as the types of characteristics that are essential (compassion, consistency, self-sacrificing). The analysis of moral issues highlights the relation of age to context, as the moral concerns salient for the older adults are found to be different from those with which the younger adults articulate. In addition to being one of the first systematic reports of moral conceptions at different points in adulthood, this chapter shows that context and development are as intertwined near the end of life as they are at its beginning.

Conclusions

In sum, the contributions in this book provide the groundwork for investigating the social contexts of morality from a developmental perspective. This includes defining context in terms of salient aspects of experience, such as the nature of social relationships, social interactions, and social events, and in terms of dimensions of social judgments, such as the ways in which judgments and beliefs influence the structure and interpretation of the social context. We believe that these approaches to studying context shed new light on the origins, acquisition, and sequencing of morality in social development.

References

Asch, S. (1952/1987). *Social psychology.* Oxford: Oxford University Press.
Blasi, A. (1980). Bridging moral cognition and moral action: A critical review of the literature. *Psychological Bulletin, 88,* 1–45.
Blum, L. (1987). Particularity and responsiveness. In J. Kagan & S. Lamb (Eds.), *The emergence of morality in young children* (pp. 306–337). Chicago: University of Chicago Press.
Brown, R., & Herrnstein, R. (1975). Moral reasoning and conduct. In R. Brown & R. Herrnstein, *Psychology* (pp. 289–340). Boston: Little, Brown.

Damon, W. (1977). *The social world of the child.* San Francisco: Jossey-Bass.

Damon, W. (1983). *Social and personality development.* New York: Norton.

Darley, J. M. (1993). Research on morality: Possible approaches, actual approaches [Review of *Handbook of moral behavior and development*]. *Psychological Science, 4,* 353–357.

Dietrichson, P. (1964). When is a maxim fully universalizable? *Kant-Studien, 55,* 143–170.

Dunn, J. (1988). *The beginnings of social understanding.* Cambridge, MA: Harvard University Press.

Dworkin, R. (1993). *Life's dominion.* New York: Knopf.

Eisenberg, N. (1982). *The development of prosocial behavior.* New York: Academic Press.

Estes, W. K. (1993). Cited in J. M. Darley. Research on morality: Possible approaches, actual approaches [Review of *Handbook of moral behavior and development*]. *Psychological Science, 4,* 353–357.

Feldman, D. H. (1980). *Beyond universals in cognitive development.* Norwood, NJ: Ablex.

Freud, S. (1930/1961). *Civilization and its discontents.* New York: Norton.

Grusec, J., Dix, T., & Mills, R. (1982). The effects of type, severity and victim of children's transgressions on maternal discipline. *Canadian Journal of Behavioural Science, 14,* 276–289.

Grusec, J., & Goodnow, J. (1994). Impact of parental discipline methods on the child's internalization of values: A reconceptualization of current points of view. *Developmental Psychology, 30,* 4–19.

Grusec, J., & Pederson, J. (1989, April). *Children's thinking about prosocial and moral behavior.* Paper presented at the Biennial Meeting of the Society for Research in Child Development, Kansas City, KS.

Hart, D. (1992). *Becoming men: The development of aspirations, values, and adaptational styles.* New York: Plenum Press.

Hartshorne, H., & May, M. S. (1928–1930). *Studies in the nature of character: Vol. 1. Studies in deceit; Vol. 2. Studies in self-control; Vol. 3. Studies in the organization of character.* New York: Macmillan.

Hay, D. F. (1994). Prosocial development. *Journal of Child Psychology and Psychiatry, 35,* 29–71.

Hoffman, M. (1982). Development of prosocial motivation: Empathy and guilt. In N. Eisenberg (Ed.), *Development of prosocial behavior* (pp. 281 – 313). New York: Academic Press.

Hume, D. (1739/1969). *A treatise of human nature.* (E. C. Mossnew, Ed.). Harmondsworth, England: Penguin.

Kant, I. (1785/1959). *Foundations of the metaphysic of morals.* (Lewis White Beck, Trans.). Indianapolis: Bobbs-Merrill.

Keil, F. (1986). On the structure of dependent nature of stages in cognitive development. In I. Levin (Ed.), *Stage and structure: Reopening the debate* (pp. 144–163). Norwood, NJ: Ablex.

Killen, M., Breton, S., Ferguson, H., & Handler, K. (1994). Preschoolers' evaluations of teacher methods of intervention in social transgressions. *Merrill-Palmer Quarterly, 40,* 399–416.

Kohlberg, L. (1969). Stage and sequence: The cognitive-developmental approach to socialization. In D. A. Goslin (Ed.), *Handbook of socialization theory and research* (pp. 347–480). Chicago: Rand-McNally.

Kohlberg, L. (1984). *Essays on moral development: Vol. 2. The psychology of moral development.* San Francisco: Harper and Row.

Krappmann, L., & Oswald, H. (1991). Problems of helping among ten-year-old children: Results of a qualitative study in natural settings. In L. Montada and H. W. Bierhoff (Eds.), *Altruism in moral systems* (pp. 142–158). Toronto: Hogrefe and Huber.

Kurtines, W. M., & Gewirtz, J. L. (Eds.). (1991). *Handbook of moral behavior and development* (Vols. 1–3). Hillsdale, NJ: Lawrence Erlbaum.

Latane, B., & Darley, J. M. (1970). *The unresponsive bystander: Why doesn't he help?* Englewood Cliffs, NJ: Prentice-Hall.

Maccoby, E., & Martin, J. (1983). Socialization in the context of the family: Parent–child interaction. E. M. Hetherington (Ed.) *Handbook of child psychology: Vol. 4. Socialization, personality and social development* (4th ed., pp. 1–101). New York: Wiley.

Milgram, S. (1974). *Obedience to authority.* New York: Harper and Row.

Murdoch, I. (1970). *The sovereignty of good.* New York: Schocken.

Nucci, L. P. (1981). The development of personal concepts: A domain distinct from moral or societal concepts. *Child Development, 52,* 114–121.

Nucci, L. P. (1984). Evaluating teachers as social agents: Student's ratings of domain appropriate and domain inappropriate teacher responses transgressions. *American Educational Research Journal, 21,* 267–378.

Nunner-Winkler, G., & Sodian, B. (1988). Children's understanding of moral emotions. *Child Development, 59,* 1323–1338.

Piaget, J. (1932). *The moral judgment of the child.* New York: Free Press.

Putnam, R. A. (1990). The moral life of a pragmatist. In O. Flanagan & A. O. Rorty (Eds.), *Identity, character, and morality: Essays in moral psychology* (pp. 67–89). Cambridge, MA: MIT Press.

Ross, H., & Lollis, S. P. (1989). A social relations analysis of toddler peer relationships. *Child Development, 60,* 1082–1091.

Ross, L., & Nisbett, R. E. (1991). *The person and the situation: Perspectives on social psychology.* Philadelphia: Temple University Press.

Saltzstein, H. (1994). The relationship between moral judgment and behavior: A social-cognitive and decision-making analysis. *Human Development, 37,* 299–312.

Siegler, R. S. (1984). Mechanisms of cognitive growth: Variation and selection. In R. J. Sternberg (Ed.), *Handbook of human intelligence* (pp. 897–971). Cambridge: Cambridge University Press.

Smetana, J. G. (1985). Preschool children's conceptions of transgressions: The effects of varying moral and social-conventional domain-related attributes. *Developmental Psychology, 25,* 499–508.

Taylor, C. (1989). *Sources of the self.* Cambridge, MA: Harvard University Press.

Turiel, E. (1983). *The development of social knowledge.* Cambridge: Cambridge University Press.

Turiel, E., Killen, M., & Helwig, C. (1987). Morality: Its structure, functions, and vagaries. In J. Kagan & S. Lamb (Eds.), *The emergence of morality in young children* (pp. 155–243). Chicago: University of Chicago Press.

Turiel, E., & Smetana, J. G. (1984). Social knowledge and social action: The coordination of domains. In W. M. Kurtines & J. L. Gewirtz (Eds.), *Morality, moral development, and moral behavior: Basic issues in theory and research* (pp. 261–282). New York: Wiley.

Walker, L., & Taylor, J. H. (1991). Family interactions and the development of moral reasoning. *Child Development, 62,* 264–283.

Wilson, J. Q. (1993). *The moral sense.* New York: Free Press.

Youniss, J. (1980). *Parents and peers in social development.* Chicago: University of Chicago Press.

Zahn-Waxler, C., & Radke-Yarrow, M. (1990). Origins of empathic concern. *Motivation and Emotion, 14,* 107–130.

Part I

The acquisition of morality

1 The social construction of character in toddlerhood

Dale F. Hay, Jennifer Castle, Carol A. Stimson, and Lisa Davies

Character is this moral order seen through the medium of an individual nature.
Ralph Waldo Emerson

Introduction

In this chapter, we consider morality in everyday life from the perspective of individual differences. We define individual differences in the language of descriptive statistics, as variation within a distribution of scores. Nearly 40 years ago, Cronbach (1957) drew attention to the fact that the psychologists who study individual differences, as opposed to general trends, almost represent a different discipline; he argued that there were actually two "disciplines of scientific psychology." Members of the two disciplines have different concerns with respect to sampling and measurement issues, and tend to employ different statistical techniques (correlation and regression as opposed to analysis of variance designs).

With respect to developmental research in particular, Appelbaum and McCall (1983) raised similar issues, pointing out that any developmental theory must account for differences among individuals as well as describing the average trajectory followed by the overall population. In many areas of developmental research, a focus on individual differences has almost supplanted the study of average trends: Consider, for example, the extent to which the study of attachment relationships has been so greatly influenced by the use of Mary Ainsworth's Strange Situation paradigm (Ainsworth, Blehar, Waters, & Wall, 1977) for the measurement of individual differences (for a review see Belsky & Cassidy, 1994). The patterns of attachment described by Ainsworth are now thought to be significant because they are stable over time and predict later developmental outcomes. In other words, in the language of psychometrics, they are reliable and thought to have predictive validity and thus cannot be dismissed as merely random variation.

23

In other areas of developmental research, including the study of moral understanding, there continues to be much interest in the general capacities and performance of the average young human, and the analysis of variation in capacities and performance is less well advanced. Our aim in this chapter is to explore some ways in which individual differences can be studied in the moral domain. Thus, we may ask, when in the course of development are stable individual differences in moral attributes first observed? How do they consolidate over time? And are they first discernible in children's own actions, or in adults' interpretations of those actions? Are they perhaps first identifiable with respect to overt prosocial actions and adherence to social conventions, rather than understanding of moral principles per se?

In posing any questions about individual differences in psychological phenomena, it is helpful to focus on a general construct or related set of constructs with respect to which individuals may vary (see Cronbach & Meehl, 1955). One might of course describe some individuals as more moral than others, or perhaps more morally advanced than others. Judgments of this sort must be made, for example, when church authorities are deciding whom to canonize. However, in the more ordinary reaches of human life, it seems useful to focus on constructs that subsume moral decision making but also include attention to social conventions and behavioral and emotional responsiveness to the needs of others.

In developmental analyses, it is also important to move beyond theoretical discussions of the existence of universal moral norms, which is a philosophical concern that is difficult to translate into a scientific question. That is, if we assume the universality of any given moral principle, we are essentially accepting the null hypothesis; the claim can be shaken by even one contradictory piece of empirical evidence. Any one of us might accept the universality of any given moral principle as axiomatic – the authors of this chapter differ among themselves in whether their accounts of moral development would spring from such an axiom – but it is assuredly difficult to treat the universality of moral principles as a theorem. Therefore, in sketching out patterns of individual difference in this general domain of human life, it becomes helpful to focus on social conventions and norms as well as moral issues.

Hence, to address these issues in the present context, we have found it useful to return to an old-fashioned phrase: *character* (see also Hay, Castle, & Jewett, 1994). In this chapter, we define character as an individual's *general approach to the dilemmas and responsibilities of social life,* a responsiveness to the social world that is supported by emotional reactions to the distress of others, the acquisition of prosocial skills, knowledge of social conventions, and construction of personal values. In our view, use of the term *character* emphasizes the fact that, in the course of growing up, individuals develop a *general approach to the social world* that includes adherence to moral rules of a given society and social conventions, but also is much influenced by other dimensions of temperament, personality, and intellectual style. Thus, in adult life, any society may contain many individuals "of good character" who hold quite differing views with respect to the great moral debates of their time as well as the more niggling, morally tinged issues, such as whether it is right to use private medical care or send one's children to private schools. Over the life course an individual is confronted with many such social and ethical dilemmas; the way in which he or she pursues a consistent yet flexible path around such issues may be described in terms of his or her character.

Furthermore, use of the construct of character provides us with a general framework in which to integrate three types of evidence relevant to theories of moral understanding and moral action: (1) behavioral evidence about the origins and development of prosocial actions (for reviews see Eisenberg & Mussen, 1989; Hay, 1994; Radke-Yarrow, Zahn-Waxler, & Chapman, 1983); (2) behavioral and physiological evidence about emotional responsiveness, empathy, and guilt (see Eisenberg & Strayer, 1987; Zahn-Waxler, Cole, & Barrett, 1991); and (3) cognitive evidence about social understanding and comprehension of moral principles, as represented by various other chapters in this volume. Diverse topics such as sharing, helping, empathy, and guilt can all be seen as relevant to the emergence of character (see Hay et al., 1994). Furthermore, use of the term *character* permits us once again to move beyond contemporary analyses of temperament and personality (for a review see Engfer, Walper & Rutter, 1994) to consider the role of motivation in social development.

When the phrase *character development* was in fashion, it represented a meaningful domain of inquiry for developmental psychologists, as evinced by a major review by Vernon Jones (1946) in Carmichael's *Handbook of Child Psychology*. In the first part of this century there was considerable interest in the stability and coherence of individual differences in the moral realm. This tradition is perhaps best represented by Hartshorne and May's (1930) classic study of individual differences in honesty and resistance to temptation. In his review, Jones attempted to integrate the literature on moral development into a more general psychological perspective and was particularly at pains to distinguish the construct of character from those of morality and temperament. The distinctions he made are still quite helpful to researchers in the domain of moral development, whereas attempts are still made to relate a child's approach to the social world to temperament and personality on the one hand (see Engfer et al., 1994) and cognitive understanding on the other (see Baron-Cohen, 1994; Dodge, 1991).

In the first place, Jones (1946) emphasized the importance of the conative as well as the cognitive in the development of character, and the fact that humans have the capacity to adhere to new principles and reinvent their own characters as they move through life:

Morality concerns itself with conformity to existing standards of a given time or place. Character does not necessarily imply such conformity. . . . This does not mean, of course, that character is not related to morality. It means that character is a more dynamic and more inclusive concept. In character development much more attention is given to volitional factors and to individual creativeness in the realm of goals to be achieved. . . . If we add to morality the ability to reconstruct one's values and the volitional powers sufficient to direct conduct progressively toward such evolving values, then we have character. (p. 707)

At the same time Jones was at pains to note that character does not simply reduce to temperament, although temperamental features (and other personality variables) may indeed influence the development of character:

Whether a person is good-tempered, sanguine, phlegmatic, melancholic, or choleric is certainly of interest to anyone rating him for practical purposes of living or working with him, and no claim can be made that such characteristics have no relation to character. Strictly speaking, however, the readiness and capacity of an individual for such relatively prevailing affective experiences are not central to the problem of his character. . . . character concerns itself more with the volitional powers of the individual and the directions or goals of his striving. (p. 708)

What is old-fashioned about Jones's account is the emphasis placed on the *motivational* aspects of an individual's character. In other words, in the context of the psychology of his time, Jones was concerned with the conative as opposed to the cognitive or affective dimensions of character – with will rather than thoughts or feelings. In this view, character development is bound up with the exercise and control of something we might call "moral motivation." Thus a goal for parents in any culture is not simply to acquaint their children with the social norms and moral imperatives of the culture, but also to try to foster motivation to act in accordance with those norms and imperatives. In other words, as parents, we don't just want our children to be polite, we want them to *want* to be polite. As children grow older, their parents and others see them as more or less likely to show such moral motivation – that is, to differ in character.

Jones (1954) contributed a revised chapter on character development to the second edition of the *Handbook*. However, in the third edition of *Carmichael's Handbook* (Mussen, 1970), this was replaced by a chapter by Hoffman (1970) on *moral development,* in which Piaget's and Kohlberg's general theories of moral development featured prominently. The term *character* was no longer included in the index, save for one reference to Hartshorne and May's Character Education inquiry. In our view, this marks a sea change in thinking about moral development that then concentrated developmental psychologists' attention on normative developmental processes and cognition, as opposed to individual differences and motivation. Our aim here is primarily a conceptual and methodological one: to explore some ways in which to redress the balance between normative and individual difference-oriented approaches to the study of moral development.

One would certainly not want to return to the drive theories of the 1940s and 1950s and so, in our own thinking about character formation, we have found it necessary to think the motivational dimensions of character as inextricably bound up with affect, behavior, and cognition. Thus, much current work on prosocial behavior, which we see as central to the concept of character, focuses on the emotional and cognitive underpinnings of prosocial acts (see Hay, 1994). Thus moral motivation might be seen to emerge in parallel with a cognitive understanding of social dilemmas and with emotional responsiveness to the concerns of others; the causal links across the affective, conative, and cognitive dimensions of character are yet to be specified.

In a recent review of literature relevant to the topic of character development (Hay et al., 1994), we identified several dimensions of character that undergo development during the lifespan. These include (1) sensitivity to the emotions and needs of others; (2) cooperative versus competitive orientations toward the use of common resources; (3) provision of care to infants, the elderly, the ill, and others in need; (4) helping others to meet their goals, through active helping or more passive compliance and obedience; (4) social problem-solving skills that permit the successful resolution of conflict with others; (5) the development of standards for truth telling and trustworthiness; (6) awareness of and adherence to social conventions and moral norms. We also argued that character development is fundamentally linked to the development of a sense of self and entails self-regulation, self-evaluation, and self-reflection.

We believe that each dimension of character development that we have identified is actively constructed, modified, and reflected upon by an individual throughout the lifespan. However, we also believe that this is one area of individual development where Cooley's (1902) concept of the "looking glass self" is apposite. Some differences in character may be speculated about by parents and others before their behavioral manifestations are apparent, and the views of family members and others may in fact shape character.

To explore this bidirectional process, in the current chapter we have focused on one particular example from the dimensions of character described in our model of character formation (Hay et al., 1994): the cooperative versus competitive use of resources. Individuals may be characterized as relatively generous or selfish – likely to share resources freely with other persons or to keep them for their own private use. We believe that the origins of this particular dimension of character lie in the very early prosocial impulses of infants and toddlers. The tendency to share resources with other person, including one's own agemates, emerges shortly before the first birthday (Hay, Caplan, Castle, & Stimson, 1991; Rheingold, Hay, & West, 1976). However, individual differences in early tendencies to share or refrain from sharing have not been examined in any detail. In this chapter, therefore, we ask when, if ever, in early development individual differences in the tendency to share with peers become stable over time.

Should systematic individual differences be identified in early patterns of sharing resources, it is unclear what factors might account for their origin. Some investigators have argued for the heritability of prosocial behavior, whereas others have focused on social learning processes (for a review see Hay et al., 1994). We are particularly interested in the extent to which parents' views of their children's characters might become a formative influence on the children's tendencies to share or refrain from sharing. In particular, with respect to our interest in the "looking glass self," we consider the extent to which individual differences in early tendencies to share or not are mirrored by the opinions of others. Thus, for the purposes of this chapter, we have asked, When do mothers start to think about their children as generous or selfish? And to what extent do mothers' attributions parallel children's own tendencies to share with others? Are the mothers' attributions themselves stable over time? And furthermore we have considered how one main difference between individuals, their gender, influences both children's own prosocial actions and the views their mothers hold about them. Gender is currently a major concern for theories of moral reasoning and the development of the moral emotions; some theorists claim that females and males follow gender-differentiated pathways throughout life, and that this is particularly the case with respect to moral reasoning and the moral emotions (see, e.g., Gilligan, 1982; Zahn-Waxler et al., 1991).

In sum, in this chapter we explore some ways of studying the emergence of systematic individual differences in children's use of resources. We ask whether such differences are stable over time, whether the differences are linked to mothers' attributions about the children's relative selfishness or generosity, and whether they basically reduce to differences between girls and boys. We begin, however, by a review of some studies of sharing in the first year of life, which by and large have charted group trends and ignored the question of difference among individuals.

Observed use of common resources in the first years of life

Shortly before the first birthday, infants characteristically begin to offer food and other objects to their companions – their mothers, fathers, sisters, brothers, peers, other adults, even dogs (see Rheingold et al., 1976). At around the same time, infants also begin to show objects to other persons at a distance, and to engage in coordinated use of them, a behavior we termed *partner play* (Rheingold et al., 1976). When infants first begin to extend objects toward another person's hand or lap, they have some difficulty letting go; however, in the second year of life, they are as likely to give an object away to a companion as to extend and then withdraw it. However, all of these actions, even the tendency to show objects at a distance and to extend objects without relinquishing them, meet the dictionary definition of sharing, in which one person affords to another "the partial use or enjoyment of a thing, though it may merely imply the mutual use or enjoyment" (see Hay & Rheingold, 1983, for a fuller discussion of the definition of the early sharing behaviors).

In any one assessment, infants vary in the frequency with which they share; however, these individual differences are not often explained by experimental manipulations. Infants share new toys as often as familiar ones, unique toys as well as those that are available in duplicate, and scarce resources as well as those that have been amply provided (Hay et al., 1991; Rheingold et al., 1976). Neither modeling nor reinforcement seems to increase the likelihood of sharing (Hay & Murray, 1982; Rheingold, 1973); however, adults' requests for an object and their attempts to engage infants in a game of give-and-take reliably increase the rate of sharing (Hay & Murray, 1982). The latter experience of playing give-and-take with a friendly adult promotes subsequent sharing in a different setting with the mother (Hay & Murray, 1982).

Individual differences in the frequency of sharing on any one occasion are therefore difficult to interpret. What is more compelling is the apparent universality of early sharing. It seems that virtually all normal infants show, offer, and give objects to others; 100% of the 18-month-old infants tested in a series of studies in North Carolina (Rheingold et al., 1976) showed or gave and 100% of the 18-month-old British children to be described in this sample did so as well. Furthermore, the early sharing behaviors have been noted across cultures and by investigators writing in other historical epochs (for a review see Hay & Rheingold, 1983). Thus, the most meaningful individual difference seems to be one of the basic capacity to share at all, not the rate of sharing on any given occasion. Indeed, some theorists claim that infants who never share objects with others are showing early signs of autism (see Sigman & Mundy, 1993). It has therefore been argued that early sharing may qualify as a precursor to the mature social understanding that is absent in autistic individuals (see Baron-Cohen, 1994).

Although the tendency to share with others seems well-nigh universal in the second year of life, there is some evidence from cross-sectional studies that it declines thereafter. A number of investigators have noted that prosocial behavior, including sharing, occurs at low rates in preschool classrooms (for reviews see Caplan, 1993; Hay, 1994). It was initially thought that these low rates of sharing in the preschool years represented the starting point for prosocial development, to be followed by a linear increase in sharing and other prosocial behaviors over the school years (see Bryan & London, 1970). However, increased attention to prosocial activities in the first 2 years of life has challenged this view.

It now appears that there may be an actual decline in prosocial behavior from infancy to childhood. For example, in a laboratory setting, 3-year-olds share less with their mothers than 2-year-olds do, the 3-year-olds calling their mother's attention to things with words, not gestures (Cook, 1977). Cooperative games with peers that entail the exchange of objects decline over the second year (Eckerman, Davis, & Didow, 1989) and 2-year-olds are less likely than 1-year-olds to share in response to a peer's expression of interest in an object (Hay et al., 1991). Thus, to the extent that sharing is a behavior that most toddlers show but not necessarily at high rates, and that declines to even lower rates over the early childhood years, investigation of individual differences may be limited by floor effects. It is important therefore to move beyond the analysis of rates of sharing and consider exactly how individuality in prosocial behavior may be manifesting itself.

We believe that, as the universality of early prosocial action declines, meaningful individual differences do in fact emerge (see also Hay, 1994). Thus, in particular, we expect individual differences in prosocial activities, including the use of common resources, to become stabler and more coherent as children grow older. This particular hypothesis about sharing is in line with theorists who have claimed that infancy is a period in development that is relatively canalized – where individual variation is less striking than the rapid developmental progression taken by members of the species as a whole (e.g., Bronson, 1985; McCall, 1981). In this view, both biologically and socially derived variations among individuals do not become apparent until after the canalized period.

In testing this hypothesis, Bronson (1985) observed the social behavior of children in the first, second, and third trimesters of the second year. In the third trimester, there was a greater range of behavior, indicating more differences among individuals, and individual children's behavior was stabler from session to session. Furthermore, the social behavior shown in the third trimester predicted the children's social adjustment in nursery school at age $3\frac{1}{2}$ years, whereas the earlier assessments were less predictive. In this chapter, we ask similar questions about toddlers' use of common resources: Does the frequency of sharing become increasingly variable with age? Do individual differences in the rate of sharing stabilize as children grow older?

Preliminary evidence for individual differences in rates of sharing

In our first studies of early sharing, the major emphasis was on documenting the occurrence of this achievement at early ages and on identifying factors that increased its occurrence (Rheingold et al., 1976). Therefore small samples of 15- to 18-month-old toddlers were tested under a number of experimental conditions; these studies showed a considerable range in the frequency with which the children shared, but no attempts were made to examine the coherence or stability of those individual differences, apart from the particular experimental manipulations that were being made. We have therefore reexamined those data to see if there was indeed any evidence for stability of individual differences across different types of sharing, different trials (which usually contrasted two different experimental conditions), and different social partners. These figures must of course be treated with caution due to the very small sample sizes and the fact that various experimental manipulations were being made. Nonetheless, they reveal interesting patterns.

For example, in one small sample ($N = 12$), 18-month-old children were observed sharing with their mothers and with unfamiliar persons, in two different trials. In both trials the mother and an unfamiliar adult sat together in the room; a variety of toys were available. In the first trial the adult maintained a pleasant but passive presence; in the second trial, the adult explicitly asked the children for particular toys. Two forms of sharing were examined – actual offers of objects into the persons' hands or laps and a more distal form of sharing interest in an object, showing it to other persons while at some distance from them.

Both distal and proximal forms of sharing with the mother showed stability across trials, despite the shift in experimental conditions, with the adult explicitly asking for toys in the second trial. The stability coefficients were r (11) = .62 for showing objects from a distance, and r (11) = .69, $p < .05$, for placing objects in the mother's hand or lap. Thus the children tended to be consistent over time in the extent to which they showed and gave objects to their mothers, regardless of what the adult was doing.

In contrast, none of the children gave objects to the adult in the first trial, when the adult was merely sitting and chatting to the mother. In the second trial, when the adult asked for particular items, few children explicitly offered objects to the adult. However, they were rather more likely to show the adult various objects, and the tendency to show objects to the adult in the second trial was reliably associated with the tendency to give objects to the mother in that trial, r (11) = .76, $p < .05$. Showing objects to the adult in the second trial was also positively though not reliably associated with the rate of giving objects to the mother in the first trial.

Thus, in this small sample, individual children seemed more or less likely to share what they saw and found of interest in the environment with others. Their tendencies to do so were consistent over time and across partners, although in general they were more likely to bring things physically to their mothers but bring unfamiliar adults' attention to interesting items at a distance. In this sample, the proximal and distal forms of sharing with the mother were not reliably associated; however, in a Canadian sample of toddlers between 12 and 24 months of age, positive associations were found between showing and giving objects to the mother (Hay, 1979).

We conducted similar analyses of another study involving a different small sample in which 18-month-olds were observed with their fathers. Here fewer strong associations were found; nevertheless, the tendency to give objects to the father in one trial was moderately, positively associated with the tendency to do so in a second trial, r (19) = .43. Taken together with observations that sharing with the mother is reliably associated with the tendency to play cooperative games with her (Hay, 1979), there is reason to explore such individual differences further. In other words, one of the core strands of character in the model we have proposed (Hay et al., 1994) – the tendency to use communal resources cooperatively rather than competitively – may have its origins in these early patterns of consistent sharing across time and across partners in toddlerhood. We now seek to explore this possibility in a somewhat larger sample that has been studied longitudinally. First, however, it is necessary to consider some factors that might promote individual differences in children's use of resources.

Factors that might account for individual differences in character

Socialization versus vulnerability

If there are indeed systematic individual differences in the way in which young children share resources, where do those differences come from? Most of the studies we have undertaken so far have shed little light on the correlates of any individual differences in early sharing. It is perhaps important to begin considering this issue with respect to general models of prosocial development that have been offered with respect to somewhat older children, those of preschool age and older. One can see two somewhat opposing models in the literature on prosocial development (for a review, see Hay, 1994). The first, more traditional model sees the capacity for prosocial action as a favorable outcome of the socialization process. It assumes that children are taught explicitly to share and cooperate with and nurture others, through the basic social learning processes of reinforcement, modeling, and instruction. The implication is that more mature, "better socialized" children will be more likely to engage in prosocial activities. This model implicitly guided the various experimental attempts to increase the rate of children's prosocial activities that characterized studies of prosocial development in the 1960s and 1970s (for reviews see Bryan & London, 1970; Radke-Yarrow et al., 1983).

More recently the socialization model has been challenged, partly as a function of findings from observational studies that show classroom teachers rarely reward or encourage prosocial behavior (for a review see Caplan, 1993), and partly as a function of the move away from social learning theory within developmental psychology. Current work places much more attention on children's cognitive understanding and emotional regulation in social situations, and puts much less emphasis on the acquisition of particular classes of social behavior (for a review see Hay, 1994). One implication of this revised view is that prosocial behavior is not necessarily seen as a good thing in all social circumstances (see Caplan, 1993). And thus a second general model now guides work in this area: a model in which prosocial activity is seen as something that can be taken to excess and that may be accompanied by high levels of guilt and failures to protect the self.

Perhaps the most provocative discussion about individual differences in early prosocial development, in which the second model obtains, comes from the work of Carolyn Zahn-Waxler and her colleagues, who have focused on the children of depressed mothers. Zahn-Waxler has concentrated her attention largely on the emotional as opposed to behavioral dimensions of prosocial behavior, with a particular focus on children's empathic concern and sympathetic interventions in the face of another's distress (see Zahn-Waxler & Radke-Yarrow, 1990; Zahn-Waxler, Radke-Yarrow, Wagner, & Chapman, 1992). Such sympathetic interventions often include sharing resources with the distressed persons, for example, when a child brings a peer a comforting object such as a teddy bear.

In these studies, children whose mothers have suffered from manic-depressive illness show *more* concern for the distress of others than do children whose mothers have been emotionally healthy (Zahn-Waxler, Cummings, McKnew, & Radke-Yarrow, 1984). Such children are also *less* likely than the children of well women to engage in conflict with their siblings (Hay, Vespo, Zahn-Waxler, & Radke-Yarrow, 1993). Children of depressed women are *more* likely than the children of well women to respond sympathetically when their mothers simulate distress, although that is also affected by the security of the attachment relationship with the mother and by the child's own level of behavioral problems: Children in a secure relationship with a depressed mother are particularly likely to display prosocial behavior (Radke-Yarrow, Zahn-Waxler, Richardson, Susman, & Martinez, 1994).

Taken together, these studies indicate that individual children who show prosocial behavior at especially high rates may be doing so in response to their early experience with distressed parents. Their preoccupation with the concerns of others may place the children themselves at risk for later psychopathology (see Zahn-Waxler et al., 1991). In this line of thinking, it is vulnerable children – those who have been asked to be parent substitutes for their own parents and siblings – who are most likely to be prosocial children.

The role of gender

One point of convergence between models is the prediction that girls, as opposed to boys, would be especially likely to exhibit prosocial activities. The traditional socialization view would suggest that girls are more amenable to the socialization process, perhaps depending more on the good opinions of others than boys do. The vulnerability model, as expressed by Zahn-Waxler and her colleagues (Zahn-Waxler et al., 1991), suggests that particular demands may be placed on girls in distressed families and that, in consequence, girls may be especially likely to feel excess levels of guilt and responsibility for other persons. In general, both traditions imply that character development follows gender-typical pathways throughout the lifespan.

Despite these strong predictions from two quite different traditions, however, the literature does not yield consistent findings on this point. One trend seems to be that teachers and parents see greater differences between girls and boys than are apparent in children's own reports of their activities or in direct observations (for a review see Hay, 1994). The extent of gender differences shown seems to depend on the particular form of prosocial behavior that is being studied and the way in which it is measured (Eisenberg & Lennon, 1983; Eisenberg & Mussen, 1989). Even where there are strong predictions that girls will perform differently than boys will – for example, in terms of the use of the principles of caring versus justice in moral decision making (see Gilligan, 1982) – that is not always the case (see Smetana et al., 1991; Snarey, Reimer, & Kohlberg, 1985). Thus, one of our major concerns here is to examine gender differences with respect to a particular strand of character development, the sharing of common resources, both in terms of the children's actual observed behavior and in the views their mothers hold about their generosity and selfishness.

The role of parental attributions

The great strength of the social learning approach that dominated studies of prosocial development in the 1960s and 1970s was the emphasis on children's important social relationships with parents, siblings, and peers and on the way in which social experiences shape the capacity for prosocial action. However, the mechanistic emphasis on modeling and reinforcement processes that characterized traditional social learning theory no longer seems adequate to account for the complexities of children; the roles of cognition and emotion need to be read into the equation (see Hay, 1994).

What may be lost, however, in the swing to the study of cognitive and emotional processes is the importance of significant social relationships, as opposed to the individual child's own reasoning powers and emotional responsiveness. The analysis of parents' effects on their children's prosocial activities needs to be extended beyond the study of specific behavioral processes like modeling and reinforcement. In particular, we believe that the systematic individual differences in prosocial activities emerging during the toddler period are at least partly derived from the constructions parents and other adults place on children's activities. Thus, parents begin to see their children as differing in character, and the labels they develop may guide their actions in ways so that different children in the same family may have quite different interactive experiences (see Plomin & Daniels, 1987). It is thus important to study the importance of those parental labeling processes.

With respect to the present example, the strand of character pertaining to the use of common resources, it appears that parents initially pay little attention to their infants' attempts to share. When infants offer objects to their parents, the parents often say "Thank you" and name the objects (West & Rheingold, 1978), but they rarely take the behaviors seriously. When parents are asked to report when their children began to offer or give objects, they admit that they have really never noticed these activities (Rheingold et al., 1976). In some cases, perhaps when infants are taking rather a long time to share a series of objects, or are sharing bits of sticks or stones or other somewhat disreputable items, sharing may be actively discouraged (Rheingold et al., 1976). It thus seems unlikely that parents' initial attributions about this aspect of their children's characters would derive from their observations of early sharing. Early prosocial behavior is seen as playful at best or annoying at worst (see Caplan, 1993).

Rather, it seems likely that much more attention would be paid by adults to young children's sharing under duress with siblings and peers. At the point in development when toddlers acquire a younger sibling or begin to enter into playgroups or nursery schools, parents may begin to pay much more attention to sharing. Thus it seems likely that parents' characterizations of children as selfish or generous consolidate as the children grow older. Nonetheless, it is unclear whether the parents' attributions in fact mirror children's actual prosocial activities.

To address this issue of the emergence of parental attributions about their children's character, we shall examine some data collected in the course of our longitudinal study of prosocial development, using an instrument we called the Toddler Personality Inventory or TPI. In this sample, we were only able to interview one parent, the mother; it is quite possible that mothers and fathers would disagree about their children's prosocial tendencies, as they do about behavioral problems (Sharp, Hay, Pawlby, Schmucker, & Kumar, 1994). Thus we can only generalize from the present findings to mothers, not fathers.

Mothers were asked to rate their children on a number of dimensions, particularly focusing on the tendencies to show prosocial as opposed to aggressive and uncooperative behavior. Adminstration of the TPI at different times in the course of the study permitted analyses of the stability and consolidation of the mothers' attributions. In this chapter, we shall focus on three particular attributions that mothers make with respect to the use of common resources: generosity, possessiveness, and selfishness.

Thus, to summarize, we shall now examine some preliminary data from our own longitudinal study of prosocial development to explore the possibility that individual differences in character, both as inferred from observations of an individual's actions and as manifested in another's views about that person, emerge over the first years of childhood. We focus throughout on one particular strand of character, an individual's generous or selfish approach to the sharing of common resources, as our basic illustrative example. The analyses we present here are not complete and are intended to illustrate some ways in which investigators of prosocial development can try to identify meaningful individual differences; they obviously do not provide a complete description or an explanation of such differences.

The South London study of prosocial development

In the course of our study, we observed 65 children living in two South London communities. The children's names had been obtained from age and sex registers in two medical practices. Both practices served a heterogeneous population of families, predominantly working-class but with a substantial proportion of middle-class families. Three age cohorts were contrasted, the groups having a mean age of 18, 24, and 30 months when the study began. Observations were made again 6 months after the initial assessment, so that the cohorts were then at a mean age of 24, 30, and 36 months of age, respectively. Use of this design means that there are replication samples at 24 and 30 months of age, although not at 18 and 36 months.

Procedure

On each occasion, each focal child was observed at home for 45 minutes, in the presence of the mother, a familiar peer, and the peer's mother. The observational situation was designed to resemble an ordinary visit by a mother and child to another mother and child's home. The focal child has been asked to invite the peer her own child knew best, along with that child's mother. Most of the studies of early sharing have been conducted in laboratory playrooms under very carefully controlled conditions, often with previously unacquainted toddlers meeting each other for the first time (e.g., Hay et al., 1991; Rheingold et al., 1976). In contrast, in this longitudinal study, we wished to observe early prosocial relations under natural conditions. Thus we used home observations and placed virtually no restrictions on the situation. If siblings and/or the father or other adult relatives would normally be present on such occasions, they were not excluded from our observations. The mothers were asked to behave in any way they naturally would and the children were permitted to move freely around the house and garden. The children might be engaging in many different types of activities, not simply those constrained by a particular set of toys presented in a laboratory setting. Thus, in this study, we were trying to see how common the sharing behaviors might be in a familiar, as opposed to a novel setting, and whether individual patterns of the use of resources might stand out against much background noise. In terms of the distinction recently made by Hartup, French, Laursen, Johnston, and Ogawa (1993), we were attempting to study children in an open-field rather than a closed-field setting. The particular toys the children were playing with and the activities they chose to pursue might indeed affect the rate of sharing; we were concerned to see whether any individual tendencies to share rather a lot or rather a little would nonetheless be apparent.

An observer carrying a hand-held video camera followed the focal child; a warm-up period in which the children were acclimated to the camera preceded the 45 minutes of observation. Sharing with peers was recorded from the video records in the course of transcribing all initiations and reactions made by the two children to each other, using an adapted version of the PICS (Peer Interaction Coding System) first used in a laboratory study of 12- and 24-month-old peer triads (Caplan, Vespo, Pederson, & Hay, 1991; Hay et al., 1991). Instances where one child offered an object to the other – that is, extended an object toward the other child's hand or lap – were recorded. Review of the transcripts then led to the removal of instances where the object was playfully tossed or rolled toward the recipient, so that we are now examining "literal" offers of objects into the peer's hand or lap.

Mothers of the focal children were interviewed, using the TPI, on four occasions throughout the longitudinal study. In Wave 1 of testing, the mothers were interviewed on the occasion of the peer visit and then again two weeks later. The same procedure was followed in Wave 2 of testing. Thus we were able to examine the short-term stability of the mothers' judgments at each wave of testing, as well as the long-term stability of their characterizations of their children over the 6-month period.

Do individual differences increase with age?

Observed rates of sharing

As we noted, Bronson (1985) claimed that individuality increases over the second year of life. She based this claim on three observations: Scores on various measures of social behavior showed greater variability as the children grew older, stability from one assessment to the next increased as the children grew older, and prediction to behavior in preschool could only be made from observations in the last trimester of the second year, not from earlier observations. Here we do not have the possibility of looking at the children's behavior in a preschool setting, so have only asked the first two questions about children's frequency of sharing with familiar peers: First, do the distributions of sharing scores show greater variability at the older ages? And, second, is the tendency to share with a familiar peer more likely to be stable over time for the older children?

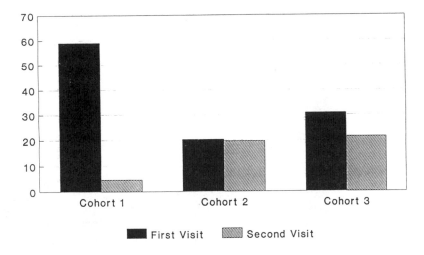

Figure 1.1. Variance in sharing scores: Cohort differences and trends over time.

Variability at different ages. The cohort-longitudinal design used in this study introduces some complexity into the question of whether variability increases with age. The variances shown by each age cohort at each time of testing are presented in Figure 1.1. Bronson's hypothesis that variability would increase with age was not confirmed in this sample. For all the age cohorts, scores were less variable in the second visit than in the first; the decline in variability was most obvious for the youngest cohort, who showed the greatest variance at Time 1 and the lowest at Time 2. If one just looks at the scores at the first visit, the cross-sectional comparisons show a curvilinear pattern, and indeed the variance shown by the 18-month-olds is significantly larger than that shown by the 30-month-olds, $F(20, 21) = 2.90$, $p < .05$ (see Hays, 1963, for a discussion of the use of the F distribution to compare sample variances). Only if one looks exclusively at the scores from the second visit does one see a pattern conforming to Bronson's (1985) hypothesis: Indeed, the variability shown by Cohort 3, now 36 months of age, is greater than that shown by Cohort 1, now 24 months of age, $F(18, 18) = 4.68$, $p < .05$. The difference in variability between the 24- and 30-month-olds at the time of the second visit is also significant, $F(19, 18) = 4.30$, $p < .05$. These findings draw attention to the facts that one must be very cautious in interpreting any trends over time where just a single cohort is studied and that cross-sectional comparisons may not be replicated in a second cohort.

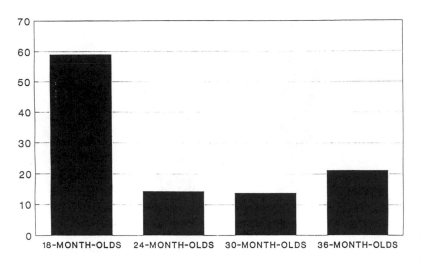

Figure 1.2. Variance in sharing scores: Age comparisons (cohorts combined at 24 and 30 months).

In this sample, it is possible to look at variability at the ages of 18, 24, 30, and 36 months of age by combining across cohorts at 24 and 30 months of age (Figure 1.2). Here we see a pattern opposite to that predicted by Bronson (1985), with the greatest variability shown at 18 months, followed by a decline in variability, with a slight rise at 36 months. Only some comparisons can be made here, as there is overlapping membership of the different distributions on which this graph is based. The comparison of the 18-month-olds with the 36-month-olds (Cohort 1 at Time 1 vs. Cohort 3 at Time 2) shows significantly greater variability in the younger group, in contrast to Bronson's hypothesis, $F(20, 18) = 2.79, p < .05$. Furthermore, the contrast between the 24-month-olds (Cohort 2 at Time 1 and Cohort 1 at Time 2) and the 36-month-olds (Cohort 3 at Time 2) shows that the apparent increase in variability is not a significant one. Thus, if anything, variability in sharing seems to decrease, not increase, as children grow older.

Stability of individual differences. Bronson (1985) also predicted that an increasing individuality in children's social behavior is also manifested by increasing stability of individual differences as children grow older. Thus, in our example, the tendency to share with a peer on two occasions, spaced 6 months apart, should be more consistent for the older cohorts than for the younger ones. Some support was found for this hypothesis of greater stability of sharing in the older cohorts. The association between sharing on one occasion and the next, six months later, was $r(18) = .01$ for the youngest cohort and $r(19) = .19$ for the middle cohort, but $r(18) = .62, p < .05$ for the oldest cohort. Use of the r to z transformation showed that the stability coefficients shown by Cohorts 3 and 2 were significantly greater than that shown by Cohort 1, $z = 2.022, p < .025$, one-tailed, and $z = 1.67$, $p < .05$, one-tailed, respectively. (One-tailed tests were used because of the directional nature of the hypothesis being tested.) Thus, individual differences in the tendency to share with peers would appear to be consolidating in the second half of the third year of life. However, this cross-sectional finding might reduce to cohort differences, not true changes in age in the stability of individual differences.

Maternal attributions

We can now ask the same two questions about mother's attributions about their children: Are the maternal ratings showing greater variability over time? And do individual differences, as rated by the mothers, appear to be more stable in the older cohorts? We start, however, by considering the preliminary question of whether mothers are generally more likely to characterize older children as generous or selfish.

Mothers' use of the moral terms. Even the mothers of the youngest children in the sample felt able to rate their children in terms of the moral attributes of generosity and selfishness. None of the mothers considered the term *generous* to be not applicable to their children's behavior across all four assessments; only 8.3% of mothers considered the term *selfish* not applicable across the four assessments. In general, as might be expected, the average mother considered her child somewhat generous ($M = 3.8$, $SD = 0.5$) and not very selfish ($M = 1.9$, $SD = 1.2$).

Mothers' judgments of selfishness were stable over a 2-week period at each wave of testing, $r = .65, p < .01$ in Wave 1 and $r = .57, p < .01$ in Wave 2. A lesser degree of stability over 2 weeks was found for mothers' judgments of generosity; stability over the 2-week period was low to moderate at both waves of testing, $r = .37, p < .05$ in Wave 1 and $r = .24$ in Wave 2.

Variability at different ages. A search for patterns of changing variability with age is somewhat hampered by the restricted range used for items on the TPI. But, with this caveat, we repeated the analyses done for the observed rates of sharing. Variance in mothers' ratings of selfishness and generosity for the three age cohorts at both times of testing is shown in Figure 1.3. No support for the hypothesis of greater variance in the older cohorts was found at either time of testing; none of the variances differed significantly. Similarly, when cohorts were combined so that 18-, 24-, 30-,

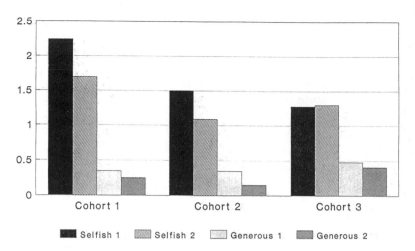

Figure 1.3. Variance in attributions: Cohort differences and trends over time.

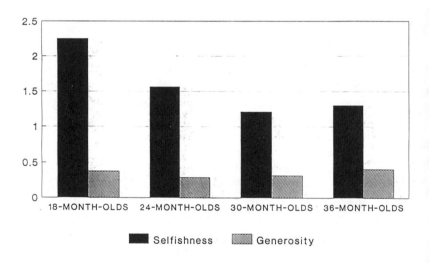

Figure 1.4. Variance in attributions: Age comparisons (cohorts combined at 24 and 30 months).

and 36-month-olds could be contrasted, no significant differences amongst variances were observed (Figure 1.4).

Stability of mothers' attributions over time. We noted earlier that children's observed rate of sharing seems to consolidate into a stable trait in the oldest cohort, as indicated by the stability of individual differences over 6 months. Rather different patterns were found for the mothers' attributions. Ratings of generosity were only moderately stable over time within the three age groups. In contrast, the stability of the mothers' ratings of selfishness was remarkably high in the youngest cohort ($r = .88$), moderate in the middle cohort ($r = .47$), and also very high in the oldest cohort ($r = .85$). Because one-tailed tests were used, only the difference between the middle and oldest cohorts is significant, $z = 2.24$, $p < .05$. The difference between the youngest and middle cohorts, although also substantial ($z = 2.58$), is shown in the direction opposite to the hypothesis being tested. Thus the mothers' ratings do not generally show a pattern of greater visibility in the older cohorts, although there is a significant difference in the stability of the ratings of selfishness for the two older cohorts.

Links between the mothers' attributions and observed rates of sharing with peers

The preceding analyses suggest that sharing with peers is a stabler trait in the oldest cohort; mothers' ratings of selfishness are also stable over time in that cohort, although ratings of generosity are not. What, then, might be the relation between children's sharing and the mothers' ratings, for this oldest cohort and for the sample as a whole?

In general, the mothers' judgments about generosity and selfishness were almost completely unrelated to the children's overt sharing with peers. For the sample as a whole, at the first visit, the correlation between sharing with the peer and ratings of selfishness and generosity was $r = .02$ and $r = -.003$, respectively. At the time of the second visit, the correlations between overt sharing with the peer and the mothers' ratings were $r = -.04$ for selfishness and $r = -.15$ for generosity.

For the oldest cohort, for whom individual differences in each variable seemed to be stabilizing, the associations between the mothers' words and the children's deeds were of somewhat greater magnitude, but nonetheless not significant. For that cohort, at the time of the first visit, sharing with peers was slightly negatively related to both maternal ratings, $r = -.13$ for selfishness and $r = -.11$ for generosity. On the second occasion, there was a moderate association with selfishness; children who shared more with their peers were seen as somewhat less selfish by their mothers, $r = .35$. However, sharing with peers was also negatively associated with the ratings of generosity; children who shared more often were seen by their mothers as less generous, $r = -.21$. Thus, in general, at least in this sample, no great correspondence was found between the children's observed prosocial activity and their mothers' opinions.

Gender differences

The preceding analyses suggest that mothers' attributions about their children's selfishness – a negative judgment with respect to a moral category – are quite stable over 6 months; their positive judgments about generosity are less stable. Thus there is consistency over time in a negative characterization of individual children but not a positive one. Furthermore, the mothers' stable judgments about selfishness are not highly related to the children's actual behavior with familiar peers. What might account for the consistency of the mother's views? One possibility is that the mothers are making their judgments about selfishness and generosity on the basis of firmly held stereotypes about gender roles; if so, the mothers' ratings may be based more on their expectations for particular characteristics in their sons and daughters than on the children's actual behavior.

As we noted earlier, both the traditional socialization model and the more recent vulnerability perspective predict that girls will show prosocial behavior more frequently than boys will. It therefore seems likely that mothers themselves might subscribe to such a view and rate daughters as more generous and less selfish than sons are. This gender-based difference in attributions may have no basis in reality, thus accounting for some of the discrepancy between mothers' views and children's actual behavior. To test this possibility, we examined gender differences in observed sharing and in the mothers' ratings. Because it seems possible that gender differences begin to consolidate after the second year of life (see Hay, 1994, for a fuller discussion), we tested for associations with gender in a model that also includes age cohort as a factor.

Gender differences in observed rates of sharing with peers

A 2×3 gender by age cohort multivariate analysis of variance on the frequency of sharing during each visit revealed a reliable gender by cohort interaction, multivariate $F (4, 104) = 2.57$, $p < .04$, Pillais criterion. Univariate tests and inspections of the discriminant function coefficients showed that the effect was primarily due to differences in sharing on the second occasion, $F (2, 52) = 4.49$, $p < .02$. In the youngest cohort, girls share somewhat less often than boys do, $M = 1.4$ versus $M = 2.6$; in the middle cohort, boys share more often than girls, $M = 5.1$ versus $M = 1.7$; and in the oldest cohort, the reverse holds, with girls sharing more often than boys, $M = 5.1$ versus $M = 1.5$. The overall main effects of age and gender showed no significant difference. Thus the more stereotypical pattern of girls showing more prosocial activity than boys emerged only in the oldest cohort, at the second time of testing (when the children were 36 months of age). Across the sample as a whole, girls shared somewhat more often than boys did on the first occasion, $M = 5.0$ versus $M = 3.3$, whereas boys shared somewhat more often than girls did on the second occasion, $M = 3.1$ versus $M = 2.7$, but these main effects were not significant.

Effects of gender on maternal attributions

There was no effect of gender on mothers' ratings of generosity, nor did gender interact with age cohort to influence those ratings. There was indeed a reliable main effect of gender on mothers' ratings of selfishness, multivariate $F(2, 53) = 3.26, p < .05$. Inspection of the univariate tests and discriminant function coefficients suggested that this was primarily attributable to the mothers' judgments during the first wave of testing, $F(1, 24) = 6.60, p < .01$. On that occasion, girls were rated as significantly more selfish than boys were, $M = 2.3$ versus $M = 1.5$. Thus the mothers held opinions that actually ran counter to gender role stereotypes.

Gender did not interact with age cohort to influence the mother's judgments of selfishness; however, there was a reliable multivariate main effect of age, multivariate $F(4, 108) = 2.76, p < .032$. This was attributable to differences in the judgments made during the second wave of testing, $F(2,54) = 3.35, p < .05$. The middle cohort, now 30 months of age, was seen as the most selfish, the oldest cohort, now 36 months of age, the least ($M = 2.19$, $M = 2.31$, and $M = 1.43$ for the youngest, middle, and oldest cohorts, respectively).

Thus, in general, it appeared that during the first wave of testing gender was the more salient factor influencing mothers' judgments about their children's selfishness, with girls seen as more selfish than boys. On the second occasion, although there was still a nonsignificant trend for girls to be seen as more selfish than boys, age seemed a more important determinant of the mothers' views. In general, the discordance between mothers' views and children's behavior was not explained by the mothers' holding stereotypical attitudes. If anything, at least by 36 months of age, girls' and boys' behavior was more stereotypical than were their mothers' opinions.

Gender and individuality

It still seems possible, however, that individuality is influenced greatly by gender. This is seen in a comparison of the stability coefficients for girls and boys in each of the age cohorts. (Obviously the cell sizes grow small when making such a comparison, so these findings are provided for descriptive purposes only.) For the children in the youngest cohort, who show virtually no consistency in sharing from the first visit to the next, there is in fact moderate stability for the girls, $r = .35$, but inconsistency for the boys, $r = -.26$. In the middle cohort, there is really little consistency over the 6-month period for either gender, $r = .03$ for the girls and $r = .12$ for the boys. However, for the oldest cohort, where there appears to be considerable stability over time, quite different patterns are shown by the girls and the boys. The girls' tendency to share with familiar peers is very stable over the 6-month period, $r = .70$. In contrast, the boys are only moderately consistent, $r = .28$. If such patterns were found in a larger sample, they would suggest that, as girls and boys enter the preschool years, sharing with peers is a stabler characteristic of individual girls, but a more variable characteristic of individual boys. Given the fact that prosocial behavior, including sharing, greatly influences children's judgments about their classmates (Denham, McKinley, Couchoud, & Holt, 1990), this disparity could have important implications for girls' and boys' adjustment to the preschool settings and their social reputations.

Gender-related links between mothers' attributions and observed sharing

If girls' tendencies to share with peers are indeed stabler over time than boys' are, does this account for the discrepancy with mothers' reports? We examined associations between the children's rates of sharing at each occasion and their mothers' judgments of selfishness and generosity. No higher levels of association were found for girls than for boys. It seems that, in this sample, mothers' judgments about generosity and, particularly, selfishness were internally consistent but fairly unrelated to what the children were actually doing with their familiar peers.

Summary and conclusions

The aim of our chapter was primarily conceptual and methodological. We wished to illustrate ways in which one could begin to explore the developmental origins of differences in character. In the course of our illustrative analyses, stable individual differences were demonstrated for children's rates of sharing with peers and mothers' judgments about their selfishness. However, there was virtually no relation between the two pieces of information about the child's character. There are at least two possible reasons for this discrepancy, beyond obvious concerns about measurement error in all the variables.

First, it is possible that, when making these judgments, a mother is reflecting on her own relationship with the focal child, not on the child's relation with peers. We do not yet have detailed analyses of the children's prosocial activities with the mother; however, in the first wave of testing, we examined the alacrity with which children shared with their mothers and peers by computing latency to share with each partner. The latency to share with the mother was indeed correlated with the mother's ratings of selfishness; the more selfish a child was rated, the longer he or she took before sharing with the mother. This association was somewhat stronger in the younger cohorts than in the oldest group.

Second, it is possible that links between mothers' attributions and children's behavior might be discerned at a more global level of analysis; in general, reliable individual differences are often observed when composite measures or patterns of behavior, rather than frequency counts, are used (see, e.g., Waters, 1978). Thus it might be useful to examine judgments about selfishness or generosity in the context of related traits. Furthermore, it might be useful to compare children who never shared with peers with those who shared at least once. Factor analyses of the various traits rated on the TPI had yielded a factor that we labeled *contentiousness,* comprising the traits selfishness, possessiveness, aggression, moodiness, and interest in toys. Children who never shared with their peers at all were seen as reliably more *contentious* than were those who exhibited some degree of sharing. It must be said, however, that children who shared not at all were seen as reliably less *selfish* than those who shared at least once, $M = 0.9$ versus $m = 2.01$, $F(1, 57) = 4.42$, $p < .05$. It does seem that the global pattern, rather than the individual judgment of selfishness, was associated with the children's overt activity.

These considerations suggest that Cooley's (1902) notion of the "looking glass" self is still worth studying empirically, but that the process of doing so is a rather complex one. It should be noted that, in other strands of character, such as the tendencies to show empathic reactions or to be aggressive, similar discrepancies are found across raters and forms of measurement (see Eisenberg & Lennon, 1983). Our exploration of these issues has led to the following conclusions:

1. There is really very little evidence for increasing variability in sharing between 1.5 and 3 years of age. If anything, the overall level of variance seems to decrease as children grow older.

2. Nonetheless, in this sample, it was the oldest cohort that showed the greatest stability over a 6-month period, suggesting that individual differences in sharing may indeed be consolidating in the second half of the third year of life, particularly for girls. However, it is completely possible that this pattern would not be shown at the same ages in a different

cohort. The current design has drawn attention to the importance of cohort differences as well as age differences, and thus this particular pattern requires replication.

3. Mothers' negative attributions are extremely consistent over time, their positive attributions less so. The mothers seemed to have very little problem with making such global judgments about their children's character; apparently even 18-month-olds can be rated as more or less selfish in a way that is consistent over a 6-month period. Mothers' judgments about their children's selfishness are affected by the child's gender and age, but relatively unaffected by the children's actual tendency to share with a familiar peer. One suspects that sibling relationships and sharing with less well acquainted children might also affect the mother's judgments.

4. By and large, mothers see girls as more selfish than boys; however, the difference in sharing by girls and boys is affected by cohort membership. The stereotypical pattern of girls sharing more than boys do is found only in the oldest cohort. This finding is in line with others that show very little in the way of gender differences in prosocial activities prior to 2 years of age but the emergence of gender differences in the preschool years (see Hay, 1994). It is of considerable interest to know whether the mothers' more negative views of their daughters – their tendency to think of girls as being more selfish than boys are – come to influence the girls' own prosocial activities. Such a link might be profitably explored within the vulnerability model developed by Zahn-Waxler and her colleagues (1991).

In general, then, there seems to be a great deal to learn about individuality in the moral realm. Studies of moral understanding have moved beyond monolithic developmental frameworks to take up issues such as gender differences (e.g., Gilligan, 1982) and cultural underpinnings of moral reasoning (e.g., Snarey et al., 1985). It is important, however, to move still beyond essentialist arguments such as Gilligan's notions of different moral trajectories for females and males and consider the fact that women are not all alike, just as men are not all alike. Gender stereotyping did not seem to account for all the manifestations of individuality in our sample, and there are many correlates beyond gender that need to be explored. Within the population of women, individuals differ in character; some may be caring, others callous. Similarly, individual men differ in character. We continue to believe that the emergence of individuality is affected by children's own behavioral propensities and the views that parents and others hold about them; but charting these connections is by no means an easy task. Our illustrative analyses show just how complex a task it may turn out to be.

References

Ainsworth, M. D. S., Blehar, M., Waters, E., & Wall, S. (1977). *Patterns of attachment: Observations in the strange situation and the home.* Hillsdale, NJ: Lawrence Erlbaum.

Appelbaum, M., & McCall, R. (1983). Design and analysis in developmental psychology. In P. H. Mussen (Series Ed.) & W. Kessen (Vol. Ed.), *Handbook of child psychology: Vol. 1. History, theory, and methods* (pp. 415–476). New York: Wiley.

Baron-Cohen, S. (1994). Children's theories of mind: Where would we be without the intentional stance? In M. Rutter and D. F. Hay (Eds.), *Development through life: A handbook for clinicians* (pp. 303–318). Oxford: Blackwell Scientific.

Belsky, J., & Cassidy, J. (1994). Attachment. In M. Rutter and D. F. Hay (Eds.), *Development through life: A handbook for clinicians* (pp. 373–402). Oxford: Blackwell Scientific.

Bronson, W. (1985). Growth in the organization of behavior over the second year of life. *Developmental Psychology, 21,* 108–117.

Bryan, J. H., & London, P. (1970). Altruistic behaviour by children. *Psychological Bulletin, 73,* 200–211.

Caplan, M. (1993). Inhibitory influences in development: The case of prosocial behavior. In D. F. Hay & A. Angold (Eds.), *Precursors and causes in development and psychopathology* (pp. 169–198). Chichester: Wiley.

Caplan, M., Vespo, J. E., Pederson, J., & Hay, D. F. (1991). Conflict over resources in small groups of one- and two-year-olds. *Child Development, 62,* 1513–1524.

Carmichael, L. (1954). *Manual of child psychology* (2nd ed.). New York: Wiley.

Cook, K. (1977). *The verbal and nonverbal sharing of 2- and 3-year-old children.* Unpublished master's thesis, University of North Carolina at Chapel Hill.

Cooley, C. H. (1902). *Human nature and the social order.* New York: Scribners.

Cronbach, L. J. (1957). The two disciplines of scientific psychology. *American Psychologist, 12,* 671–684.

Cronbach, L. J., & Meehl, P. E. (1955). Construct validity in psychological tests. *Psychological Bulletin, 52,* 281–302.

Denham, S. A., McKinley, M., Couchoud, E. A., & Holt, R. (1990). Emotional and behavioral predictors of preschool peer ratings. *Child Development, 61,* 1145–1152.

Dodge, K. A. (1991). Emotion and social information processing. In J. Garber & K. Dodge (Eds.), *The development of emotion regulation and dysregulation* (pp. 159–181). Cambridge: Cambridge University Press.

Eckerman, C. O., Davis, C. C., & Didow, S. M. (1989). Toddlers' emerging ways of achieving coordination with a peer. *Child Development, 60,* 440–453.

Eisenberg, N. D., & Lennon, R. (1983). Sex differences in empathy and related capacities. *Psychological Bulletin, 94,* 100–131.

Eisenberg, N., & Mussen, P. H. (1989). *The roots of prosocial behavior in children.* Cambridge: Cambridge University Press.

Eisenberg, N., & Strayer, J. (1987). *Empathy and its development* (pp. 292–316). Cambridge: Cambridge University Press.

Engfer, A., Walper, S., & Rutter, M. (1994). Individual characteristics as a force in development. In M. Rutter & D. F. Hay (Eds.), *Development through life: A handbook for clinicians* (pp. 79–111). Oxford: Blackwell Scientific.

Gilligan, C. (1982). *In a different voice: Psychological theory and women's development.* Cambridge, MA: Harvard University Press.

Hartshorne, H., & May, M. A. (1930). *Studies in deceit.* New York: Macmillan.

Hartup, W. W., French, D. C., Laursen, B., Johnston, M. K., & Ogawa, J. R. (1993). Conflict and friendship relations in middle childhood: Behavior in a closed-field situation. *Child Development, 64,* 445–454.

Hay, D. F. (1979). Cooperation interactions and sharing between very young children and their parents. *Developmental Psychology, 15,* 647–653.

Hay, D. F. (1994). Prosocial development. *Journal of Child Psychology and Psychiatry, 35,* 29–71.

Hay, D. F., Caplan, M., Castle, J., & Stimson, C. A. (1991). Does sharing become increasingly "rational" in the second year of life? *Developmental Psychology, 27,* 987–993.

Hay, D. F., Castle, J., & Jewett, J. (1994). Character development. In M. Rutter & D. F. Hay (Eds.), *Development through life: A handbook for clinicians* (pp. 319–349). Oxford: Blackwell Scientific.

Hay, D. F., & Murray, P. (1982). Giving and requesting: social facilitation of infants' offers to adults. *Infant Behavior and Development, 5,* 301–310.

Hay, D. F., & Rheingold, H. L. (1983). The early appearance of some valued behaviors. In D. L. Bridgeman (Ed.), *The nature of prosocial development: Interdisciplinary theories and strategies* (pp. 73–94). New York: Academic Press.

Hay, D. F., Vespo, J. E., Radke-Yarrow, M., & Zahn-Waxler, C. (1993). *Patterns of sibling conflict when the mother is depressed.* Paper presented at the European Developmental Psychology Conference, Bonn.

Hays, W. (1963). *Statistics.* New York: Holt, Rinehart, and Winston.

Hoffman, M. L. (1970). Moral development. In P. H. Mussen (Ed.), *Carmichael's manual of child psychology* (Vol. 2, pp. 261–359). New York: Wiley.

Jones, V. (1946). Character development in children: An objective approach. In L. Carmichael (Ed.), *Manual of child psychology* (pp. 701–751). New York: Wiley.

Jones, V. (1954). Character development in children – An objective approach. In L. Carmichael (Ed.), *Manual of child psychology* (2nd ed., pp. 781–832). New York: Wiley.

McCall, R. B. (1981). Nature–nurture and the two realms of development: A proposed integration with respect to mental development. *Child Development, 52,* 1–12.

Mussen, P. H. (Ed.) (1970). *Carmichael's manual of child psychology* (Vol. 2). New York: Wiley.

Plomin, R., & Daniels, D. (1987) Why are children in the same family so different from each other? *Behavioral and Brain Sciences, 10,* 1–16.

Radke-Yarrow, M., Zahn-Waxler, C., & Chapman, M. (1983). Children's prosocial dispositions and behaviors. In P. H. Mussen (Series Ed.) & E. M. Hetherington (Vol. Ed.), *Socialization, personality, and social development* (pp. 469–545). New York: Wiley.

Radke-Yarrow, M., Zahn-Waxler, C., Richardson, D. T., Susman, A., & Martinez, P. (1994). Caring behavior in children of clinically depressed and well mothers. *Child Development, 65,* 1405–1414.

Rheingold, H. L. (1973). Independent behavior of the human infant. In A. D. Pick (Ed.), *Minnesota symposium on child psychology* (pp. 178–203). Vol. 7, Minneapolis: University of Minnesota Press.

Rheingold, H. L., Hay, D. F., & West, M. J. (1976). Sharing in the second year of life. *Child Development, 47,* 1148–1158.

Sharp, D., Hay, D. F., Pawlby, S., Schmucker, G., & Kumar, C. (1994). The impact of postnatal development on boys' intellectual development. Manuscript submitted for publication.

Sigman, M. D., & Mundy, P. (1993). Infant precursors of childhood intellectual and verbal abilities. In D. F. Hay & A. Angold (Eds.), *Precursors and causes in development and psychopathology* (pp. 123–144). Chichester: Wiley.

Smetana, J. G., Killen, M., & Turiel, E. (1991). Children's reasoning about interpersonal and moral conflicts. *Child Development, 62,* 629–644.

Snarey, J. R., Reimer, J., & Kohlberg, L. (1985). Development of social-moral reasoning among kibbutz adolescents: A longitudinal cross-cultural study. *Developmental Psychology, 21,* 3–17.

Waters, E. (1978). The reliability and stability of individual differences in infant–mother attachment. *Child Development, 48,* 489–494.

West, M. J., & Rheingold, H. L. (1978). Infant stimulation of maternal instruction. *Infant Behavior and Development, 1,* 205–215.

Zahn-Waxler, C., Cole, P., & Barrett, K. C. (1991). Guilt and empathy: Sex differences and implications for the development of depression. In J. Garber & K. Dodge (Eds.), *The development of emotion regulation and dysregulation* (pp. 243–272). Cambridge: Cambridge University Press.

Zahn-Waxler, C., Cummings, E. M., McKnew, D., & Radke-Yarrow, M. (1984). Altruism, aggression and social interactions in young children with a manic-depressive parent. *Child Development, 55,* 112–122.

Zahn-Waxler, C., & Radke-Yarrow, M. (1990). Origins of empathic concern. *Motivation and Emotion, 14,* 107–130.

Zahn-Waxler, C., Radke-Yarrow, M., Wagner, E., & Chapman, M. (1992). Development of concern for others. *Developmental Psychology, 28,* 126–136.

2   Morality, autonomy, and social conflict

Melanie Killen and Larry P. Nucci

Morality and autonomy are two central features of social life. Morality refers to principles of how we ought to treat others, and autonomy refers to the goals of the individual. The relationship between rules that guide our actions for treating others (morality) and our struggle to become an individual (autonomy) is fundamental to our social existence, and yet, our understanding of this important relationship has been eclipsed by the multitude of ways that the connections between morality and autonomy have been characterized as well as how these terms have been defined. Philosophers (e.g., Kant, 1785/1959) and psychologists (e.g., Freud, 1930/1961) have typically viewed morality as the struggle between the egoistic and selfish desires of the self and the rational and legitimate concerns of the treatment of others. From these views morality is the achievement of the suppression of the self-interested, self-motivated individual. Recently, these views have been called into question. Philosophers have critiqued Kantian morality because of its impoverished moral self. In Kantian morality there is little room for placing value on social relationships and nonmoral personal goals (see Williams, 1981). Likewise, psychologists have argued that human nature is not as aggressive and selfish as Freud has characterized it (Kagan, 1984; Turiel, 1983). These analyses call for a substantive reexamination of the relationship between morality and autonomy, particularly in the field of moral development where morality and autonomy are central concepts.

Piaget's theory (1932), which provided the foundation for current research on moral development, conjoined morality and autonomy by contrasting an autonomous morality with a morality of constraint. In that account, autonomy refers to moral judgments that are based on criteria of justice or reciprocity that form a logical, socially equilibrated moral posi-

We thank Daniel Hart, Judith Smetana, and Heidi Zolot for helpful comments on the manuscript. Part of the research was supported by a Spencer Foundation grant and a Wesleyan Project Grant awarded to the first author.

52

tion independent of social convention and authority. Moral autonomy in Piagetian theory is a developmental achievement reflecting a triumph of reason and reciprocity over egocentrism and unilateral respect for authority. From our perspective, Piaget's use of the term *autonomy* is limited because it leaves out legitimate considerations of the individual, that is, nonmoral autonomous goals. We believe that a focus on the emergence of "moral autonomy" ignores legitimate aspects of the nonmoral self that we think are important and have been overlooked.

Other critiques of the Piagetian view have concentrated on gender and cultural biases, which we believe also misrepresent the relationship between morality and autonomy. For example, some have criticized the cognitive-developmental model for expressing a primarily male orientation to interpersonal relations in which personhood is equated with disconnected autonomous individualism, and morality is the impersonal, "objective," resolution of the competing interests of persons through justice and rational norms (Gilligan, 1977, 1986). This male orientation is contrasted with a putatively predominantly female moral orientation of care, which is based on a view of self as connected with others rather than differentiated and autonomous. Viewing moral autonomy as a male orientation, however, does not provide an adequate answer for how females (and males) weigh nonmoral, personal considerations of the self when making moral decisions.

The equation of autonomy with individualism has also been identified as a cultural orientation. Western cultures are said to be oriented to autonomy and individualism, and non-Western cultures are thought to be oriented to the group and collectivism (Shweder, Mahapatra, & Miller, 1987; Triandis, 1989, 1990). In our analysis, we will discuss the various ways in which this perspective has implications for understanding the development of autonomy and morality. Further, autonomy has also been defined in opposition to morality by those who equate autonomy with self-interested individualism. For example, Robert Bellah and his colleagues (Bellah, Madsen, Sullivan, Swidler, & Tipton, 1985) contrast the moral person with the autonomous individual who is much less concerned for others than for himself or herself. Interestingly, some elements of this oppositional view of morality and self-interest are also contained in constructivist theories of moral development that define higher levels of moral development in terms of moral autonomy. Kohlberg (1969, 1971), for instance, characterized the early phases of moral development as entailing a shift from a focus on self (egoism) to a moral focus on others.

These contradictory views of autonomy in relation to morality have obscured both the ways in which moral and personal developments transpire, as well as the ways in which concerns for the self and moral concerns for others interact. Our position is that morality and personal autonomy are interrelated, coexisting aspects of social functioning that operate throughout the lifespan of individuals in all cultures. Persons are simultaneously individualistic and other-directed, autonomous and interdependent (Nucci & Lee, 1993; Turiel, Killen, & Helwig, 1987).

Goals of the chapter

In this chapter we explore the heterogeneous nature of social development by looking at the emergence of children's morality and autonomy in their social interactions. We will look at two types of social exchanges. First, we will examine how children resolve conflicts between their self-interests and the needs of others in peer exchanges. Our emphasis is on peer conflicts in which both parties have a legitimate stake, and in which resolution, as opposed to domination by one party or the other, requires both an assertion of one's own needs and attendance to the needs of the other in order to arrive at a fair or caring outcome. Conflicts of this sort contain both elements of autonomy (identifying one's legitimate claims) and morality (being fair and caring toward the other), and, thus, theoretically, entail reciprocal or bidirectional thinking.

Second, we will look at how children, through their interactions with adults, establish a personal discretionary area of behavior. We will examine exchanges involving children's attempts to differentiate their areas of discretion or choice from behaviors that fall within the authority or interests of others. In these cases, conflicts arise over an authority's attempt to regulate the child's behavior, and the child's sense that an issue is or ought to be a personal matter for the child to decide. In these exchanges, the primary agenda of the child is the establishment of autonomy. Autonomy in the sense of establishing an area of personal discretion or behavioral choice is what we refer to as the personal domain (Nucci, 1981; Smetana, Chapter 7, this volume), which appears to be critical for the formation of personal identity and sense of agency (Damon & Hart, 1988; Nucci & Lee, 1993).

We will argue that children's emergent morality and their sense of autonomy can be seen interacting in the context of the two forms of social conflict (peer and adult–child). Because the role of culture is important in structuring the social interactions children experience, we will also describe the ways in which cultures contribute to the meanings children ascribe to the social experiences that influence their construction of morality and sense of personal autonomy.

Theoretical background

In Piaget's (1932) pioneering work on moral judgment, morality was defined as autonomy, judgments that are independent of authority and external pressure – that is, judgments that refer to principles of justice, not to authority dictates or external consequences. The term *autonomy* was borrowed from Kantian theory. As the moral philosopher Schneewind (1986) describes it:

> The term "autonomy" came into moral philosophy rather late. It was taken over from political discussion, where it referred straightforwardly to the ability of a society or group to make its own laws. The responsibility for its adoption lies with Kant, who used it for the central idea of his ethical theory, namely, that morality is constituted by the requirement that we act out of respect for moral laws that we ourselves make. (p. 64)

This definition does not consider the individuality of persons but the independence of social thought, and this was the aspect of morality that Piaget theorized to be the hallmark of moral development. In their discussion of Piaget's use of the term autonomy, Davidson and Youniss (1991) note that: "To put it another way, the construction of identity and the construction of morality are aspects of the *same construction*" (p. 112). Autonomy refers to the liberation of social thought from external influences. From Piaget's perspective early moral reasoning was characterized by several qualities, all of which pertained to the lack of independence in moral decision making. Moral realism (the term he used to describe early moral thinking) was characterized by three features: (1) a heteronomous orientation (the child evaluates moral acts in terms of authority commands and dictates); (2) a belief in the "letter rather than the spirit of the law" (the child evaluates moral acts in terms of the written rule); and (3) an objective rather than subjective conception of responsibility (the child focuses on actual consequences rather than "unobservable" intentions of acts). Together these features reflected a strict rule orientation rather than a recognition and understanding of principles of justice.

As we mentioned, Piaget's theory did not include legitimate nonmoral considerations, such as personal identity and development. We believe that it is important to distinguish "legitimate nonmoral concerns" from "selfish" concerns. Whereas many social conflicts involve a "clash of blind desires," other conflicts involve legitimate concerns of the self that sometimes have to be weighed with moral ones, such as personal projects (e.g., getting an education), personal goals (e.g., establishing a career), and personal hobbies (e.g., listening to opera). Examples of personal issues within the United States include the content of one's correspondence and self-expressive creative works, one's recreational activities, one's choice of friends or intimate associates, and actions that impact the state of one's own body (Nucci, 1981; Nucci, Guerra, & Lee, 1991; Smetana, Bridgeman, & Turiel, 1983). While the specific content of the personal is influenced by cultural norms (Miller & Bersoff, 1992), identification of a personal set of actions is thought to manifest broader core requirements for establishing personal boundaries for the self as an object and related requirements (for personal agency, continuity, and uniqueness) for establishing a sense of self as a subject (Nucci & Lee, 1993). Accordingly, we argue that individuals within all cultures seek to establish areas of personal choice in response to this set of fundamental psychological requirements (see Nucci, in press).

Interestingly, moral philosophers, such as Williams (1981) and Scheffler (1982) have argued that Kantian morality is overly stringent because it does not take nonselfish concerns of the self, such as personal projects (e.g., educating oneself), into consideration. They argue that it may not be irrational for the individual to weigh such considerations when making moral judgments. Williams (1981) asserts:

It is a real question, whether the conception of the individual provided by the Kantian theories is in fact enough to yield what is wanted, even by the Kantians; let alone enough for others who, while equally rejecting Utilitarianism, want to allow more room than Kantianism can allow for *the importance of individual character and personal relations in moral experience.* (p. 5; emphasis added)

Likewise, Piaget did not theorize about the importance of the individual or personal relations in moral development. He did not consider how legitimate concerns of the individual arise out of reciprocal peer interactions. Yet, children develop a sense of fairness and justice through a reciprocal recognition that the desires of others are similar to the desires of the self. In order to recognize principles of fairness one has to see the other as having needs that are similar to one's own needs and desires. Implied in this process is the development of autonomy (how one wants to be treated). In Piaget's theoretical formulation, morality and autonomy were intertwined aspects of the same developmental process, yet the primary focus of the research was on moral knowledge. Knowledge about the self and self-identity were not investigated.

We assert that children's conceptions of the personal are distinct from their understandings of morality. Conceptions of what is personal can interact with children's morality in two ways. First, moral reciprocity requires some degree of individuation on the part of the actors involved in any moral exchange. At the heart of social conflict around object disputes, for example, is the notion that what is mine – that is to say, what belongs to *me* – is morally separable from what belongs to you. Second, the identification of a personal area of actions is necessary in a more general sense for the child's construction of conceptions of rights (Nucci & Lee, 1993). Although moral structures of just reciprocity require that rights and protections granted oneself be extended to others, moral conceptions of justice and human welfare do not in and of themselves provide the means to identify personal rights and freedoms. This treatment of rights is consistent with philosophical arguments that ground the notion of rights in the establishment of personal agency (Dworkin, 1977; Gewirth, 1978, 1982). Gewirth (1978), for example, argues that personal freedom is a necessary good since freedom is necessary for the continuation of agency. Because freedom is a necessary good, agents logically hold that they have a right to claims to freedom. In developmental theory, concept of the personal serve to identify freedom as a necessary good for maintaining agency and uniqueness. The content of the personal domain is the content of the individual's identified freedoms. One function of the personal, then, is to provide the source and the conceptual justification for the individual's claims to freedom. Extensions of such freedoms to others transform individual claims into moral conceptions of rights (Nucci, in press).

Surprisingly little is known about how children integrate legitimate concerns of the personal and of the self with concerns for others and how this process contributes to children's acquisition of moral concepts. Damon's (1977) research on children's conceptions of the fair distribution of resources showed that children as young as 7 and 8 years of age weigh legitimate claims of the self with moral ones when resolving sharing disputes. How children resolve conflicts provides also an important source for studying children's emerging coordination of the needs of the self with the needs of others. Children's engagement in active resolutions of conflicts provides them with opportunities to develop social and moral knowledge; when children are confronted with another person's perspective they are forced to reconsider their own viewpoint (see Berkowitz, 1985; Damon, 1983; Hay, 1984; Hay & Ross, 1982; Piaget, 1932; Shantz, 1987; Shantz & Hartup, 1992). Thus, analyses of conflict among young children reveal their constructions of morality and autonomy.

Coordination of autonomy and morality through conflict resolution

It has been theorized that conflict plays a key role in the acquisition of new concepts in development. This stems from many theories (Baldwin, 1906; Freud, 1930/1961; Piaget, 1975/1985; Riegel, 1979) but Piaget's theory of equilibration has been the most influential in developmental research. Piaget (1975/1985) postulated that states of disequilibrium promote the child to seek solutions to problems and thus move to a higher level of understanding. Interpersonal conflicts are theorized to produce change because children are forced to take different viewpoints in order to maintain equilibrium (and social harmony) among interactants (see Bearison & Gass, 1979; Berkowitz, 1985; Nucci & Killen, 1991; Shantz & Hartup, 1992). Thus, the experience of conflict resolution is important for the construction of knowledge.

How children resolve conflicts has involved very little empirical scrutiny despite its central importance in human development. Much of what motivates the research is the notion that conflict facilitates change, yet this is very difficult to study empirically. Hence, the work has usually been very descriptive (What issues generate conflicts? How do gender and age influence methods of conflict resolution? How are conflicts resolved by teachers, by peers?) rather than theoretically motivated.

A small group of studies conducted from a theoretical perspective has tested hypotheses about change in development. These studies have shown that social interaction leads to advancement on both cognitive (Bearison & Gass, 1979; Doise & Mugny, 1979) and social-cognitive tasks (Berkowitz, 1985; Damon & Killen, 1982; Kruger, 1993; Kruger & Tomasello, 1986). Interestingly, the phenomena of conflict and conflict resolution have appeal for many investigators from a wide range of different perspectives and disciplines. Conflict resolution is a major focus of research in discourse processes (Garvey & Shantz, 1992; Grimshaw, 1990) and in ethological fields (Cords, 1988; de Waal, 1989).

From our viewpoint, an understudied aspect of conflict resolution is the way in which it demonstrates the emergence of autonomy and the coordination of autonomy and morality. An examination of the research literature on children's conflicts reveals a number of findings that are informative about both the moral nature of peer exchanges and the emergence of the autonomy of the individual, despite the lack of explicit focus on this topic (see Hay, 1984; Hay & Ross, 1982; Killen, 1991; Killen & Turiel, 1991; Ross & Conant, 1992). In the next section, we will discuss these features of children's social conflicts and demonstrate that they reveal how morality and autonomy are essential aspects of social exchanges. These studies have investigated the types of issues that generate conflicts, the justifications given, the resolutions, and the roles that adults and peers play in such exchanges.

Issues, justifications, and resolutions of conflicts

In general, conflict episodes are defined as instances in which one person "protests, retaliates, or resists the actions of another" (see Hay, 1984; Shantz, 1987). Research on the issues that generate conflicts in middle-class U.S. samples has shown that the most common form of conflict between young children stems from object disputes (sharing toys) followed by structuring activities (such as role playing); few conflicts stem from physical harm or aggression. Object disputes and physical harm have been typically referred to as "moral" because of the presence of a victim (e.g., someone gets his or her toys taken away; someone gets hurt) in contrast to conflicts stemming from social coordination (how to play a game) or social order (how to sit at juicetime), which do not involve a victim (Killen & Turiel, 1991).

In her review of the literature, Shantz (1987) makes the important point that conflicts should be differentiated from aggression. Not all conflicts are aggressive in nature. In support of this, it is interesting that object disputes (nonaggressive forms of interaction) predominant in young children's exchanges over acts of hitting and exclusion (aggressive forms). Conflicts over resources and those that stem from the infliction of physical harm both involve a "victim," but they are distinguished from each other in several important ways, particularly with respect to issues of autonomy.

Although both object disputes and aggressive acts involve "victims," the negative intrinsic consequences associated with physical harm and aggression are irreversible, unlike the consequences associated with object disputes, which can be "repaired." "Wrongs" can be made "right" through negotiation with the distribution of objects (e.g., one can give the toy back to the rightful owner); however, one cannot undo the harm that has been inflicted on another person during a conflict involving aggression. Thus, the most common form of conflict among children, object disputes, is constructive from a moral viewpoint because such disputes can be negotiated through social interaction. Most important for our argument, object disputes serve as a powerful source for asserting autonomy. In fact, the crux of object disputes is a struggle between the needs of the self ("I want that truck") and the needs of others ("You have three trucks and she doesn't have any!").

An examination of the types of justifications that children give during disputes provides one means for determining whether the autonomous claims of the self are legitimate or selfish. For example, the statement "I want it and you can't have it because I don't like you" would be considered selfish and less legitimate than the justification, "I want it because I am making a house and I need that block for my door," or "I want it because you have already had a turn with it and I haven't had a chance to use it yet." The latter two cases are considered more legitimate than the former instance because they tap two types of legitimate concerns: (1) a statement of autonomy: "I want it for a project I am making," and (2) a statement of morality: "I want it because it's fair." In the first example ("I want it and you can't have it because I don't like you"), autonomy is pitted against morality ("I want it" at the expense of thinking about the needs of others). In the second example, autonomy is identified as a personal project (building a house), and in the third example, autonomy is identified as a personal right (it's fair). Determining which form of autonomy is reflected in children's utterances is not easy; systematic study of the context of children's behavior and judgment is required in order to determine the meaning of the justification. Understanding young children's use of justifications during disputes is important, however, because it provides the first evidence for the emerging conceptualization regarding the coordination of the needs of others and the needs of the self with the emerging awareness of claims of entitlement, fairness, and justice.

Several investigators have pointed to the increased use of legitimate justifications regarding entitlement to objects from toddlerhood to preschool age in middle-class populations (Corsaro, 1985; Dunn & Munn, 1987; Eisenberg & Garvey, 1981; Ross & Conant, 1992). Preschool children frequently use justifications for making claims to objects; their entitlements are usually based on: (1) possession, (2) prior possession, or (3) ownership of objects (Ross & Conant, 1992). Ross and Conant (1992) report that the majority of conflicts with preschoolers are won by the initial possessor of the object under dispute. For example, in an observational study, toddlers who had just picked up a toy lost it 55% of the time, but toddlers who had it for awhile lost it 38% of the time (Bronson, 1981). Thus, one criterion that children use to base a judgment of entitlement is the length of engagement with a toy, which establishes temporary possession for the child; in some cases children view this as a legitimate basis for possession and they refrain from taking the object away from the possessor under these conditions.

A child who asserts his or her own autonomy regarding the possession of an object has a claim that is legitimately recognized by children of the same age. Similarly, Eisenberg-Berg, Haake, & Bartlett (1981) found that children who were told they were owners of objects possessed them longer, and they were more likely to make ownership claims, whereas nonowners gave them up sooner. The moral qualities present in these exchanges center around the recognition of the rights of others; the autonomous qualities pertain to the respect for the individual's claims to objects.

In a longitudinal study, Dunn and Munn (1987) examined the types of justifications that mothers and siblings used during conflict episodes in the home. In contrast to most research, which has been conducted with preschool (and older) children, they examined very young children's use of justifications. They found that the use of justifications increased with age from 18 months to 36 months. In addition, the types of justifications that children used were analyzed. The use of justifications referring to material consequences increased between 18 and 24 months, and between 24 and 36 months. Mothers' use of justifications about material consequences also increased as their children got older. In addition, children used justifications referring to their own feelings, social rules, and others' feelings. Interestingly, these justifications reflect both autonomy and morality; children gave reasons that reflected individualistic concerns (their own feelings), as well as consequences of actions (material consequences), and others' feelings. These findings suggest that justifications regarding morality and autonomy coexist in early development; one does not precede the other as has been postulated in traditional cognitive-developmental theory (Kohlberg, 1969; Piaget, 1932).

Research has also shown that when children use justifications during conflict episodes, the chance of the conflict ending is increased more than when children protest without articulating any reason for their actions. In fact, fewer conflicts arise when children give justifications for their actions than when they do not (Eisenberg & Garvey, 1981). These findings provide a partial explanation of what it is about peer interaction that is important in moral development: Peers reinforce the use of justifications by other peers in social exchanges. In contrast, adults often encourage compliance and acquiescence and do not encourage the use of reasons and justifications, especially by children who are perceived to be instigators.

How a conflict is resolved is an important indicator of the role that conflict plays in moral development. The types of resolutions that have been documented in young children's conflict exchanges include compromise, bargaining, negotiation, reconciliation, acquiescence, appealing to an adult, retaliation (physical or verbal), retribution (physical or verbal), topic dropping (or changing to a new activity), and observer or adult intervention (Hay, 1984; Killen & Turiel, 1991; Shantz, 1987; Shantz & Hartup, 1992). These resolutions vary the degree to which the needs of others are recognized (e.g., compromise) or not recognized (e.g., retribution).

Conflicts resolved through compromise provide a very different experience for children than ones resolved through retribution or appeal to an adult. Compromising involves a coordination of the needs of others with the needs of the self, whereas retribution is unilateral. If one child instigates a conflict and the topic is dropped (after the recipient protests the instigating action), then there is no clear indication that either child was aware of the needs of the other. However, if the topic is dropped but one child offers a compromise, then there is an indication that one child has taken the other child's viewpoint into consideration. One disadvantage of adult intervention is that it prevents children from having the opportunity to work out conflicts on their own and to develop a sense of self-efficacy. This does not mean that adult intervention is always negative or that peer compromises are never motivated by self-interest. There may be times when adult intervention is important because adults can point out intrinsic consequences of acts to children in ways that peers cannot. Yet, working out conflicts without adult intervention can foster a sense of autonomy and self-reliance in children in ways that are not apparent when adults mediate children's conflicts. In order to compromise one must recognize the needs of another in a way that appealing to an adult does not require. Because compromising requires refraining from a purely self-interested point of view, it has been theorized to lead to more mature forms of mutual respect and morality.

The empirical research on children's peer conflict shows that the least successful resolution strategies are sheer insistence on one's way and the use of physical or verbal aggression (Shantz & Shantz, 1985), and the most successful ones are those based on compromises, conditional statements, counterproposals, and reasons (e.g., those that reflect a sensitivity to the other's interests and needs) (Eisenberg & Garvey, 1981; Putallaz & Gottman, 1981). These findings suggest that the use of justifications ("I want it because X") reduces conflict. Thus, in some cases, nonmoral, nonselfish reasons are effective in resolving conflicts. When adults are present in children's conflict episodes, however, the events take on a different meaning. Adults can provide reasons for what makes an action wrong as well as communicate their view of children's self-efficacy and autonomy.

Adult influence on peer relations

Piaget (1932) first raised the provocative point that parents inhibit, rather than teach, moral development. His theory was based on the notion that parent–child relationships are not ones of equality. Only relations of equality, such as peer relations, provide the experiential basis for children to develop notions of equality and fairness. Youniss (1980), Damon (1977), and Turiel (1983) have also argued for an explanation of the acquisition of moral development based on the child's construction of knowledge rather than a direct learning from parents and adults. A central issue in this debate is the nature of peer interaction and its importance for the child's construction of morality. The empirical findings for this issue present a mixed picture on the role of the adult. Some findings support the notion that parents and teachers inhibit children's peer initiation of methods of conflict resolution whereas other research findings suggest that parents facilitate it (Ross & Conant, 1992).

As an example, Ross, Tesla, Kenyon, and Lollis (1990) examined mothers' interventions in their 20- and 30-month-old children's object disputes with peers and found that mothers supported the rights of the other child 90% of the time and were inconsistent in using principles of entitlement. Mothers did not support their own child's possession status; in fact, mothers often argued against possession and ownership ("Let her play with it because she doesn't have one like that at home"). Neither possession nor ownership guided the mothers' actions. Thus, mothers' behavior was not always consistent with principles of fairness, nor was it consistent with common justifications used by children at this age. Further, mothers were not supportive of the child's autonomy because issues of fairness were given priority over issues of autonomy (e.g., "let her have it even though it's yours"). These findings indicate that direct modeling of parental behavior is probably an inadequate explanation for the acquisition of morality because mothers are not consistent in their feedback to children regarding these forms of experience. Other sources of experience, such as peer interaction, must contribute to the child's construction of concepts of morality and a sense of personal autonomy.

Peer relations and adults' influence on conflict resolution

We now turn to a discussion of several studies conducted to examine how children resolve conflicts in different settings, taking into consideration how these interactions reveal aspects of the child's emerging sense of morality and autonomy. The research was designed to investigate the issues that generate conflicts, the methods of resolutions, and the different roles that peer and adult–child interaction play in the process of resolving conflicts (Arsenio & Killen, in press; Killen, 1989; Killen & Naigles, 1995; Killen & Sueyoshi, 1994; Killen & Turiel, 1991; Rende & Killen, 1992). In several studies, preschool-aged children were observed in two settings: (1) a peer group situation in which children were videotaped in triads in a nursery school playroom where they were given the opportunity to play with toys for 15 minutes without any adults present, and (2) nursery school free-play in which children were observed during regular school time when adults are present. These two settings have been referred to as closed-field and open-field, respectively, due to relative contextual constraints placed on the nature of play (Hartup, French, Laursen, Johnston, & Ogawa, 1993).

Observations of children's conflicts and resolution methods

In one study (Killen & Turiel, 1991), analyses were conducted on the source of conflict and the type of resolution in each of these two settings. The predominant source of conflict in the semistructured peer group situation was sharing toys (76%), whereas the source of conflict was more varied in the free-play setting. Although sharing toys was still the most frequent source (33%) of conflict in the free-play, other sources of conflict contributed to the overall percentage of disputes (e.g., physical and psychological harm, structuring activities, social order rules, friendship expectations). These findings were not surprising; children were asked to play with toys in the peer session for 15 minutes and it was expected that most of the conflicts would be about how to share the toys. What was surprising were the long, complex negotiation exchanges children engaged in over the use of objects in the peer triad situation. In the peer group setting, children engaged in negotiation exchanges that involved bargaining, trading toys, and third-party intervention (e.g., "I'll give you this yellow block if you give him that truck and he gives you the little cup"). In addition, children used a range of statements to indicate their entitlement ("I want it because I need it to make a bridge," "I want it because I don't have any," "I want it because you have three cars and I have none," "I want it because I haven't had it yet").

In semistructured peer groups 36% of the conflicts were resolved by children alone, whereas during free-play only 19% of the conflicts were resolved by children alone. Thus, a setting that was conducive to object disputes revealed complexities in children's methods of conflict resolution not often witnessed during free-play situations. There are several possible reasons that children generated longer resolution sequences in the peer groups than during the free-play setting: (1) In peer groups, children were asked to engage in sustained play whereas during free-play children change activities at a high rate (usually every 1–2 minutes); (2) children interacted with the same two partners for 15 minutes over four sessions whereas during free-play children change play partners at a high rate; and (3) adults were absent whereas during free-play adults often intervene in children's conflicts (sometimes before children have a chance to work them out on their own).

The results for the types of resolutions that occurred (topic dropped, child-generated, adult-generated) during free-play (for three free-play settings combined) showed that adults intervened in conflicts stemming from physical harm more than any other type of moral conflict (60% as opposed to 27% for psychological harm, 48% for object disputes, and 48% for use

of space disputes). Conflicts stemming from social order were largely resolved by adults (66%) and very rarely by children (7%) and sometimes
dropped (26%). Object disputes were more often resolved by children
(24%) than any other source of conflict. These findings reveal that even
during free-play children resolved object disputes despite the presence of
adults. This bears on the issue of morality and autonomy and the tension
between the two in several ways.

First, when adults intervene in children's interactions they limit children's opportunities to develop independence and autonomy and, in particular, how to resolve conflicts on their own without external assistance.
Yet, limiting children's opportunities to develop self-reliance often outweighs the alternative course of action (ignoring the event), which could
result in a moral infraction (e.g., someone getting hurt, someone being
deprived of play materials). Thus, adults, especially teachers, make decisions to give priority to autonomy or morality depending on the nature of
the consequences of an action. When parents and preschool teachers were
interviewed in a study to be described below in more detail, it was shown
that teachers were more willing than parents to subordinate the moral
consequences of acts to the priority of fostering autonomy in young children (e.g., "sometimes children need to struggle a little bit with the toys in
order to learn how to work out conflicts on their own").

Second, studies have shown that not all forms of adult intervention have
the same effect; some methods are more appropriate for facilitating children's morality and autonomy than other techniques. Walker and Taylor
(1991) videotaped family interactions and found that when parents used
supportive suggestions, children's moral reasoning was facilitated more
often than when parents used challenging statements. Further, Nucci and
Turiel (1978) observed how adults intervened in children's naturally occurring transgressions in the preschool and found that their methods varied
depending on the type of transgression. Adults used emotion statements
and explanations with moral transgressions (e.g., hitting, not sharing toys)
more often than with social-conventional ones (e.g., not running, wearing a
smock for painting, sitting at juicetime) in which they used commands and
disorder statements. Interestingly, children responded to moral transgression more often than to social-conventional ones. It is not known whether
this is because children understand the intrinsic consequences of moral
transgressions earlier than they understand social-conventional ones or
because adults use statements that focus on consequences when discussing
moral acts more than when discussing social-conventional acts; further
examination is needed.

In the preschool setting, we propose that when adults explain the nature of the intrinsic consequences to children (e.g., "she won't have any toys if you take them"), this helps children to focus on the perspective of the recipient of the act. In addition, methods of intervention that involve a request for the children to work it out themselves (e.g., "You kids should be able to work this out by yourself next time") assist children's abilities to develop a sense of autonomy and self-efficacy. These methods differ from straightforward commands (e.g., "Give it back") or rule statements (e.g., "You have to give those toys back because you know the rule at our school says that you have to share"), which neither provide children with information intrinsic to the act (morality) nor indicate that they can work it out themselves (autonomy).

Children's evaluations of adult intervention methods

Two studies were conducted to investigate how children evaluate adult methods of intervention in children's transgressions and conflicts (Nucci, 1984; Killen, Breton, Ferguson & Handler, 1994). In the study by Nucci (1984), elementary-school-aged children were asked to evaluate teachers who used different types of teacher intervention methods: domain appropriate and domain inappropriate. Domain appropriate statements were ones in which the teachers' explanation matched the domain of the transgression (a moral statement for a moral transgression, a social-conventional statement for a social-conventional transgression). Domain inappropriate statements were ones in which the teachers' explanation did not match the domain of the transgression (moral statement for a social-conventional transgression, social-conventional statements for a moral transgression). Nucci found that elementary-school-aged children rated teachers who used domain-appropriate statements as better teachers than the ones who used domain-inappropriate methods. Interestingly, children preferred teachers who spoke about transgressions in terms similar to their own understanding of what made the acts wrong.

In a related study, Killen, Breton, Ferguson, and Handler (1994) examined preschool-aged children's judgments about teacher intervention methods. Preschool children were interviewed regarding their evaluation of teacher intervention methods for four types of transgressions, two moral (hitting, not sharing toys) and two social-conventional ones (standing rather than sitting at juicetime, and playing with Legos in the sandbox). Children ($3\frac{1}{2}$, $4\frac{1}{2}$, and $5\frac{1}{2}$ years old) were asked to make two types of judgments. The first was a choice between two types of explanations (domain appropriate and domain inappropriate) and the second was a choice between the use of teacher intervention (time-out) and teacher-directed non-intervention (letting the children work it out on their own).

For the first judgment, the majority of children (57% for moral and 70% for social-conventional) preferred teachers to use domain-appropriate methods of intervention (e.g., telling an instigator who doesn't share toys to give some back "because it's not fair to the others who do not have any") rather than domain-inappropriate ones (e.g., telling an instigator who doesn't share toys to give some back "because it will make a mess when he has all of the toys on his side of the table"). For the second judgment, the majority of children (72%) preferred teachers to intervene rather than to let children work it out on their own (for both moral and social-conventional transgressions).

These results present two pictures of young children's social judgments. On the one hand, children understand the intrinsic consequences of acts (as evidenced by their preference for teachers to be domain consistent). On the other hand, children prefer teachers to intervene and use time-out rather than to let children work out conflicts on their own. The first judgment reveals young children's social and moral orientation; young children prefer teachers to explain conflicts in terms of the intrinsic consequences. The second judgment reveals aspects of children's nonautonomous orientation; young children prefer teachers to intervene in their conflicts rather than to let them work it out on their own. There are two possible interpretations of these findings. Children may prefer teachers to intervene because that's what teachers do, or they may prefer teachers to intervene because they think that is the best thing for them to do. Children's justifications for their answers support the latter interpretation. Children made statements like "the teacher should send the instigator to 'time-out' so he/she won't hurt anyone anymore." This suggests that children believed that the best thing for the teacher to do would be to remove the instigator from the situation because he or she was going to continue provoking conflicts. In future research we plan to ask children about whether teachers should let children work out conflicts on their own when the participants are friends and when they are nonfriends in order to determine if children's assumptions about the history of interactions among the participants influences their judgment about when teachers should intervene in children's conflicts and transgressions.

Mothers of preschool children were administered the same interview as the children for direct comparisons with children's evaluations of teachers' intervention strategies (Killen, LaFleur, & Beyers, in preparation). All mothers preferred teachers to use domain-appropriate explanations for moral transgressions (100%) and for social-conventional transgressions such as playing with Legos in the sandbox (87%); not all mothers believed that teachers should use moral explanations or social-conventional explanations for the social-conventional conflict about standing at juicetime (47% preferred social-conventional, "domain-appropriate" language and 52% preferred moral language). Mothers made sharp distinctions about the types of conflicts that teachers should let children work out on their own. No mothers thought that teachers should let children work out hitting conflicts on their own but 58% believed that teachers should let children work out conflicts about sharing toys. About one-third (33% and 25%) of the mothers preferred teacher-directed nonintervention for the two social-conventional conflicts (Legos and juicetime). The majority of mothers preferred teachers to use explicit statements regarding the social and moral nature of transgressions but were selective in the types of transgressions that mothers preferred teachers to let children work out on their own.

So far these studies have indicated that autonomy is an important dimension of children's interactions in the preschool setting and that it can be distinguished from children's moral interactions. Autonomy is a developing and emerging aspect of young children's lives, which is revealed in their justifications during conflict episodes and their evaluations of teacher methods of intervention. We did not find any gender differences in children's use of justifications and evaluations, which raises questions about the theory that autonomy is a male orientation, as has been articulated by Gilligan (1977) and her colleagues.

Another way in which autonomy has been contrasted with morality is in terms of cultural orientation, as we mentioned at the beginning of the chapter. Much recent research has described non-Western cultures, such as Japan, as being collectivistic and Western cultures as individualistic (Markus & Kitayama, 1991; Triandis, 1989). One of the assumptions of this dichotomy is that autonomy is a Western trait or characteristic. Non-Western morality is oriented to the group rather than to the individual and autonomy is not valued or emphasized in non-Western cultural teachings (Shweder, 1991). In order to determine the universality of the integral aspects of autonomy and morality in children's social interactions and social judgments, the first author conducted a study in two preschool settings in Tokyo, Japan (Killen & Sueyoshi, 1994).

Morality and autonomy in Japanese children's social interactions

In a study by Killen and Sueyoshi (1994), we were interested in several aspects of morality and autonomy in Japanese preschool social interactions.

First, we were interested in how morality and autonomy get expressed in Japanese children's interactions, particularly in methods of conflict resolutions. Second, we were interested in how Japanese children and adults make judgments about teacher methods of intervention that indicate preferences for different types of explanations.

Part of the motivation for our study was to reexamine the ways in which the two constructs, morality and autonomy, were portrayed by Tobin, Wu, and Davidson (1989) in their ethnographic study on preschool children's daily activities in three cultures, Japan, China, and the United States. In their study, Tobin et al. refer to the Japanese as oriented to "gentle groupism," the Chinese as oriented to "authoritarian groupism," and the Americans as exhibiting individualism. Japanese educators emphasize the importance of "groupism" through structured group activities, the use of school uniforms, large class sizes, a deemphasis on individual differences among children, and a rewarding of children's efforts, not abilities. In contrast, American educators promote "individualism" through individualized attention, small class sizes, and an emphasis on fairness, justice, rights, autonomy, self-reliance, creativity, and competition among children. In essence, Tobin et al. assert that morality, defined as fairness and rights, and autonomy, defined as self-reliance, are features of American preschool life, not reflective of Japanese or Chinese culture.

The research reported by Tobin et al. was in the form of a rich narrative, documenting the daily lives of preschool children in different cultures. One limitation of the research reported in their book, however, is that it was anecdotal. The authors did not aim to systematically observe children's behavior according to a standard set of categories applied to each culture. For example, Japanese preschool behavior was organized under headings such as "Group Life" (p. 38), "Class Size and Student/teacher Ratios" (p. 36). American preschool behavior was organized under headings such as "Liberty" (p. 137), "Self Reliance and Independence" (p. 138), "Freedom of Choice and Variety of Experience" (p. 139), "Freedom and Constraint" (p. 141), "Individualism" (p. 144), and "Liberty, Equality, and Fraternity" (p. 146). Tobin et al. did not report whether they found groupism in the U.S. preschool or self-reliance, freedom, individualism, or liberty in the Japanese preschool. Regarding conflict resolution, Tobin et al. referred to these exchanges as reflecting the American sense of justice, rights, and liberty ("justice and the process of negotiation is a middle-class American approach to conflict resolution" [1989, p. 167]). Further, Tobin et al. interpreted the U.S. children's ability to resolve conflicts on their own as reflecting the emerging sense of self-reliance and autonomy in the U.S. culture. Thus, one goal of our study (Killen & Sueyoshi, 1994) was to reexamine Tobin et al.'s portrayal of morality and autonomy in the Japanese preschool culture.

Our study was designed to investigate the types of issues that generate conflicts, how children resolve them, and the roles that teachers play in such exchanges. In addition, children, parents, and teachers were interviewed about methods of conflict resolution. The interview we administered to children and mothers in Japan was identical to the one we used in the U.S. study, with modifications in the picture drawings and names of children (in pilot observations we found that the conflicts depicted in the interview stories were frequently occurring events in the Japanese setting). First, findings for the observational study will be reported and then the results for the interview study.

Observations in Japanese preschool settings

For the observational part of the study, preschool-aged children in a day-care (hoiken) classroom located in a middle-class section of Tokyo participated in the study. Twenty-nine children were observed for four 15-minute sessions (totaling 1 hour per child) during free-play time, which resulted in 148 conflict episodes. The conflicts were recorded and then translated by Sueyoshi with the help of a professor of education at a university in Tokyo. We discovered that conflicts were frequent, everyday occurrences in Japan, just as they are in the United States. (Lina Sueyoshi spent several months in the daycare prior to recording conflicts in order to become familiar with the setting.) Analyses were conducted on the source of the conflict, the method of resolution, the gender of the instigator, and the type of conflict (unilateral or mutual). Here is a sample excerpt of a conflict among Japanese children:

> Obs. #82. Setting: Free-play, outdoors.
> Hana: [Is drawing a girl in a notebook that children use to draw in.]
> Aichan: I want to draw, too!
> Hana: You'll have to wait because I'm still drawing.
> Aichan: [Not listening to her] I want to draw!
> Hana: Can you wait just a little bit longer? I haven't finished drawing all the hair yet.
> See [pointing to the hair].
> Aichan: I want to draw! You're not being fair!
> Hana: [Patiently] Just a little bit more, okay? I'm almost done.
> Aichan: Okay. [She walks away and comes back later to draw.]

What struck us about this conflict episode was the similarity between this conflict exchange and ones recorded for the American sample. In this episode, the simultaneous expression of autonomy ("I want to draw") and morality ("You're not being fair") is verbalized by the child who wants to draw. Furthermore, the children worked out the conflict through a compromise (one child asks the other to wait until she is done drawing and the other child walks away and comes back later to draw). This observation counters some of Tobin et al.'s statements that Japanese children do not express concerns for autonomy and justice.

The quantitative analyses of the observations revealed that the majority of children's conflicts (47%) stemmed from social order (e.g., structuring activities). The second most frequent source of conflict (30%) was the distribution of resources (e.g., object disputes and turn taking). Of the conflicts categorized as distribution of resources, 31% were object disputes and 69% were turn taking. Only 9% of all conflicts stemmed from object disputes. Conflicts that stemmed from psychological harm (14%) included exclusion, name calling, and teasing. Very few conflicts stemmed from physical harm (8%). Thus, just as with the U.S. data, children had many conflicts about structuring activities and very few about the infliction of physical harm. Most conflicts involving a "victim" were about object disputes and turn taking rather than physical harm or exclusion.

The major difference between the Japanese and American preschool sources of conflict was that Japanese children had very few object disputes (only 9%) and American children typically have a large number of object disputes (see Shantz, 1987). Yet, Japanese children had many conflicts about turn taking. For example, children had turn-taking disputes about the use of the jump rope and the swing. The differences between object disputes and turn taking have to do, in part, with the available resources and physical setting. Japanese preschool children spend more time outside than do American preschool children. Activities such as use of the swing, jump rope, slide, and climbing apparatus generated more conflicts about turn taking than activities involving block play and crafts, which generated more conflicts about object disputes. In both types of conflicts, however, competing claims have to be weighed and reasons can be provided for determining who gets access to the resource. Although it can seem as if Japanese children do not focus on fairness because they have few object disputes, many of the Japanese conflicts about turn taking involved discussions about rights and fairness as evidenced in the protocol reported here. Children had frequent disputes about whose turn it was to hold the jump rope and to swing. In addition, children asserted their rights by referring to the amount of time someone has already had with a desired resource ("you have had it a long time"). Interestingly, initial possessors of object disputes won the disputes 64% of the time replicating American findings (reported by Ross & Conant, 1992) that children acknowledge past possession of an object as a legitimate claim.

Analyses regarding the types of resolutions to conflicts showed that adults rarely played a role in resolving children's conflicts. Most conflicts were resolved by children through compromising and bargaining (30%), reconciliation (21%), or letting the topic drop (26%). Adults intervened in 18% of the conflicts; of these, 16% involved explanations from the adult (only 2% involved adult command and rule statements). The breakdown for the source of conflict by resolution type shows that, for physical harm, the predominant method of resolution was adult intervention (33%); the rest of these conflicts were resolved by children or dropped. The predominant form of resolution for conflicts stemming from psychological harm was child-generated methods (57%) or topic dropped (33%); adults rarely played a role (10%). Distribution of resources was generally resolved with child-generated methods (57%); 29% were dropped, and 15% were resolved by adults. And for conflicts about structuring activities, the majority were resolved by children (54%); 22% involved adult intervention (18% with explanations and 4% without explanations), and 25% were dropped. These findings are in contrast to the American sample because adults played a very minor role in resolving conflicts in Japan whereas adults played a significant role in resolving children's conflicts in the U.S. study reported here.

Other researchers also have observed that Japanese nursery school teachers rarely intervene in children's conflicts (Lewis, 1984; Tobin et al., 1989). This has been interpreted in different ways. Tobin et al. have argued that the lack of teacher intervention reflects the group orientation of Japanese culture because preschool class sizes tend to be large, thus minimizing the teacher–child interaction and increasing the group interaction. Other researchers have pointed to the self-reliance that adult nonintervention fosters in young children in Japan (Lewis, 1984). By not intervening in children's conflicts, teachers encourage self-reliance in young children. Yet, self-reliance has been categorized as a feature of Western, not non-Western cultures. Thus, one interpretation of nonintervention is that it reflects a collectivistic, non-Western view and the other interpretation is that it reflects a Western, individualistic perspective.

We propose that both aspects are part of Japanese culture; the group and the individual are emphasized in different ways. Japanese teachers explained their nonintervention approach in terms of promoting autonomy in young children ("children will learn to resolve conflicts on their own if we do not intervene too quickly"). An interesting finding was that adults rarely used command statements when intervening in children's conflicts. When they intervened, they used explanations and rationales. What made this approach remarkable was that teachers were able to use explanations even with a large preschool class size (1 teacher for 25 students) relative to American standards (2–3 teachers for 15 children). American teachers stated that they preferred to use explanations over command statements, but when the class sizes got large they had to resort to the use of commands and rule statements. Interestingly, Japanese teachers do not seem to have this problem. This feature of adult–child interactions also contrasts to general cultural characterizations of collectivistic cultures. It is usually expected that collectivistic cultures do not place the same emphasis on reasoning and judgment as is done in individualistic cultures. Tobin et al. (1989) invoked this characterization when describing the American preschool, which they said encouraged "children to use words to express their positive feelings as well as to resolve disputes" (1989, p. 152). Yet, we found that Japanese teachers repeatedly intervened in children's conflicts by asking them whether they had told the other children of their concern, desire, or intention. As an example, consider the following protocol:

Setting: Three children, Isumi, Koji, and Takuma, are drawing pictures. Koji taps Takuma on the head. He repeats this several times. After a few minutes, Takuma retaliates by pushing Koji. They begin hitting each other. Another child, Sayuki, goes and tells the teacher. A few seconds later, the teacher comes running over.

Teacher: Why are you crying, Takuma?
Takuma: Because Koji hit me in the head [sobbing].
Teacher: Tell Koji that you don't want to be hit in the head.
Takuma: I did.
Koji: [Steps away from Takuma, fidgeting with his fingers.]
Teacher: Why don't you say it one more time?
Takuma: I said it many times.
Koji: No, he only said it only once.
Teacher: [Turning to Koji] Koji, you're supposed to stop even if he says it once! Why did you hit him?
Koji: [No answer.]
Teacher: [Directing herself back to Takuma] Takuma, you've got to stop crying and tell him. If you don't tell him why you don't want him to do that, Koji won't understand why he can't do it.

In this example, the teacher emphasizes the use of reasoning and judgment. The teacher tells the recipient to inform the instigator that hitting is wrong, and to explain why it is wrong. What differs from this account as compared with American teacher methods of resolution is that the teacher did not chastise the instigator (e.g., "don't hit him") nor did the teacher point out the harm on her own (e.g., "you hurt him"). Instead the teacher focused on communication and methods of reconciliation (e.g., "tell him that you don't want to be hit"). The teacher did not refrain from using reasoning but refrained from punishing the instigator. A positive aspect of this approach is that it reduces the use of aggression to gain adult attention, which is often interpreted as a cause for American children's instigating behavior (to gain attention from the teacher).

We found that teachers' tendency to intervene in children's conflicts varied by the source of the conflict. Conflicts stemming from physical harm were resolved by teacher intervention more than by any other method. The way that teachers intervened differed from American methods but not along the stereotyped cultural characterizations. We found that Japanese teachers used reasoning and judgment as part of their intervention strategy. The teachers made attempts to promote peer interaction, a Piagetian concept! In fact, children's free-play social interactions resembled the videotaped peer group sessions reported in the Killen and Turiel (1991) study conducted in the United States. In those peer group sessions, adults were absent and American children engaged in long deliberations about conflicts, not recorded during free-play. In Japan, children had long conversations during free-play, a setting in which adults were present but rarely intervened.

Interviews with Japanese children and mothers

In order to better understand how Japanese children and mothers evaluate teacher methods of intervention, Japanese children ($N=20$) and mothers ($N=20$) were interviewed with the same interview given to the American children and mothers (Killen & Sueyoshi, 1994). The interview was translated by the second author of the study with help from the local preschool directors. As described (see Killen et al., 1994), subjects were administered four conflict stories (hitting, not sharing toys, playing with Legos in the sandbox, and standing at juicetime) and were asked to make two judgments: (1) a choice between two teacher explanations, domain appropriate and domain inappropriate; and (2) time-out (punishment) and nonintervention.

As indicated in Table 2.1, the Japanese children and mothers were remarkably similar to each other when assessing the types of explanations teachers should give to children when intervening in transgressions. The majority of Japanese children preferred domain-appropriate explanations for social-conventional transgressions (80% and 70% for Legos and juicetime) and for one of the moral transgressions, not sharing toys (65%). Like the American children (Killen et al., 1994), Japanese children preferred teachers to explain hitting in social-conventional, rather than moral terms (only 35% preferred domain-appropriate moral explanations for the hitting story). This meant that children preferred teachers to use explanations that focused on the

Table 2.1. *Percentage of preferences for teacher intervention and teacher-directed nonintervention by Japanese children and mothers*

	Children (N = 20)	Mothers (N = 20)
Domain-appropriate teacher intervention methods		
Sharing	65	100
Hitting	35	100
Legos	80	60
Juicetime	70	55
Teacher-directed nonintervention ("Work it out")		
Sharing	70	90
Hitting	70	35
Legos	80	95
Juicetime	70	55

Notes: Domain appropriate = moral statements for moral conflicts; social-conventional statements for social-conventional conflicts; sharing = sharing toys; hitting = hitting with a plastic shovel in the sandbox; Legos = playing with legos in the sandbox; juicetime = standing rather than sitting at juicetime.
Source: Killen and Sueyoshi (1994).

disturbance created when one child hits another child rather than on the pain that will occur.

Our interpretation of children's response to the hitting story is that children interpreted the disturbance as another moral consequence of the act of hitting. In the "domain-inappropriate" picture card, the teacher points to a child covering his ears because of the commotion being created by one child hitting another child (in the "domain-appropriate" picture card, the teacher points to the recipient of the hitting behavior who looks unhappy). For some children, this may have been interpreted as another harmful consequence of the act (making the story a "mixed-domain" event). The results for children's justifications support this interpretation. Children justified their choice of the domain inappropriate explanation by referring to the harm that occurred to the child covering his or her ears during the transgression. (Also, in a previous study, Killen et al., 1994, we found this judgment to be age-related.)

As shown in the table, all Japanese mothers (100%) preferred teachers to use domain-appropriate methods for moral transgressions and the majority preferred domain-appropriate methods (60% and 55%) for social-conventional transgressions. Japanese, as well as American mothers, preferred teachers to talk about the harm occurring or the unfairness when one child hit another or took someone's toy, rather than to talk about the disturbance or the mess.

Japanese children (and mothers) were very different from the American sample, however, regarding their views about whether teachers should let children work out conflicts on their own. The majority of Japanese children ($M=75\%$ for all transgressions) preferred teachers to let children work out conflicts on their own; the majority of Japanese mothers preferred this method (for all transgressions except for hitting in which only 35% preferred teachers to let the children "work it out"). This is in direct contrast to the American sample where a minority of children preferred teachers to let children work it out (only 25% of American children preferred teacher-nonintervention over "timeout"; Killen et al., 1994).

These findings were surprising because they suggest that Japanese mothers prefer teachers to encourage autonomy and self-reliance in their children. The implications are that autonomy and morality are both present in American and Japanese cultures. We propose that cultural differences are primarily in how morality and autonomy are coordinated. At times, teachers and parents emphasized autonomy ("sometimes they have to "fight it out" to gain confidence and assert their own position") in each culture, and, at other times, adults stressed the importance of moral considerations ("you should give that toy to her because she hasn't had it yet and you have had it a long time"). How these two considerations are coordinated in different situations varies in each culture.

What becomes clear in our observations and interviews with children in both American and Japanese cultures is that conflictful exchanges in young children provide an important opportunity for children to negotiate these two central features of social development, morality and autonomy. Rather than considering conflicts as a clash between moral and selfish desires, we believe it is important to acknowledge the nonmoral, *nonselfish* claims made by young children. Just as in adult life, when personal projects (getting an education), personal ambitions (working on a career), and personal hobbies (listening to opera) are legitimate, nonmoral, nonselfish goals, so too are the types of considerations children often articulate in their conflicts with one another. In the next section, we explore the way in which issues in the personal domain get expressed in adult–child interactions in everyday life.

Social conflict and children's personal domain

The peer conflicts described in the preceding sections, entailing attempts by children to establish moral equilibriums between their own needs or wishes and those of others, are complemented by another set of social interactions from which children construct concepts about areas of behavior that are a matter of personal choice and privacy rather than moral or social regulation. This set of actions comprises what we have called the personal domain (Nucci, 1981; Smetana, Chapter 7, this volume) and our emphasis in this section will be on children's exchanges with adults.

The establishment of a personal domain is part and parcel of what it means to have social autonomy. The construction of what is private or personal, however, is not an autochthonous achievement involving only the child's claims to freedom of action. It is socially constructed out of negotiation and input from others (Nucci, 1994). We have already seen how extensions of personal freedoms to personal control over objects enter into children's negotiations involving sharing. During childhood some of the most important of these interactions occur in the give-and-take of friendships during which issues of personal boundaries are dealt with in a context defined by their interpersonal connectedness (Sullivan, 1953). For, unlike the moral exchanges discussed earlier in this chapter, the child's exercise of choice often takes place in the context of relationships that are inherently asymmetric. Since children are dependent on adult protection, nurturance, and teaching, a child's freedom of action is almost always at the mercy of adults. This is especially the case in relations between children and parents, where issues of adult authority and responsibility coexist with parental tendencies to invest their own familial and personal identities in their children. Thus, although children's sense of fairness and reciprocity is constructed largely out of interactions with peers, children's constructions of personal freedom are substantially tied to their attempts to negotiate within their asymmetric relations with adults.

Adult–child interaction and the personal

Social conflicts dealing with personal issues were the subject of a recent study examining the social interactions of 20 middle-class mothers and their 3- or 4-year-old children (Nucci & Weber, in press). This study examined how interactions pertaining to personal matters differed from interactions regarding interpersonal regulation. Mother–child dyads were observed during four activity periods over a span of 3 days. Trained coders classified event sequences as moral, conventional, prudential (issue of self-harm), personal, or mixed. For the most part, interactions around uncontested personal issue involved social messages from the mothers indicating recognition that the child's activity was one of personal choice. Mothers did so in two ways. In some cases mothers simply stated so directly as in the following example.

> Mother: If you want, you can get your hair cut. *It's your choice.*
> Child: I only want it that long – down to here. [Child points to where she wants her hair cut.]

More typically, the social messages mothers directed to children about personal issues were in the form of offered choices such as in the following exchange:

> Mother: You need to decide what you want to wear to school today.
> Child: I wear these.
> Mother: Okay, that's a good choice.

In this interaction, the mother conveyed through an offered choice that dress is a matter for the child to decide. The child might accordingly infer that such behavior is personal. Through both direct and indirect forms of communication mothers indicated a willingness to provide children areas of personal discretion. Not all events involving personal issues, however, were uncontested. Mothers and children engaged in negotiation in about one-quarter of the events involving personal issues. Conflicts also arose over mixed events. Approximately 90% of the mixed events observed in the study involved overlap with the personal domain. Mothers engaged in negotiations with their children in the context of such mixed events about half of the time. This is illustrated in the following interaction.

> Mother: Evan, it's your last day of nursery school. Why don't you wear your nursery sweatshirt?
> Child: I don't want to wear that one.
> Mother: This is the last day of nursery school, that's why we wear it. You want to wear that one?
> Child: Another one.
> Mother: Are you going to get it, or should I?
> Child: I will. First I got to get a shirt.
> Mother: [Goes to the child's dresser and starts picking out shirts.] This one? This one? Do you know which one you have in mind? Here, this is a new one.
> Child: No, it's too big.
> Mother: Oh, Evan, just wear one, and when you get home, you can pick whatever you want, and I won't even help you. [Child puts on shirt.]

This case presents a conflict between a dress convention (wearing a particular shirt on the last day of school) and the child's view that dress is a personal choice. The mother acknowledged the child's resistance and attempted to negotiate, finally offering the child a free choice once school is over. This example illustrates several things. For one, the mother provided direct information to the child about the convention in question, "This is the last day of nursery school, that's why we wear it." At the same time, the mother exhibited an interest in fostering the child's autonomy and decision making around the issue. The child's resistance, which conveyed the child's personal interest, was not simply cut off, but was guided by the mother, who linked it to the child's autonomy: "Are you going to get it, or should I? . . . you can pick whatever you want, and *I won't even help you.*" In the end, there was compromise. The child got to choose, but within a more general conventional demand (enforced by the mother) that he wear a shirt.

The verbal exchange in this example is further illustration that the mothers in this study acted in ways that indicated an understanding that children should have areas of discretion and personal control. The excerpt also illustrates ways in which children, through their resistances, provided mothers with information about the *child's* desires and needs for personal choice. Analyses of the individual responses provided by children indicated that assertions of prerogative and personal choice did not occur to the same degree across all forms of social interaction, but were disproportionately associated with events involving personal issues. Assertions of prerogative and choice comprised 88% of children's responses in the context of mixed events, and 98% of their responses in the case of predominantly personal events. In contrast, such responses comprised less than 10% of children's statements in the context of moral or prudential events, and about 25% of their responses to conventional events. These behavioral measures indicate that middle-class preschool-aged children have differentiated conceptions of the personal from matters of interpersonal social regulation. Interviews conducted with the children revealed that they viewed personal, but not moral or conventional behaviors as one's that should be up to the "self" and not the mother to decide.

This observational study (Nucci & Weber, in press) provided evidence that children play an active role in relation to their mothers, and provide feedback in the form of requests and resistances to their mothers that afford mothers information regarding the child's claims to areas of personal control. This feedback is not simply a generalized resistance to adult authority (Brehm & Brehm, 1981; Kuczinski, Kochanska, Radke-Yarrow, & Girnius-Brown, 1987), but a delimited set of claims to choice over a personal sphere. This is most evident in cases of mixed events, and suggests that mothers open to their children's feedback have direct access to information about their own children's needs for a personal domain. At the same time, these conflicts over what children regard as personal issues provide children with information about the social boundaries of their personal freedom. Thus, the construction of what is personal appears to be a reciprocal system entailing an interplay between children's claims to freedom, and social feedback confirming or constraining those claims. Smetana's (1989) work on adolescent–parent conflicts indicates that similar types of child resistance to adult control over what children view as personal continues throughout development as children move away from status as dependents and subordinates to status as adults (see also Youniss & Smollar, 1985).

Cultural factors

Given the interactive social basis for the child's construction of the personal, it is not surprising to find that cultural variations exist in the specific content of what gets included within the personal domain. Recent work in India has provided evidence of cultural variations in what gets treated as a matter of personal choice as opposed to interpersonal moral obligation (Miller & Bersoff, 1992; Chapter 8, this volume). Other research has demonstrated that cultures differ in how personal "rights" are distributed according to gender (see Wainryb & Turiel's Chapter 9, this volume). Despite these variations, however, we do know that conceptions about personal issues are not confined to so called Western individualist cultures, and that conflicts between adolescents and parents over issues concerning adolescents' personal freedom are likewise evident across cultures. Yau and Smetana (1994), for example, reported that Chinese adolescent–parent relations were not without conflict (although less so than in the United States), and that conflicts were over the same types of issues as their American counterparts. Most interesting for our purposes here is that the adolescents in their study positioned their arguments in terms of exercising personal jurisdiction.

At the present time, however, we have no cross-cultural ethnographic or observational data that directly examine cultural variations in how interactions between children and adults play themselves out over children's personal issues. The most direct look at culture and class effects on children's and parents' views of children's personal autonomy has been conducted in Brazil (Nucci, Camino, & Sapiro, 1993). Interviews of 240 northeastern Brazilian children and adolescents from four social classes and three ages (6–8, 10–12, 14–16 years of age) revealed class differences in the tendency of children to view issues as personal. Lower-class children were less likely than middle-class children to view personal issues as ones that children rather than parents should control. However, by age sixteen, the majority of children across all social classes treated personal issues in the same way, that is, as actions children, rather than parents, should determine. In the second portion of their research, Nucci et al. (1993) found similar class differences in Brazilian mothers' views of children's personal autonomy. In their study they interviewed 120 lower- and middle-class mothers from the southern and northeastern regions of the country. The southern region of Brazil is culturally similar to Europe and North America, whereas the northeast is more traditional and has been characterized as a collectivist culture (Triandis, 1990).

Findings from the interviews with mothers revealed regional and class differences in the ways in which mothers viewed the personal domains of their children. Mothers from southern Brazil and middle-class mothers from both the southern and northeastern regions were more likely to treat children's personal items as ones the children should have choice over, and were more likely to see such issues as negotiable than were mothers from northeastern Brazil or lower-class mothers from either region. There were age effects associated with these regional and class differences in the mothers' views that paralleled findings with the northeastern Brazilian children. Lower-class mothers from both regions of Brazil stated that children under the age of 10 should not be allowed to have decision-making authority over any of their actions because they believed their children had not matured sufficiently to have the reasoning capacity to form personal opinions and might make choices that would be impractical or harmful to themselves. Middle-class mothers from both regions of Brazil, however, stated that children should have decision-making authority over some personal actions in order to develop their emerging personal autonomy, agency, and competence. In contrast with their views about young children, the majority of Brazilian women across social classes stated that adolescents should have freedom of choice over personal issues. Interestingly, Brazilian mothers from all of the groups including lower-class mothers of young children responded affirmatively to the question of whether it was important for a child to develop a sense of individuality. Mothers across classes and regions tended to use similar reasons, which expressed a desire for their children to establish uniqueness, autonomy, competence, and agency. In other words, mothers irrespective of social class or culture expressed concerns for children's autonomy and individuality.

These studies with Brazilian children and mothers indicate that Brazilian children treat a class of actions as matters that are "personal" and within their area of privacy and individual regulation. Furthermore, they provide evidence that Brazilian mothers also differentiate between areas of children's activity that mothers should control, and areas that are in the children's personal sphere and should be left to children to determine. What is perhaps most important is that these data provide evidence for Brazilian conceptions of personal autonomy and individuality that are in many respects similar to such conceptualizations in so-called "individualistic" cultures.

In sum, cross-cultural studies of children's personal autonomy provide a complex picture indicating that caution needs to be exercised in any effort to extend research about children's areas of personal choice to members of non-Western or traditional cultures. In taking these cultural factors into account, however, it is important to resist tendencies to view cultures as homogeneous and to assume that personhood and the individual are concepts of concern only to what are referred to as individualistic cultures. While notions of "self" like beliefs about the personal are culturally variable, all cultures contain some differentiated view of self, and members of all cultures appear to hold idiosyncratic individual views of themselves as distinct persons with particular interests (Spiro, 1993). Expression of the self through actions in the personal domain both instantiate those individual characteristics of "self" but also enact the rights or freedoms accorded members of a given cultural group. Coordinations of "rights" through resolutions of interpersonal conflicts in childhood and adolescence are, thus, at once the spontaneous inventions of individual children responding to fundamental psychological and social realities, and the expression of the cultural context in which they take place. Variations in these constructions of the personal are thus connected to cultural and individual variations in what counts as a moral issue. A productive area for future research on children's sociomoral development, then, would be on the cultural variations in children's interactions and conflicts over the personal.

Conclusions

In this chapter, one of our goals was to demonstrate the ways in which legitimate claims of the self are a part of the everyday lives of children and are central for the acquisition and formation of morality in development. We believe that it is important to conceptualize autonomy as an integral part of morality, rather than as a lesser form of it, its polar opposite, a gender orientation, or a cultural dimension. Our data stemmed from children's social interactions in preschool settings, peer groups, and with parents in the home. These naturalistic contexts provided rich sources of information for determining the nature of children's statements about, reflections on, and evaluations of fairness, justice, autonomy, personal entitlement, and self-efficacy. Only through a detailed analysis of children's interactions in familiar, everyday settings, can the form of their concerns and obligations be understood. Further, analyses of children's peer and adult–child interactions in these cultural contexts will better enable us to grasp the complexity and interweaving nature of autonomy and morality in development.

References

Arsenio, W., & Killen, M. (in press). Preschoolers' emotions and conflicts during small group play. *Early Education and Development.*

Baldwin, J. M. (1906). *Social and ethical interpretations of mental development.* New York: Macmillan.

Bearison, D., & Gass, S. T. (1979). Hypothetical and practical reasoning: Children's persuasive appeals in different social contexts. *Child Development, 50,* 901–903.

Bellah, R., Madsen, R., Sullivan, W., Swidler, A., & Tipton, S. (1985). *Habits of the heart: Individualism and commitment in American life.* New York: Harper and Row.

Berkowitz, M. (Ed.). (1985). *Peer conflict and psychological growth: New directions for child development.* San Francisco: Jossey-Bass.

Brehm, S. S., & Brehm, J. W. (1981). *Psychological reactions: A theory of freedom and control.* New York: Academic Press.

Bronson, W. C. (1981). Toddlers' behavior with agemates: Issues of interaction, cognition, and affect. In L. P. Lipsitt (Ed.), *Monographs on infancy.* Norwood, NJ: Ablex.

Cords, M. (1988). Resolution of aggressive conflicts by immature long-tailed macques (*Macaca fascicularis*). *Animal Behavior, 36,* 1124–1135.

Corsaro, W. (1985). *Peer culture in the early years.* Norwood, NJ: Ablex.

Damon, W. (1977). *The social world of the child.* San Francisco: Jossey-Bass.

Damon, W. (1983). *Social and personality development.* New York: Norton.

Damon, W., & Hart D. (1988). *Self-understanding in childhood and adolescence.* Cambridge: Cambridge University Press.

Damon, W., & Killen, M. (1982). Peer interaction and processes of change in moral reasoning. *Merrill-Palmer Quarterly, 28,* 347–367.

Davidson, P., & Youniss, J. (1991). Which comes first, morality or identity? In W. M. Kurtines & J. L. Gewirtz (Eds.), *The handbook of moral behavior and development* (Vol. 1, p. 105–121). Hillsdale, NJ: Lawrence Erlbaum.

de Waal, F. (1989). *Peacemaking among primates.* Cambridge, MA: Harvard University Press.

Doise, W., & Mugny, G. (1979). Individual and collective conflicts of centrations in cognitive development. *European Journal of Social Psychology, 9,* 105–108.

Dunn, J., & Munn, P. (1987). The development of justification in disputes. *Developmental Psychology, 23,* 791–798.

Dworkin, R. (1977). *Taking rights seriously.* Cambridge, MA: Harvard University Press.

Eisenberg, A., & Garvey, C. (1981). Children's use of verbal strategies in resolving conflicts. *Discourse Processes, 4,* 149–170.

Eisenberg-Berg, N., Haake, R. J., & Bartlett, K. (1981). The effects of possession and ownership on the sharing and proprietary behaviors of preschool children. *Merrill-Palmer Quarterly, 27,* 61–68.

Freud, S. (1930/1961). *Civilization and its discontents.* New York: Norton.

Garvey, C., & Shantz, C. U. (1992). Conflict talk: Approaches to adversarial discourse. In C. U. Shantz and W. W. Hartup (Eds.), *Conflict in child and adolescent development* (pp. 93–121). Cambridge: Cambridge University Press.

Gewirth, A. (1978). *Reason and morality.* Chicago: University of Chicago Press.

Gewirth, A. (1982). *Human rights: Essays on justification and application.* Chicago: University of Chicago Press.

Gilligan, C. (1977). In a different voice: Women's conceptions of self and morality. *Harvard Educational Review, 47,* 481–517.

Gilligan, C. (1986). Remapping the moral domain: New images of the self in relationship. In

T. Heller, M. Sosna, & D. Wellbery (Eds.), *Reconstructing individualism: Autonomy, individuality, and the self in Western thought* (pp. 237–252). Stanford, CA: Standford University Press.

Grimshaw, A. (1990). *Conflict talk.* Cambridge: Cambridge University Press.

Hartup, W. W., French, D., Laursen, B., Johnston, M., & Ogawa, J. (1993). Conflict and friendship relations in middle childhood: Behavior in a closed-field situation. *Child Development, 64,* 445–454.

Hay, D. F. (1984). Social conflict in early childhood. In G. Whitehurst (Ed.), *Annals of child development* (pp. 1–44). Greenwich, CT: JAI.

Hay, D. F., & Ross, H. (1982). The social nature of early conflict. *Child Development, 53,* 105–113.

Kagan, J. (1984). *The nature of the child.* New York: Basic Books.

Kant, I. (1785/1959). *Foundations of the metaphysics of morals* (Lewis White Beck, Trans.). Indianapolis: Bobbs-Merrill.

Killen, M. (1989). Context, conflict, and coordination in early social development. In L. T. Winegar (Ed.), *Social interaction and the development of children's understanding,* (pp. 119–146). Norwood, NJ: Ablex.

Killen, M. (1991). Social and moral development in early childhood. In W. Kurtines & J. Gewirtz (Eds.), *Handbook of moral behavior and development* (Vol. 2, pp. 115–138). Hillsdale, NJ: Lawrence Erlbaum.

Killen, M., Breton, S., Ferguson, H., & Handler, K. (1994). Preschoolers' evaluations of teacher methods of intervention in social transgressions. *Merrill-Palmer Quarterly, 40,* 399–416.

Killen, M., LaFleur, R. & Beyers, J. (in preparation) *Mothers', fathers', and teachers' evaluations of ideal and practical methods of conflict resolution in the preschool setting.* Unpublished manuscript.

Killen, M., & Naigles, L. (1995). Preschool children pay attention to their addressees: Effects of gender composition on peer disputes. *Discourse Processes, 19,* 329–345.

Killen, M., & Sueyoshi, L. (1994, June). *Conflict resolution in Japanese preschool settings.* Paper presented at the 24th Annual Meeting of the Jean Piaget Society, Chicago.

Killen, M., & Turiel, E. (1991). Conflict resolutions in preschool social interactions. *Early Education and Development, 2,* 240–255.

Kohlberg, L. (1969). Stage and sequence: The cognitive developmental approach to socialization. In D. Goslin (Ed.), *Handbook of socialization: Theory and research.* (pp. 347–480). Skokie, IL: Rand McNally.

Kohlberg. L. (1971). From *is* to *ought:* How to commit the naturalistic fallacy and get away with it in the study of child development. In T. Mischel (Ed.), *Cognitive development and epistemology* (pp. 151–235). New York: Academic Press.

Kruger, A. C. (1993). Peer collaboration: Conflict, cooperation, or both? *Social Development, 2,* 165–182.

Kruger A. C., & Tomasello, M. (1986). Transactive discussions with peers and adults. *Developmental Psychology, 22,* 681–685.

Kuczinski, L., Kochanska, G., Radke-Yarrow, M., & Girnius-Brown, O. (1987). A developmental interpretation of young children's non-compliance. *Developmental Psychology, 23*(6), 799–806.

Lewis, C. (1984). Cooperation and control in Japanese nursery schools. *Comparative Education Review, 28,* 69–84.

Markus, H., & Kitayama, S. (1991). Culture and the self: Implications for cognition, emotion, and motivation. *Psychological Review, 98,* 224–253.

Miller, J., & Bersoff, D. M. (1992). Culture and moral judgment: How are conflicts between justice and interpersonal responsibility resolved? *Journal of Personality and Social Psychology, 62,* 541–554.

Nucci, L. P. (1981) The development of personal concepts: A domain distinct from moral or societal concepts. *Child Development, 52,* 114–121.

Nucci, L. P. (1984). Evaluating teachers as social agents: Student's ratings of domain appropriate and domain inappropriate teacher responses transgressions. *American Educational Research Journal, 21,* 267–378.

Nucci, L. P. (1994). Mother's beliefs regarding the personal domain of children. In J. G. Smetana (Ed.), *Parental beliefs: Causes and consequence for development* (pp. 81–97). San Francisco: Jossey-Bass.

Nucci, L. P. (in press). Morality and personal freedom. In E. Reed & E. Turiel (Eds.), *Values and cognition.* Hillsdale, NJ: Lawrence Erlbaum.

Nucci, L. P., Camino, C., & Sapiro, C. (1993, July). *Mother's and children's concepts of areas of children's personal autonomy and social regulation in the United States and Brazil.* Paper presented at the biennial meeting of the International Society for the Study of Behavioral Development, Recife, Brazil.

Nucci, L. P., Guerra, N., & Lee, J. Y. (1991). Adolescent judgments of the personal, prudential, and normative aspects of drug usage. *Developmental Psychology, 27,* 841–848.

Nucci, L. P., & Killen, M. (1991). Social interactions in the preschool and the development of social and moral concepts. In B. Scales, M. Almy, A. Nicolopoulou, & S. Ervin-Tripp (Eds.), *Play and the social context of development in early care and education* (pp. 219–233). New York: Teachers College Press.

Nucci, L. P., & Lee, J. Y. (1993). Morality and autonomy. In G. G. Noam & T. E. Wren (Eds.), *The moral self* (pp. 123–148). Cambridge, MA: MIT Press.

Nucci, L. P., & Turiel, E. (1978). Social interactions and the development of social concepts in preschool children. *Child Development, 49,* 400–407.

Nucci, L. P., & Weber, E. (in press). Social interactions in the home and the development of young children's conceptions of the personal. *Child Development.*

Piaget, J., (1932). *The moral judgment of the child.* New York: Free Press.

Piaget, J. (1975/1985). *The equilibration of cognitive structures: The central problem of intellectual development* (T. Brown & K. Thampy, Trans.). Chicago: University of Chicago Press.

Putallaz, M., & Gottman, J. (1981). Social skills and group acceptance. In S. Asher & J. Gottman (Eds.), *The development of children's friendships* (pp. 116–149). Cambridge: Cambridge University Press.

Rende, R., & Killen, M. (1992). Social interactional antecedents of object conflict. *Early Childhood Research Quarterly, 7,* 551–563.

Riegel, K. F. (1979). *Foundations of dialectical psychology.* New York: Academic Press.

Ross, H. S., & Conant, C. (1992). The social structure of early conflict: Interaction, relationships, and alliances. In C. U. Shantz & W. W. Hartup (Eds.), *Conflict in child and adolescent development* (pp. 153–187). Cambridge: Cambridge University Press.

Ross, H. S., Tesla, C., Kenyon, B., & Lollis, S. P. (1990). Maternal intervention in toddler and peer conflict: The socialization of principles of justice. *Developmental Psychology, 26,* 994–1003.

Scheffler, S. (1982). *The rejection of consequentialism.* Oxford: Clarendon Press.

Schneewind, J. (1986). The use of autonomy in ethical theory. In T. Heller, M. Sosna, & D. Wellbery (Eds.), *Reconstructing individualism: Autonomy, individuality, and the self in Western thought* (pp. 64–75). Stanford, CA: Stanford University Press.

Shantz, C. U. (1987). Conflicts between children. *Child Development. 58,* 283–305.

Shantz, C. U., & Hartup, W. W. (Eds.). (1992). *Conflict in child and adolescent development.* Cambridge: Cambridge University Press.

Shantz, C. U., & Shantz, D. W. (1985). Conflict between children: Social-cognitive and sociometric status. In M. W. Berkowitz (Ed.), *Peer conflict and psychological growth: New directions for child development* (pp. 3–21). San Francisco: Jossey-Bass.

Shweder, R. (1991). *Thinking through cultures.* Cambridge, MA: Harvard University Press.

Shweder, R., Mahapatra, M., & Miller, J. (1987). Culture and moral development. In J. Kagan & S. Lamb (Eds.), *The emergence of morality in young children* (pp. 1–82). Chicago: University of Chicago Press.

Smetana, J. G. (1989). Adolescents' and parents' reasoning about actual family conflict. *Child Development, 60,* 1052–1067.

Smetana, J. G., Bridgeman, D., & Turiel, E. (1983). Differentiation of domains and prosocial behavior. In D. Bridgeman (Ed.), *The nature of prosocial development: Interdisciplinary theories and strategies.* New York: Academic Press.

Spiro, M. (1993). Is the Western conception of the self "peculiar" within the context of the world's cultures? *Ethos, 21,* 107–153.

Sullivan, H. S. (1953). *The interpersonal theory of psychiatry.* New York: Norton.

Tobin, J., Wu, D., & Davidson, D. (1989). *Preschool in three cultures: Japan, China, and the U.S.* New Haven, CT: Yale University Press.

Triandis, H. C. (1989). The self and social behavior in differing cultural contexts. *Psychological Review, 96,* 508–520.

Triandis, H. C. (1990). Cross-cultural studies of individualism and collectivism. In J. J. Berman (Ed.), *Nebraska Symposium on Motivation, 1989: Vol. 37. Cross-cultural perspectives* (pp. 41–133). Lincoln: University of Nebraska Press.

Turiel, E. (1983). *The development of social knowledge.* Cambridge: Cambridge University Press.

Turiel, E., Killen, M., & Helwig, C. (1987). Morality: Its structure, functions, and vagaries. In J. Kagan & S. Lamb (Eds.), *The emergence of morality in young children* (pp. 155–243). Chicago: University of Chicago Press.

Walker, L., & Taylor, J. H. (1991). Family interactions and the development of moral reasoning. *Child Development, 62,* 264–283.

Williams, B. (1981). *Moral luck.* Cambridge: Cambridge University Press.

Yau, J., & Smetana, J. G. (1994). *Adolescent–parent conflict among Chinese adolescents in Hong Kong.* Unpublished manuscript, University of Hong Kong.

Youniss, J. (1980). *Parents and peers in social development.* Chicago: University of Chicago Press.

Youniss, J., & Smollar, J. (1985). *Adolescents' relations with mothers, fathers, and friends.* Chicago: University of Chicago Press.

3 Children's conceptions of sociomoral affect: Happy victimizers, mixed emotions, and other expectancies

William Arsenio and Anthony Lover

Affects, by being represented, last beyond the presence of the object that excites them. This ability to conserve feelings makes interpersonal and moral feelings possible and allows the latter to be organized into normative scales of values. (Piaget, 1954/1981, p. 44)

Well, the boy who pushed him off would probably feel happy at first, but he'd be sad too. Happy cause he got a turn by pushing the other kid off, and sad because he knows how he'd feel if someone did that to him. (an 8-year-old child)

In this chapter we focus on two basic questions: What emotions do children expect various sociomoral acts to produce, and how do these emotional expectancies influence children's sociomoral behavior? Our underlying goal is to examine how children's understanding and behavior involving common, everyday sociomoral events (e.g., acts of victimization, helping and sharing, and potential adult and child sanctions) are influenced by the emotional outcomes they expect these events to produce. In other words, how are the more or less prescriptive limits of children's interpersonal behaviors, the essential sociomoral "do's" and "don'ts" (Emde, Johnson, & Easterbrooks, 1987), related to children's conceptions of sociomoral affect? We will present a theoretical model and related research based on the ideas that children remember the emotions that are linked with particular social events, and that they use these emotion–event links to anticipate future emotion outcomes and to plan their behavior accordingly.

Historically, emotions and affective processes have long played an important role in socialization-based research emphasizing the adult-to-child transmission of moral values. For example, the affective quality of adult–child relationships, the emotional intensity of disciplinary encounters, and children's emotional responses to rewards and punishment have all been addressed as part of this literature (see, e.g., Kochanska, 1993; and Maccoby, 1980, for a related review). In contrast, emotions have generally been deemphasized in cognitive-developmental studies that focus on children's construction and abstraction of moral principles from peer–peer interactions (Gibbs & Schnell, 1985). More recently, however, some have questioned the need and desirability of dividing affect and cognition into such distinctly separate theoretical frameworks (e.g., Gibbs, 1991; Hoffman, 1991). Turiel (1983), for example, has observed that the cognitive-developmental view that moral prescriptions are generated, in part, "from the perceptions of the consequences to the victims" (p. 35) is fundamentally compatible with the socialization view that effective parental inductions involve "reasoning with the child, and in the process, highlighting the effects of the child's actions to himself or herself and to others" (p. 176). Furthermore, several cognitive-developmental studies have shown that both children and adults often specifically refer to the emotional consequences of transgression in justifying their sociomoral actions and judgments (e.g., Arsenio & Ford, 1985; Nucci & Turiel, 1978; Smetana, 1984) much as successful parental inductions typically include a focus on the emotional consequences of children's behaviors (e.g., Hoffman, 1983; Zahn-Waxler, Radke-Yarrow, & King, 1979).

We are interested in expanding on this shared theoretical focus on emotional outcomes in the present chapter. It will be argued that the social meaning of emotions (e.g., Bretherton, Fritz, Zahn-Waxler, & Ridgeway, 1986), and emerging cognitive abilities are combined in children's conceptions of sociomoral affect, and that these affect–event links can provide children with important insights into the underlying reasons for why certain sociomoral acts are regulated (see also Hoffman, 1981, 1983, and 1987 on the informational and motivational roles of sociomoral affect). These issues are addressed in four major sections. The outline of a general model of the formation and use of emotion–events links is presented in the first section. This is followed by a brief second section describing some studies that illustrate the major components of this model including: (1) children's conceptions of emotional outcomes and how these conceptions vary depending on the specific nature of the sociomoral context involved; and (2) the connections between individual differences in conceptions of sociomoral affect and children's sociomoral behavior. The first two sections address more general issues regarding situational sociomoral affect. In contrast, the last two parts of the chapter focus on a narrower but important subset of affective conceptions associated with acts of victimization. Specifically, the third part summarizes recent findings that indicate that children often expect victimizers to feel happy, and the fourth part describes possible explanations and theoretical implications of this "happy victimizer" conception.

Conceptions of sociomoral emotions: Outline of a model

A pair of 2-year-old preschool friends are playing in the sandbox. One child is holding an attractive toy bulldozer, when the other child hits her friend and grabs the toy away. The injured child cries and attempts to hit her friend back, but a teacher intervenes. The two friends do not play together for the remainder of their outside time. Similar scenes are observed over the next few months. Then one day, one of the two children smiles while reaching for her friend's toy and asks, "Can I have it?" Her friend lets her have a turn.

How can we explain this important developmental transition away from victimization toward attempted sharing and turn taking? One possible explanation, and the focus of this chapter, involves the role of situational affect. As Harris (1985, 1989) and others (e.g., Bandura, 1986; and Lazarus, 1991) have noted, many of our behavioral decisions are influenced by "an anticipation of the way that we will feel in some future situation. A child's readiness to go to school, to brave the dentist, to seek out a new friend, or to run away from punishment is based on an appraisal of how he or she will feel when facing these situations" (Harris, 1985, p. 162). In other words, the children's conceptions of situational affect, that is, the links between specific situations and their associated affective outcomes, provide them with a powerful way of anticipating the emotional outcomes and resulting emotional meaning of a wide array of social behaviors. This should be especially true for sociomoral events that involve very affectively charged events, such as acts of victimization, sharing and helping, and potential peer and adult sanctions. Getting back to the 2-year-olds, they may have gradually learned that simply hitting and grabbing their friend's toy has an undesirable set of emotional consequences – the friend becomes sad and/or angry, adults become upset, and the positive emotions of cooperative play are disrupted. (Note – it is not being claimed that the affective conceptions need to be explicitly conscious for them to influence children's reasoning and behavior [see, e.g., Lazarus, 1991, on the conscious vs. cognitive distinction].)

The basic details of the previous example are relatively brief, but even a slightly more elaborated model of situational sociomoral affect requires a number of other important assumptions and considerations (Table 3.1). For example, any model of situational affect, whether sociomoral or not, is based on research indicating that people often remember the affective states, such as the emotional antecedents and consequences that are con-

Table 3.1. *A four-step model of affect and cognition in sociomoral development*

Step 1 Children experience and witness a wide range of affectively laden sociomoral events.	Various types of sociomoral events (e.g., prosocial vs. victimization) typically have different patterns of emotional consequences. Children's affective sociomoral experiences are highly differentiated by type of event.
Step 2 Children form cognitive representations of sociomoral events that include affective regularities.	Although different types of sociomoral events exist, within types of events children tend to have similar affective reactions and conceptions because of basic similarities in the meaning and function of human emotions.
Step 3 Affective sociomoral knowledge informs subsequent social reasoning and guides behavior.	Children can use affective conceptions to anticipate the likely outcomes of different sociomoral behaviors before acting. Socioemotional relationships, however, may promote, inhibit, or distort the nature and use of underlying affective knowledge.
Step 4 Children coordinate knowledge of affective consequences to form more general sociomoral principles.	For example, prohibitions regarding acts of victimization are constructed from an extensive knowledge of resulting emotional consequences. Commonalities in outcomes ("I don't like how it feels to get hit, my friend doesn't like how it feels," etc.) provide the "raw material" from which principles such as fairness are abstracted.

nected with various events (e.g., Blaney, 1987; Bower, 1981; and see also Piaget, 1954/1981). There may be important questions about the accuracy of these memories and the possible role of cognitive distortions (see e.g., Dodge, 1991), but it is increasingly clear that emotions do not simply happen and then disappear. Rather, emotions appear to be routinely stored as part of our basic cognitive and social-cognitive representations so that affect–event links are likely to be ubiquitous.

This core assumption (the linking of affect and situation) is actually the second step of our larger four-step model of situational sociomoral affect.

Even before children connect affect and sociomoral situations, they are exposed to a wide range of very different sociomoral events both as participants and observers (Step 1 of the model). For example, victimization and prosocial acts tend to elicit very different emotional displays in recipients (compare Arsenio, Lover, & Gumora, 1993, and Denham, 1986). Repeated exposures to events with similar emotional outcomes then allow children to form generalized scripts of prototypes linking events and emotions (Hoffman, 1983). So, children might come to believe that being victimized will make them feel sad or angry, whereas being shared with is seen as typically making them happy (Step 2). In the end, children will understand different sociomoral events in terms of their typical emotional consequences, and as we have described, they can use this knowledge to anticipate the likely consequences of their behavior. Conceptions of the situational affective consequences of sociomoral behavior inform children's subsequent social reasoning and guide their related sociomoral behavior (Step 3).

The first three steps of this model are an attempt to elaborate some of the implicit assumptions underlying most studies on situational affect (e.g., Barden, Zalko, Duncan, & Masters, 1980; Lewis, 1989; Strayer 1986, 1989). Specifically, not all social or sociomoral events are likely to elicit similar emotions. Consequently, children will extract different affect–event links depending on the particular nature of the event, and this affective information will help them anticipate various behavioral outcomes. Step 4 is more uniquely associated with sociomoral affect. In this final step, it is proposed that children coordinate their knowledge of sociomoral affect to form more general sociomoral principles. For example, children who understand that they do not like to have their possessions stolen begin to coordinate this knowledge with their conceptions that friends, acquaintances, and even enemies seem to feel the same way. In addition to coordinating event–emotion regularities across different relationships, children may also begin to coordinate event–emotion links across different types of sociomoral events that share certain underlying features. The commonalities in the expected emotional outcomes of being a target of theft, a target of undeserved aggression, and target of verbal abuse might all be combined to form a concept of unfair victimization. In this view, conceptions of sociomoral affect provide the raw material from which more general, abstract sociomoral principles are formed using a variety of cognitive abilities. In essence, children's sense of fairness and concern for others' welfare (to take just one sociomoral principle) are constructed from an extensive knowledge of the emotional consequences of acts involving victimization.

Several additional features of this model need to be mentioned at this point. First of all, although different events are likely to be associated with different emotional outcomes, for a given event, children will share a degree of consensus about the associated emotional consequences. To be sure, there are emotionally ambiguous events, and there are unique personal factors that will influence expected outcomes (see especially Gnepp, 1989), but, for example, nearly all children expect that someone will feel sad or angry after being unfairly victimized (Arsenio, 1988) or will feel happy after succeeding at some important task (Barden et al., 1980). The existence of these consensually shared conceptions indicates that many affect–event links are not idiosyncratic, probably in large part because of the basic similarities in the meanings and functions of human emotions (see, e.g., Izard, 1977, and Plutchik, 1980, and especially Ekman, 1993, on cross-cultural similarities in emotion–event links).

Another aspect of this model (Steps 3 and 4) is that children's conceptions of sociomoral affect will also be subject to important distortions and biases. Despite the existence of normative links between various sociomoral events and emotions, there are also likely to be important differences in how children view particular emotional outcomes. For example, there is some evidence that aggressive children view victimization more positively than their peers (e.g., Perry, Perry, & Rasmussen, 1986) and that threats of aggression are especially likely to distort aggressive children's social cognitive functioning (e.g., Dodge & Somberg, 1987; and see also Dodge, 1991). In part, these different views may reflect children's accurate understanding of their own unique interpersonal histories, so that aggressive children may view aggression more positively because of their greater history of successful victimization. Other biases, however, may reflect actual affective distortions stemming, for example, from the influence of ongoing mood states on the availability of subsequent affectively charged memories (Clark & Isen, 1982). The existence of normative or consensually shared conceptions of sociomoral affect along with major individual differences in these conceptions is both expected and consistent with related social-cognitive studies (see, e.g., Dodge & Feldman, 1990).

A final comment is needed before discussing some of the empirical evidence for the various steps of this model. Although much of the preceding discussion emphasizes the idea that children extract their conceptions of sociomoral affect directly from their own experiences, it is clear that adults also provide children with a powerful set of situational affective information (see, e.g., Zahn-Waxler et al., 1979 and Hoffman, 1983, on moral inductions). Much of the present chapter reflects the "direct experience" (i.e., nonsocialization) view, but it must be acknowledged that there is a potentially complex relationship between adult-transmitted and child-derived conceptions of sociomoral affect. For some events there may be close parallels between adult emotional communications and children's own conceptions of situational affect. This may help to explain the relative success of parental inductive techniques in moral socialization, in that adults may intuitively focus on emotional consequences that are clearly related to children's own experiences and conceptions, "Look what you did! Don't you see you hurt Amy – don't ever pull hair" (Zahn-Waxler et al., 1979, p. 327).

Whether these parallels exist for all types of sociomoral events is an open question that will not be directly addressed in this chapter.

Conceptions of sociomoral emotions: Some research findings

In this section we provide a brief summary of some of our research on aspects of this general model. Much of this work, to date, has focused on Step 2 and, to a lesser degree, Step 3 of this model – namely, children's conceptions of sociomoral affect. Several questions have been of particular interest, including whether children distinguish among several categories of sociomoral events in terms of their emotional outcomes, whether children also distinguish between the anticipated reactions of different participants within types of events, and whether there is any evidence that conceptions of situational sociomoral affect are implicated in children's subsequent sociomoral reasoning or behavior.

One study (Arsenio, 1988) is especially useful for beginning to address these issues. Given some of the results from earlier research (e.g., Arsenio & Ford, 1985), it was expected that children would view different domains or categories of sociomoral events as tending to elicit different emotional outcomes – so there would be some specificity in affect–sociomoral event links. Six categories of sociomoral events were included based on evidence that children make meaningful conceptual and behavioral distinctions among inhibitive morality, active morality, distributive justice, prosocial morality, conventions, and personal events (Damon, 1977; Eisenberg, 1982; Nucci, 1981; Tisak & Ford, 1986; Turiel, 1983 [see Table 3.2 for brief descriptions and examples]). All of these events were considered so-ciomoral in that they share a common focus on the more or less prescriptive limits of interpersonal behavior (the "ought" and "ought not" of social interactions), but they also clearly differ in important ways. For example, in the most studied distinction, the results of more than 40 studies (see Turiel, Killen, & Helwig, 1987) indicate that children distinguish between the more contextually based social organizational limits of conventional events from the more universal aspects of inhibitive moral events that involve explicit issues of fairness and victimization. Similarly, distinctions

Table 3.2. *Sociomoral rule systems*

Rule system	Description
Inhibitive morality	Events involving victimization and unfairly depriving others of their rights (Turiel, 1983): For example, one child steals another child's toy. Stimulus stories adapted from Arsenio & Ford (1985) and Nucci (1981).
Active morality	Interventions on the behalf of victimized others (Tisak & Ford, 1986): For example, a child stops another child from unfairly hurting a third child. Stimuli adapted from Tisak (1986) and Tisak & Ford (1986).
Conventional	Events that, although somewhat arbitrary in content, promote the smooth functioning of social groups (Turiel, 1983): For example, a child violates a school rule in the presence of a teacher by wearing a bathing suit to class. Stimuli adapted from Nucci (1981) and Weston & Turiel (1980).
Personal	Events that primarily affect the actor, and that consequently are often viewed as outside moral and conventional regulation (Nucci, 1981): For example, a child writes something in a notebook during recess, and the teacher requires the child to reveal what was written. Stimuli adapted from Nucci (1981).
Distributive justice	Events involving the distribution of group-earned resources (Damon, 1977): For example, one child equitably divides the earnings that three classmates received for delivering newspapers. Stimuli adapted from Damon (1977, 1980).
Prosocial morality	Events in which private resources are used to create beneficial outcomes for others (Eisenberg, 1982): For example, one child helps another child pick up a game that was dropped accidentally. Stimuli adapted from Eisenberg (1982) and Eisenberg-Berg & Hand (1979).

between positive "oughts" (prosocial and active morality) and negative "ought nots" (inhibitive morality and conventions), although less directly studied (Eisenberg, 1982, but see Tisak & Ford, 1986, and Kahn, 1992), represent a major division within the sociomoral literature. In terms of this chapter, these sociomoral categories were seen as providing fundamentally different social contexts, each of which constrains (though does not dictate [see Turiel, 1983]) children's social reasoning and behavior, including their probable conceptions of emotional outcomes.

In part 1 of this two-part study, kindergartners, third graders, and sixth graders were presented with events representing the six types of sociomoral events and were asked to assess the likely emotional consequences of these events for various participants including actors, targets, and observers. Overall, children's conceptions of these emotional consequences were found to be highly differentiated, ranging from the generally positive emotional expectations for simple low-cost prosocial acts and the equitable distribution of group resources (distributive justice) to the expectations for highly negative emotions following types of victimization (including inhibitive and active morality).

One interesting and illustrative contrast involves the emotions selected for prosocial and active morality. In a wider sense, both of these types of events are prosocial in that active morality involves helping someone who is being victimized, and these prosocial events involved low-cost helping and sharing. Yet, children expected that the prosocial actors and recipients would generally feel quite happy, whereas they attributed somewhat mixed, but basically negative emotions to active moral actors and recipients. On one hand, these distinctly different emotion outcomes confirm the theoretical importance of not simply reducing all types of sociomoral events to one undifferentiated domain. More concretely, the expected positive outcomes for simple prosocial events help to explain why some prosocial acts are used to help regulate ongoing mood states (negative state relief; see, e.g., Cialdini & Kenrick, 1976), since children's conceptions reveal a belief that they will "feel happy by doing good" (cf. Moore, Underwood, & Rosenhan, 1984). In contrast, the more mixed emotional expectations for active moral events may help to explain why it is often difficult for children and adults to intervene in acts of victimization even when they think that they should (cf. Latane & Darley, 1968). In both cases, children's conceptions of emotion outcomes may help to clarify previous research issues.

As expected, children also anticipated different emotional consequences for participants within some categories of sociomoral events. For example, although inhibitive moral events (acts of victimization) were seen as eliciting extremely negative emotions in victims and observers, children expected that victimizers would feel somewhat happy. (Additional research on the "happy victimizer" expectancy and its potential significance for children's views of victimization are described in extensive detail in the last two sections of this chapter.)

In the second part of this study the focus was on whether conceptions of sociomoral affect might have any utility for children's subsequent reasoning (Step 3 of the model). Children were presented with depictions of event actors' and targets' emotional reactions and they were asked to judge which of two sociomoral events was more likely to have elicited the depicted emotional reactions. The details of this task are somewhat complicated (see Arsenio, 1988, pp. 1614 (General Design) and 1616–1617), but appropriate emotion–event links were originally determined in part 1 of this study. So, for example, it was known that most subjects expected simple acts of helping and sharing would make both actors and recipients feel happy. Consequently, in one part 2 trial (out of 18 total trials) children saw a line drawing depicting both a happy actor and target, and they had to select whether these emotions had been elicited when one child shared a game (vignette a) or one child pushed another off a swing (vignette b).

Unlike in part 1, there were significant age-related changes in part 2, with third and sixth graders showing higher levels of accuracy than kindergartners. Yet, all three age groups were able to use the affective information to infer eliciting sociomoral events at greater than chance levels. In an important sense, then, the links between sociomoral events and emotions are reversible: Children can begin with either the associated emotion or the sociomoral event to make some inferences about the missing part of the affect–event link. Stated somewhat differently, affect–event links are usually seen in terms of anticipating the emotional consequences of events, but it is clear that associated affects can also help to infer the nature of a sociomoral event when other information is missing or ambiguous – for example, the "guilty look" parents and children use to guess who just stole a cookie or broke the living room window (see also the extensive literature on social referencing).

A final study goal was to assess whether there were also important individual differences in addition to these broadly shared consensuses regarding sociomoral affect. Specifically the relationships between children's part 1 and part 2 performance were examined. For each child a score was calculated for conceptions of sociomoral affect by comparing the child's own conception with the group norm. (So, for example, if a child said he expected someone who shared to be sad and most other subjects expected that that prosocial target would be happy, that child received a certain "deviation" score. The more consensus there was for a conception, the greater the deviation score would be for a child's nonconsensual conception. Consequently, the total of each child's deviation scores indicated how much overall consensus the child shared with the group regarding the affective outcomes of sociomoral events.) It was found that children's overall part 1 consensus score related quite significantly to their accuracy in part 2. The more a child's part 1 score differed from consensual conceptions, the fewer trials (out of 18) the child got right in part 2. Children with unusual conceptions of sociomoral affect were less successful at linking normative affective information with associated sociomoral events.

Unpublished data (Arsenio, 1986) from that study provide additional evidence for the significance of individual differences in children's conceptions of sociomoral affect. Children's teachers were asked to rate each subject's sociomoral behavior in the six different sociomoral categories included in the study using 7-point scales. A total teacher score that reflected the adequacy or inadequacy of children's sociomoral behavior, was found to be linked with children's part 1 and part 2 performance. Overall, children who were rated by teachers as having less adequate sociomoral behavior were more likely to have unusual conceptions of sociomoral affect in part 1, and to be unable to link affective information with associated events in part 2. (Correlations were performed separately for each grade because different grade-level regression slopes emerged. Five of the six relevant correlations were in the expected direction, and four of six correlations were significant despite the much smaller N's [$N = 24$ for each grade vs. a total sample N of 72].)

Collectively these results provide some support for the claims underlying Step 2 and Step 3 of our sociomoral model. On average, children across a wide age range (5 to 12 years) were found to have quite systematic conceptions of sociomoral affect, which revealed a sensitivity to both the type of sociomoral event and the specific role of the event participant. Differences in sociomoral contexts were reflected in differing affect–event and affect–event–participant links. Assessing whether these different affect–event links actually influence social reasoning and behavior is, however, somewhat more complex, and the evidence is more indirect. The part 2 results do suggest situational affect could be useful for subsequent social reasoning, although it remains to be shown that such conceptions actually are used in meaningful ways.

In a more recent study (Arsenio & Fleiss, in press) we attempted to address questions about the actual utility of children's conceptions of sociomoral affect in a somewhat different way. We reasoned that if there are important connections between conceptions of sociomoral affect and related behavior, then groups with distinctly different sociomoral behaviors should also have different sociomoral conceptions. Obviously, such group comparisons cannot establish that behavioral differences are a direct result of different conceptions. Results from a related literature (involving comparisons of juvenile delinquents' and more normal children's moral reasoning [Smetana, in press]), however, suggested that this research strategy would help to clarify some of the initial connections between behavior and situational affect.

Forty-eight children were individually interviewed regarding their conceptions of the emotional outcomes of inhibitive and prosocial moral, conventional, and personal events (described within Table 3.2) for event actors and recipients. In addition, children were asked to provide rationales to clarify why they had selected particular emotional outcomes. One-half of the sample was split between second and fifth graders from a racially heterogeneous elementary school, and the other half was from a similar age group of children who had been referred to a mental health facility for conduct problems involving acts of theft, property damage, physical cruelty, aggressiveness, and defiance of social limits and authorities (i.e., meeting DSM III-R [American Psychiatric Association, 1987] criteria for either Oppositional Defiant Disorder or Conduct Disorder). The groups did not differ in race or ethnicity, cognitive functioning, or maternal education.

Overall, both groups demonstrated the same systematic and differentiated conceptions of sociomoral affect that were observed by Arsenio (1988). For example, both groups expected prosocial events of low-cost sharing and helping to make actors and recipients feel mostly happy, and that moral victims would feel very negatively. However, a number of important group differences also emerged. For acts of victimization (inhibitive morality), behaviorally disruptive (BD) children expected both victims and victimizers to feel much less fear than did typical children. In addition, compared to their peers, BD children explained victimizers' emotions with more references to desirable material and psychological consequences and fewer references to the loss, harm, and unfairness resulting from victimization. In other words, BD children expected that victimizers would focus more on the gains resulting from their acts of victimization and less on victims' losses. Collectively, these results suggest that BD children view victimization in more positive terms for victimizers, and that they attempt to minimize the negative consequences, or at least the fear, resulting from victimization (see also Boldizar, Perry, & Perry, 1989; Perry et al., 1986; Slaby & Guerra, 1988).

Another potentially important group difference emerged in children's conceptions of low-cost prosocial acts of sharing and helping. Compared with their peers, BD children were less likely to focus on the positive consequences that actors' helping and sharing had created for prosocial recipients, and more on the fact that actors had been able to refrain from harming or victimizing someone else. For both inhibitive (victimization) and prosocial events, it appears that when BD children assess *actors'* emotions, they are less likely than their peers to also focus on the potential consequences for event *recipients* (a topic covered at length later in this chapter). A final, even more pervasive group difference was that BD children selected more "simplistic" emotion outcomes (i.e., "happy" or "sad" vs. other emotions) for all sociomoral rule systems than did typical children. This finding is especially striking since the happy/sad positive-to-negative valence distinction is a rudimentary emotion dimension available to even young preschoolers (Bretherton, et al., 1986). It is unclear, however, whether these results mean that BD children are being influenced by some unexplained "developmental lag" in this area.

One unresolved issue is whether BD children's conceptions of sociomoral affect are simply different from those of typical children (i.e., atypical) or whether they are truly inaccurate (deficient). Questions about group accuracy will be difficult to answer until more is known about the actual emotions children experience during sociomoral encounters (Step 1 of the model, and see the conclusion of this chapter). Yet, regardless of their ultimate accuracy, BD children's conceptions of sociomoral affect would be likely to promote more victimization and a variety of less sophisticated sociomoral behaviors.

Happy victimizers, mixed emotions, and conceptions of victimization

Children's conceptions of sociomoral emotions may help to clarify a number of theoretical issues, including the role of positive emotional expectancies in prosocial behavior (negative state relief), and distinctions between "simple" prosocial behavior and acts of bystander intervention. One of the most intriguing and potentially important findings to emerge from this literature, however, involves the "happy victimizer," that is, children's belief that victimizers will feel happy after successful acts of victimization rather than scared, guilty, or even some mix of positive and negative valence emotions. We believe that the developmental shift from the "happy victimizer" expectancy observed in younger children to the more mixed emotional expectancies of older children may reflect a moral transition of major significance in children's lives. Consequently, a large part of the remaining chapter is devoted to exploring this transition in some detail. It will be argued that young children begin by viewing victimization in terms of two separate sets of emotional reactions, typically the happiness of the victimizer and the sadness or anger of the victim, whereas older children begin to integrate these reactions so that the pain and loss of the victim act to modify and reduce the victimizer's happiness. The first few sections will address both the existing empirical evidence for the happy victimizer finding and its potential theoretical significance. This discussion is then followed by several sections which focus on the potential cognitive and affective contributions underlying this moral transition.

Initial evidence and significance

One of the first descriptions of the happy victimizer finding was in a study by Barden et al. (1980). They presented kindergartners, third, and sixth graders with a variety of social events, and then asked subjects to imagine how they would feel if they were the event actor by selecting from one of five emotions – happiness, sadness, fear, anger, and neutral affect ("just ok"). Although there were only a couple of age-related shifts for particular types of events, one of the most pronounced changes involved acts of undetected dishonesty, that is, where an actor stole something without getting caught. While most third and sixth graders expected to feel scared, nearly half of the kindergartners expected to feel happy after the theft, probably, the authors speculated, because 4-year-olds focused on the material gains resulting from the act.

In a subsequent study these authors (Zelko, Duncan, Garber, & Masters, 1986) also examined adult expectancies regarding children's emotional conceptions: "since adults are integral in home and school settings as socializing agents, it is important to consider . . . how closely adults' implicit theories of affect approximate those of children themselves" (p. 109). Adult subjects were given the same events and emotion choices as in the earlier study, and one-third of the sample predicted the preschoolers' responses, one-third the third graders', and one-third the sixth graders'. In general, adults were quite accurate at predicting third and sixth graders' responses, but they were less accurate at predicting preschoolers' responses, especially those for acts of undetected dishonesty. Adults primarily expected preschoolers to select fear (36%) and neutral affect (23%) as emotional consequences, but instead preschoolers emphasized happiness (41%), and split their remaining choices among the other emotions. The authors concluded that there is a significant discrepancy in how adults and preschoolers appear to view acts of undetected dishonesty, and that this gap might have important implications for our understanding of children's moral development.

We were also struck by the potential significance of these findings for a number of reasons. It seems clear that if young children really do expect positive emotional consequences for victimizers, then this conception would help to perpetuate a continued pattern of attempted victimizations. For example, in their research on the social cognitive mediators of aggression, Perry and Perry and their colleagues and others have found connections between children's outcome expectancies (Boldizar et al., 1989; Perry et al., 1986; Slaby & Guerra, 1988), that is, the expected consequences of acts of victimization, and children's aggressive behavior. Specifically, aggressive elementary school children are more likely to view aggression as producing more positive outcomes for the self, and they are less concerned about causing suffering in the victim than their nonaggressive peers. Although these studies focused on individual differences in aggression, they also raise concerns about the behavioral consequences of young children's seemingly normative expectation that acts of victimization will make victimizers feel happy.

A second reason for concern stems from the Zelko et al. (1986) study. The finding that many adults do not know that young children view victimization positively is especially problematic since it will act to undermine adults' socialization efforts with children. Unless children are actually "caught in the act," adults might make incorrect assumptions about how children view victimization, and resulting adult–child moral discussions and encounters will often be at cross purposes. And even when adults do catch their young children in the act of victimizing others, they will tend to misinterpret and be confused by childrens' developmentally normative reaction of happiness. ("Don't you ever laugh when you take your brother's toy!" [see also Dunn, 1988, on the frequency on young children's positive affect during transgressions].)

Finally, this happy victimizer conception seems to conflict with the core assumptions of several influential sociomoral theories (e.g., Hoffman, 1987; Turiel, 1983; Zahn-Waxler & Kochanska, 1990) in which an awareness of victim harm, a sense of empathic distress, and a fear of external sanctions should all lead children to expect that victimizers will feel *negative* emotions, such as sadness, fear, and/or guilt. Despite some of the major theoretical differences between socialization and cognitive-developmental accounts of children's sociomoral development (e.g., Gibbs & Schnell, 1985), recent versions of both theories emphasize that children's awareness of victims' pain and loss should reduce the frequency of future acts of victimization (see also Turiel, 1983). Neither theory seems to predict that children will attribute extensive positive emotions to victimizers.

Sociomoral studies and happy victimizers

With these issues in mind, we took a closer look at some of our previous research in which conceptions of victimization had been at least a partial focus. In one part of a study on the affective roots of moral and conventional distinctions (Arsenio & Ford, 1985), first and third grade children rated the affective consequences of moral transgressions for event victims, victimizers, and observers on a 5-point scale (-2 = very negative emotions to $+2$ = very positive emotions). Although children expected that they would feel slightly negative as an observer (-0.53) and that victims would feel very negative (-1.57), they also expected that victimizers would feel slightly positive ($+.46$ [Arsenio, 1985]). More than one-half of both first and third graders selected positive emotions both for victimizers who committed acts of undetected dishonesty, and acts of physical victimization that produced material gains. On the one hand, then, these findings extended those of Barden et al., 1980, and Zelko et al., 1986: Apparently, happy victimizer conceptions are not limited to acts of undetected theft. In contrast to Barden et al., however, we did not find that the happy victimizer conception disappeared by third grade. It appeared to us that this finding might apply to both a wider range of moral acts and a wider age range of children. (Yet, one important unresolved issue is the role of concrete, material gains in children's happy victimizer expectancy. Most of the acts of victimization used as stimulus stories in this literature produce obvious gains for the victimizer, but it is less clear how children view victimization that results in psychological and other less tangible gains [see the conclusion].)

Similar results were observed in a subsequent study using methods adapted from those used by Barden et al. (Arsenio, 1988; see previous discussion for details). Kindergartners, third, and sixth graders attributed overwhelmingly negative emotions to victims (98% sad, angry, or scared), while at the same time more than half of the kindergartners and third graders (56% and 59%) expected victimizers to feel happy. In fact, the discrepancy between the emotions attributed to victims and victimizers was greater than the emotion difference observed between any two characters in the five remaining sociomoral categories. A subsequent study (Arsenio, Berlin, & O'Desky, 1989) indicated that children also provide quite different rationales for victims' and victimizers' emotions. Victims' negative emotions were often explained in terms of the unfairness of the act ("it just wasn't fair that someone took his toy without asking him first" [46% of rationales]). In contrast, victimizers' emotions, especially happiness, were explained in terms of the material gains produced by acts of victimization ("now she's got the toy she wanted" [62% of victimizer rationales]).

The moral attributional shift: Research by Nunner-Winkler and Sodian

Although the happy victimizer conception had been observed and highlighted in several earlier studies, Nunner-Winkler and Sodian (1988) were the first to examine it explicitly in some detail. The authors proposed that moral events are likely to produce intense conflicting feelings in that "a person who violates a moral rule may, for instance, experience joy at the success of his or her forbidden behavior and or shame, guilt, and remorse at his or her immoral behavior" (p. 1323). They proposed that children's emotional expectancies will influence their behaviors, and that the expectation of unpleasant feelings like shame and remorse, in particular, are essential elements in children's moral motivation.

These issues were assessed in a 3-part study of 4-, 6-, and 8-year-olds' conceptions of moral emotions. In part 1, children were presented with two moral situations, one in which a child resisted stealing candy, and another in which the child succumbed and stole the candy. In general, 4- and 6-year-olds attributed more positive emotions to the actor who stole the candy than 8-year-olds (74%, 40%, and 10% positive emotions, respectively), and 4- and 6-year-olds expected the actor who resisted stealing to feel more negatively than 8-year-olds (57%, 71%, and 41%, respectively, with 6- to 8-year-olds differing significantly). Despite using a variety of manipulations to emphasize victims' pain and loss, parts 2 and 3 of the study confirmed that 4- to 6-year-old children expect victimizers to feel happy, surprisingly even in one condition where a victim was pushed off a swing and lay on the ground crying and bleeding!

Nunner-Winkler and Sodian interpreted the overall results in terms of a moral attributional shift. That is, young children have a basic outcome orientation in which they expect victimizers to feel happy if they attain a desired, often material, goal. In contrast, older children have a more intrinsically moral orientation: They expect victimizers to feel negatively because of their awareness of the victim's pain as well as the external standards applying to such acts. But what could explain such a moral transition? One possibility that they raised was a "conflicting emotions" hypothesis. Essentially, in this view, children really do attribute both positive and negative emotions to victimizers, such as happiness due to gains from victimization and empathic sadness for the victim. Younger children, however, may be incapable of easily producing both types of consequences because of some underlying cognitive constraints that make it difficult to acknowledge mixed emotions in *any* situation, whether sociomoral or not (e.g., Harter & Buddin, 1987). In other words, young children might have both positive and negative emotions associated with their memory for acts of victimization, but positive emotions may be more available perhaps because on average they are somewhat stronger, or perhaps because existing stimulus stories unwittingly emphasized victimizers' gains and deemphasized victims' losses. Nunner-Winkler and Sodian, however, rejected this hypothesis since even extreme efforts to manipulate the salience of victim harm (e.g., the "crying and bleeding" condition just described) did little to change children's belief that victimizers are happy. The authors reasoned that if children really do attribute mixed emotions to victimizers, then focusing attention on the victim's pain should at some point lead children to report other negative victimizer emotions that exist as part of their larger representation of victimizers' emotions.

The moral conflict: Research by Arsenio and Kramer

Although our own earlier evidence supported the happy victimizer conception, it did not confirm the major moral attributional shift reported by Nunner-Winkler and Sodian. Whereas they found a drop in happy victimizer expectancies from 80% in 4-year-olds to 10% in 8-year-olds, we found that this expectancy was relatively stable across a wider age range (e.g., 55% of 6-year-olds and 50% of 8-year-olds in one study [Arsenio & Ford, 1985; Arsenio, 1985], and 56% of 5-year-olds, 59% of 8-year-olds, and 40% of 11-year-olds in another study [Arsenio, 1988]). Yet, our previous studies addressed a wide range of different sociomoral conceptions, and victimizer conceptions were only a minor aspect of this research. The importance of the happy victimizer finding and unresolved issues about the age and nature of the moral attributional shift lead us to conduct a study with an explicit focus on children's conceptions of emotions and victimization.

Forty-eight children (4-, 6-, and 8-year-old boys and girls), participated in this two-part study (Arsenio & Kramer, 1992). In the first part, children were read a story closely resembling the one used by Nunner-Winkler and Sodian in which a child steals another child's candies from his or her school (or preschool) locker. However, we asked children about reactions of *both* victimizers and victims, rather than providing them with adult experimenter-derived victim emotions, which might not correspond with their actual beliefs (cf. Zelko et al., 1986). For example, young children might rationalize their happy victimizers conceptions by believing that victims are not really harmed. Subjects were also free to assess either the emotional consequences for the victim or victimizer first. Presumably, if young children are more focused on the positive material outcomes of victimization, they will be more likely to assess victimizers first, whereas any increasing moral orientation in older children might lead them to assess the victim first.

We found that all but one 4- or 6-year-old and that the majority of 8-year-olds (11 of 16) expected victimizers to feel either "good" or "happy," and all subjects expected victims to feel negative emotions, including "sad," "bad," and a few "angry" (although 8-year-olds were significantly less likely to attribute positive emotions to victimizers than the other two age groups). Based on these results, it seemed quite unlikely that the "happy victimizer" conception resulted from any obvious attempt to minimize or deny victims' losses.

Does this mean that children are completely unmoved by the victim's plight when they think about the victimizer? One finding suggested perhaps not. Although there were no age-related differences in children's decisions

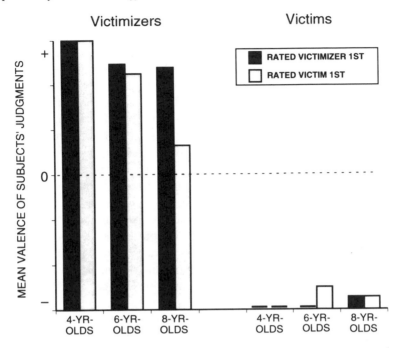

Figure 3.1. Judgments of the positive-to-negative valences of victimizers' and victims' emotional responses as a function of whom children decided to assess first.

to rate either victims or victimizers first, there was one interesting order effect. Eight-year-olds who decided to assess *victims* first (about one-half of this age group) subsequently judged that victimizers would be less happy than all other children (Figure 3.1). Perhaps 8-year-olds who rated victims first were directed to the costs of victimization, and this awareness then moderated their expectation of victimizer happiness. Because the order of rating victims and victimizers was not experimentally manipulated, however, it was equally possible that 8-year-olds who rated victims first did so because they were more oriented to the costs of victimization to begin with (i.e., order per se did not alert them to the victim's loss).

Consequently, in part 2 we attempted to assess whether other forms of highlighting the victim's loss might influence children's judgments of victimizers' emotions. Friendship manipulations were emphasized, with victims and victimizers described as friends, and in one condition the subject was even described as being victimized by a known close friend. Friendships were emphasized for two major reasons. For one, children are likely to be more sensitive to moral considerations within the context of ongoing friendships (e.g., Killen, 1990; Youniss, 1980), especially, it seemed, when they are described as being victimized by a close friend. This focus on friendship would also help to address an important but little examined explanation for the happy victimizer, namely the victimizer as "bully." Perhaps children believe that the victimizers portrayed in these studies differ from most typical children. Subjects might assume that lying, cheating, stealing, and physical harm are not normative behaviors for children, and consequently that someone who is described mostly with references to his or her misdeeds might simply be a "bully" or a "naughty" child. Describing victims and victimizers as friends and including a known friend as story protagonists would begin to address this concern.

Despite the multiple attempts to increase the salience of the harm generated for victims in part 2, once again all but one of the younger children expected victimizers to feel "good" or "happy" and victims to feel "sad," "bad," or "mad," and all subjects expected victimizers to feel more positively than victims. Eight-year-olds, however, seemed somewhat more influenced by the salience manipulations as they attributed positive emotions to victimizers for slightly more than one-half of their judgments (19 of 32), and their quantitative ratings of victimizers' emotions (on a 3-point scale) were significantly less positive than those of younger children. Surprisingly, children's judgments for two friendship conditions (victim and victimizers as friends vs. subject being victimized by a known friend) did not differ. The fact that children expected their own close friend to feel happy after victimizing them does, however, suggest that conceptions of happy victimizers are not limited to bullies or other "bad characters" (see also Nunner-Winkler & Sodian, 1988).

Children's emotion judgments and other data that were collected on their rationales for these judgments suggest that younger children almost exclusively attribute happiness to successful victimizers, and that a majority of 8-year-olds would seem to agree. Yet, there was some other research that raised questions about the completeness of these findings. Results of several studies (e.g., Glasberg and Aboud, 1982; Harter & Buddin, 1987; Harter & Pike, 1984) indicate that young children are more likely to select positive emotions and deny negative emotions for a variety of social-cognitive tasks than their older peers. This "positive bias" might have little effect on judgments of victims because children's own experiences in this role have been so overwhelmingly negative, but, we reasoned, if more mixed feelings are connected with victimizers, then young children might initially find it easier to report the positive feelings connected with victimizing. Previous studies never probed children further once they provided

Table 3.3. *Number of judgments indicating that victimizers could feel other than initially selected emotions*

Age	Probe level			
	1	2	3	4
4	2	1	7	22
6	21	8	3	0
8	28	4	0	0

Note: Subjects were asked three increasingly explicit probe questions; 1 = least, 3 = most explicit. Level 4 responses = victimizer feels only initial emotion. Each subject made judgments for two stories.

initial more positive emotions, so that any additional negative emotion attributions could have remained untapped.

After children provided their emotion judgments and rationales in part 2, they were also asked a series of increasingly direct probe questions to assess whether they believed that victimizers could be feeling any other emotions in addition to the one(s) they originally provided. For the initial probe children were simply asked whether the victimizer could be feeling anything else. If the subject said "no" he or she was then asked whether the victimizer could feel an emotion of the opposite valence from the emotion the subject had originally selected. A "no" answer for this probe resulted in a final probe most easily illustrated with an example. "You said your friend was happy when she got your swing. What if she looked at you on the ground and saw that you were very sad. Could she be feeling anything besides happy?"

The probe question results revealed that 6- and 8-year-olds provided additional victimizer emotions for the initial least directive probe for more than two-thirds of their judgments, and all of their responses were of the opposite valence from the emotions originally selected (Table 3.3). In other words, the great majority of children who initially said the victimizer felt "happy" or "good" responded to the question "could he/she be feeling anything else" by saying "sad," "bad," or "angry." And this additional, opposite valence victimizer emotion emerged even though it is somewhat easier for children to attribute two similar valence emotions (e.g., "happy" and "glad") than two different valence emotions to a single target (Harter & Buddin, 1987). There was, however, an alternative explanation involving the potential demand characteristics of the probe methodology that needed to be addressed before taking these results too seriously. Perhaps older children interpreted the probe questions as meaning "if someone asks you something twice or more it means that your first answer was probably wrong, so give a different answer." We addressed this concern by using the identical probe methodology to interview an additional group of children about possible alternative valence emotions in *victims*. As expected, we found that children rarely attributed any opposite valence emotions to victims (2 of 18 subjects), which suggested that the observed changes for victimizers were unlikely to be the result of the probe methodology itself.

At this point it would be useful to describe a related cross-national study briefly (Kim, 1993) before summarizing and discussing our results. A group of 120 children (30 4-, 6-, 8-, and 10-year-olds) in Seoul, Korea, were recently presented with the same stories used in part 2 of the Arsenio and Kramer study (1992), and then asked to assess the emotional reactions of victims and victimizers and to provide rationales for their judgments. Results revealed that all of the Korean children expected victims to feel negative emotions (sadness, anger, and fear) due to the victims' materials losses (although older children also mentioned significantly more moral factors, such as fairness and reciprocity concerns). The great majority of the younger Korean children also expected that victimizers would feel happy (92%, 87%, and 85% of 4-, 6-, and 8-year-olds) because of the concrete gains resulting from their acts of victimization, with the beginning of a decline in happy victimizer expectancies beginning at age 10 (56%). Although no probe data are available for the Korean children, the overall similarities in two samples seem clear: All subjects expected victims to feel negatively, and nearly all of the 4- and 6-year-olds expected victimizers to feel happy. Older children (age 8 in the United States and 10 in Korea), however, are somewhat less likely to attribute positive emotions to victimizers.

These results seem to suggest that children attribute quite mixed emotions to *acts of victimization,* but not to the *victimizers* within those acts, that is, children typically attribute very intense opposite valence emotions to victims and victimizers, but the majority of all age groups initially expected victimizers to feel happy. These findings, however, are qualified by the probe results in important ways. Most 6- and nearly all 8-year-olds responded to the least-direct probe question by providing an opposite valence emotion for victimizers but not for victims. In other words, most older children who said victimizers were happy also went on to mention negative emotions, but they rarely expected victims to feel anything but sad or angry. So, although there was no age-related *reversal* in conceptions of victimizers (positive to negative emotions as in Nunner-Winkler & Sodian, 1988) there was a subtler shift from 4-year-olds' view that victimizers are simply and exclusively happy to 8-year-olds' tendency to view victimizers as feeling more mixed or conflicting emotions.

The picture that emerges from children's conceptions of victimization suggests that they come to see a basic moral conflict: Essentially to victimize is to gain desirable outcomes and feel happy, to be victimized is to lose what is yours and to feel sad, angry, and the like. It appears that 4-year-olds view victims and victimizers as having two separate noninteracting sets of emotional conceptions to a single event. In contrast, by 6 to 8 years of age children seem to expect that the positive emotions of victimizers will be modified by the negative emotions of victims, that is, victims' and victimizers' emotions are being coordinated into a larger understanding of victimization.

We believe that this shift from viewing victimization as involving two separate sets of emotional reactions (victimizer and victim) to viewing victimization as a single set of coordinated and interacting reactions is a critical transition in children's larger moral development. Children's understanding of reciprocity, fairness, and justice may all depend on an early ability and tendency to coordinate the emotional reactions of victims and victimizers, both to understand and to feel that the victim's pain and loss will moderate one's own happiness regarding the gain produced by "successful" acts of victimization. But just how does this transition occur? Why do children come to believe that victimizers will feel mixed emotions rather than simple glee? And what processes and mechanisms are responsible for this transition? These admittedly complex questions are the focus of the next few sections, involving potential cognitive constraints on children's understanding of multiple emotions, a Piagetian description of affect and memory, and brief discussion on how children's "emotional history" (e.g., levels of empathy and attachment histories) may influence their conceptions of moral emotions.

Cognitive constraints and the moral transition

One possible explanation for the shift in children's conceptions of victimizers involving underlying cognitive constraints was first suggested by Nunner-Winkler and Sodian (1988). Perhaps younger children are unable to attribute mixed emotions to moral victimizers because of their larger inability to understand that *any* situation, not just those involving victimization, can produce mixed emotions in a single person (Arsenio & Kramer, 1992). This hypothesis stems from a growing literature (e.g., Donaldson & Westerman, 1986; Harris, 1983; and see Harter & Whitesell, 1989, for a review) on children's general understanding of simultaneous emotions, and especially the results of an influential study by Harter and Buddin (1987).

Harter and Buddin (1987) extrapolated from both Piagetian research findings and the neo-Piagetian skill theory of Fischer (1980) to argue that "just as he or she has difficulty integrating two physical judgments such as height or width in a conservation task, a child might be expected to have difficulty integrating two emotions, particularly if these were perceived as opposites" (p. 388). Guided by earlier findings (Harter, 1983), the authors proposed that two dimensions are particularly important in children's understanding of simultaneous emotions, the valence of the emotions (positive or negative) and the target of these emotions, that is, whether they are directed at one person or situation or multiple targets. Interviews of 126 subjects between the ages of 4 and 12 indicated that children exhibit a highly systematic and scalable sequence of 5 stages in their understanding of simultaneous emotions. So, for example, the ability to attribute same valence emotions to situations (e.g., happy and proud) emerged as a prerequisite for the ability to attribute mixed valence emotions. In fact, the most advanced and complex developmental acquisition was children's understanding that one person could feel mixed emotions about the same event – precisely the same ability that would be needed to understand that victimizers could feel mixed emotions.

Based on these findings, we thought that it might be important to examine the links between children's tendency to attribute mixed emotions to moral victimizers and their larger ability to understand mixed emotions in nonmoral situations. Although Harter and Buddin found that an understanding of same target, opposite valence simultaneous emotions typically emerged around age 11, results from a number of other studies indicate that children are able to understand mixed emotions much earlier when they are not required to generate examples of these situations themselves (e.g., Donaldson & Westerman, 1986; Harris, 1983; see especially Fischer, Shaver, & Cornochan, 1990, p. 113). Consequently we (Arsenio & Kramer, 1991) expected that at least some of the older children in our 4- to 8-year-old sample would reveal an understanding of mixed emotions in nonmoral situations.

As part of the Arsenio and Kramer (1992) study, children were presented with a mixed emotions task adapted from Harris (1983). Children were read stimulus stories in which they were told that they had found their lost bike but that the bike had been damaged. Different manipulations emphasized either that the bike was found (positive emotion condition), that it was damaged (negative condition), or a combination of elements (mixed condition). After each condition children were asked if they would feel happy, sad, mad, and/or scared, and they were told that they could chose as many emotions as they wished. Children were then asked a final question about two children who disagreed as to whether someone could feel happy and sad at the same time, and why (see Arsenio & Kramer, 1991; and Harris, 1983,

Experiment 3, for details). Children's tendency to acknowledge mixed emotions was then assessed in two ways. If they judged that the mixed emotion condition would elicit mixed emotions, *and* that the positive and negative conditions would elicit only positive and negative emotions, respectively, they were scored as understanding mixed emotions. Alternatively if they said "yes" to the final question ("can someone feel happy and sad at the same time") and they could give an explanation for this judgment, they were also scored as understanding mixed emotions. Using these two criteria, we found that only 2 4-year-olds, but 14 6-year-olds and all 16 8-year-olds were able to understand nonmoral mixed emotions.

The next important question involved how closely children's understanding of mixed events in nonmoral situations paralleled their conceptions of victimizers' emotions. Children's conceptions of mixed emotions in moral victimizers were assessed using their response to the initial probe question following their emotion judgments for victims and victimizer ("could [the victimizer] feel anything else?"). Subjects who responded "yes" to this probe and then provided an emotion of the opposite valence from their original victimizer judgment were scored as having attributed mixed emotions to victimizers. Overall, 42 to 48 subjects showed a similar level for mixed emotions in moral and nonmoral situations, Thirteen 4-year-olds scored "no" for both, 12 6-year-olds scored "yes" for both, and the 16 8-year-olds scored "yes" for both (1 6-year-old scored "no" for both). Perhaps as important, for all but 2 subjects an ability to attribute mixed emotions in the more general nonmoral situation was a prerequisite for mixed emotions in the moral situation. As expected, then, the cognitive ability to understand mixed emotions outside of moral contexts appears to underlie children's ability to attribute mixed emotions to moral victimizers.

Although this single assessment of nonmoral emotions was only a small component of a larger study (included in Arsenio & Kramer 1991, but not 1992), these results do suggest some intriguing possibilities for future research. If this link between children's general understanding of mixed emotions and their attribution of mixed emotions to victimizers is confirmed, then it would help to explain 4-year-olds apparent belief that victimizers are happy regardless of the victim's losses. Underlying cognitive constraints may mean that young children are more morally "obtuse" than "resistant." Converging evidence on children's "theory of mind" and their cognitive abilities may also prove revealing. Some studies in this area already suggest that children's understanding of how the intentional mental states of a social dyad can interact (such as victimizer's positive emotions and victim's negative emotions) may require second-order recursive abilities that only merge by age 5 or 6 (Astington, Harris, & Olson, 1988).

Yet, ultimately, even if underlying cognitive constraints do play an important role in children's conceptions of moral emotions, these constraints will only provide a partial explanation for why children begin to modify their conceptions of victimizer happiness. As Fischer et al. (1990) noted, the emergence of cognitive abilities makes it *possible* for children to believe that a situation may elicit multiple emotions (i.e., cognitive abilities play a necessary but not sufficient role), but their actual tendency to do so may depend on a variety of other social and emotional factors.

The happy victimizer: Theory and implications

Piaget and affect

Why then do children come to view victimization and particularly victimizers in terms of mixed emotions? A general understanding of mixed emotions may promote this transition, but why should a belief that victims feel overwhelmingly negative emotions compel children to change their initially positive views of victimization? As one of our adolescent subjects said, "I wouldn't care if he felt sad cause I stole his jacket. Why should I? I've got a great jacket, and if that other kid was stupid enough to leave it in his locker – tough!" Yet, somehow most children do begin to feel that the emotions of victims actually matter to victimizers, that seeing or even expecting the victim's negative feelings alters the simple happiness of getting something the "easy way."

One intriguing explanation for this victimizer transition is suggested in Piaget's writings on affect and cognition (especially his book *Intelligence and Affectivity* [see also Cowan, 1981, 1982]). The details of this explanation are somewhat complex, but two interrelated elements are central: (1) emotions are not simply experienced and then forgotten, but rather they are stored as an important part of our basic representations/ understandings of various sociomoral events; and (2) the dynamics of this victimizer transition closely parallel those Piaget used to describe conflicts of the will in general.

The first part of this explanation is familiar from the beginning of this chapter, "affects, by being represented, last beyond the presence of the object that excites them" (Piaget, 1954/1981, p. 44). In other words, emotions do not simply happen and then disappear, but rather, given the nature of human cognition, emotions are routinely included as part of our representations of a wide variety of events. These emotion–cognition links then accumulate and develop over time to form a complex web of memories linking experienced emotions and the situations and people that precede and follow these emotions (see the growing recent literature on the situational antecedents and consequences of emotions [e.g., Masters & Carlson, 1984; Stein & Levine, 1989; Stein, Trabasso, & Liwag, 1993]). As a result, children may come to remember that being a victimizer can sometimes lead to happiness and gain, whereas being a victim produces loss and negative emotions. The question remains, however, how these potentially "remembered affects" influence children's moral development, and, more precisely, how are they implicated in the "victimizer transition"? The second aspect of this transition requires a brief description of what Piaget called "the problem of the will" before returning to specifically moral issues.

Piaget's examination of the will begins with William James's classic conflict: In the middle of preparing a lecture, a scholar happens to notice that it is a beautiful day outside. For a few moments the scholar feels a strong desire to put down the lecture and go out to enjoy the day, but in the end a sense of obligation or duty prevails, and he or she completes the lecture. Piaget argues that this illustration contains two elements that are central to all real exercises of the will. Initially there must be a conflict between two impulses or tendencies, and eventually the initially weaker impulse must predominate over the stronger impulse (although we might argue that there can still be a conflict even if the initially stronger impulse predominates in the end).

To understand how and why duty and obligation eventually prevail, Piaget claims that it is useful to begin by viewing acts of the will as "affective analogues" of what occurs in intellectual decentration. In the conservation of liquids task, for example, (see the earlier discussion of Harter & Buddin, 1987), the young child learns to free himself or herself from the perceptual pull of focusing exclusively on the height of the liquid by exercising logical abilities such as reversibility and negation. Acts of will, it is claimed, function in a similar way. "Therefore, the act of will consists here simply in relying upon a decentration, upon something that is exactly analogous to the reversibility of the intellectual operation and which consists in subordinating the actual value, the desire, to a larger scale of (permanent, coordinated, and reversible) values" (Piaget, 1962, cited in Bearison & Zimiles, 1986). In other words, the impulse – wanting to stop work to enjoy a beautiful day – initially has such a strong affective pull that for the moment continuing work becomes a weaker priority. The affective intensity of going outside, however, gradually becomes subsumed by the more powerful, but temporarily less available set of affectively charged memories associated, for example, with the scholar's pride in his or her teaching competence and an awareness of a larger sense of professional responsibility. This transition or affective decentration may begin the moment when the scholar realizes that to go outside it will be necessary to stop writing the lecture. With this shift in attentional focus or decentration the affects associated with completing the lecture are more fully remembered and, in essence, reactivated since, "when a person recalls past situations, he *relives* values as well as memory images" (Piaget, 1954/1981, p. 64 [emphasis added]). In the end the scholar continues writing the lecture because the more extensive and powerful affective memories associated with completing the task have greater affective strength than the feelings associated with enjoying a beautiful day.

The important parallel here is that exercises of the will, in general, and the victimizer transition, in particular, both involve subordinating immediately salient affectively charged impulses to initially less charged memories. Specifically, younger children's moral conceptions suggest that they are initially overcome by the gain and happiness produced by victimization, the immediate egocentric pull felt by the victimizer. In older children, this impulse becomes weakened and perhaps even replaced by a focus on the accompanying loss, sadness, and anger of the victim. Described in terms of the will, the immediate pull of victimizing others for material gain becomes less powerful in comparison with an emerging and countervailing set of affective values emphasizing the unfairness of deliberately harming others for selfish gains. Still, questions remain. Namely, what are the origins of these "countervailing values" and how do they gain their affective power?

Piaget's answer focuses on the role of children's social relationships, and, especially, their peer interactions. In his terms, a prototypical peer interaction might start when Child 1 engages in a "negative expenditure of effort" while interacting with Child 2, that is, Child 1 acts in a way that benefits Child 2, but at some loss of time, energy, or resources to Child 1. In turn, Child 2 appreciates this action and feels a sense of debt toward Child 1, which leads Child 2 to attribute a positive value toward Child 1 in the form of feeling goodwill. At the same time, Child 1 feels a sense of satisfaction about his or her original action (see figure 1, p. 46 in *Intelligence and Affectivity*). It is easy to imagine further Child 2 returning the favor, and to see how "moral feelings originate from feelings of goodwill towards others who have given pleasure" (p. 47). With the help of emerging cognitive abilities, these affectively positive reciprocal exchanges become conserved (remembered) and organized into more permanent structures of fixed values.

Several aspects of this example are especially interesting. One is the emphasis on how *positive* features of social interactions may underly children's subsequent understanding and behavior regarding acts of *victimiza-*

tion. Imagine two children with a history of positive interactions (close friends). When these children get into conflicts with each other, their emotional ties or "goodwill" should lead them to think twice before victimizing each other. Perhaps more important, even when one friend does victimize the other, the victimizer is likely to experience his friend's loss in a fairly direct and immediate fashion. The potential joy resulting from victimization is tempered by the pain of a friend who has brought joy in the past. In this view, the existence of prior affective ties, especially a history of positive reciprocity, lays a groundwork from which the child is likely to alter his or her initial conception that victimization is a highly effective way to produce material and psychological gains. Expressed as a conflict of the will, the shallower, short-term emotional gains produced by victimization are outweighed by the deeper emotional ties resulting from friendship.

Clearly, children's affective relationships are only the first step in Piaget's description of moral development in *Intelligence and Affectivity.* Memories of early affective experiences provide the raw material and some motivational power for emerging moral principles, but children must also learn to apply these principles to people with whom they have no emotional ties or even negative ones. It is not enough to refrain from harming one's friends only to feel free to harm strangers or one's enemies. Yet, even a description of this initial moral transition highlights the joint contributions made both by children's cognitive abilities, including memories of previous sociomoral encounters and the abstractions drawn from these encounters, and their affective experiences, including their social relationships with various peers and adults.

Another less obvious implication of this description of moral origins involves the effects of stable individual differences in peer relationships on children's moral understanding and behavior. Although many of children's peer–peer affective relationships may tend toward equality and reciprocity (Piaget, 1932; Youniss, 1980), there is also the potential for gross inequalities in that "a person can give more than he receives or even give without receiving" (Piaget, 1954/1981, p. 47). Occasional imbalances in reciprocity are probably typical, but if, for a variety of reasons, this imbalance persists and becomes chronic, then children should be expected to construct coherent, but "nonnormative" sets of moral values from their memories of these affectively charged experiences. In other words, if a child's peer relationships are routinely characterized by something less than "the goodwill" described by Piaget, then that child will also have a different set of affectively charged relationship experiences and memories from which to construct his or her understanding of victimization. In turn, these chronic affective imbalances are likely to have a number of long-term consequences, including certain difficulties in integrating the emotional experiences of victims and victimizers.

Peer relationships and conceptions of victimization

We have argued that the victimizer transition (i.e., the age-related shift away from viewing victimizers as feeling strictly happy) depends, in part, on the pattern of children's relationships, and, consequently, that stable individual differences in these relationship patterns will affect children's conceptions of moral emotions. In essence, children's cognitive abilities may allow them to construct moral principles, but these abilities do not dictate the nature of the affective experiences that provide the raw material for these principles. According to Piaget's example, when children are joined together by positive feelings and reciprocal goodwill, they should be less likely to separate their feelings as victims and victimizers within that relationship. In contrast, children with weak or dysfunctional peer relationships will lack the emotional ties or social bonds that could transform their initial views of victimization.

To date, little direct evidence supports these broad claims about the links between children's peer relationships, their conceptions of sociomoral affect, and their related behavior. Two existing literatures, however, may prove especially helpful for addressing some of these ideas; the literature on children's sociometrically determined peer status, and that on the social consequences of children's attachment status. In both of these areas some studies already link children's interpersonal histories and their tendencies to victimize others, and some ongoing research is specifically designed to assess children's conceptions of sociomoral affect. We provide here a brief summary of relevant work in both of these areas.

A great number of studies on children's peer status and its consequences (see, e.g., Asher & Cole, 1990, for a review) have shown that many children develop relatively stable peer–peer interactive patterns in which they are routinely rejected, neglected, or sought out by their peers, and that this peer status often quickly generalizes to entirely new settings. There are, unfortunately, young children who very definitely experience pervasive patterns of ill will in their interactions with other children, and, as Denham, McKinley, Couchoud, and Holt (1990) have shown, there are also children as young as 3 and 4 who behave more prosocially toward their peers and who are liked more as a result. In addition, it is already known that a pattern of victimization including aggressiveness is the single strongest predictor of peer rejection (Coie, Dodge, & Kupersmidt, 1990), and that peer rejection and aggressiveness are associated with a variety of children's social-cognitive deficits (including difficulties in emotion recognition [Denham et al., 1990; Vosk, Forehand, & Figueroa, 1983] and evaluations of provocation [Crick & Ladd, 1990]).

Based on these overall findings, Lemerise and Bush (1994) at Western Kentucky University have recently begun to examine whether children with different peer statuses also differ in how they view the emotional consequences of victimization. They have already administered sociometric and "happy victimizer" interviews (see Arsenio & Kramer, 1992, part 2) to over 465 children between the ages of 4 and 9 with a special interest in comparing rejected/aggressive and accepted/nonaggressive children's judgments. Subsequent analyses will focus on several potential differences both in children's emotion judgments as well as their justifications for these judgments. In terms of children's emotion judgments, it is expected that older aggressive/rejected children may attribute fewer mixed and more positive emotional outcomes to victimizers than will older accepted/nonaggressive children. It is also proposed that even when aggressive/rejected do attribute mixed emotions to victimizers, they will do so for different reasons than their peers. Aggressive children are expected to explain victimizers' mixed emotions with more self-focused rationales – for example, victimizers' happiness may sometimes be tempered by the potential fear of getting in trouble. In contrast, when nonaggressive accepted kids explain victimizers' emotions they will be more likely to focus on the needs and desires of the victims (e.g., the victim's pain), rather than on additional victimizer concerns.

The comprehensive nature of their sample will also make it possible for Lemerise and Bush to examine less obvious differences in the moral conceptions of other sociometric groups. For example, it would be interesting to know how the social isolation of certain peer-neglected children affects their conceptions of moral emotions. On one hand it may be that a certain amount of peer conflict is needed for children to develop clear conceptions regarding the emotional consequences of victimization, and, consequently, peer-neglected children may have less of a sense of either the potential rewards of being a victimizer or the losses resulting from being victimized. On the other hand, peer-neglected children may be so concerned about the losses resulting from victimization that they may form highly fearful conceptions that might reinforce their social isolation. It will also be interesting to compare more sociometrically average children and accepted/nonaggressive children to assess, for example, whether accepted children's moral attributions reveal a more other-focused empathic orientation. In any case, this study should begin to clarify some of the important connections between children's peer relationships and their conceptions of sociomoral emotions.

This last section focuses on the somewhat more speculative potential connections between children's attachment status, their beliefs about moral emotions, and, ultimately, their behavior (see also Emde et al., 1987). With its emphasis on adult–child relationships and the primacy of adult contributions, attachment theory seems more closely linked with typical socialization theories of children's moral development than with Piagetian-based cognitive developmental theories. Yet, despite these deep and nontrivial differences, attachment theory and the social cognitive model underlying this chapter both share an emphasis on the pivotal role of reciprocity in affectively mediated relationships and the long-term consequences of these relationships.

Some of these larger commonalities are especially clear in a study by Troy and Sroufe (1987) on the connections between children's attachment status and their patterns of victimization. The 28 subjects in their research were initially part of a larger prospective study in which children's maternal attachment status was assessed at 12 and 18 months using the Ainsworth Strange Situation. Several years later, when these children were between the ages of 4 and 5 and attending preschool, they were paired together to play with a same gender peer for seven 15-minute sessions. Groups were formed representing all possible combinations of attachment histories, and the videotapes of children's interactions were assessed by three observers. Subsequent analyses revealed striking group differences in these preschoolers' patterns of victimization depending on their earlier attachment status. Out of the total 14 dyads, all 5 of the pairs in which a child with an avoidant attachment history was paired with an insecurely attached child (either avoidant or ambivalent) were characterized by a clear and pervasive pattern of victimization. In contrast not 1 of the 8 dyads in which there was at least one securely attached child there showed a pattern of victimization (the remaining dyad included two ambivalently attached children). The authors noted that these group differences were highly significant despite the relatively small number of dyads involved in the study.

We believe that the early attachment history of all the children involved in this study can be seen to meaningfully relate to the relationships they formed in the preschool free play situation. Specifically, because of an early relationship marked by a consistent pattern of caregiver insensitivity, rejections and abuse, children with an avoidant attachment history have clearly internalized models of both exploiter and exploited. (p. 170)

In their discussion Troy and Sroufe go on to suggest two related explanations for why children's attachment status is such a powerful predictor of their victimization behavior 3 to 4 years later. The more proximal cause is the relationship between children's attachment status and their general pattern of interactions with peers. Other attachment-related studies have shown, for example, that insecurely attached children express fewer positive emotions to their peers, are less empathic, and are generally less socially competent with their peers (e.g., Sroufe, Schork, Motti, Lawroski, & LaFreniere, 1984). Consequently, insecurely attached children are less likely to have had positive peer relationships and accumulated "goodwill" and, therefore, would lack the strong affective bonds that ultimately make the pain and loss of the victim matter to the victimizer. (Note that the parallels between this explanation and the one given for peer status may stem from similarities in the social-relational deficits of insecurely attached and peer-rejected children.)

A related and ultimately more basic explanation involves the "working models" (e.g., Kobak & Sceery, 1988; Main, Kaplan, & Cassidy, 1985) or social expectations that children generate from their early attachment relationships with adults. This explanation begins with the observation that insecure attachment patterns are typically the result of parental nonresponsiveness and especially a tendency to ignore or selectively attend to infants' emotional signals (e.g., Bretherton, 1985; Egeland & Sroufe, 1981; George & Main, 1979). As a consequence of this early experience, children who are insecurely attached (especially avoidantly attached children) are likely to form "working models" of relationships that reflect, in part, a core belief in the emotional nonreciprocity of others. Namely, based on their first interpersonal experiences, these children learn that their feelings do not readily modify or alter the behaviors and feelings of their primary attachment figures. In turn, this early failure in emotional reciprocity will promote a pattern of victimization, not because these children are unaware of victims' pain and loss, but because insecurely attached children do not believe that someone else's emotional response has any direct relevance for their own emotional reactions and understanding. Although few children are likely to form such an extreme working model of relationships (see George & Main, 1979, and Main & George, 1985, however, on abused children's interactions with peers), even partial tendencies in this direction may weaken children's concern for victims by undermining their expectancies for emotional reciprocity.

We (Arsenio, Shea, & Sacks, 1994) are currently assessing some of these proposed connections by comparing the attachment status and conceptions of sociomoral emotions in two groups of male adolescents. One group of 20 adolescents is from a special educational program that is offered as an alternative to juvenile detention, and the control group of 20 adolescents is from a demographically comparable high school. (The two groups do not differ in terms of SES, race/ethnicity, and reading ability scores.) All subjects were given individual interviews in which they completed self-report measures of attachment status (Collins & Read, 1990) and empathy (Bryant, 1982), in addition to being asked about the probable emotional outcomes of different acts of victimization.

As expected, delinquent adolescents are significantly more likely to describe themselves as being insecurely attached than the control adolescents (16 of 20 insecure vs. 8 of 20 insecure, respectively). Additional links are expected between subjects' attachment status and their conceptions of sociomoral affect: Specifically, insecurely attached subjects are expected to view victims and victimizers as having discrete emotional reactions, with victimizers primarily seen as happy and victims as angry and scared. Although analyses have only begun, there is already some evidence for this last hypothesis. Delinquent subjects are significantly less likely than controls to attribute mixed emotions to victimizers, and they require more probe questions to alter their view that victimizers are feeling happy. Subsequent analyses of subjects' rationales for these judgments and their quantitative ratings of emotions (along a 5-point scale) should help to clarify this finding. Still, the lack of mixed emotion conceptions in behaviorally disturbed adolescents seems consistent with the claim that they would be less likely than their peers to integrate the emotions of victims and victimizers.

Conclusion

In this chapter we have presented a theoretical model and some empirical evidence regarding children's conceptions of sociomoral affect and how these conceptions can inform children's sociomoral reasoning and behavior. Some aspects of this model clarify the assumptions underlying all work on situational affect, whether sociomoral or not, and these claims are likely to be uncontroversial. For example, children (and adults) tend to remember the emotions they experience in a wide range of personally and socially significant events, and these affect–events links will help them to anticipate the likely outcomes of related future events. The clear affective salience of common, everyday sociomoral events involving victimization, the sharing of individual and group resources, and child and adult sanctions should provide children with an especially rich source of potential information for informing and guiding their subsequent sociomoral reasoning and behavior. In fact, the evidence presented suggests that children have highly differentiated conceptions regarding these familiar sociomoral events, reflecting a sensitivity both to differences in the social contexts of various sociomoral acts (e.g., victimization vs. prosocial acts) as well as the various roles people can play within these events (e.g., victims vs. victimizers). Some indirect evidence was also presented indicating that conceptions of sociomoral affect may influence behavior: As expected, children who exhibited less acceptable forms of sociomoral behavior differed somewhat from their peers in the emotional outcomes they anticipated for sociomoral behaviors.

The somewhat controversial claim that these affect–event conceptions provide the "raw material" for the construction of abstract sociomoral principles was illustrated with a single extended example in the last two sections of the chapter. It appears that young children expect moral victimizers to feel happy after their transgressions because of the potential gains produced by victimization, but that by age 8 or so an important development transition results in children attributing more mixed emotions to victims. We argued that this change reflects a shift from viewing victimization in terms of two separate noninteracting sets of conceptions about victims' and victimizers' emotions, to a more coordinated understanding of victimization in which victimizers are seen as responding to the pain and loss of the victim.

The critical question then became "how and why does this transformation take place?" The role of cognitive limitations was acknowledged, but in the end, interpersonal reciprocity and affectively mediated relationships were seen as fundamental in this transition. Using Piaget's example involving conflicts of the will, the initially more affectively salient gains produced by acts of victimization become subordinated to the more long-term affective considerations involved in friendships and other social relationships. What starts in the context of friendships and close relationships, however, must also be extended to strangers, new acquaintances, and even one's enemies. We proposed that children's moral principles originate from their emotional experiences, but that they must then also cognitively abstract certain extensions of these principles. In its simplest form this may involve inferences such as "I don't like how it feels when someone steals my toy, my friend doesn't like that either, so this new kid probably won't like it." As we noted earlier, the emergence of morality depends on a variety of cognitive abilities, including memories for affective events and abstractions of commonalities in these events, as well as the pattern of affectively mediated relationships a child has experienced with peers and adults. In this view, morality is not the "blind" result of unreasoned and unexamined emotions, nor is it a set of coldly rational and impersonal cognitive principles.

We want to conclude by highlighting what we see as some important issues for future research in this area. One major issue is the seeming gap between children's conceptions of the positive consequences of victimization for victimizers, and other evidence suggesting that even very young children are sensitive to the pain and loss of victims (e.g., Hoffman, 1983;

Zahn-Waxler et al., 1979). The extensive literature on the development of empathy, for example, suggests that when children victimize others they will find themselves involuntarily experiencing the negative emotions of their victims (Hoffman, 1975, 1987). Consequently, even fairly young children should not expect victimizers to feel simple happiness (see, e.g., Miller & Eisenberg's 1988 review article on the link between aggression and empathy).

One explanation for this gap is that children may actually experience mixed emotions as victimizers long before they can express these feelings, much as Harris (1987) has argued about their abilities with mixed emotions in general. This explanation, however, does not seem to address 4-year-olds' overwhelmingly positive view of victimization: even if they are only able to choose a single victimizer emotion, it is unclear why that emotion should nearly always be a positive one. Alternatively, it may be that early empathic tendencies are more fragile than previously expected, especially given evidence that parental abuse (e.g., Main & George, 1985) and less extreme deficits in parental emotional reciprocity (reflected in children's insecure attachment) are already known to undermine children's empathy. Yet, ultimately, neither explanation for the wide gap between the young children's supposed empathic tendencies and their conceptions of victimization seem especially convincing. Future research directed to this issue should provide especially important insights into children's larger views of victimization.

Another important unresolved issue concerns the accuracy of children's sociomoral conceptions, that is, to what extent do children's conceptions of various sociomoral emotions actually correspond to the emotions they experience in these contexts. Questions about the accuracy of affect–event links were raised in one of the first studies in this field (Barden et al., 1980), but, to date, there is almost no research on this topic. (A few studies have addressed children's expressed emotions in various social contexts [e.g., Arsenio & Killen, in press; Arsenio et al., 1993; Denham 1986; Fabes & Eisenberg, 1992], but not the connections between these emotions and children's related conceptions.) Research on this topic would help to determine whether there is a lag between children's emotional experiences and their conceptions of sociomoral affect, or whether children's conceptions are fundamentally different from their actual experiences. Resolving questions about the accuracy and timing of the links between children's conceptions and their actual experiences of emotions will be another essential task for researchers interested in sociomoral affect.

A final issue involves the role of material gain in children's happy victimizer expectancy. Nearly all of the acts of victimization used in this research produce tangible, material gains for victimizers, whether through stealing some desirable object or obtaining some advantage by not having to wait for one's turn. What about those acts that involve intimidation, domination, and other forms of more strictly psychological victimization? Do children have a general expectation that victimization produces positive consequences even when the benefits are less obvious? In their research, Nunner-Winkler and Sodian (1988, experiment 2) found that 4- to 6-year-olds expect victimizers to feel happy following victimizing acts that produced both tangible and nontangible gains. It is not known, however, whether these findings apply to older children as well, and whether there are meaningful differences in how children view victimization that does or does not produce obvious benefits. These issues need to be assessed more systematically if we are to understand the full extent of children's initially positive views of victimization.

In conclusion, we have argued that children's conceptions of sociomoral emotions allow them to anticipate the likely consequences of their sociomoral behaviors, and that these emotion–event expectancies provide children with critical information for the construction of more abstract moral principles. Much of this discussion focused specifically on children's conceptions of victimization, and the proposed transition from viewing victimizers as feeling happy to viewing them as feeling more mixed emotions (reflecting an underlying integration of victimizers' gains and victims' losses). Evidence was presented suggesting that this transition in children's conceptions of victimization may apply to children of other cultures, and that delinquent children may view the emotional consequences of victimization differently than their peers. Throughout, we have tried to emphasize that neither affective nor cognitive contributions are really sufficient to explain this transition: A complex combination of "remembered affects," interpersonal relationships, and developing cognitive skills are all involved. Consequently, debates about whether either cognition or affect is more important, or even over which of these two precedes in a temporal sense are not likely to be especially revealing (e.g., Lazarus, 1984, vs. Zajonc, 1984). At the same time, we believe that a meaningful explanation of children's sociomoral development will require an equally detailed account of the structure and function of both affective and cognitive contributions. In the end, it will not be sufficient to compare affect to the "gasoline which activates the motor of an automobile but does not modify its structure" (Piaget, 1954/1981, p. 5), or to liken cognition to a slightly elaborated "funnel" that affects the flow but not the content of affectively charged socialization experiences that are transmitted from adults to children.

References

American Psychiatric Association. (1987). *Diagnostic and statistical manual of mental disorders* (3rd ed., rev.). Washington, DC: American Psychiatric Association.

Arsenio, W. (1985, April). *Children's posttransgressional affective conceptions and social-cognitive judgments.* Paper presented at the biennial meeting of the Society for Research in Child Development, Toronto.

Arsenio, W. (1986). *Affective components of social cognition and their relation to behavior.* Unpublished doctoral dissertation, Stanford University.

Arsenio, W. (1988). Children's conceptions of the situational affective consequences of sociomoral events. *Child Development, 59,* 1611–1622.

Arsenio, W., Berlin, N., & O'Desky, I. (1989, April). *Children's and adults' understanding of the emotional consequences of sociomoral events.* Paper presented at the biennial meeting of the Society for Research in Child Development, Kansas City.

Arsenio, W., & Fleiss, K. (in press). Behaviorally disruptive and typical children's conceptions of sociomoral affect. *British Journal of Developmental Psychology.*

Arsenio, W., & Ford, M. (1985). The role of affective information in social-cognitive development: Children's differentiation of moral and conventional events. *Merrill-Palmer Quarterly, 31,* 1–18.

Arsenio, W., & Killen, M. (in press). Preschoolers' emotions and conflicts during small group table play. *Early Education and Development.*

Arsenio, W., & Kramer, R. (1991, April). *Happy victimizers and their victims: Children's understanding of moral affect and multiple emotions.* Paper presented at the biennial meeting of the Society for Research in Child Development, Seattle.

Arsenio, W., & Kramer, R. (1992). Victimizers and their victims: Children's conceptions of the mixed emotional consequences of victimization. *Child Development, 63,* 915–927.

Arsenio, W., Lover, A., & Gumora, G. (1993, March). *Emotions, conflicts, and aggression during preschoolers' freeplay.* Paper presented at the biennial meeting of the Society for Research in Child Development, New Orleans.

Arsenio, W., Shea, T., & Sacks, B. (1994). *Attachment status and empathy in adolescents' conceptions of victimization.* Unpublished manuscript.

Asher, S., & Coie, J. (1990). *Peer rejection in childhood.* Cambridge: Cambridge University Press.

Astington, J., Harris, P., & Olson, D. (1988). Introduction. In *Developing theories of mind* (pp. 1–15). Cambridge: Cambridge University Press.

Bandura, A. (1986). *Social foundations of thought and action.* Englewood Cliffs, NJ: Prentice-Hall.

Barden, R., Zelko, F., Duncan, S., & Masters, J. (1980). Children's consensual knowledge about the experiential determinants of emotion. *Journal of Personality and Social Psychology, 39,* 968–976.

Bearison, D., & Zimiles, H. (1986). Developmental perspectives of thought and emotion: An introduction. In D. Bearison, & H. Zimiles (Eds.), *Thought and emotion: Developmental Perspectives* (p. 1–10). Hillsdale, NJ: Lawrence Erlbaum.

Blaney, P. (1987). Affect and memory: A review. *Psychological Bulletin, 99* (2), 229–246.

Boldizar, J., Perry, D., & Perry, L. (1989). Outcome values and aggression. *Child Development, 60,* 571–579.

Bower, G. (1981). Mood and memory. *American Psychologist, 36,* 129–148.

Bretherton, I. (1985). Attachment theory: Retrospect and prospect. In I. Bretherton & E. Waters (Eds.), *Growing points of attachment theory and research* (pp. 3–35). *Monographs of the Society for Research in Child Development, 50* (1–2, Serial No. 209).

Bretherton, I., Fritz, J., Zahn-Waxler, C., & Ridgeway, D. (1986). Learning to talk about emotions: A functionalist perspective. *Child Development, 57,* 529–548.

Bryant, B. (1982). An index of empathy for children and adolescents. *Child Development, 53,* 413–425.

Cialdini, R., & Kenrick, D. (1976). Altruism and hedonism: A social development perspective on the relationship of negative mood and helping. *Journal of Personality and Social Psychology, 34,* 907–914.

Clark, M., & Isen, A. (1982). Toward understanding the relationship between feeling states and social behavior. In A. Hastorf & A. Isen (Eds.), *Cognitive social psychology* (pp. 73–108). New York: Elsevier.

Coie, J., Dodge, K., & Kupersmidt, J. (1990). Peer group behavior and social status. In S. Asher & J. Coie (Eds.), *Peer rejection in childhood* (pp. 17–59). Cambridge: Cambridge University Press.

Collins, N., & Read, S. (1990). Adult attachment, working models, and relationship quality in dating couples. *Journal of Personality and Social Psychology, 58,* 644–663.

Cowan, P. (1981). Preface to J. Piaget, *Intelligence and affectivity: Their relationship during child development* (T. Brown & C. Kaegi, Trans. and Eds.). Palo Alto, CA: Annual Reviews Monograph.

Cowan, P. (1982). The relationship between emotional and cognitive development. In D. Cicchetti & P. Hesse (Eds.), *Emotional development* (pp. 49–80). San Francisco: Jossey-Bass.

Crick, N., & Ladd, G. (1990). Children's perceptions of the outcomes of social strategies: Do the ends justify the means? *Developmental Psychology, 26,* 612–620.

Damon, W. (1977). *The social world of the child.* San Francisco: Jossey-Bass.

Damon, W. (1980). Patterns of change in children's social reasoning: A two-year longitudinal study. *Child Development, 51,* 1010–1017.

Denham, S. (1986). Social cognition, prosocial behavior, and emotion in preschoolers: Contextual validation. *Child Development, 57,* 194–201.

Denham, S., McKinley, M., Couchoud, E., & Holt, R. (1990). Emotional and behavioral predictors of preschool peer ratings. *Child Development, 61,* 1145–1162.

Dodge, K. (1991). Emotion and social information processing. In J. Garber & K. Dodge (Eds.), *The development of emotion regulation and dysregulation* (pp. 159–181). Cambridge: Cambridge University Press.

Dodge, K., & Feldman, E. (1990). Issues in social cognition and sociometric status. In S. Asher & J. Coie (Eds.), *Peer rejection in childhood* (pp. 119–155). Cambridge: Cambridge University Press.

Dodge, K., & Somberg, D. (1987). Hostile attributional biases among aggressive boys are exacerbated under conditions of threat to the self. *Child Development, 58,* 213–224.

Donaldson, S., & Westerman, M. (1986). Development of children's understanding of ambivalence and causal theories of emotion. *Developmental Psychology, 22,* 655–662.

Dunn, J. (1988). *The beginnings of social understanding.* Cambridge, MA: Harvard University Press.

Egeland, B., & Sroufe, L. (1981). Developmental sequelae of maltreatment in infancy. In R. Rizley & D. Cicchetti (Eds.), *Developmental perspectives in child maltreatment* (pp. 77–92). San Francisco: Jossey-Bass.

Eisenberg, N. (1982). *The development of prosocial behavior.* New York: Academic Press.

Eisenberg-Berg, N., & Hand, M. (1979). The relationship of preschoolers' reasoning about prosocial moral conflicts to moral behavior. *Child Development, 50,* 356–363.

Ekman, P. (1993). Facial expression and emotion. *American Psychologist, 48,* 384–392.

Emde, R., Johnson, W., & Easterbrooks, M. (1987). The do's and don'ts of early moral development: Psychoanalytic tradition and current research. In J. Kagan & S. Lamb (Eds.), *The emergence of morality in young children* (pp. 245–276). Chicago: University of Chicago Press.

Fabes, R., & Eisenberg, N. (1992). Young children's coping with interpersonal stress. *Child Development, 63,* 116–128.

Fischer, K. (1980). A theory of cognitive development: The control and construction of hierarchies of skills. *Psychological Bulletin, 87,* 477–531.

Fischer, K., Shaver, P., & Cornochan, P. (1990). How emotions develop and how they organize development. *Cognition and Emotion, 4,* 81–127.

George, C., & Main, M. (1979). Social interactions of young abused children: Approach, avoidance, and aggression. *Child Development, 50,* 306–318.

Gibbs, J. (1991). Towards the integration of Kohlberg's and Hoffman's moral development theories. *Human Development, 34,* 88–104.

Gibbs, J., & Schnell, S. (1985). Moral development "versus" socialization: A critique. *American Psychologist, 40,* 1071–1080.

Glasberg, R., & Aboud, F. (1982). Keeping one's distance from sadness: Children's self-reports of emotional experience. *Developmental Psychology, 18,* 287–293.

Gnepp, J. (1989). Children's use of personal information to understand other people's feelings. In C. Saarni & P. Harris (Eds.), *Children's understanding of emotions* (pp. 151–180). Cambridge: Cambridge University Press.

Harris, P. L. (1983). Children's understanding of the link between situation and emotion. *Journal of Experimental Child Psychology, 36,* 490–509.

Harris, P. L. (1985). What children know about the situations that provoke emotions. In M. Lewis & C. Saarni (Eds.), *The socialization of emotion* (pp. 161–186). New York: Plenum.

Harris, P. L. (1987, March). *Developmental change in children's understanding of mixed and masked emotions.* Paper presented at the workshop on Transition Mechanisms in Cognitive-Emotional Development: The Longitudinal Approach, Grachen, Switzerland.

Harris, P. L. (1989). *Children and emotion: The development of psychological understanding.* Oxford: Blackwell.

Harter, S. (1983). Children's understanding of multiple emotions: A cognitive-developmental approach. In W. Overton (Ed.), *The relationship between social and cognitive development* (pp. 147–194). Hillsdale, NJ: Lawrence Erlbaum.

Harter, S., & Buddin, N. (1987). Children's understanding of the simultaneity of two emotions: A five-stage developmental acquisition sequence. *Developmental Psychology, 23,* 388–399.

Harter, S., & Pike, R. (1984). The pictorial scale of perceived competence and social acceptance for young children. *Child Development, 55,* 1969–1982.

Harter, S., & Whitesell, N. (1989). Developmental changes in children's understanding of single, multiple, and blended emotion concepts. In C. Saarni & P. Harris (Eds.), *Children's understanding of emotions* (pp. 81–116). Cambridge: Cambridge University Press.

Hoffman, M. (1975). Developmental synthesis of affect and cognition and its implications for altruistic motivation. *Developmental Psychology, 11,* 607–622.

Hoffman, M. (1981). Perspectives on the difference between understanding people and understanding things. In J. Flavell & L. Ross (Eds.), *Social-cognitive development* (pp. 67–81). Cambridge: Cambridge University Press.

Hoffman, M. (1983). Affective and cognitive processes in moral internalization. In E. Higgins, A. Ruble, & W. Hartup (Eds.), *Social cognition and social development: A sociocultural perspective* (pp. 236–274). Cambridge: Cambridge University Press.

Hoffman, M. (1987). The contribution of empathy to justice and moral development. In N.

Eisenberg & J. Strayer (Eds.), *Empathy: A developmental perspective* (pp. 47–80). Cambridge: Cambridge University Press.

Hoffman, M. (1991). Comment on J. Gibbs article, "Towards the integration of Kohlberg's and Hoffman's moral development theories." *Human Development, 34,* 104–110.

Izard, C. (1977). *Human emotions.* New York: Plenum.

Kahn, P. (1992). Children's obligatory and discretionary moral judgments. *Child Development, 63,* 416–430.

Killen, M. (1990). Children's evaluations of morality in the context of peer, teacher–child, and familial relations. *Journal of Genetic Psychology, 151,* 395–410.

Kim, S. (1993). *Children's understanding of emotions in moral transgressions.* Unpublished doctoral dissertation, Yonsei University, Seoul, Korea.

Kobak, R., & Sceery, A. (1988). Attachment in late adolescence: Working models, affect regulation, and representations of self and others. *Child Development, 59,* 135–146.

Kochanska, K. (1993). Towards a synthesis of parental socialization and child temperament in early development of conscience. *Child Development, 64,* 325–347.

Latane, B., & Darley, J. (1968). Group inhibition of bystander intervention in emergencies. *Journal of Personality and Social Psychology, 10,* 215–221.

Lazarus, R. (1984). On the primacy of cognition. *American Psychologist, 39,* 124–129.

Lazarus, R. (1991). *Emotion and adaptation.* New York: Oxford University Press.

Lemerise, E., & Bush, M. (1994). *Children's understanding of the emotions of victims and victimizers: Developmental and peer status differences.* Manuscript in preparation.

Lewis, M. (1989). Cultural differences in children's knowledge of emotional scripts. In C. Saarni & P. Harris (Eds.), *Children's understanding of emotions* (pp. 350–374). Cambridge: Cambridge University Press.

Maccoby, E. E. (1980). *Social development: Psychological growth and the parent–child relationship.* New York: Harcourt, Brace, and Jovanovich.

Main, M., & George, C. (1985). Responses of abused and disadvantaged toddlers to distress in agemates: A study in the daycare setting. *Developmental Psychology, 21,* 407–412.

Main, M., Kaplan, N., & Cassidy, J. (1985). Security in infancy, childhood, and adulthood: A move to the level of representation. In I. Bretherton & E. Waters (Eds.), *Growing points of attachment theory and research* (pp. 66–104). *Monographs of the Society for Research in Child Development, 50* (1–2, Serial No. 209).

Masters, J. C., & Carlson, C. R. (1984). Children's and adults' understanding of the causes and consequences of emotional states. In C. Izard, J. Kagan, & R. Zajonc (Eds.), *Emotions, cognition, and behavior* (pp. 438–463). Cambridge: Cambridge University Press.

Miller, P., & Eisenberg, N. (1988). The relation of empathy to aggressive and externalizing/antisocial behavior. *Psychological Bulletin, 103,* 324–344.

Moore, B., Underwood, B., & Rosenhan, D. (1984). Emotion, self, & others. In C. Izard, J. Kagan, & R. Zajonc (Eds.), *Emotions, cognition, and behavior* (pp. 464–483). Cambridge: Cambridge University Press.

Nucci, L. (1981). The development of personal concepts: A domain distinct from moral or societal concepts. *Child Development, 52,* 144–121.

Nucci, L., & Turiel, E. (1978). Social interactions and the development of social concepts in the preschool child. *Child Development, 49,* 400–407.

Nunner-Winkler, G., & Sodian, B. (1988). Children's understanding of moral emotions. *Child Development, 59,* 1323–1338.

Perry, D., Perry, L., & Rasmussen, P. (1986). Cognitive social learning mediators of aggression. *Child Development, 57,* 700–711.

Piaget, J. (1932). *The moral judgment of the child.* London: Routledge and Kegan Paul.

Piaget, J. (1962). Will and action. *Bulletin of the Menninger Clinic, 26*, 138–145.
Piaget, J. (1954/1981). *Intelligence and affectivity: Their relationship during child development* (T. Brown & C. Kaegi, Trans. and Eds.). Palo Alto, CA: Annual Reviews Monograph.
Plutchik, R. (1980). *Emotion: A psychoevolutionary synthesis.* New York: Harper and Row.
Slaby, R., & Guerra, N. (1988). Cognitive mediators of aggression in adolescent offenders: 1. Assessment. *Developmental Psychology, 24*, 580–588.
Smetana, J. (1984). Toddlers' social interactions regarding moral and conventional events. *Child Development, 55*, 1767–1776.
Smetana, J. (1990). Morality and conduct disorders. In M. Lewis & S. Miller (Eds.), *Handbook of Developmental Psychopathology* (pp. 157–179). New York: Plenum.
Sroufe, A. L., Schork, E., Motti, F., Lawroski, N., & LaFreniere, P. (1984). The role of affect in social competence. In C. Izard, J. Kagan, & R. Zajonc (Eds.), *Emotions, cognition, and behavior* (pp. 289–319). Cambridge: Cambridge University Press.
Stein, N., & Levine, L. (1989). The causal organization of emotional knowledge: A developmental study. *Cognition and Emotion, 3*, 343–378.
Stein, N., Trabasso, T., & Liwag, M. (1993). The representation and organization of emotional experience: Unfolding the episode. In M. Lewis & J. Haviland (Eds.), *Handbook of emotions* (pp. 279–300). New York: Guilford.
Strayer, J. (1986). Children's attributions regarding the situational determinants of emotion in self and others. *Developmental Psychology, 51*, 815–822.
Strayer, J. (1989). What children know and feel in response to witnessing affective events. In C. Saarni & P. Harris (Eds.), *Children's understanding of emotions* (pp. 259–289). Cambridge: Cambridge University Press.
Tisak, M. (1986). Children's conceptions of parental authority. *Child Development, 57*, 166–176.
Tisak, M., & Ford, M, (1986). Children's conceptions of interpersonal events. *Merrill-Palmer Quarterly, 32*, 291–306.
Troy, M., & Sroufe, A. (1987). Victimization among preschoolers: Role of attachment relationship history. *Journal of the American Academy of Child Psychiatry, 26*(2), 166–172.
Turiel, E. (1983). *The development of social knowledge: Morality and convention.* Cambridge: Cambridge University Press.
Turiel, E., Killen, M., & Helwig, C. (1987). Morality: Its structure, functions and vagaries. In J. Kagan & S. Lamb (Eds.), *The emergence of morality in young children* (pp. 155–243). Chicago: University of Chicago Press.
Vosk, B., Forehand, R., & Figueroa, R. (1983). Perceptions of emotion by accepted and rejected children. *Journal of Behavioral Assessment, 5*, 151–160.
Weston, D., & Turiel, E. (1980). Act–rule relations: Children's concepts of social rules. *Developmental Psychology, 16*, 417–424.
Youniss, J. (1980). *Parents and peers in social development.* Chicago: University of Chicago Press.
Zahn-Waxler, C., & Kochanska, G. (1990). The origins of guilt. In R. Thompson (Ed.), *Nebraska Symposium on Motivation, 1988: Vol. 36. Socioemotional Development* (pp. 183–258). Lincoln; University of Nebraska Press.
Zahn-Waxler, C., Radke-Yarrow, M., & King, R. (1979). Child rearing and children's prosocial initiations toward victims of distress. *Child Development, 50*, 319–330.
Zajonc, R. (1984). On the primacy of affect. *American Psychologist, 39*, 117–123.
Zelko, F., Duncan, S., Barden, R., Garber, J., & Masters, J. (1986). Adults' expectancies about children's emotional responsiveness: Implications for the development of implicit theories of affect. *Developmental Psychology, 22*, 109–114.

Part II

Social judgment in different contexts

4 Obedience to authority in children and adults

Marta Laupa, Elliot Turiel, and Philip A. Cowan

March 16, 1993, was the 25th anniversary of the My Lai massacre, an incident in which American soldiers in Vietnam fired on and killed unarmed Vietnamese men, women, and children under orders from their commanding officer. History provides many examples of such incidents, in which individuals harm or kill others under orders from authority, Nazi Germany's Final Solution being one notable example. Volumes have been written in an attempt to explain such actions, which have been referred to as crimes of obedience (Arendt, 1964; Kelman & Hamilton, 1989). Experimental studies, such as those of Milgram (1963, 1974) and Haney, Banks, and Zimbardo (1973) have demonstrated the existence of obedience to authority in laboratory settings as well. Persons commit acts that cause serious harm, or which they believe will cause serious harm, to others and which they would not under normal conditions commit, in obedience to commands from persons they consider legitimate authorities.

Of interest to psychologists are not only those individuals who obey authority in these instances, but those who disobey. At the My Lai massacre, as well as during the Holocaust, there were individuals who refused to obey orders to kill innocent civilians, often at considerable personal risk. Similarly, in the Milgram experiments, there was less than complete obedience; some people refused to obey after various levels of shock had been reached. Further, Milgram found varying levels of obedience when using different experimental conditions. Clearly, obedience to authority is not an all or nothing phenomenon. What is in need of explanation is not only acts of criminal obedience, but both obedience and disobedience across and within individuals in different situations.

Researchers in developmental psychology are, of course, interested in the developmental origins of behaviors of obedience and disobedience. From a developmental perspective, different theories have offered differing explanations for the phenomenon of obedience to authority. Socialization theories describe social development as a process by which children,

131

under the influence and direction of authority, adopt the social norms of their group. Development entails greater adherence to such norms with increasing age. More recent variations of this view characterize different cultures as being more or less oriented toward duty and obedience to authority (Shweder, Mahapatra, & Miller, 1987). Children in such cultures adopt the obedience and duty orientation that is transmitted to them by adults in their culture. However, laboratory studies, as well as naturally occurring events, demonstrate that individuals' orientations toward authority are not unitary or homogeneous (Milgram, 1963, 1974). Laboratory studies (Martin, Lobb, Chapman, & Spillane, 1976; Shanab & Yahya, 1977) show that children also obey under certain circumstances and disobey in others, demonstrating considerable heterogeneity in orientation toward authority across ages 6 to 16 years.

Another view is offered by traditional cognitive-developmental theory, which originated with the work of Piaget (1932/1965). Whereas socialization theories are primarily concerned with behavior, this approach is concerned with the development of children's social reasoning, as well as the relation of their reasoning to their behavior. This view proposes that over the course of development, in contrast to a growing adherence to social norms and authority dictates, children become more autonomous and less authority-oriented. In this view, the young child has a heteronomous orientation toward adult authority that is absolute and unquestioned, such that the very content of the child's morality derives from the acceptance of adult authority dictates as moral absolutes. With development, children are able to form judgments of morality independent of authority and become autonomous in their social reasoning. Thus, with development comes not greater conformity and adherence to authority commands, but greater independence, in both thought and action, from authority commands. The gradual development toward autonomous reasoning does not replace heteronomy, however. Both orientations coexist in adulthood and individuals may draw from either orientation when given commands by authorities in different situations.

In this chapter we propose a third view, which differs from both socialization and traditional cognitive theories. This view derives from research indicating that children conceptualize the social world in three distinct domains: the moral, the social-organizational, and the psychological (Turiel, 1983; Turiel & Davidson, 1986; Turiel, Killen, & Helwig, 1987). These domains form structured subsystems of thought through which the child's experiences are organized. Children construct concepts within each domain out of distinct and qualitatively different social interactions and experiences. Children's social development does not arise out of being socialized to obey authority, nor does an orientation toward authority comprise a stage in children's social-cognitive development. Rather, children's concepts of authority are complex, interacting with, and being influenced by, concepts in each domain.

Recent research undertaken within the domain perspective has shown that there are three important components to children's authority reasoning, closer examination of which can shed light on both obedience and disobedience in situations such as My Lai, as well as in more ordinary, everyday events. These three components are: (1) the type of command, (2) the attributes of the authority figure, and (3) the social context. Children as young as 4 years of age have been shown to consider the type of command issued when making authority judgments, rejecting commands of authorities they consider morally unacceptable (Laupa, 1994; Laupa & Turiel, 1986, 1993; Smetana, 1988a, 1988b, 1989; Tisak, 1986; Weston & Turiel, 1980). Further, children as young as 4 years of age have been shown to judge authorities with respect to attributes they possess, such as social position (position in a specific social context) and knowledge (Laupa, 1991, 1994; Laupa & Turiel, 1986). Finally, children have been shown to judge the legitimacy of authorities with regard to the social context in which an authority interaction takes place (Laupa, in press; Laupa & Turiel, 1993).

Within this framework, judgments of obedience to authority do not entail solely considerations of morality. Children's authority judgments always incorporate all three components: type of command, authority attributes, and social context. Because of this differentiation in children's reasoning, it is possible for a conflict to arise between authority and morality. This conflict can most often be seen in conflicting judgments of legitimacy and obedience. An example of this would be a situation such as the My Lai massacre in which a person judges an authority to be legitimate based on his possession of certain authority attributes (the second component), while judging that the command itself (the first component) should not be obeyed. Thus, a closer examination of the development of the different components of children's authority judgments can be applied to understanding behaviors of obedience and disobedience to authority both inside and outside the family.

In this chapter we first review theories from the cognitive-developmental perspective, all of which describe children's authority concepts as developing through distinct levels. We then describe our position, which considers that children's authority concepts, and social knowledge more generally, are differentiated with respect to distinct conceptual domains. We then address the issue of the development of authority concepts more directly and present a framework for understanding children's authority judgments as involving three distinct components. Finally, we present an account of the development of children's concepts of authority within three domains of knowledge, using the three-component framework and drawing on results of recent research that has investigated children's concepts about obedience and disobedience to authority in different contexts.

Cognitive-developmental theories

The traditional view of children's authority concepts comes from the work of Piaget (1932/1965). Piaget did not directly study children's authority concepts; his aim was to investigate children's moral development. He believed that the genesis of moral obligation is children's acceptance of commands from persons whom they respect. Thus, children's concepts of authority are an integral aspect of their moral cognitions; the first persons whom children respect and whose commands they accept are adult authorities.

Piaget described three qualitatively different levels in the child's consciousness of moral rules; in each can also be seen a description of the child's authority concepts. The very young child (aged 2 to 5 years) exists in an essentially premoral state. Children at this level engage in individualized, ritualistic behaviors without a feeling of necessity or obligation. The child is aware of a host of regulations or expectancies emanating from the environment, but does not differentiate among them in any way. This level can also be considered to be preauthority in that the child has not yet formed the notion of any external, environmental source of obligation to follow these rules. Such an obligation will initially arise out of respect for powerful adult authorities.

When the feeling of obligation toward rules arises (at approximately 5 years of age), the child has reached the level of heteronomy characterized by a rigid acceptance of adult rules and dictates as external, fixed, and absolute. A central aspect of the heteronomous orientation is the child's unilateral authority relations with adults whom the child conceives of as omniscient and virtually supernaturally powerful. Thus, their concepts of authority are unilateral and adult-centered. This shift in the child's consciousness is not accompanied by a shift in behavior toward absolute obedience to all authority commands. However, in keeping with their heteronomous orientation, children at this stage do not make moral judgments that are independent of authority; they do not distinguish among rules that prevent harm to persons (e.g., "do not hit") and those which prevent disorder or messiness (e.g., "do not eat spaghetti with your hands"). All such rules are the expectations of mysterious "big people" whose reasons cannot be fathomed, but who must be obeyed.

The final level is that of autonomy in which the obligatory nature of rules arises out of the respect that the child holds for the group, of which he or she is an equal and participating member. The child no longer accepts as absolute the dictates of adult authorities, but submits himself or herself to the rules generated by the group using the principles of mutual respect and cooperation. Through these experiences children construct independent moral judgments based on self-generated moral principles, rather than authority dictates. At this level the child approaches equality with adults and no longer views it as necessary to defer to their authority. Thus, in this account, young children are unable to conceive of adults as anything other than superior and infallible beings. This view of adults as all-powerful is inextricably linked to young children's moral reasoning.

Since Piaget's early work on the topic, a number of researchers in the area of children's social cognition have conducted investigations that bear, directly or indirectly, on children's concepts of authority relations (Damon, 1977; Selman, 1980; Youniss, 1980; Youniss & Smollar, 1985). The first of these studies to investigate children's authority concepts directly was done by Damon (1977), who investigated children's reasoning about the legitimacy of, and obedience to, both adult authorities (parents) and peer authorities (team captains) across a range of issues and contexts. Children across this age range (4 to 11 years) exhibited a variety of reasoning about both parents' and peers' authority. Children's responses showed a progression from reasoning focused on the self's desires, through reasoning based on physical attributes of the authority, to reasoning based on consideration of the authority's knowledge and skills.

Other work on children's social concepts relevant to the issue of authority is that of Selman (1980), who has described the development of children's perspective-taking abilities and applied this framework to the understanding of children's concepts of various interpersonal relationships, including the parent–child relationship. The aspects of the parent–child relationship he has investigated and which bear on authority issues include the formation of the parent–child relationship (why parents have children), obedience, punishment, and conflict resolution. Selman has described levels of development of children's reasoning about these issues, which are assumed to be reflective of underlying development in children's perspective-taking capacity. Children first see parents as essentially existing to meet children's needs. They later develop a unilateral concept of parental authority in which parents love their children and children respond with obedience. In this system, parents use punishment to educate and protect the child. In later childhood children's concepts of the parent–child relation become more reciprocal; parents are seen in terms of the emotional support they give children. Obedience is no longer viewed as absolute, but voluntary, and punishment is viewed as a form of communication. Finally, in early adolescence parents are seen as persons with psychological characteristics and parents and children are seen to interact with mutual respect.

In related research, Youniss (1980; Youniss & Smollar, 1985) has described changes that occur in the parent–child relationship from childhood to adolescence. Middle-school-aged children view the parent–child relationship as unilateral and maintained by the child's obedience. Adolescents view their relationship with their parents in ways more similar to a friendship – as a mutual relationship that does not entail unilateral obedience.

All of these descriptions of the development of the child's authority reasoning are consistent with Piaget's description of the child's moral development. The very young child is characterized as unable to differentiate between the self and other. Because the child cannot conceive of an authority external to the self giving commands that are potentially in conflict with the child's own desires, there is no real concept of authority. The school-aged child is described as taking a unilateral perspective toward authority as residing in powerful, omniscient adults whose role is to control the child's behavior and whom the child is bound to obey. Finally, adolescents are described as viewing the parent–child relationship as reciprocal, and the parents' authority as legitimized by their superior knowledge and skills. Taken as a whole, children are described in all these formulations as increasing in the extent to which they view adults as their equals; the parents' authority consequently declines.

Domain theory

In the research that resulted in his description of levels of authority reasoning, Damon (1977) found that young children reject a parent's authority to give certain commands, such as the command to steal. This type of finding, which was not included in Damon's analysis of developmental levels, actually contradicts the central proposition of traditional theories that young children do not distinguish among different types of authority commands or rules. Furthermore, results of recent studies show that young children do not accept all authority dictates and that they make distinctions among different types of acts and rules (Nucci, 1981; Nucci & Turiel, 1978; Smetana, 1981, 1984; Turiel, 1983).

The latter research supports the claim that children conceptualize social acts and rules in distinct conceptual domains (Smetana, 1983; Turiel & Davidson, 1986; Turiel et al., 1987). One of these, the moral domain, refers to concepts of the welfare and rights of persons. Moral rules are those which prohibit acts that violate the welfare or rights of persons, such as rules against hitting and stealing. A second domain refers to concepts of social organizations and systems and the conventions associated with their efficient functioning. Social conventional rules are those which serve to coordinate interactions of persons within these social systems, such as rules regarding forms of address or table manners. The third domain refers to concepts of the psychological characteristics of persons, such as their beliefs, ideas, feelings, and intentions. Part of the conceptualization of the psychological domain is the concept of personal issues, which are considered to be a person's own business and outside the jurisdiction of moral concern or social regulation. Choice of friends or style of dress (Nucci, 1981) are examples of such issues. Children across a wide age range have been shown to discriminate between events pertaining to different domains, and reason about them differently depending on the specific domains to which they pertain (see Smetana Chapter 7, this volume, for further details).

Consistent with the domain approach, recent research has shown that children's concepts of authority are differentiated with respect to the content of the command given (Damon, 1977; Laupa & Turiel, 1986, 1993; Tisak, 1986; Tisak & Tisak, 1991; Weston & Turiel, 1980). Acts affecting persons' rights or welfare (the moral domain) are judged by children to be neither alterable by nor contingent on authority. This research has shown that children reject commands from even otherwise legitimate authorities if the command is judged to be morally unacceptable. In contrast, regarding conventional rules that regulate the functioning of social systems, authorities are judged to be legitimate when giving commands consistent with the conventional system.

Recently, Smetana has undertaken a series of studies (1988a, 1988b, 1989) of preadolescent and adolescent children's concepts of the authority of parents across domains. Smetana has found that very little disagreement exists between parents and children regarding the parents' authority to regulate their children's moral and conventional behavior. Conflict occurs primarily regarding personal issues and regarding what Smetana and others have referred to as "mixed-domain" issues – issues that incorporate elements of more than one domain, or which can be interpreted by various persons as pertaining to different domains. Issues over which conflict occurs are interpreted by the adolescent as personal issues, outside the jurisdiction of regulation by authority. The same issues may be seen by the parents as conventional, and thus legitimately subject to regulation by parental authority. Issues regarding the performance of household chores, or the adolescent's personal appearance, often fall in this category. Thus, these findings support the claim that children conceptualize authority within distinct domains; children judge the parents' jurisdiction over the child to be limited in the moral and personal domains in different ways.

Family authority study

Before going on to further discussion of the three components of authority judgments, we must note that in our account of the development of children's concepts of authority we draw throughout the chapter on data from a previously unpublished study by the authors, which we refer to as the Family Authority Study. The purpose of the Family Authority Study was to investigate children's reasoning about the attributes of parental authorities across three domains. The primary focus was on children's reasoning about the attributes parents possess that legitimize their authority over their children, in contrast to the content of the command or rule that the parent enforces, which has been the focus of much previous research (Smetana, 1988a, 1988b, 1989; Tisak, 1986; Weston & Turiel, 1980). In particular, the focus was on children's reasoning about parents' legitimacy to punish children, and parents' power to exact obedience from children even in cases where children do not judge their commands to be legitimate. Since the study has not been published previously, a brief description of the methods and analysis of these data is necessary.

The subjects in this study were 15 4th, 18 7th, and 17 10th graders attending public schools in the San Francisco Bay area. Approximately equal numbers of subjects in each grade were male and female (overall 46% male and 54% female). Subjects were administered an interview in two parts. The purpose of the first part of the interview was to elicit from subjects spontaneous examples of family rules and expectations corresponding to moral, social-organizational, and psychological issues. Toward this aim, subjects were asked a series of questions about expectations in their family (What are the things that people are supposed to do or not supposed to do in your family? Are there ways that your mother/father expect you or want you to be?). Subjects were then asked a set of questions regarding "psychological rules," which refer to expectations that their parents and other family members have of them regarding their psychological characteristics (Are there feelings you are not supposed to let anyone know about? Is it all right to be happy, angry, sad in your family?). Of the spontaneously generated rules, one moral rule, one conventional rule, and one psychological rule were chosen for subjects for further interviewing.

The second part of the procedure consisted of in-depth interviews regarding each of these three rules or expectations in the family. For each expectation, subjects were asked five sets of questions. The first set of questions, "Rule status," corresponds to the first component of authority judgments, that of the domain of the act being regulated. These questions were aimed at evaluating children's judgments of the rule or expectation regarding the act, how it originated and how children learned of it. The next three sets of questions, "Legitimacy to command," "Legitimacy to punish," and "Power," correspond to the second component of authority judgments, that of authority attributes. These questions are aimed at assessing children's judgments of the origins and justification for parents' and others' authority over children in each of the three domains, in particular, what authority attributes these persons possess that legitimize their authority commands. The question set "Power" focuses on different persons' ability to enforce rules in cases where they might not normally be considered legitimate – for example, a parent commanding a child to hit, or a child commanding his or her sibling. In these cases the ability to coerce obedience may be particularly important. The last set of questions, "Social context," corresponds to the final authority component, that of social context. These questions are aimed at assessing children's reasoning about parental and other authority across contexts. The five sets of questions are as follows:

> *Rule status:* Subjects were asked to evaluate each rule (Is it a good rule?) and to state how they learned of its existence, whether it is in fact a rule, or simply "something that everyone knows," and why.
>
> *Legitimacy to command:* Subjects were asked whether parents can command the child to obey the rule, whether they will still be able to command the child to obey the rule when the child is an adult, and why.
>
> *Legitimacy to punish:* Subjects were asked what parents do when children transgress, whether parents can punish children's transgressions, whether parents will still be able to punish transgressions when the child is an adult, and why.
>
> *Power:* Subjects were asked whether parents can change the rule to its opposite (e.g., require children to hit, or prohibit them from doing chores), whether they can punish children for transgressing the altered rule, what children do when the parent transgresses the existing rule, whether children can punish parents' transgressions, whether children can enforce a sibling's obedience to the rule, and why.

Social context: Subjects were asked if the child's teacher from
school can command the child to obey the rule in his or her own
home, what parents would do about a transgression that occurred in the home of the child's friend, whether they can punish the child for such a transgression, and why.

Each subject was interviewed about one rule from each domain. The
criteria for choosing rules about which to interview subjects were that the
rule was spontaneously mentioned by the subject and that there was a clear
family expectation regarding the behavior. Among moral rules, 43% of
subjects were interviewed about hitting, 11% about stealing, and 46%
about lying. Among conventional rules, 89% of subjects were interviewed
about doing chores and 11% about other conventional rules such as brush-
ing teeth and going to bed at a certain time. Among psychological rules,
17% of subjects were interviewed about "being a good student," 44%
about "being nice" or "not showing anger," 17% about "showing respect,"
and 10% about "being open."

For each question subjects were required to make a yes or no judgment,
and then to give reasons or justifications for their judgment. Justifications to
responses were coded using a system adapted from previous research
(Laupa, 1991; Laupa & Turiel, 1986, 1993). Questions of legitimacy to command, legitimacy to punish, power, and social context all ask about the
legitimacy of, or obedience to, persons issuing various commands in various
settings, and all were coded with the same set of justifications. Justifications
were of three major types. Act-oriented justifications pertain to the nature
of an act commanded or its consequences. Authority-oriented justifications pertain to the attributes of the person giving the command, including
adult status, knowledge, authority position, and delegated social position.
Punishment-oriented justifications pertain to the potential for, or avoidance
of, punishment. Responses to all yes or no questions were tested for sex
differences. The number of significant differences found was approximately
that expected by chance; sex differences were not considered further.[1]

We now turn to an account of the development of children's concepts of
authority within three domains of social knowledge. First, we explain more
fully the three components involved in children's authority judgments. We
consider children's concepts of how adults and peers function as authorities
(i.e., in establishing and enforcing rules and delegating authority) across
and within different social contexts, and how development in each domain
relates to children's conceptualization of the bases for authorities' legitimacy. In doing so, we refer to the Family Authority Study, as well as other
relevant research.

Three components of authority judgments

Any situation in which one individual issues a command to another can be seen as an instance of an authority interaction. In each case, judgments must be made about both the legitimacy of the authority (Is it all right for the individual to issue the command?) and obedience to the authority's command (Should the person receiving the command obey it?). The three identified authority components of command type, authority attributes, and social context always enter into children's authority judgments, at least implicitly. Part of an attempt to illuminate behaviors of obedience and disobedience involves explicit consideration of these different components.

Type of command

We have seen that there is evidence that the legitimacy of authority varies across domains – that is, children will reject authorities who give commands or make rules that children judge to be morally unacceptable or which violate what children conceive to be their boundaries of personal autonomy. These considerations constitute the first component of authority judgments, the type of command, which is always taken into account in judgments about any given authority interaction. However, research focusing on the domain to which the act pertains does not delve deeply enough into how children reason about the characteristics of persons in authority, or explain situations in which people *do* obey immoral commands. Thus, further investigation is needed to explore the aspects of authority reasoning that are involved in such events. Conversely, in addition to obeying immoral commands, persons sometimes reject or disobey commands that are morally acceptable because they issue from a source that is not considered legitimate for some other reason. Thus, authority concepts involve more than a simple consideration of the domain of behavior being regulated. Recently researchers have investigated other factors involved in children's reasoning about legitimacy and obedience to authority commands.

Authority attributes

Authority attributes are characteristics possessed by persons that render them legitimate as authorities and compel obedience to their commands. Children have been found to consider three authority attributes when judging the legitimacy of school authorities: adult status, knowledge (skill or expertise in a particular area relevant to the commands being given), and social position (an official authority position or role in a given social organization). When considering the legitimacy of school authorities, such as teachers and principals, children take into account these three factors and weigh them differently depending on the specific context (Laupa, 1991, 1994; Laupa & Turiel, 1986, 1993). In these studies children across the ages of 4 to 13 years were asked to evaluate the legitimacy of individuals with different combinations of the three attributes. Children were also asked to choose between individuals with different attributes who give contradictory or opposing commands. Although children are aware of adult status, it does not figure largely in their judgments of school authorities. Children accept as legitimate authorities at school both adults and children with social position (e.g., persons who were hired for or chosen to do the job) whether or not they are knowledgeable. Many children also accept as authorities adults and children with knowledge but no social position. In contrast, adult status is not considered as important. With the exception of preschoolers, children are no more likely to accept an adult as an authority than a child when other attributes are held constant. In addition, even preschool-aged children choose obedience to a person with either social position or knowledge, in contrast to one with adult status, when the two are put in opposition.

This work is the first to demonstrate that children reason about the social position of authorities in a given social-organizational system when making legitimacy and obedience judgments. The results are in contrast to studies showing that children's authority judgments are based largely on considerations of adult status and knowledge (Damon, 1977) or the nature of the parent–child relation (Selman, 1980; Youniss, 1980; Youniss & Smollar, 1985). One reason that these studies found that children focus on adult status and knowledge in their authority judgments may be that the research examined children's reasoning about parents as authorities, rather than teachers and other school authorities. The school as a social-organizational system is very clearly defined. It has clear physical limits (the boundaries of the playground) and clear temporal limits (the hours of the school day). Persons' roles in the system are unambiguous; the principal is in charge of the school, the teacher is in charge of the class. Results of studies by Laupa and her colleagues show that children conceptualize the school in this way.

In contrast, the social organization of the family is more ambiguous. It does not have clear physical limits (the parents' authority over the child may not be limited only to their home) and it does not have clear temporal limits (the parents' authority over the child may not be limited only to a certain time of day). This is not to say that the family is not an organized system. However, it is probably more difficult for children to reason explicitly about the family as a system and the place of the parent as an authority in the system. Both the family authority data and other recent research (Laupa, in press) have shown that children do have some understanding of the authority position of parents in the family. Recall that in the Family Authority Study children were asked to judge the legitimacy of parents to enforce an existing rule in each domain (Legitimacy to command). Children's acceptance of the legitimacy of parents as authorities is based in part on reasoning about adult status and knowledge, as it is with school authorities. However, children also reason about the parent's role as an authority in the family. The parents are seen as the family members with the responsibility for raising and taking care of the child. Further, the parents are legitimate in enforcing children's obedience to family rules because they brought the child into the world and provide for the child economically. In addition, as in studies of school authorities, adults other than the parent are not accepted as authorities by children at home, even when they have knowledge attributes, because they are not members of the family and do not have the responsibility for the child's upbringing (that is, they lack an authority position in the family). Thus, reasoning about parental authority is similar to reasoning about school authority in that it involves considerations of the authority's social position, as well as adult status and knowledge.

Social context

Authority interactions involve at least two persons, one in a dominant and one in a subordinate position. Thus, the authority attribute of social position is not really a characteristic of a person, but a description of a social relation that holds between two individuals within a given social-organizational system. Because authority is a social relation and not a characteristic of a person, it may vary across different social and physical contexts. That is, a teacher, who is considered a legitimate authority at school, may not be considered legitimate in a public park. A parent, who is considered a legitimate authority at home, may not be considered legitimate at school. The family authority data show that children's concepts of parents' legitimacy vary across contexts. Recall that subjects were asked about a parent punishing a child for a transgression of a rule at home and in another child's home in which the rule does not apply (Social context). Fifty percent of subjects overall reported that their parents *would* punish them for transgressions of rules at home, whereas only 29% reported that their parents *would* punish them for committing the same transgression in a friend's home. Further, whereas 87% of subjects judged that their parents *can* punish them for such transgressions at home, only 60% judged that their parents *can* punish them for committing the same transgression in a friend's home. Thus, the parents' authority is limited by context.

Conversely, subjects were also asked if their teacher from school could issue commands to them at home. Overall, only 21% of subjects judged that the teacher's commands would be legitimate in their home. These results are consistent with other studies (Jancaterino, 1982; Laupa & Turiel, 1993) that have shown that children will, for the most part, reject school authorities who give commands or attempt to establish rules outside the school (e.g., in a public park or a child's home) and that children give precedence to home rules over school rules. Thus, children's authority judgments can be seen to involve considerations of the social context in which the authority interaction is taking place.

The development of authority concepts within three domains

Having elaborated the three components of authority judgments, we now turn to the development of authority concepts within three domains of social knowledge. We consider how authority judgments are influenced by act considerations in each domain, how development in each domain is related to children's conceptualizations of the bases for authorities' legitimacy, and how authorities function across and within different contexts.

The moral domain

The moral domain comprises concepts regarding the welfare and rights of persons. Ample evidence has shown that children take into account the moral acceptability of the command when judging authorities and reject commands of authorities that they judge are morally unacceptable. In these cases, other authority considerations (i.e., attributes, context) can be rendered irrelevant; the morally unacceptable command will be rejected. However, one can also observe cases in which immoral commands are issued and some subordinates choose to obey. An example would be a military officer who orders soldiers to kill civilians. In examining these cases, it is important to make a distinction between the legitimacy of a person to issue commands and whether those commands should or should not be obeyed. It is possible for judgments of legitimacy and obedience to come into conflict. In order to look at possible conflicts more closely, we must first make a distinction between children's reasoning about sources of legitimacy and their reasons for obedience.

Legitimacy and obedience. In reviewing research on children's reasoning about authority attributes, we have focused primarily on legitimacy and its sources, the two primary sources being the attributes of knowledge and social position. This research has also shown that children make judgments about obedience to authority commands in different ways than they do about legitimacy. Children take two factors into account more often when making obedience judgments than when making legitimacy judgments. The first factor is problem solving – whether obeying the command is likely to lead to a resolution of the problem in question. Problem solving, to some extent, is associated with the attribute of knowledge. As described earlier, children take into account the type of act being regulated when making authority judgments; they are more likely to accept authority commands they judge will lead to a desirable outcome (e.g., a solution to a particular problem) (Laupa, 1991; Laupa & Turiel, 1986). To the extent that an authority's legitimacy arises out of his or her knowledge relevant to solving a particular problem, it would be advisable to obey him or her because obedience is likely to lead to a resolution of the problem. In cases where an authority's legitimacy is based on knowledge, it is rare for judgments of legitimacy and obedience to conflict. An authority may be highly knowledgeable in a particular content area. If the child is unable to judge whether the authority's command will lead to a resolution of a particular problem, then the child will most likely accept the command because it comes from a knowledgeable source. The child has no basis for rejecting the authority's command in this case. However, if the authority issues a command that the child knows will not resolve the problem, then the command will be rejected regardless of the authority's other attributes.

An example of this is the Laupa and Turiel studies (1986, 1993) in which children were asked about school authorities in hypothetical situations who gave commands aimed at preventing or causing harm. Children judged that teachers giving commands aimed at preventing harm should be obeyed, in part due to their knowledge attributes. When a teacher tells children how to resolve a dispute they should obey because the teacher knows better than they do how to resolve the problem. However, when a teacher gave a command that, if obeyed, would lead to harm, children unanimously rejected her authority. Thus, in cases where the authority's legitimacy is based on knowledge, the authority's attributes cannot come into conflict with his or her command. An authority's knowledge will be negated if he or she gives an obviously incompetent or unacceptable command.

In contrast, in cases where an authority's legitimacy arises from social position, judgments of legitimacy and obedience may conflict. The example of an officer ordering soldiers to kill civilians would be such a case. The officer's authority in this case does not derive from knowledge attributes, but from a social position within a particular social-organizational system. Even if the person receiving the command judges that the command is not legitimate, the person issuing the command has the legitimizing attribute of social position, and thus there may be important reasons for obeying his or her unacceptable command. These reasons ordinarily involve consideration of the person's ability to punish.

Power and punishment. It has been found (Laupa, 1991; Laupa & Turiel, 1986) that, regarding school authorities, children reason about punishment only with respect to obedience and not legitimacy. Children do not reason that school authorities are legitimate because they have the ability to punish. However, they do reason that it is advisable to obey them in order to avoid punishment. The same is found regarding parents as authorities (Laupa, in press). Obedience to, and not legitimacy of, commands from parents and siblings is justified on the basis of avoidance of punishment. Further, children reason about punishment primarily with regard to obedience to individuals who hold a social position. Children are aware that the possession of knowledge and/or adult status alone do not enable one to inflict punishment. The power to inflict punishment requires that the person hold a social position in a particular social context. Thus, obedience is linked to considerations of punishment, and the ability to punish is linked to social position.

Whereas these studies looked at children's reasoning about the rationales for obedience, one of which is avoidance of punishment, the Family Authority Study investigated children's reasoning about whether and why parents are legitimate in punishing children (Legitimacy to punish). Reasons given for the legitimacy of punishment by parents were similar to those given for legitimacy of commands of parents. They focused on adult status, knowledge, and authority position. Children are also aware of the parents' economic power; parents are legitimate and can punish because they have economic resources that the child does not have, which enable them to punish the child.

This type of reasoning can also be seen in children's responses to questions about parents' authority over their children after they are grown. The majority of children (56% to 78% across the three rules) rejected the authority of parents to enforce these rules when their children are grown. The majority of children (88% to 92% across the three rules) also rejected the authority of parents to punish when the children are grown. In addition to reasoning that the child is now an adult and the parent no longer has superior knowledge, children also reason that the parents do not have authority or power to enforce their commands because the child no longer lives with the parent and is now economically independent. Thus, parents both lack the legitimacy to punish their adult children and the power to enforce their commands. This is not to say that parents might not compel their adult child to obey through persuasion or emotional coercion, but that children do not judge that it is legitimate for the parents to do so after the child is grown.

Although legitimate social position and the power to punish often coincide, as in the case of a teacher or parent, one can imagine an individual having the power to inflict punishment without the corresponding social legitimacy. This would be the case for dictators and criminals in the political and social realm, and older siblings in the realm of the family, all of whom have a kind of physical power over those they command even though those receiving their commands may not consider them to be legitimate. In the Family Authority Study children were asked if children could enforce siblings' obedience to family rules (Power). The majority of subjects (64% to 82% across questions) reject the legitimacy of a child to enforce siblings' obedience to family rules, whether the sibling is younger or older, primarily because siblings lack adult status or delegated social position. However, one study (Laupa, in press) found that children accept the legitimacy of younger siblings in authority over older siblings if they have an authority position delegated by a parent. Children judged that a 10-year-old child could be "in charge" of a 12-year-old sibling if the parent had delegated this position. Thus, older siblings do not have legitimate authority over their younger siblings simply due to superior size and physical power, but both older and younger siblings can gain authority by delegation.

Children were also asked, regarding each rule, whether they could enforce their parents' obedience to the rule, and punish their parents for transgressions. A few children (9% to 14%) reported that they could, primarily by using emotional coercion (e.g., acting upset until the parent complies). In addition, many subjects (36% to 43%) stated that they could advise their parents to obey the rule or that they should have the right to compel them to obey, but that they lacked any coercive power to enforce their command. The remainder of subjects (43% to 57%) reported that they simply have no authority over their parents and cannot tell them to obey family rules or compel their obedience. For both conventional and psychological rules, fourth graders were significantly more likely than older subjects to judge that they have no authority over their parents, whereas older subjects said that they do have, or should have such authority. However, with regard to moral rules, there was no age difference; fourth graders were as likely as older children to report that they do have or should have authority to enforce their parents' obedience of moral rules. Thus, with increasing age children judge that the parent–child authority relation is, or at least should be, reciprocal in the areas of conventional and psychological regulation. Fourth graders take this view only when reasoning about moral rules.

Children recognize that parents' power over their children is considerable, even when their commands are not legitimate. Subjects in the Family Authority Study were asked whether parents could change a moral rule to its opposite (e.g., require a child to hit or steal) and whether they could punish for transgressions of the transformed rule (Power). Thirty-six percent of subjects judged that parents could change the rule and require children to commit immoral acts. This is not to say that they would be correct in doing so, but that they have the authority to do so. Many of these subjects explicitly stated that the parents have the power to do this, even though they do not have the right. The remaining 64% of subjects judged either that the parent could not institute such a rule because it would be wrong to do so, or that such a rule would be irrelevant because they would simply refuse to obey it. It is important to note that children who accept the authority of parents to make such a rule do not judge that an immoral act becomes moral when a parent commands it. They are, however, recognizing that parents have sufficient power over their children that they could make and enforce such a rule and that children may have to obey them.

Thus, judgments of obedience are related to reasoning about legitimacy, reasoning about punishment, and considerations of command type. All are related in children's reasoning, but are not one and the same. In a number of different ways individuals may be coerced into obeying, even possibly acting in ways they judge are immoral, given the right combination of these factors. A person may have physical power, without the legitimacy to use it for punishment or coercion. This person may compel obedience if the power is great enough (e.g., children reject the legitimacy of a child to command or punish a younger sibling but the younger sibling may be forced to obey through sheer coercion). A person may have the legitimacy to issue a command and the legitimacy to punish due to social position, even in cases where the command is not legitimate (e.g., children judge that a parent can require children to commit acts of harm, because they have social and coercive power). The last example is the typical situation in which a crime of obedience may occur. Any or all of these elements may be salient in any given authority interaction and may influence children's potential obedience or disobedience.

Moral authority and heteronomy. In contrast to cases in which persons lack legitimacy, but compel obedience through coercion, there are cases in which persons lack legitimacy but gain obedience for other reasons. A person may have the legitimacy to issue a command due to knowledge attributes, without having the legitimacy to punish. This person's commands will be obeyed if the child judges them to be acceptable (e.g., children sometimes accept commands from knowledgeable adults because they lead to favorable outcomes, although the adult has no legitimacy to punish disobedience). A person may have the moral authority to issue a command, without possessing any authority attributes, and thus lack the accompanying power to enforce commands through punishment (e.g., children judge that they should be able to compel parents to obey them in some cases, but they lack the power to do so). Children are most likely to accept a command from a person who has no authority attributes at all in the case where the command serves a moral end, for example, the prevention of harm (Laupa & Turiel, 1986, 1993). In these cases, the individual has a sort of moral authority that lends legitimacy without an official authority position being absolutely necessary. Similarly, the Family Authority Data show that while children are for the most part rejected as authorities over their siblings, they are accepted more regarding moral rules than conventional or psychological rules, showing the importance children give to regulating moral behavior. However, in these cases of "moral authority" the person has no real power: no authority position, no special knowledge that would confer authority on him or her, and no ability to punish.

This sort of moral authority should be distinguished from what Piaget and others have referred to as heteronomy. Heteronomy, in Piaget's theory, is the acceptance of adult dictates as fixed and absolute. The parent has authority not because his rules are in accord with the demands of morality, but because his rules define what is morally acceptable behavior. This acceptance of adult dictates is closely tied to the conception of adults as overwhelmingly physically and socially powerful. Ample evidence has shown that children do not reason about adult commands in this way – they do not make judgments of right or wrong based on authority. However, results of some studies suggest that young children reason about parents as all powerful authorities (Damon, 1977; Selman, 1980; Youniss, 1980; Youniss & Smollar, 1985), which, while not an indication of moral heteronomy, does suggest a sort of heteronomous orientation to authority. More recent studies show young children able to conceptualize authority with respect to social position and not solely adult status (Laupa, 1991, 1994; Laupa & Turiel, 1986). Although these findings seem inconsistent, they can be understood by considering that children's reasoning about parents' superior knowledge and power are part of their psychological concepts, that is, concepts of others' psychological characteristics and attributes.

The psychological domain

The psychological domain is comprised of concepts of the self and the psychological qualities of persons, including feelings, beliefs, ideas, and intentions. Researchers have investigated the development of both children's concepts of self (Damon & Hart, 1988) and children's concepts of others' psychological states, an area that has been generally referred to as "theories of mind" (Astington, Harris, & Olson, 1988). Another important part of children's concepts in the psychological domain are concepts of personal issues – areas of behavior that are not legitimately subject to regulation by authority, but are within the bounds of one's personal choice and jurisdiction (Nucci, 1981). There are two areas of children's psychological concepts that interact with and influence their authority concepts – the child's concepts of the psychological attributes of persons in authority and the child's concepts of parental authority over the development of the child's own psychological attributes.

Psychological concepts, authority attributes, and moral judgments. To the extent that knowledge is an important attribute that confers legitimacy on a person as an authority, children's inferences about others' knowledge will be important in their authority judgments. In one study, children were asked about authorities with social position (teachers and peer authorities at school) who were presented as lacking the knowledge to solve problems among children on the playground (Laupa, 1991). Older children and adolescents (ages 8 to 13 years) judged these persons on the basis of their attributes as they were depicted, that is, they either judged them to be legitimate authorities because of their social position, or to not be legitimate authorities because of their lack of knowledge. However, some young children (ages 6 to 7 years) persisted in judging these persons as knowledgeable even when they were presented as lacking knowledge, and considered them to be legitimate as authorities. These subjects were unable to differentiate knowledge and social position, rejecting the idea that someone in a social position could lack knowledge. For young children, not being able to differentiate knowledge from social position may lead them to accept as authorities persons whom older children may reject.

Recent research (Raviv, Bar-tal, Raviv, & Houminer, 1990; Raviv, Bartal, Raviv, & Peleg, 1990) has shown that children's view of parents and teachers as knowledgeable experts decreases with age in certain content areas, while remaining stable in others. Although the child's judgment of a parent or teacher as knowledgeable is not by itself enough to confer legitimacy on that person's commands, it is likely that children's acceptance or rejection of different persons as authorities in different situations is influenced by their conceptions of these persons' expertise. An understanding of how children conceptualize various persons' knowledge and expertise would thus inform our understanding of their authority concepts.

Judgments about authorities' knowledge can also be seen when children consider the legitimacy of persons in authority to give commands that children judge to be wrong. Children do not base their judgments of the rightness of commands on their source. However, in their reasoning about the legitimacy of authority, they make judgments based on what they believe the authority knows or thinks. For example, when subjects in the Family Authority Study were asked whether parents could change a moral rule to its opposite (e.g., requiring a child to hit or steal) subjects took into account what they know about the way their parents think about making rules. A few children (16%) judged that the parents could change the rule and enforce the change because the parents think they are doing the right thing; in their judgment the new rule is better. This does not mean that the child agrees that the parents are right, but children recognize that the parents' legitimacy stems in part from the fact that they make rules that, to the best of their knowledge, are in the best interests of their child. Several children reasoned that if the parents decide it is right, for example, to hit, then it *is* right, but their reasoning shows their basic judgment of the wrongness of hitting hasn't been influenced by the parents' new rule (e.g., if parents allow children to hit they will hurt each other and thereby learn that hitting is wrong).

These results are similar to those of studies of children's concepts of God's authority to command persons to commit acts that harm another (such as to steal or hit) (DeLong, 1991; Nucci, 1985; Nucci & Turiel, 1993). In these studies, subjects rejected the idea that God's commands could make it right for one person to harm another. However, some subjects attempted to coordinate their concepts of God's goodness with their moral concepts and reasoned that if God gave a command that appears to lead to harm, there must be an ultimately good outcome that they cannot comprehend. This reasoning is similar to that of children in the Family Authority Study who attempt to discern the good in a parental rule, for example, to hit siblings. In both cases, the subjects' judgment of the authority's command is influenced by their assumptions about the person's (or God's) superior knowledge. As noted earlier, young children are not heteronomous in their moral reasoning; they do not make moral judgments based on authority commands. However, children of all ages have concepts of the psychological characteristics of parents and other adults, who are generally viewed as highly knowledgeable. These concepts enter into their judgments about these persons' legitimacy as authorities, and the legitimacy of their commands.

Parents' authority to regulate the development of their children's psychological characteristics. Another way in which concepts of authority and concepts of psychological qualities interact throughout developments is in children's reasoning about the authority of parents to regulate children's own psychological qualities. By expectations regarding psychological qualities we mean something different from expectations regarding moral and conventional behavior. Parents make moral and conventional rules regarding specific behaviors, such as hitting or chores. Psychological rules or expectations apply to children's personal qualities, rather than to specific behaviors. Examples of psychological rules are parents' expectations that the child "be a nice person" or "be a good student." Although there may be specific behaviors that the child must perform in order to display these qualities, the expectation is about the quality itself, not the specific behaviors.

Children's concepts of parents' psychological expectations are related to, but differ from, what have been described as personal concepts. Concepts of the personal domain involve behaviors that pertain only to the self and are not legitimately subject to regulation by authority, such as choice of friends or clothing, rather than personal or psychological qualities. Children and adolescents reject the authority of parents to regulate behaviors in the personal domain (Nucci, 1981; Smetana, 1988a, 1988b, 1989; Tisak, 1986), and several studies have investigated the areas of behavior children judge to be within their own and not their parents' jurisdiction. However, no research had previously investigated children's concepts of parents' authority over their personal or psychological qualities, involving such matters as intellectual attributes, or the expression of feelings. To what extent do children view parents as having authority to determine or to alter their children's psychological qualities?

The family authority data show that psychological expectations are more implicit for children than expectations about moral and conventional behavior. Subjects were asked how they first learned of the different expectations. Although the majority of subjects reported that parents had explicitly made the expectation known to them in each domain (moral 84%, conventional 91%, and psychological 71%), the percentage is somewhat lower for psychological than for moral and conventional expectations. Further, when asked if the expectation is a rule, or just something members of the family know, significantly more subjects reported that moral and conventional expectations are rules (42% and 45%) than that psychological expectations are rules (17%). When moral and conventional expectations are judged to be rules, it is because they are explicit, parents enforce them, and children are punished for transgressions. When psychological expectations are judged not to be explicit rules, it is because they are explicit, not enforced, not always obeyed, and transgressions are not always punished.

Although children generally accept the legitimacy of parents to regulate their psychological qualities, they do not do so in the same way that they accept their parents' regulation of moral and conventional behavior. Children across the ages of 9 to 15 years consider their parents legitimate in having these psychological expectations of their children. Reasons given are similar to reasons for legitimacy over conventional and moral behavior; parents have a responsibility to care for their children and guide their development and they have age and knowledge superior to the child that enable them to do this. However, significantly fewer subjects consider parents legitimate in punishing for transgressions of psychological (69%) than conventional and moral rules (93% and 98%). Those subjects who reject the legitimacy of the parent to punish for psychological transgressions insist that psychological qualities cannot be regulated by parents (because a person's feelings cannot be altered by others), or that they should not be regulated by parents (because children should have autonomy over their psychological qualities), although parents can make their expectations known. Below is an example of a tenth-grade girl responding to questions about a family rule to "talk stuff out."

WOULD (YOUR PARENTS) HAVE THE RIGHT TO PUNISH YOU FOR NOT SHOWING YOUR FEELINGS?
Oh, never, no.
HOW COME?
Because showing your feelings is up to you. I mean, it's a good idea to open up and it's good to be honest, but my parents or no one can get mad at you for not expressing yourself.
WELL, HOW COME THEY CAN PUNISH YOU FOR LYING BUT THEY CAN'T PUNISH YOU FOR NOT BEING OPEN?
Because I think feelings and telling the truth are different things. Feelings is like, expressing yourself, it's more, it has to do more with you. Lying, to me, is more a thing that can hurt other people but not showing your feelings could probably hurt you more than someone else.

This subject, while acknowledging her parents' right to punish children's moral transgressions, sees the regulation of psychological qualities as personal and thus beyond the control of persons other than the self.

Children believe that parents have great influence over the origins of their children's psychological qualities. The majority of children (71%) reported that they learned what was desirable behavior in this regard from their parents, rather than deciding for themselves. The majority of children (70%) also reported that the idea did not originate with their parents, but that their parents originally learned what was desirable from their own parents, thus passing it from one generation to the next. In addition, children judge that once a psychological characteristic or behavior pattern has been set, it can not easily be changed. For example, recall that children were asked whether parents could change a rule to its opposite (e.g., requiring a child to hit or to be mean, prohibiting chores) and punish a transgression of the new rule. Negative judgments were sometimes (14% to 40%) justified with reasoning that once a parent had expected certain behaviors or certain qualities from a child over a period of years, it was either unreasonable or impractical to attempt to institute a rule change. Below are examples of responses to questions about parents changing a rule and requiring children to lie or hit.

(10th-grade female)
HOW COME THEY . . . CAN'T SAY "NOW WE WANT YOU TO LIE?"
Because they've already established something that's so permanent that they can't change it without having a big argument over it because I can go back and say, "Hey, remember when you said this and this and this and you make me think that way and now that's the way I think and you can't just overnight change me like that."
WOULD YOUR PARENTS HAVE THE RIGHT TO PUNISH YOU FOR TELL-ING THE TRUTH WHEN THEY SAID "WE WANT YOU TO LIE"?
No, because they taught me this and I would say, "Hey, that's not right. You taught me this way. This is the way it's in my head. I've got it straight now and, you know, it's not going to change in my head because that's the way you put it and that's the way I think now and that's the way I believe is right and you can't punish me for something that you put in me and not the way you taught me."

(7th-grade female)
WOULD YOUR PARENTS HAVE THE RIGHT TO PUNISH YOU NOW FOR NOT HITTING?
No.
HOW COME?
Because they told you to begin with that you weren't supposed to hit and you've learned that's the way that you're supposed to go about it and . . .
SUPPOSING THEY WANT YOU TO HIT NOW?
Well, I still say that I wouldn't hit because, you know, once again I've been taught not to and I've been brought up that way and now when I think about it I would say that I think that I shouldn't hit and so even if it means disobeying them, I wouldn't hit.

These subjects view their moral judgments as having originated with their parents, but as no longer susceptible to change. Further, if such a change in the rule were made, many subjects (50% to 64%) reported that they simply would not obey the new rule. Thus, children are implying that, if parents start early enough, they can teach their child anything: to be mean, to be a slob, or to hit siblings routinely. Once the training has taken affect, the child gradually becomes more autonomous and the parents lose their influence.

As we have noted, children have been found to conceptualize a personal domain over which parents do not have jurisdiction as authorities (Nucci, 1981; Nucci & Lee, 1993; Smetana, 1986, 1988a, 1988b, 1989; Tisak, 1993). With increasing age, children judge a greater number of issues to be in the personal domain and, thus, they view less of their behavior to be under their parents' jurisdiction. Autonomy in adolescence thus develops out of adolescents' conflicts with parents regarding those issues increasingly defined by the adolescent as personal and by the parents as conventional (Smetana, 1988a, 1988b, 1989; Chapter 7, this volume). However, results of the Family Authority Study show that, despite children's insistence on a personal domain over which their parents do not have jurisdiction, they view parents as having tremendous influence over the development of their psychological qualities, as well as their moral and conventional behavior. Children judged it appropriate that parents have expectations regarding their psychological qualities; many even thought it appropriate for parents to punish transgressions. As children assert their autonomy, they are, to some extent, asserting the autonomy to be the person they think their parents brought them up to be.

The social-organizational domain

A large part of the function of authority is to create and enforce rules in the conventional domain, defined as comprising those rules which serve to regulate efficiently the functioning of the social system. Whereas moral rules are conceptualized by children as independent of authority regulation or social consensus, and personal rules as outside the jurisdiction of authority regulation, conventional rules can be created and defined by authority. Recent research has shown that children's developing authority concepts are related to their underlying concepts of social organizations and institutions. The influence of social-organizational concepts on children's authority judgments can be seen in their reasoning about authority with respect to social position, social context, and delegation of authority, all of which are important to conventional regulation.

Social position. One can see the development of children's reasoning about social organizations in their reasoning about the social position of authorities in interaction with conventional rules systems. As has already been noted, children consider social position of school officials to be of great importance in legitimizing their authority at school (Laupa, 1991; Laupa & Turiel, 1986, 1993). Children clearly consider social position more important than adult status, judging as legitimate children with authority positions but not adults without authority positions.

However, social position is not equally important to children at all ages. Development in reasoning about social position with respect to authority can be seen in children's coordination of social position with knowledge attributes (Laupa, 1991). Young children (6 to 7 years of age) rely more on knowledge in making authority judgments, choosing persons with knowledge over persons with social position when the two conflict. Grade-school-aged children are more conflicted in their judgments, unable to coordinate knowledge and social position, whereas children in early adolescence give clear priority to social position. Young children are also more likely to consider a person with knowledge but not social position to be legitimate as an authority, whereas older subjects reject such a person as an authority. In addition, young children are more likely than older ones to accept a person as legitimate in instituting new rules in a setting in which he or she holds no authority position (e.g., a principal making rules in a public park) (Laupa & Turiel, 1993). Overall, young children are aware that persons can hold social positions that legitimize their authority in different contexts, but they do not consider social position as important for authority judgments as do older children.

Children's judgments regarding the contextual boundaries of different authority vary depending on the type of social position the authority holds. Children's judgments regarding the bounds of parental authority differ from those of other authorities, such as school authorities. Children judge parents to have broader jurisdiction than teachers across contexts. Whereas teachers are, for the most part, limited to the jurisdiction of the school, parents' jurisdiction extends out of one's home into other contexts such as the school and others' homes. In the Family Authority Study, most subjects (74% to 80%) reported that their parents would take action, such as get angry, talk to them, or punish them, if they transgressed their own family's moral or psychological rule at a friend's home. Most subjects (63% to 78%) judged that parents would be legitimate in punishing them for such a transgression. In addition, children have also been shown to accept the jurisdiction of parents over their own children at school (Laupa, in press).

However, the jurisdiction of the parent is also limited by context. Children in the Family Authority Study restrict the parents' authority to punish for transgressions of conventional rules in a friend's home (34% positive responses), more so than for transgressions of moral or psychological rules (78% and 63% positive responses). Children reason that parents do not have legitimacy to regulate their children's conventional behavior in a social system of which they are not members, that is, another family. Similarly, the legitimacy of parents to give commands in school is limited when their commands come into conflict with those of a teacher (Laupa, in press).

Delegated authority. Consistent with their conceptualization of authority as existing within hierarchically organized social systems, children recognize authority as something that can be delegated from one person to another within the system. Children as young as 4 years of age accept a child as a legitimate authority at school when the position is delegated from a person in a higher position, such as a teacher or principal. Children with delegated authority have greater legitimacy than adults without such a position. Similarly, children recognize the delegation of authority in the family; the family authority data, as well as other research (Laupa, in press), show that siblings are not considered legitimate authorities over one another unless the role has been delegated by the parents. Even younger siblings are accepted as authorities over older siblings in limited cases, but only if the position is delegated by the parents, showing the relative importance of delegated position, in contrast to age. Overall, findings show that children conceptualize authority within hierarchically organized social systems. Children's developing concepts of social systems, the ways in which they are organized, and how they function influence their authority judgments – judgments of who is dominant and who is subordinate in authority relations across contexts and situations.

The family context of obedience

In studying children's and adolescent's understanding of authority and obedience, it was not our intention to provide support and guidance for families. Nevertheless, the findings may be informative and even consoling to members of both older and younger generations. Despite the challenges that children and especially adolescents make to parents' rules, parents can be reassured that their sons and daughters (most of them) actually believe strongly in the legitimacy of parental authority in the domains of morality and convention, and accord parents a major role in shaping their psychological development. Despite the feeling that parents are trying to limit their autonomy, adolescents can be reassured that much of the conflict between them and their parents may lie in discrepant understandings about whether certain issues reside in the personal domain, and not (in most cases) in their parents' deliberate attempts to quash their individuality.

A strong finding of the Family Authority Study is that children as young as fourth graders do not treat all adult authority as equivalent. They have clearly differentiated views about the legitimacy of parents' authority and believe that parents' authority extends over a wider array of contexts than the authority of other adults. In part, this wider authority extended by children to their parents can be seen as coming from parents' special role in child rearing, and their power to distribute daily rewards and punishments. It is also possible that parental authority stems not only from role and power considerations, but also from the fact that the relationship between parents and their children, whether positive, negative, or ambivalent, is often unique in both emotional quality and intensity.

It is important to note that although children and adolescents believe that parental authority is broad in scope, it is also seen as limited. Parents are not the rule makers and rule enforcers in every domain (moral, conventional, psychological/personal) and in every social context (home, school, friends' houses). Whether an adult rule should be obeyed, then, depends on who the adult is, what the rule is, and where the potential transgression occurs. Given these conclusions, it would be useful to speculate on the ways in which social-cognitive studies of authority and obedience and family interaction studies of parent–child conflict can mutually enrich each other.

Social cognition contributions to studies of family conflict. Issues of authority and obedience arise in the daily life of the family because explicit or implicit rules are frequently disobeyed, whereupon family conflict often ensues. Family researchers who study parent–child conflict (e.g., Patterson, 1991) tend to focus on parent and child controlling behaviors, and on the regulation or dysregulation of affect during family conflict. Disobedience is usually coded as one of many subcategories of "externalizing" or "aggressive" behavior. Smetana's research (1988a, 1989) underlines the growing potential for intrafamily conflict as emerging adolescents include more and more rules as falling within the personal domains, whereas their parents continue to view these same rules as conventional. Conflict has cognitive as well as emotional components. Disagreements about whether a rule should be obeyed, then, may often be confounded with disagreements about whether the parents have legitimacy to make and enforce the rule (e.g., about the adolescent's personal appearance). Interviews with family members may provide new information that adds to our understanding of the circumstances under which some rules function as triggers for family conflict whereas others do not.

Family studies contributions to social-cognitive studies of authority and obedience. To urge that the social-cognitive research paradigm be used as a complement to observation of family interaction does not imply that *judgments* about authority and obedience necessarily correspond to obedient *behavior.* Despite the fact that children accord parents legitimacy in making and enforcing moral and conventional rules, and agree that these rules should be obeyed, children's behavior frequently contradicts their beliefs. Similarly, parents' explicit statements of rules and punishments do not guarantee that they will enforce the rules even in the face of flagrant violations.

Nevertheless, a combination of family observation and social-cognitive methods has the potential to answer some interesting questions about the relation between authority and obedience in judgment and action. All of these questions about judgment and behavior raise issues about individual differences, often not a concern of social-cognitive researchers. A combination of social-cognitive and family behavioral research could answer some important questions about whether individual differences in family functioning are associated with individual differences in children's judgments, and whether individual differences in family members' judgments about authority and obedience affect the relationships in the family.

Recent findings indicate that there are strong connections among the quality of family relationships, parenting styles, and children's development (Conger et al., 1992; Cowan & Cowan, 1992; Cox, Owen, Lewis, & Henderson, 1989). Family interaction studies would be helpful in differentiating between cases where individuals' beliefs about authority and obedience are congruent with their obedient or disobedient behavior, and cases where obedience beliefs and behavior contradict each other. Second, data concerning the quality of parent–child and other family relationships (marital, sibling) might help to answer the question of whether judgments concerning legitimacy of authority vary with the quality of family transactions. For example, are parents who establish positive relationships with their children more likely to be accorded the authority to make and enforce rules? Conversely, is it possible that parents who behave in certain punitive or inconsistent ways toward their children, their spouses, or others will lose legitimacy, in the children's view, to make and enforce rules and dispense punishments. The answer would probably vary by domain, with less effect of family relationship quality on rules in the moral domain (provided children judge the rules to be morally acceptable) and more in the conventional and psychological domains. It seems to us that a mutual exploration of social cognition and family interaction has great promise for our understanding of authority and obedience as it plays out in the day-to-day lives of children and parents.

Conclusions: Crimes of obedience

Research on the ways children and adolescents think about authority, considered in this chapter, amply demonstrates that children's authority judgments are quite differentiated; children consider each of the three authority components in their legitimacy and obedience judgments. These types of differentiations in reasoning are consistent with what is known about the issue, raised at the outset, of "crimes of obedience" in which the demands of morality conflict with those of authority. As stated earlier, obedience to authority is not an all or nothing phenomenon, and both obedience and disobedience require explanation. Perhaps most illustrative of the phenomenon are the findings of Milgram's (1963, 1974) classic experimental studies in which subjects were instructed to administer what they thought were painful electric shocks to fellow subjects in a supposed learning experiment. In the first study (Milgram, 1963), the majority of subjects continued to administer shocks, despite the learner's protests, in obedience to commands from the experimenter. The results have been interpreted as involving subjects' attempts to coordinate concerns of two domains (Turiel & Smetana, 1984). On the one hand, the subject has a moral concern with not committing actions that may harm another person. On the other hand, the subject has a social-organizational concern with upholding the rules of the particular social organization he or she has agreed to enter. Subjects must weigh and coordinate these concerns, which, in this case, can lead to different courses of action.

The results of several different experimental conditions (Milgram, 1974) support the proposition that subjects' behaviors are affected by their consideration of the moral features of the situation. This consideration corresponds to the first authority component, that of type of command. For example, one set of experimental conditions involved varying the proximity of the "victim" to the subject who was administering the shocks. The closer the victim was in physical proximity to the subject, the fewer the subjects who administered the maximum level of shock. Thus, increasing the salience of the moral consequences of the command (by making the harm to the victim more noticeable) led to lower levels of obedience. Although such experimental research has not been done with children, hypothetical interviews with children demonstrate that when the possible harm arising from an authority command is made salient, children recommend disobedience to the command (Laupa & Turiel, 1986, 1993).

Similarly, another set of experimental conditions supports the proposition that subjects' behaviors are affected by their consideration of features of the situation corresponding to the second authority component, that of authority attributes. In this situation the primary social-organizational aim for subjects is to carry out the orders given by the experimenter (an authority) in order to complete the experiment successfully. Variations of experimental conditions that affect subjects' judgments of the legitimizing authority attributes of the experimenter should lead to varying levels of obedience. This was found to be the case; various manipulations of the role and physical location of the experimenter lead to lower levels of obedience.

For example, two variations involve manipulation of the experimenter's social position. In one, the experimenter is called out of the room and leaves a subject (who is actually a confederate of the experimenter) to give the orders, without instructing him as to what level of shock is to be used. In the experimenter's absence, the confederate decided to increase progressively the level of shock. In this case, a nonauthority does have a delegated authority position, but he has not been given jurisdiction to choose the voltage level. In another case, a subject gave the commands while the experimenter served as victim. The procedure continued until the experimenter himself demanded to be released from the chair in which he was receiving shocks. In this condition, not only did the person lack delegated jurisdiction, but his commands were being contradicted by those of someone in higher authority, that is, the experimenter himself. Very few subjects in these variations obeyed to the maximum level. Analogously, when given hypothetical interviews, a majority of grade-school-aged children reject the authority of adults who do not hold a social position in the context in which they are issuing commands.

Other experimental conditions influence subjects' judgments of the authority's knowledge attributes. In one variation, two authorities gave contradictory commands (at some point one authority gave the command to continue and the other to stop). No subjects continued to the maximum level of shock in this condition; 90% broke off at the point where the disagreement began. This type of disagreement between authorities who are at equivalent levels in the organizational hierarchy is not resolvable by subjects; there is no way for subjects to determine who is higher in command. In addition, such disagreement can lead subjects to question the authorities' superior knowledge. The experimenters are allegedly highly trained experts who are conducting a scientific experiment with procedures the subject knows little or nothing about. Subjects have no way of determining which authority has greater knowledge or better judgment in this case, but they may easily come to the conclusion that one or both of them are not as knowledgeable as they previously assumed. Analogously, in hypothetical interviews, children are least likely to accept the authority of an individual who lacks knowledge and whose social position is in question.

Another experimental condition suggests that subjects are also influenced by considerations of punishment. In this condition, the authority leaves the room and issues commands by telephone from another location. In this case, only 20% of subjects continued to the maximum level of shock. An interesting feature of this condition is that several subjects disobeyed the experimenter by continuing to shock at the lowest level while reporting to the experimenter by phone that they were increasing the level of shock in obedience to his commands. "Secret" disobedience of this type suggests the possibility that subjects' obedience was due, at least in part, to fear of sanctions. If the concern were with carrying out the aims of the experiment, subjects would either obey the experimenter, or refuse to obey when the moral concerns outweighed the social-organizational ones. However, if the concern is to avoid punishment, subjects can achieve this end by leading the experimenter to believe they have obeyed.

Finally, another variation provides an example of subjects possibly being influenced by a consideration of sanctions. In this experimental condition, two confederates of the experimenter posed as subjects in the experiment and, at predetermined voltage levels, one and then the other refused to continue. The percentage of subjects administering the maximum shock in this case was only 10%. After having defied the authority the confederates remain in the laboratory room, thus giving the appearance to the subject that ordinary subjects can defy the authority's orders and suffer no sanctions because of it. If fear of punishment is a factor in subjects' decision to continue, then one would expect this condition to be associated with less obedience. Another possibility is that the condition contributed to subjects judging the authority to be less knowledgeable than they had originally thought. In the same way that conflict between two authorities may lead to the subject questioning their knowledge, the existence of other ordinary persons questioning the authority may contribute to the subject doubting the authority's knowledge. Again, research into children's reasoning about such issues shows an analogous drop in recommendations of obedience to individuals who lack the ability to inflict punishment.

There is a parallel, therefore, between the influences of domain, attributes of the authority, and context on adults' behaviors in the Milgram experiments and the way children and adults reason about authority. When making authority judgments, children take into account the type of act being regulated. In addition, they consider the person's official social position in a given social-organizational system in coordination with the social context in which the command is being given. They also consider the person's knowledge attributes in light of the command given and the likely outcome if it is obeyed. Finally, children consider the person's ability to inflict punishment, whether legitimate or nonlegitimate.

The investigation of children's authority concepts with regard to authority attributes and social context has demonstrated the importance of social-organizational reasoning in children's authority judgments. In contrast, traditional-stage-oriented theories that describe global changes in the parent–child relation to a large extent focus on the children's understanding in the psychological domain, that is, how they conceptualize the psychological attributes of parents and other adults. Children are described as developing more sophisticated role-taking abilities that enable them to understand better their parents as persons (Selman, 1980). This understanding allows for a more equal parent–child relation as the child gets older (Youniss, 1980; Youniss & Smollar, 1985). These descriptions only partially explain children's authority concepts, to the extent that they incorporate children's concepts in the psychological but not the moral or social-organizational domains.

There is no simple relationship between one's judgments about an authority and his or her commands and one's obedience or disobedience to those commands. In this chapter we have demonstrated that obedience to authority is not an all-or-nothing phenomenon by making explicit the components that go into children's and adults' authority judgments in both conflicting and nonconflicting situations. We have described the ways in which obedience and disobedience can be analyzed by looking at how individuals coordinate these components in their reasoning. Evidence of the importance of these coordinations can be seen both in experimental studies with adults, as well as studies of children's reasoning about hypothetical situations. These findings support the proposition that reasoning about the three authority components, particularly the attributes of those giving authority commands, is central to judgments of an authority's legitimacy and subsequent obedience or disobedience.

Note

1. Percentages reported in text are descriptive except where statistically significant findings are specifically noted.

References

Arendt, H. (1964). *Eichmann in Jerusalem.* New York: Viking Press.

Astington, J. W., Harris, P. L., & Olson, D. R. (1988). *Developing theories of mind.* Cambridge: Cambridge University Press.

Conger, R. D., Conger, K. J., Elder, G. H., Jr., Lorenz, F. O., Simons, R. L., & Whitbeck, L. B. (1992). A family process model of economic hardship and adjustment of early adolescent boys. *Child Development, 63,* 526–541.

Cowan, C. P., & Cowan, P. A. (1992). *When partners become parents: The big life change for couples.* New York: Basic Books.

Cox, M. J., Owen, M. T., Lewis, J. M., & Henderson, V. K. (1989). Marriage, adult adjustment, and early parenting. *Child Development, 60,* 1015–1024.

Damon, W. (1977). *The social world of the child.* San Francisco: Jossey-Bass.

Damon, W., & Hart, D. (1988). *Self-understanding in childhood and adolescence.* Cambridge: Cambridge University Press.

DeLong, B. (1991). *Concepts of morality and religion: The coordination of moral prescription and divine authority.* Unpublished doctoral dissertation, University of California, Berkeley.

Haney, C., Banks, C., & Zimbardo, P. (1973). Interpersonal dynamics in a simulated prison. *International Journal of Criminology and Penology, 1,* 69–97.

Jancaterino, W. (1982). *The relationships between children's understanding of social influence and their moral evaluations of harm.* Unpublished doctoral dissertation, University of California, Santa Cruz.

Kelman, H. C., & Hamilton, V. L. (1989). *Crimes of obedience.* New Haven, CT: Yale University Press.

Laupa, M. (1991). Children's reasoning about three authority attributes: Adult status, knowledge and social position. *Developmental Psychology, 27,* 321–329.

Laupa, M. 1994. Who's in charge? Preschool children's concepts of authority. *Early Childhood Research Quarterly, 9,* 1–17.

Laupa, M. (in press). Children's concepts of authority in home and school contexts. *Social Development.*

Laupa, M., & Turiel, E. (1986). Children's conceptions of adult and peer authority. *Child Development, 57,* 405–412.

Laupa, M., & Turiel, E. (1993). Authority reasoning and social contexts. *Journal of Educational Psychology, 85,* 191–197.

Martin, J., Lobb, B., Chapman, G. C., & Spillane, R. (1976). Obedience under conditions demanding self-immolation. *Human Relations, 29,* 345–356.

Milgram, S. (1963). Behavioral study of obedience. *Journal of Abnormal and Social Psychology, 67,* 371–378.

Milgram, S. (1974). *Obedience to authority: An experimental view.* New York: Harper and Row.

Nucci, L. (1981). The development of personal concepts: A domain distinct from moral or societal concepts. *Child Development, 52,* 114–121.

Nucci, L. (1985). Children's concepts of morality, societal convention, and religious prescription. In C. Harding, (Ed.), *Moral dilemmas: Philosophical and psychological reconsiderations of the development of moral reasoning* (pp. 137–174). Chicago: Precedent Press.

Nucci, L., & Lee, J. Y. (1993). Morality and personal autonomy. In G. G. Noam & T. Wren (Eds.), *The moral self: Building a better paradigm* (pp. 123–148). Cambridge, MA: MIT Press.

Nucci, L., & Turiel, E. (1978). Social interactions and the development of social concepts in preschool children. *Child Development, 49,* 400–407.

Nucci, L., & Turiel, E. (1993). God's word, religious rules, and their relation to Christian and Jewish children's concepts of morality. *Child Development, 64,* 1475–1491.

Patterson, G. R. (Ed.). (1991). *Advances in family research: Vol. 1. Depression and aggression: Two facets of family interactions.* Hillsdale, NJ: Lawrence Erlbaum.

Piaget, J. (1932/1965). *The moral judgment of the child.* London: Routledge and Kegan Paul.

Raviv, A., Bar-tal, D., Raviv, A., & Houminer, D. (1990). Development in children's perceptions of epistemic authorities. *British Journal of Developmental Psychology, 8,* 157–169.

Raviv, A., Bar-tal, D., Raviv, A., & Peleg, D. (1990). Perceptions of epistemic authorities by children and adolescents. *Journal of Youth and Adolescence, 19,* 495–509.

Selman, R. (1980). *The growth of interpersonal understanding.* New York: Academic Press.

Shanab, M. E., & Yahya, K. A. (1977). A behavioral study of obedience in children. *Journal of Personality and Social Psychology, 35,* 530–536.

Shweder, R. A., Mahapatra, M., & Miller, J. G. (1987). Culture and moral development. In J. Kagan & S. Lamb (Eds.), *The emergence of morality in young children* (pp. 1–83). Chicago: University of Chicago Press.

Smetana, J. G. (1981). Preschool children's conceptions of moral and social rules. *Child Development, 52,* 1333–1336.

Smetana, J. G. (1983). Social-cognitive development: Domain distinctions and coordinations. *Developmental Review, 3,* 131–147.

Smetana, J. G. (1984). Toddlers' social interactions regarding moral and conventional transgressions. *Child Development, 55,* 1767–1776.

Smetana, J. G. (1986). Preschool children's conceptions of sex-role transgressions. *Child Development, 57,* 862–871.

Smetana, J. G. (1988a). Adolescents' and parents' conceptions of parental authority. *Child Development, 59,* 321–335.

Smetana, J. G. (1988b). Concepts of self and social convention: Adolescents' and parents' reasoning about hypothetical and actual family conflicts. In M. R. Gunnar & W. A. Collins (Eds.), *21st Minnesota Symposium on Child Psychology: Development during the transition to adolescence* (pp. 79–122). Hillsdale, NJ: Lawrence Erlbaum.

Smetana, J. G. (1989). Adolescents' and parents' reasoning about actual family conflict. *Child Development, 60,* 1052–1067.

Tisak, M. S. (1986). Children's conceptions of parental authority. *Child Development, 57,* 166–176.

Tisak, M. S. (1993). Preschool children's judgments of moral and personal events involving physical harm and property damage. *Merrill-Palmer Quarterly, 39,* 375–390.

Tisak, M. S., & Tisak, J. (1991) Children's conceptions of parental authority, friendship, and sibling relations. *Merrill-Palmer Quarterly, 36,* 347–368.

Turiel, E. (1983). *The development of social knowledge: Morality and convention.* Cambridge: Cambridge University Press.

Turiel, E., & Davidson, P. (1986). Heterogeneity, inconsistency, and asynchrony in the development of cognitive structures. In I. Levin (Ed.), *Stage and structure: Reopening the debate* (pp. 106–143). Norwood, NJ: Ablex.

Turiel, E., Killen, M., & Helwig, C. C. (1987). Morality: Its structure, functions and vagaries. In J. Kagan & S. Lamb (Eds.), *The emergence of morality in young children* (pp. 155–243). Chicago: University of Chicago Press.

Turiel, E. & Smetana, J. G. (1984). Social knowledge and action: The coordination of domains. In W. M. Kurtines & J. L. Gewirtz (Eds.), *Morality, moral development, and moral behavior: Basic issues in theory and research.* (pp. 261–282). New York: Wiley.

Weston, D., & Turiel, E. (1980). Act-rule relations: Children's concepts of social rules. *Developmental Psychology, 16,* 417–424.

Youniss, J. (1980). *Parents and peers in social development.* Chicago: University of Chicago Press.

Youniss, J., & Smollar, J. (1985). *Adolescents' relations with mothers, fathers, and friends.* Chicago: University of Chicago Press.

5   Social context in social cognition: Psychological harm and civil liberties

Charles C. Helwig

> Ordinarily, we accept the idea of context without any question; but this is only because we do not pursue it very far. We do not see that dependence on context is a limited kind of relativism and that relativism, looked at philosophically, is hard to limit. . . . Because context is most often used in literary study, history, and social science, it is not analyzed as closely as standard philosophical questions, such as that of relativism itself. The price paid is intellectual slackness because to neglect to see where the idea leads is as intellectually unjustified as to neglect to use it. (Sharfstein, 1989, p. 59)

Recent years have witnessed an increasing recognition of the importance of context in social and cognitive development (Cohen & Siegel, 1991; Serafica, 1982; Winegar & Valsiner, 1992; Wozniak & Fischer, 1993). This has translated into calls to adapt existing developmental theories to accommodate emerging evidence of diversity and variation in psychological functioning, and has been a motivating force in spawning "new" theoretical paradigms, represented, for example, by approaches as diverse as interpretive or hermeneutic theory (e.g., Packer & Scott, 1992; Tappan, 1992) and Neo-Vygotskian theory (e.g., Cole, 1985; Rogoff, 1990; Wertsch, 1985). Empirically, appeals to address social context have generally been answered by a broadening of the scope of contextual factors examined, including detailed analyses of spheres of environmental influences (Bronfenbrenner, 1993; Bronfenbrenner & Crouter, 1983; Lerner & Lerner, 1989), accompanied by a greater emphasis on "ecologically valid" investigations of psychological processes in conditions congruent with, or closely approximating, their common applications in everyday life (Rogoff, 1990; Scribner, 1977).

Despite much recent attention, context remains one of the most poorly

Research reported in this chapter was supported by a grant from the Social Science and Humanities Research Council (SSHRC) #3-302-118-80 and by a Connaught Phase I Research Grant. I am grateful to Elliot Turiel and the editors for helpful comments on an earlier version of the manuscript.

166

understood and vaguely analyzed concepts in developmental psychology. Researchers have often proceded with intuitive, commonsense, or metaphorical definitions of context in place of close analyses of the concept tied to a consideration of the implications for theory and research. A common tendency is to equate context with environment or setting, such that anything exogenous to the individual is construed, by definition, as part of "the context" (Siegel & Cohen, 1991). Another related tendency is to investigate the "effects" of context by means of a mechanistic paradigm (Reese & Overton, 1970; Overton & Reese, 1973) in which environmental factors are considered to more or less directly determine the behaviors, cognitions, and dispositions of individual persons. This mechanistic approach has come under critique, especially by theorists adhering to an "organismic" metatheoretical paradigm (Reese & Overton, 1970; Overton, 1984), for its failure to consider the role played by an active subject in representing, construing, and interpreting social reality. From a social-cognitive point of view, analyses of the effects of social context must go beyond mere documentation of shifts in, or influences on, social judgments as a function of changing environmental conditions. In accordance with the proposition that organisms interpret or assimilate reality (Asch, 1952; Piaget, 1947/ 1960), environmental influences are mediated by cognitive processes or structures whose description and functioning must constitute a primary focus of psychological explanation. From this perspective, context and cognition are thoroughly conjoined and cannot meaningfully be separated in an antecedent–consequent causal analysis. A social-cognitive analysis of context will therefore consist of an investigation of how various aspects of situations are represented in and engage the individual's developing conceptual structures.

In this chapter, I will examine the role of social context in developmental theory *from a social cognitive point of view,* with particular emphasis on moral development. A framework will be presented for conceptualizing social context that builds on current theory and research on social-cognitive domains. The view of social context underlying this approach seeks to explain variation in judgment and reasoning as a function of diverse social concepts implicated in situational contexts as they are construed by individuals at different ages. It will be argued that this requires joint consideration of two potential sources of variation, that due to (1) the types of social and moral issues brought to bear in making a decision or judgment, and (2) developmental level, conceptualized more locally than in traditional stage theories. Research will be presented showing how the intersection of these two sources of variation can be used to illuminate our understanding of context and development in two areas: judgments of psychological harm in the elementary school years, and judgments of civil liberties and rights from young childhood through early adulthood.

Context and social cognition

The issue of context appears to have provoked extreme responses in social cognitive theory and research. Recently, a variety of "contextualist" approaches has emerged seeking to situate thinking and reasoning in culturally defined or structured praxis, belief systems, or ideology (Gergen, 1985; Packer, 1992; Rogoff, 1990, 1993; Shweder, 1986; Tappan, 1992). This approach stands in contrast to traditional structuralist stage theories of cognitive or moral development, which tend to subsume context within global structures or stages of thought (e.g., Kohlberg, 1984; Piaget, 1926/ 1975). Whereas stage theories have taken general cognitive structures as central and context as derivative, contextualist approaches (Pepper, 1942) all start with the assumption that context constitutes the primary focus of investigation. Some examples of the contextualist approach are Neo-Vygotskian theory (Rogoff, 1993; Wertsch, 1985), hermeneutic theory (Packer, 1992; Tappan, 1992), and social contructionism (Gergen, 1985; Shweder, 1986). The central assumption behind contextualism is that the psychological nature of the individual cannot be separated from the context in which human thought, emotion, and behavior naturally occur. The particular focus of the contextual analysis varies by theoretical approach, and may be directed at human functioning in concrete, real-life problem-solving activity (Neo-Vygotskianism), the products of discourse analyzed as "texts" (hermeneutic theory), or cultural ideological constructs (social constructionism). All of these approaches have in common a rejection of abstract or general cognitive structures or processes in favor of socioculturally "situated" cognitive activity.

In contextualism, the person and the situation are seen as the indissociable poles of a dynamic process (Rogoff, 1990). Accordingly, the "basic unit of analysis is no longer the (properties of the) individual, but the (processes of the) sociocultural activity, involving active participation of people in socioculturally constituted practices" (Rogoff, 1990, p. 14). In this way, contextualism is meant to offer "a unique seamlessness of individual, social, and historical (or cultural) processes" (Rogoff, 1990, p. 13).

Functionalism in general (of which contextualism is a part), and hermeneutic theory and social constructionism in particular, have all been the subject of extensive discussion and critique elsewhere (see Beilin, 1983; Kahn, 1993; Spiro, 1986; Turiel, 1989) and it is not the place here to evaluate critically these theories in detail. To summarize, contextualism has been criticized as an inherently "dispersive" explanatory paradigm failing to provide the kind of systematic explanation necessary for scientific analysis (Overton, 1984; Sharfstein, 1989). Contextualism appears to offer no a priori method for designating which contexts are of immediate theoretical relevance, nor does it say much about the generalizability of psychological processes beyond the immediate situations in which they are initially observed. Also problematic is the conceptualization of the organism–environment relation in contextualism. Contextualist theories suffer from a tendency to conflate exogenous (environmental) and endogenous (individual) levels of analysis, thereby confusing sociogenetic and ontogenetic processes in knowledge acquisition (Davidson, 1992). This comes, in part, from the explanation of knowledge as essentially a social or cultural contruct, and the use of concepts like internalization (e.g., Tappan, 1992), appropriation (Rogoff, 1990, 1993), or social transmission (Shweder, 1986; Shweder & Miller, 1985) as major explanatory developmental mechanisms. As structuralists like Piaget (1963/1968) have argued, the "psycho-sociological reductionism" encountered in contextualist theories remains incomplete as an explanation of development, and ultimately recourse to principles of internal development will be needed in order to explain fully the influences of context.

Structuralist developmental theories (Damon, 1977; Piaget, 1968/1970; Turiel, 1983) do not, of course, deny that individual and environment interact in important ways. Organism and environment are in mutual interaction with respect to functioning, and the construction of cognitive and social cognitive structures and developmental change are important products of this interaction. Transformations in systems of thought brought about through interaction with the environment constitute the explanation of developmental change in structuralist theory, rather than the internalization or appropriation of environmental structure or content. The organism/environment distinction is thus maintained as two interacting (not "indissociable") poles of a dynamic system of functioning, each of which is amenable to a structural analysis (Overton, 1994; Turiel & Davidson, 1986). In functionalist and contextualist theories this structure–function distinction is not upheld, and as a consequence these theories in effect reduce thought structures to processes of social interactions. A persistent danger in such an approach is the potential for conflating social cognition and social context.

In the area of moral development, Kohlberg's theory is exemplary of the traditional structuralist approach. The details of Kohlbergian theory are far too complex to be reviewed here (see Kohlberg, 1984, for a full account), so I will confine my discussion to a few central aspects in order to highlight the general approach and trace some of its implications for the role of context in moral reasoning. Morality is defined in Kohlbergian theory as a general or global cognitive system ("structured whole") undergoing a series of transformations in development characterized by progressive differentiations and integrations of social knowledge. Morality encompasses a wide variety of concepts pertaining to such diverse issues as rights, human welfare, social rules and laws, authority, societal roles, and sexual customs. The global definition of morality has led to the use of a methodological instrument, the moral judgment interview (MJI), containing stories or dilemmas involving conflicts between the variety of issues postulated to fall within the moral domain. The proposition that morality is a unitary system undergoing progressive differentiations provides the justification for examining reasoning in the context of conflicts embodying a wide spectrum of social concepts and categories. Judgment and reasoning assessed in these moral dilemmas is then taken as data for the generation of general descriptions (stages) of moral judgment comprising different developmental levels. A six-stage developmental sequence has been found in which moral judgment becomes increasingly abstract and differentiated from authority, punishment, social customs, and conventional regulations or existing laws (Kohlberg, 1969, 1971, 1984).

The notion of moral stages as "structured wholes" results in the requirement that stages be descriptive of moral thinking across a wide range of situations. As Kohlberg, Levine, and Hewer (1983) state, "the general empirical implication of this conception is that individuals' thinking will be manifested at a single, dominant stage when observed across instances of varying content" (p. 242). Variations in the types of social concepts or concerns under consideration are thus subsumed within the operation of the global structure, and would not be expected to have a significant effect on moral reasoning. If the proposition of structured wholes is to be valid and useful, moral reasoning should, in large measure, be defined by stage level and applied irrespective of considerations of social context.

The central proposition of general stages or levels cutting across diverse content in social and moral judgment has come under challenge. Some commentators (Fischer, 1983; Saltzstein, 1983) have questioned whether the data collected by Kohlberg and collaborators using the MJI really do show levels of consistency in responding across dilemmas compatible with the "structured whole" hypothesis. As Fischer (1983) notes:

On the Moral Judgment Interview itself, one-third of the responses fell at stages other than the individuals' modal stage, so that most individuals showed a range of at least two or three stages. Moreover, many other patterns in the data highlighted the pervasiveness of unevenness and the contributions of various environmental influences to stage of performance. Different dilemmas produced different modal stage assignments for many subjects and alternate forms of the interview produced different stages as well. (p. 99)

Researchers working close to the Kohlbergian methodology and overall approach have also found that variations in the standard dilemmas or probe questions can have a considerable effect on assessments of stages of moral reasoning (e.g., Gilligan & Belenky, 1980; Krebs, Vermeulen, Carpendale, & Denton, 1991; Leming, 1978; Linn, 1987; Sobesky, 1983). For example, Krebs et al. (1991) gave subjects, in addition to the standard Kohlbergian dilemmas, alternative dilemmas that included content relating to prosocial obligation, morality in business deals, and driving while under the influence of alcohol. When scored using Kohlberg's instrument, subjects were found to reason at significantly lower stages on these alternative dilemmas than on the standard dilemmas. For instance, 40% of subjects who scored Stage 4 on Kohlberg's test tended to exhibit Stage 2 reasoning on the impaired driving dilemma. (On some other alternative dilemmas given besides the three mentioned here more consistency with the MJI was obtained). Krebs et al. (1991) conclude that, overall, "the evidence indicates that moral judgment is sometimes homogeneous and sometimes heterogenous" with contexts exerting "varying pulls for and resistances against the activation of these stage structures" (p. 139). Kohlberg and colleagues have similarly sought to explain contextual variation in moral judgment with reference to notions like "performance factors," "downward press," and the "moral atmosphere" of institutions and environments (Colby & Kohlberg, 1987). These are the social-cognitive analogues of terms such as "resistance" and "perceptual factors," sometimes invoked to account for unanticipated decalages in cognitive development (Chapman, 1988; Inhelder & Piaget, 1959/1969; Piaget, 1971).

Interestingly, this response to contextual variation appears to constitute a move toward functionalist explanation (Beilin, 1983, 1987) and away from a structuralist (conceptual) explanation. In the face of variability in applications of global structures, researchers have tended to preserve the idea of global structure but resort to alternative, nonstructural processes in accounting for the differential application of social-cognitive structures to situational contexts. Context is dealt with "functionally," as an element or factor that impedes or facilitates the operation of globally defined social cognitive structures. Attention is thus turned toward the situational factors that induce, influence, or provoke different forms of moral reasoning. An alternative response – to reexamine the idea of global structures and to look, instead, for structural or conceptual features intrinsic to specific applications that may help explain the variation – seems not to have been considered.

The perspective on "context" to be offered here attempts to avoid some of the difficulties associated with global stage theories and purely functionalist or contextualist accounts. The purpose is to provide a more differentiated view of social cognition than that found in traditional structuralist theories, in order better to account for contextual variations in social and moral judgment. Though the analysis will mainly be in terms of social-cognitive structures, this is not to deny the ultimate importance of functional and dynamic processes in the application of these structures to social situations. A complete psychological theory will, of course, need to articulate the complex relationship between conceptual structures and psychological functioning in explanations of human behavior. But it is believed an understanding of how context is represented in the thinking of individuals at different points in development will constitute an essential component of any comprehensive explanation of social judgment and behavior.

Context, development, and social cognitive domains

Research carried out over the past decade and a half in what has been termed the "domain approach" has amassed a large body of findings suggesting that the moral judgments of children are more differentiated than has been previously assumed (see Helwig, Tisak, & Turiel, 1990; Turiel, Killen, & Helwig, 1987, for recent reviews). Counter to the expectations of global-differentiation models of moral judgment (Kohlberg, 1984; Piaget, 1932/1965), even very young children have been shown to make moral judgments exhibiting independence from punishment, authority, and social convention (Smetana, 1981; Chapter 7, this volume; Smetana & Braeges, 1990). These findings have led to the proposal that social cognition is organized into distinct conceptual systems ("domains") that undergo independent developmental transformations (Turiel, 1979, 1983; Turiel & Davidson, 1986). These conceptual systems are constructed out of the individual's interactions with the social environment. The domain of morality comprises generalizable and obligatory norms governing social interaction and is based on concepts of harm, justice, and rights. The domain of social convention comprises arbitrary and context-specific norms serving to coordinate interactions of individuals within social systems. A third domain, the psychological domain, pertains to knowledge about persons as psychological subjects, and includes concepts of intentionality, beliefs, motivation, behavior, and other concepts central to explanations of human psychological functioning and behavior (Jancaterino, 1982; Turiel & Davidson, 1986).

Social domains have been applied not only to analyses of judgment, but to analysis of the environment (context) as well (Killen, 1989, 1991; Turiel, Smetana, & Killen, 1991). Social-interactional contexts have been shown to vary in accordance with moral and conventional features. Verbal and nonverbal responses of children and adults to acts of a moral or conventional nature (usually, though not exclusively, transgressions in these studies) have been examined in preschool and elementary school contexts and in the home (Much & Shweder, 1978; Nucci & Nucci, 1982a, 1982b; Nucci & Turiel, 1978; Smetana, 1984, 1989). Social-conventional acts were associated with statements centering around aspects of social organization, such as rules or sanctions and communications from adults designed to focus the child on the disorder resulting from the act. In contrast, moral acts tended to produce reactions or statements reflecting the harmful consequences of the act for others, such as direct references to injury or loss or violations of others' rights, emotional reactions, requests for the transgressor to take the perspective of the victim, and retaliation on the part of victims. These findings from research on social domains suggest that a complementary structural analysis of both social-cognitive judgments and social environments and interactions can provide a powerful tool for understanding the complex interaction of individuals and social contexts.

This research has important implications for investigations of moral development and for the conceptualization of social context. Developmentally, the domain-specific approach differs from the global differentiation theory of Kohlberg in that it proposes that social understandings are nonunitary and that concepts of morality do not emerge out of prior concepts of social convention, authority, and punishment. Accordingly, the developmental process will be viewed, in part, as involving coordinations and integrations among diverse social concepts of different types, rather than the differentiation of one knowledge system (e.g., morality) from another (e.g., social convention). A fundamental developmental process is how social concepts are coordinated (related) in integrative conceptual structures. The kind of integration postulated in domain theory is not the general integration characteristic of global structural models (Kohlberg, 1984), but rather a more local integration specific to the particular concerns or issues being related. Two types of conceptual relations can be distinguished: within-domain and between-domain relations. Within-domain relations have not received much attention by researchers working in the domain approach, although they have been extensively investigated elsewhere. Some examples in the case of morality include coordinations of intentions and consequences in moral judgments of culpability in transgressions (Grueneich, 1982; Leon, 1980; Nummedal & Bass, 1976; Surber, 1977), and coordination of need and merit in distributive justice judgments

(Anderson & Butzin, 1978; Damon, 1975, 1977, 1980; Enright et al., 1984; Sigelman & Waitzman, 1991). Research within the domain approach has begun to examine reasoning in the context of multifaceted situations containing components from various domains (Duncan, 1986; Killen, 1990; Turiel, 1983). These studies presented subjects with "mixed" situations in which moral and social-conventional components conflict. For example, in Killen (1990), children were given a forced-choice dilemma between acting to prevent harm or acting to maintain peer group or classroom order. The findings showed considerable variation, both within and between individuals, in how moral and social-conventional considerations were coordinated. Exploring these specific patterns of coordination constitutes a focus of developmental research from the domain perspective.

Viewing development this way will require, on the subject side of the organism–environment interaction, greater attention to the specific types of concepts that may need to be coordinated in particular applications of social reasoning, and their availability at different points in development. On the environmental side, a more differentiated view of social context is needed, in accordance with the unique types of conceptual coordination problems certain environments (situations) may present at different ages. Neither social reasoning, nor environmental contexts, can be characterized in global terms.

A further implication of this view is that development may be better described as a process of understanding "embedded relations" among concepts as they are applied in complex social situations. In cases where individuals fail to judge a particular situation from the perspective of moral concepts – for example, when morality is subordinated to law or social convention as found in Kohlbergian research – it may be misleading to describe this as a (global) failure to differentiate morality from legal systems or social convention. This is because, as the research on social domains has found, in other situations even young children clearly do distinguish these concepts. An alternative interpretation of findings such as these is that, in certain situations of considerable difficulty and complexity, considerations from one domain either fail to be noticed or are subordinated to considerations from another domain. This may be done in ways that comprise inconsistencies, contradictions, and errors (Turiel & Davidson, 1986; Turiel, Hildebrandt, & Wainryb, 1991).

Defining and explaining "complexity" is, of course, the central issue. One source of complexity stems from the intrinsic features of particular concepts found within each of the social domains. Concepts clearly may vary along a continuum in their complexity. Traditionally, this has been expressed as variation from the concrete to the abstract. In moral development, relatively "concrete" moral concepts like physical harm may be easier and acquired earlier than more abstract and heavily inferential concepts like psychological harm or reciprocity. At the most abstract end of the continuum may be complex political concepts like democracy or civil liberties. In research to be presented shortly it will be argued that the interpretation-bound nature of psychological harm makes moral judgments of these acts especially difficult in certain situations for young children (Helwig, Hildebrandt, & Turiel, in press).

An additional source of complexity comes from the informational assumptions (Wainryb, 1991) from other domains that influence the application of concepts from the target domain. Moral concepts are frequently applied under factual assumptions from other domains. Individuals may fail to apply moral concepts in some situations because these situations draw upon knowledge from another domain exceeding the individual's capabilities in that area. At the most basic level, construction of the moral domain rests on prior constructions of the subject–object distinction and psychological agency (Hoffman, 1983; Turiel & Davidson, 1986). Because moral knowledge is fundamentally knowledge about how others ought to be or ought not to be treated, conceptions of actions as truly moral or nonmoral are not possible until a rudimentary psychological domain that includes conceptions of other persons is in place. Conceptions of persons themselves can be applied to social events in ways that vary across individuals and cultures. For example, Turiel et al. (1987) reanalyzed cross-cultural data on social reasoning in India to show that differences in conceptions of psychological agents contributed to cross-cultural variation in moral judgment reported by Shweder, Mahapatra, and Miller (1987). Variations in beliefs about psychological competence and rational agency may be an important factor in decisions about extending moral rights such as freedom of speech and religion to children and adolescents (Moshman, 1993).

Thorkildsen (1989) has noted an additional factor that may contribute to contextual variation in moral judgment in the form of the "implicit contracts" (Dworkin, 1977) that underlie different social-institutional practices and determine how various social goods should be distributed. Thorkildsen (1989) investigated children's moral judgments, comparing competitive situations (a contest, a test) with those where mastery of a skill was the goal, as in learning to read. Children's judgments of the fairness of various pedagogical arrangements like cooperative learning or competition were found to be highly context-dependent. Cooperative learning was judged fair in mastery situations but not in contest and test situations, whereas the opposite held true for pedagogical practices based on competition. The contractual basis of these social situations appeared to be understood as indicated by the fact that most children maintained that practices considered unfair in some situations could become fair if agreed to and adopted by the participants. Similar findings of context-specificity in children's use of principles of equality and equity in distributive justice reasoning have been reported by Siegelman and Waitzman (1991).

The idea of implicit contracts may help to explain some of the contextual variation mentioned earlier in studies conducted in the Kohlbergian approach. For example, the finding by Krebs et al. (1991) of lower-stage scores on certain economic dilemmas (e.g., whether a seller should reveal information about impending negative economic consequences on a business to a prospective buyer) might be due to specific implicit contracts defining the expectations operating in different contexts. As Krebs et al. (1991) point out, many subjects explicitly adopted a caveat emptor or "dog eat dog" approach that was specific to the business context and had the effect of pulling for lower (Stage 2) reasoning there. The implicit contract in effect in economic contexts may be more like that of a competition (Thorkildsen, 1989), differing from those in effect in either interpersonal or societal contexts. Direct investigation of the implicit contracts embedded in social situations, and how they are construed by individuals, may provide a useful avenue for further research.

The picture of social-cognitive development sketched here has much in common with contemporary "neostructuralist" positions in cognitive development (Lautrey, 1993), emphasizing local (rather than global) structural analysis, contextual constraints, and semantic aspects (e.g., informational assumptions applied in context). It is also reminiscent of a turn in Piaget's later theorizing (Piaget & Garcia, 1987/1991), where meaning or "semantic" considerations were reintroduced into formal models of cognition. These general parallels may reflect attempts to respond to similar concerns about context-specificity arising in the fields of cognitive and social cognitive development.

It is important to stress that, although I have been arguing for a "contextualization" of social and moral development, this view should not be seen as a return to a form of contextualism as a theoretical paradigm. It is still maintained that individuals *apply* their differentiated social concepts to situations, and there is therefore no reduction of social cognition to sociogenetic processes. And, though the types of theoretical constructs postulated (e.g., specific coordinations, informational assumptions) necessitate a more local analysis, it is nevertheless assumed that generalization of processes invoked to explain thought and judgment in one situation to other like situations will be possible (thus avoiding "dispersiveness"). The search for these processes, however, must be conducted with the sensitivity to context provided by a differentiated model of social-cognitive judgment and reasoning.

Judgments of psychological harm and civil liberties

In this section, this framework will be applied to interpret findings from research investigating two different moral concepts – psychological harm and civil liberties. The first study examined judgments of psychological harm, including use of information about intentions and consequences in moral evaluations, and the ability to coordinate this information with social-conventional meanings. The second study examined general concepts of freedom of speech and religion in adolescence and applications of these concepts in conflict with other issues including legal regulations, psychological and physical harm, and equality of opportunity. The third study looked at judgments of the rights of children and adults to freedom of speech and religion in the context of the family, the school, and society at large from early childhood through young adulthood.

An examination of the types of stimuli used in the domain differentiation studies discussed earlier reveals that two types of moral event are well represented: acts involving actual or potential physical harm and issues of fairness and rights. In contrast, moral events involving psychological harm are relatively poorly accounted for in the research corpus, represented by a mere four studies in the review by Turiel et al. (1987). The studies that have used as stimuli events of psychological harm provide some evidence that children conceptualize this concept in moral terms (Brendemeier, 1984; Nucci, 1986; Smetana, 1985; Smetana, Kelly, & Twentymen, 1984). Children reasoned about acts like hurting feelings, teasing, and ridiculing a physically handicapped person in accordance with the criteria defining the moral domain (however, Smetana et al. [1984] found that judgments about teasing became more universal and rule-noncontingent with age). Data from these studies are limited, however, in that either: (1) only one example of psychological harm was used in each study, or (2) psychological harm was grouped with other moral issues and not analyzed separately as a potentially contrasting category. This raises the question of whether psychological harm is conceptualized in a similar manner as other moral concepts.

Psychological harm differs from physical harm and issues of fairness in important ways. A major distinguishing feature of psychological harm concerns the role played by symbolic mediation. In psychological harm, the recipient or victim must interpret the action to experience the consequence (e.g., in a verbal insult). This is not true of other kinds of moral acts like physical harm, where the relationship between the act and its consequence is more direct, much like a "brute fact" (Searle, 1969). Even issues of fairness do not require that the victim interpret the act as a transgression for it to be possible to determine that unfairness has occurred (e.g., as when resources are distributed inequitably without the victim's awareness).[1] Psychologically harmful consequences, however, are entirely symbolically mediated through interpretations placed on actions by the recipient. This interpretation-bound feature of psychological harm has several implications. First, because interpretations can vary across individuals and social or cultural contexts, acts of psychological harm may show considerably greater context-dependence than acts of physical harm. Furthermore, psychological harm may uniquely vary by recipient's interpretation. Any act of psychological harm may be transformed into a nonharmful act, and vice versa, through corresponding changes in the recipient's interpretation (in contrast to acts of physical harm, which continue to have as components pain and damaging physical consequences despite shifts in how the act is interpreted by recipients).

These special features combine to suggest that psychological harm may interact with social-conventional systems and symbolic meanings in complex ways, posing certain problems for the development of moral judgments of these acts. In certain situations, social-conventional meanings may transform the moral nature of acts that otherwise might be seen as entailing a component of psychological harm. Social-conventional meanings here might include such things as institutional rules, cultural norms governing linguistic and symbolic communication, and rules and norms functioning in specialized contexts, such as children's games or peer group rituals. As an example of how the moral meaning of an act might be transformed through being embedded in a social-conventional meaning system, consider the academic practice of peer review. Individuals in academic settings may receive criticism – for example, from a publication review committee – that may result in a certain amount of psychological distress to the recipient. Many would not judge this event a moral transgression, since the intention of the evaluation (ideally) is not to inflict psychological discomfort, but to improve the general level of scholarship in the field and to provide "constructive criticism" of potential benefit to the recipient. An appreciation of these facts by the recipient may actually mitigate, or even eliminate, the ensuing negative psychological consequences.

The property of symbolic mediation may lead younger children to focus more on social-conventional meanings and ignore relevant moral features of acts like harmful intentions and consequences in their evaluations of certain kinds of psychological harm. Specifically, they may have problems disentangling moral features of psychologically harmful acts from social-conventional meanings when these are in conflict or tension. A context appropriate for examining these issues in school-age children is that of children's games. The game context has been defined and studied in other research (e.g., Dodsworth-Rugani, 1982; Lockhart, Abrahams, & Osherson 1977; Nucci, Turiel, & Encarnacion-Gawrych, 1983) as a social-conventional group activity with its own contextually defined rules, purposes, and goals. It is also a cooperative activity children regulate and conduct by themselves, relatively free from adult imposition (Piaget, 1932/1965). The current study (Helwig, Hildebrandt, & Turiel, 1994) investigated relations between social contexts of different types and moral judgments of intentions and consequences in children's understanding of acts of psychological and physical harm. The study focused on potential or actual moral transgressions occurring both within and outside conventional game contexts. The purpose was to determine how social-conventional meaning systems might (1) transform the moral meaning of individual acts, and (2) affect children's ability to disentangle and reason consistently about moral features of acts like intentions and harmful consequences of various types. Previous work on the role of intentions and consequences in moral judgment has shown that even young children are capable of utilizing moral intentions in making moral judgments (Farnill, 1974; Leon, 1980; Nelson, 1980; Surber, 1977; Yuill, 1984). However, this research did not place moral features of acts into conflict with contextually embedded meanings requiring children to coordinate moral and social-conventional components. It is possible that young children may have difficulty differentiating and coordinating these moral features (intentions, consequences) and nonmoral features (game rules, meanings, and procedures) in certain types of applications. The judgments of younger children may reflect confusions between the descriptive fact of psychological variation in response as a function of social context and evaluative or prescriptive orientation. That is, younger children's evaluations may tend to be more generally determined by social context rather than the particular moral features comprising specific acts. For example, younger children may show a tendency to view acts of psychological harm occurring in a game as legitimized by the game context, whereas the judgments of older children may reflect an attempt to differentiate and coordinate particular features of acts like intentions and consequences. Evidence for this hypothesis would take the form of older subjects' judgments showing more responsiveness to manipulations of moral features than the judgments of younger subjects, which, correspondingly, should be more determined by social-conventional meanings.

Subjects were 72 children evenly divided into three age groups – first grade (mean age 7;0 years), third grade (mean age 8;6 years), and fifth grade (mean age 10;9 years). Children were presented with a story narrative describing acts of actual or potential psychological harm (calling someone stupid) occurring in the context of a children's game called "smart-smart-stupid," a variant of the traditional duck-duck-goose tag-and-chase game. In this game, children are tagged and selected to participate by being tapped on the head and called "goose." The "smart-smart-stupid" substitution was used in order to provide a situation where an uninitiated player's feelings might be hurt. In the narrative, four story conditions systematically varying all possible combinations of intentions and consequences were presented. The conditions with positive intentions involved an agent who tags the recipient and says "stupid" in accordance with the game rules. In the positive consequence conditions, the recipient is familiar with the rules and is "happy to play the game." Negative consequences were introduced by having a child who is not familiar with the rules become upset and cry at being called stupid during the game. Negative intentions were introduced by having an agent deliberately try to make an uninitiated participant cry by selecting the recipient and calling him or her "stupid."

Two types of assessments were made. In the *act evaluations,* subjects were asked to evaluate the agent's action in each condition (e.g., Do you think it was *OK* or not *OK* for [agent] to tap [recipient] on the head and say stupid to him or her?). In the negative consequence conditions, subjects were also asked to evaluate the legitimacy of the recipient's emotional reactions (Do you think [recipient] should be upset that [agent] called him or her stupid in the game?). The purpose of these *legitimacy assessments* was to determine whether, in judging emotional reactions, subjects would focus on individual psychological factors such as the recipient's knowledge of the game rules, or general social contextual factors such as the conventionalized game purposes.

After all four story conditions were presented, a series of general questions was posed in order to compare children's reasoning about psychological and physical harm in and outside game contexts. Subjects were asked if it was OK or not OK to call someone stupid both in the context of the smart-smart-stupid game and outside the game context. This was to determine whether the game context could transform the meaning of an act that normally causes psychological harm outside this context. Subjects were also asked to evaluate a physical harm game in which participants push each other down in accordance with game rules. This was to determine whether game context could similarly transform the meaning of physically harmful acts. It was hypothesized that the psychological harm act would be more susceptible to contextual transformation on the basis of its symbolic mediation. Finally, subjects were asked to evaluate a "hurt feelings" game where the object was to hurt other players' feelings. This was to determine whether children could apply moral concepts of intentional harm in evaluating psychologically harmful game purposes and procedures.

Results indicated that, as expected, game context interacted differentially with acts of potential physical and psychological harm. Nearly all subjects (91%) considered it acceptable to call someone stupid in a game with rules that allow it. However, name calling that occurred outside the game was judged wrong by all but one subject. This shows that, under some circumstances, game rules or procedures can legitimize acts that normally would lead to psychological harm. This did not hold true for physical harm. All but one subject thought it would be wrong to push someone down even if it were part of the rules of a game, and all subjects negatively evaluated the physical harm game itself.

Not all acts of potential psychological harm were legitimized by game context, however. Whereas most children thought that it would be all right to play the "smart-smart-stupid" game, only 23% thought that it would be all right to play a game in which the object was to hurt other people's feelings intentionally. These results show that children were able to take into account information about moral intentions in evaluating games.

A second issue addressed in this study concerns developmental patterns in children's ability to distinguish moral features (intentions and consequences) and social conventional meanings like general game rules, purposes, and goals, in judgments of acts of psychological harm. The smart-smart-stupid game constitutes a situation where moral transgressions occur in the context of a social conventionally regulated and legitimated activity (a children's game). Although the general purposes of the game activity are nonmoral, the rule involving use of the word stupid in the selection of participants allows for the possibility of psychological harm. How would children reason about specific acts having moral components of harmful intentions and consequences occurring in the game context?

By examining patterns of responses across the four story conditions, it was possible to determine which moral features subjects were responding to in their act evaluations (e.g., intentions, consequences, or some combination of the two). A number of developmental patterns emerged. Responses that solely took into account the intentions of the transgressor tended to increase with age (only 5% of first-grade subjects showed this pattern, in contrast to 13% of third graders and 22% of fifth graders). In contrast, consequence-based responding tended to decrease with age (from 40% of first graders to only 9% of fifth graders). Interestingly, a large proportion (30%) of first graders failed to take into account *any* moral features at all, judging the act acceptable across all the story conditions. In justifying their responses they tended to focus on the game context or rules (e.g., "it's a game, so it's OK"). This pattern of response was given by only 4% to 5% of subjects in each of the older age groups. Analysis of justifications given across all story conditions revealed complementary results, with references to intentions increasing with age (from 13% of total at first grade to 36% at fifth grade) and references to the game context decreasing with age (from 29% of total at first grade, to 14% at fifth grade). These results indicate that younger children tended to focus more on the social-conventional game context in evaluating psychological harm, whereas older children more readily focus on moral features and, increasingly with age, the intentions of agents.

A similar tendency to base evaluations on the social-conventional game context is evident in first graders' evaluations of the legitimacy of negative emotional reactions experienced by recipients. In the positive intention-negative consequence condition, most of the third and fifth graders (100% and 83% respectively) thought that the recipient's reaction was appropriate, and their justifications focused on the recipient's lack of knowledge of game rules or procedures. The first graders, however, were split on this question: 52% thought that the recipient's reaction was appropriate, but 44% judged it inappropriate. Those who thought the recipient's reaction not appropriate tended to justify their responses with reference to the game context (e.g., the recipient should not be upset at being called stupid because it's a game). This age difference was even greater in the negative intention-negative consequence condition. Whereas 96% of third and fifth graders judged the recipient's reaction appropriate, only 39% of first graders did so. These results suggest that younger children exhibit a greater tendency to evaluate the legitimacy of psychological harm by reference to the social context, whereas older children place greater emphasis on the psychological perspective of the individual (the recipient's knowledge).

This study revealed a complex pattern of findings relating to the intersection of social context and moral reasoning. Judgments of physical harm were found to be largely independent of (game) context, in contrast to judgments of psychological harm. Even the youngest subjects in the study showed an understanding of the differential effect of social context on physical and psychological harm. Moreover, they were able to apply moral concepts like harmful intentions to evaluate psychologically harmful game rules or procedures, as suggested by the negative evaluations of the intentional psychological harm game found at all ages. The social-conventional game context does not "make right" all instances of psychological harm. However, when moral features of acts like intentions and consequences are in conflict with social-conventional goals, meanings, and purposes, younger children are more apt to focus on the social context, as the findings from both act evaluations and legitimacy assessments show. In these situations, younger children appear to have trouble disentangling moral features of specific acts from general social-conventional meaning systems.

The pattern of findings obtained supports the interpretation that problems in understanding embedded relations among concepts, rather than a global inability to differentiate moral and social-conventional concepts, underlie young children's difficulty in applying concepts of psychological harm in certain contexts. As findings from moral judgment research reviewed earlier suggest, young children (as young as 3 years of age in some cases) can use information about intentions in evaluating straightforward moral events. The findings from this study, however, suggest that young children's moral judgments shift to more "primitive" social-conventional or consequence-based orientations when presented with situations requiring coordination of moral features and social-conventional meanings. The traditional developmental progression from consequence to intention-based moral judgment appears to play itself out, though at older ages, in judgments of psychological harm in the game context. These findings highlight the importance of context in applications of moral judgments. Interrelations or coordinations of concepts (e.g., intentions and consequences) do not appear to follow a general pattern, but one determined by the specific features of concepts and their applications. In the current study, special properties of psychological harm (its interpretation-bound aspect) allowed psychological harm to interact in special ways with social-conventional meaning systems, making it difficult for young children to abstract out moral features like intentions and consequences in certain kinds of applications (though not in others). A more general implication of these findings may be that moral developmental patterns become recapitulated in specific applications as social cognition expands to include increasingly complex systems of embedded relations among social concepts of various types (cf. Werner & Kaplan's [1963] notion of "spiral development").

This idea may help explain certain seemingly paradoxical findings from research on civil liberties, which include basic rights like freedom of speech and religion. Sociologists and political scientists have conducted a number of surveys over several decades (beginning with Stouffer, 1955) of the general public's attitudes toward freedom of speech and religion and other rights. These surveys have consistently found that freedoms and rights are supported in some situations, but not others. For example, McClosky and Brill (1983) found high levels of support for freedom of speech when subjects were asked whether they would endorse statements put in general, abstract terms (e.g., "I believe in free speech for all no matter what their view might be"). However, when questions were posed with respect to particular situations ("A community should allow the American Nazi party to use its town hall to hold a public meeting"), substantially less support for freedoms and rights was obtained. For example, only 29% of respondents believed that members of the Nazi Party or Ku Klux Klan should be allowed to appear on public television to state their views, and a mere 14% thought that books showing terrorists how to build bombs should be available in the public library. Similar findings have been obtained in investigations of children's and adolescents' attitudes toward dissent (Zellman & Sears, 1971).

A common interpretation of these findings is that civil liberties and rights are held with little understanding or conviction among the general public (Prothro & Grigg, 1960; Sarat, 1975). This interpretation appears to be based on the assumption that concepts of civil liberties, if genuine, should constitute the only or primary determinant of moral judgment when issues of freedom are implicated. A different perspective (Helwig, 1995) is that civil liberties comprise only one aspect of moral judgment that can be coordinated with other aspects in contextualized situations. Accordingly, failure to endorse civil liberties in certain situations, especially those entailing conflicts between civil liberties and other moral concepts like harm and justice, would not by itself constitute direct evidence that concepts of civil liberties are absent or inadequately understood. Abstract or general concepts of civil liberties must be examined alongside their applications in coordination with other moral and social concepts in order to provide a full understanding of the role played by civil liberties in individuals' social reasoning, and in development. This may allow some of the paradoxes suggested by the findings of the survey research to be reconciled.

Helwig (1995) examined adolescents' and adults' conceptions of freedom of speech and religion. In this study, the judgments and reasoning of 7th and 11th graders and college undergraduates were investigated in general, in straightforward (nonconflictful) applications, and in conflict with other social and moral concepts, including legal regulations, psychological and physical harm, and equality of opportunity. The results of the study showed, first of all, that sophisticated conceptions of civil liberties emerge by adolescence and are used to evaluate social events. In their general reasoning, subjects at all ages used a diverse array of sophisticated rationales to justify why freedom of speech and freedom of religion were universal moral rights. For example, freedom of religion was seen as important for individual identity, autonomy, self-expression, and social functions such as the preservation and maintenance of group traditions deemed important. Freedom of speech was seen as important in assisting individuals in the pursuit of truth and knowledge (epistemological functions), as having social utility in contributing to the discovery of innovations facilitating social progress (a utilitarian or pragmatic function), and as a means by which moral and democratic principles are secured in political systems (e.g., by ensuring that the "will of the people" is expressed in a just political order). Subjects at all ages conceptualized freedom of speech and religion as moral or universal rights not defined by law and applying across national and cultural boundaries. It was judged wrong for governments to place general restrictions on these rights in the United States and in other countries. These abstract rights were also applied to judgments of social events including and especially in straightforward or unconflicted applications, and in some conflicts with other social and moral concepts as well.

A pattern similar to that found in the survey research (McClosky & Brill, 1983) emerged for the conflicts, in that civil liberties were often subordinated to other issues. These findings did not show anything like a general orientation, however, in that civil liberties were neither applied absolutely across situations nor always subordinated to conflicting concerns. In addition to conflicts with law, which will be discussed subsequently, the study examined conflicts between freedoms and other moral concepts like psychological and physical harm and equality. The specific issues examined were: speech containing racial slurs, speech advocating violence, speech advocating the exclusion of low-income individuals from membership in political parties, religious rituals involving physical or psychological harm, and religious proscriptions excluding low-income individuals from holding positions of authority or power in the church. Findings for these moral conflicts are given in Table 5.1, which shows the percentage of subjects judging that it would be wrong for the government to restrict freedom of speech and religion in the United States and other countries for each of the applications (in other words, those subjects who affirmed individuals' freedom to engage in the action). As can be seen from the table, civil liberties frequently were not affirmed when in conflict with other moral concepts. Several sources of variation in applications of civil liberties can be isolated. Situational or contextual variation is reflected in the different percentages of endorsement of civil liberties given in each type of conflict. Age-related or developmental variation was also found, as indicated by responses to the equality conflicts. The youngest subjects (seventh graders) were significantly more apt to subordinate civil liberties to issues of equality than were the older age groups. This was the only significant age difference found for the moral conflicts. Equality of opportunity appears to be an especially salient issue for younger adolescents,

Table 5.1. *Percentage of subjects giving freedom-affirming evaluations in conflict with other moral concepts*

Conflict type	7th grade		11th grade		College	
	Speech	Religion	Speech	Religion	Speech	Religion
Psychological harm						
United States	38	100	75	88	56	94
Other countries	33	88	69	88	56	93
Physical harm						
United States	19	44	56	62	50	38
Other countries	28	47	44	62	47	33
Equality						
United States	38	06	94	81	81	62
Other countries	50	08	87	81	80	60

Note: Percentage of subjects stating that governmental prohibition of act/practice would be wrong.
Source: Adapted from Helwig (1995).

warranting governmental intrusion into both religious spheres and public speech contexts to prevent discrimination or unfair treatment. A final source of variation reflects the heterogeneity found within age groups; civil liberties were subordinated to other moral concerns in ways that showed considerable individual differences, and there was no clear convergence toward a single pattern of response with age.

Additional developmental differences were found in applications of these rights in conflict with law. For example, 50% of seventh graders, in contrast to only a small minority of the older subjects (less than 25%, depending on age group and condition) maintained it would be wrong for individuals to violate laws restricting civil liberties, even when these laws were perceived to be unjust. Thus, although younger adolescents were able to use abstract rights concepts to evaluate laws and social systems that restrict basic freedoms, many of them nonetheless resorted to a purely legalistic perspective when considering the legitimacy of *acts* embedded within social systems held to be unjust. In contrast, older adolescents and adults tended to judge both legal restrictions on rights and acts violating restrictive laws from the perspective of abstract rights alone. This suggests a trend with age toward more integrated evaluations of legal systems and the acts embedded within those systems.

These results may have implications for moral developmental theory in general. Earlier it was noted that, in global-differentiation theories of moral judgment (e.g., Kohlberg, 1969, 1984), individuals have been found frequently to resort to legalistic ("law-and-order") reasoning to support judgments in moral dilemmas. Traditionally, this has been interpreted as a failure to differentiate morality from legal norms and social convention. However, in the present study (Helwig, 1995), at all ages abstract rights held independent of laws were used to evaluate legal systems across social contexts. This suggests that the ability to evaluate rules and social systems from a moral perspective actually *precedes* the ability to apply moral concepts consistently to social events containing conflictful moral and social conventional components. These findings appear to parallel those discussed earlier from the psychological harm study. There, young children (6-year-olds) were able to apply moral concepts to evaluate critically general rule systems (e.g., the intentional psychological harm game) but experienced difficulty in applying moral reasoning to specific acts embedded within these conventional systems. A general developmental pattern may be evident, where moral concepts of increasing abstraction and complexity are applied in straightforward situations and in evaluations of general rule systems before being applied in complex situations containing embedded relations among components from different social domains. Further research is needed on other types of moral-conventional coordinations to determine the generality of this developmental hypothesis.

In considering the flip side of the findings for civil liberties in conflict with law, it is striking that in the current study half the seventh-grade adolescents judged as permissible violations of laws restricting civil liberties. Justifications used by these subjects often mentioned the injustice of the law and the importance of civil disobedience in contributing to legal change. These findings provide a marked contrast with results of research on reasoning about rules reported by Tapp and Kohlberg (1971). These researchers asked subjects whether, in general, there were any circumstances in which a rule or law might be legitimately violated. Tapp and Kohlberg (1971) found that only a small minority (17%) of seventh-grade adolescents maintained that laws may be broken when viewed as unjust or in violation of moral principles such as individual rights. One explanation of the discrepancy between the findings of the current study and those of Tapp and Kohlberg (1971) is that judgments of the legitimacy of law violation may be specific to the concept or issue opposed to law. Young adolescents may recognize the independence of civil liberties and legal regulation more readily than they do for other moral concepts, in part as a function of their perception of civil liberties as rights "held against" authorities such as the state. Once again, this interpretation suggests that special features of moral concepts need to be considered in determining how these diverse concepts are coordinated with legal rules and conventional systems of regulation.

The research findings presented here are consistent with the proposition that social cognitive development is governed by age-related changes in local patterns of coordination among different social concepts, rather than global stages or general orientations. These may include increasingly sophisticated understandings of the embedded relations obtaining among concepts as they are applied in complex situations. The contextual variation and heterogeneity in social judgment shown in these findings is not well accounted for by global stage models.

Subsequent research (Helwig, 1993a), involving much younger subjects, has directly examined the role of social context in reasoning about freedom of speech and religion. In this study, reasoning about straightforward (i.e., nonconflicted) rights to freedom of speech and religion was assessed for three types of social context: the family, the institutional context of the school, and society at large. These contexts correspond approximately to systems of environmental structure outlined by Bronfenbrenner (1979, 1989), and can be seen as varying along a dimension from the more proximal (e.g., family) to distal (e.g., society). One issue of interest was whether concepts of abstract rights would develop first with respect to the limitations of governmental authority (the societal context) or in the more local contexts of particular social institutions, such as the family or school, with which the child is more directly familiar. The study also looked at the role of psychological agent (children vs. adults) in judgments of freedoms and rights. Controversy and disagreement abound regarding whether children should be seen as having the same "intellectual" rights as adults (Moshman, 1986; Wringe, 1981). Arguments for the restriction or curtailment of children's rights to freedom of expression and religion are often based on assumptions about the special characteristics of children as agents (e.g., their impressionability or capacity to assimilate information) or on the rights of parents or authorities to inculcate and transmit values held to be important (for a discussion of these issues in relation to adolescent rights, see Helwig, 1993b; Moshman, 1993). This is an area where psychological knowledge (e.g., concepts of persons) may be expected to impact moral judgment. Freedom of speech and religion may not be extended to young children if they are seen as lacking the requisite intellectual capacities for a mature exercise of these rights (cf. Weisstub, 1990).

Subjects were 184 children and adolescents in the first, third, fifth, and seventh grades. There was also an adult comparison sample of 24 college undergraduates. In each age group, half the subjects were given an interview pertaining to freedom of speech, while the other half were given freedom of religion (the only exception involved first graders, where 16 subjects received freedom of religion instead of the standard 24 subjects in each right/age grouping). For freedom of speech, the issue was authority prohibition of speech about rock music. For freedom of religion, the issue was authority prohibition of a hypothetical religious practice. Each example was presented in unharmful contexts; for example, the rock music in question did not contain violent or profane lyrics, and the specific religious practice involved recitation of a prayer as part of a normal religious ritual. Three conditions varying social contexts (societal, school, and family) were given, each containing two subconditions varying the agent whose rights were restricted (an adult vs. an 8-year-old child). Assessments were made of (1) the legitimacy of authority prohibition (is it OK or not OK for the authority to make a rule restricting the freedom?), (2) evaluation of the rule (is it a good or bad rule?), (3) universality (is it OK or not OK for authorities in another country to make a rule?), and (4) evaluation of rule violation (would it be OK or not OK for the agent to break the rule?).

Illustrative findings for judgments of the legitimacy of authority prohibition are found in Table 5.2. The table gives the percentage of subjects affirming freedoms in each of the conditions (i.e., the percentage of subjects stating that it would be wrong for the authority to make rules prohibiting

Table 5.2. *Judgments of children's and adults' rights to freedom of speech and religion in different social contexts*

Context	1st grade		3rd grade		5th grade		7th grade		College	
	Child	Adult	Child	Adult	Child	Adult	Child	Adult	Child	Adult
Freedom of speech										
Societal	58	62	79	79	83	96	100	100	100	100
School	58	58	79	92	79	92	83	96	92	100
Family	58	46	58	75	54	67	70	88	75	75
Freedom of religion										
Societal	81	75	88	92	96	96	96	96	100	100
School	56	75	88	96	92	88	96	100	92	100
Family	81	88	58	79	50	83	71	96	50	100

Note: Percentage of subjects stating it would be wrong for authority to make rule prohibiting freedom. For 1st grade, $N = 40$, for college undergraduates, $N = 24$, for all other age groups $N = 48$.

the freedom). Rudimentary conceptions of freedom of speech and religion appear to have emerged by 6 years of age. The majority of 6-year-olds (though only a slight majority for freedom of speech) affirmed freedoms for child and adult agents in most contexts, judging restrictions on freedom of speech and religion as wrong and outside the scope of governmental, school, and familial authority. An examination of justifications suggests that these early concepts are based on conceptions of human agency and personal choice (Nucci & Lee, 1993). Appeals for freedom were justified with reference to individual desires and wants and the prerogative of agents to act in accordance with their intentions, free from the interference of authorities.

In general, a trend toward increasing affirmation of freedoms with age is evident for most context–agent conditions. Interestingly, the relative abstractness or proximity of different contextual systems did not seem to have any affect on young children's rights concepts. The youngest subjects did not distinguish the different types of authority (governmental, school, or familial) – rights were asserted against these authorities in about the same proportions for child and adult agents. With age emerged a clear tendency to view restrictions on children's freedoms stemming from parental authority in the family as more legitimate than other types, especially for freedom of religion. Most striking, perhaps, are the low levels of affirmations of children's religious freedom in the family found in the adult comparison sample. Only 50% of the adults believed it wrong for parents to make rules restricting the religious freedom of 8-year-old children. The justifications given by adults who failed to affirm children's religious freedom frequently made reference to the inability of 8-year-olds to make informed decisions about religious membership, and the prerogative of parents to raise or socialize their children as they wish. This contrasts with the reasoning of adults who affirmed children's rights to religious freedom. These adults clearly regarded children as intellectually equipped to make such choices, viewing parental intrusion in this matter as excessive and potentially damaging. These results are consistent with studies of judgments of "personal issues" (see Smetana, Chapter 7, this volume, for an overview) showing substantial discrepancies between adults', adolescents', and children's conceptions of the personal autonomy of preadult agents in family settings. As the current study suggests, these discrepancies may be attributed, in part, to age-related variations in beliefs about the psychological characteristics of nonadult agents, an issue requiring further research.

The findings of this study point to the perhaps surprising conclusion that contextual variation in the application of concepts of freedom and rights may actually *increase* with age, at least for the issues studied here.

A greater awareness of the special characteristics of different social contexts – for example, the particular rights and obligations holding among children and adults in the familial context – as well as differences in the psychological characteristics of child and adult agents, leads to the emergence in development of more contextually sensitive applications of rights. Considerable variation appears to exist in adults' conceptions of children's intellectual capacities, a fact of importance for decisions about children's rights (Helwig, 1993b; Moshman, 1993). These findings reiterate the importance of considering "factual assumptions" from other domains, such as psychological knowledge, in determining how moral concepts like rights and freedoms are applied to concrete situations. Isolating and accounting for the relative contribution of these factors will prove an essential methodological strategy in helping to explain the manifest contextual variation in moral reasoning encountered across the age span.

Conclusions

The focus of this chapter has been on the role of social context in moral development. Earlier, the limitations of prevailing theories of social content in social cognition were discussed. It was argued that contextualist approaches do not provide clear criteria for bounding social contexts, and as a result may be susceptible to problems of dispersiveness and relativism. At the opposite pole, global stage theories attempt to encompass all social contexts within a single "structured whole," and in the process fail to adequately accommodate contextual variation in their structural models. One ramification of this was that global stage theories appear to be insufficiently "structural" in dealing with task or content variation. They dismiss context in part because they do not have a sufficiently powerful means of differentiating social contexts, to determine how different situations function *social-cognitively.* Contextual variables are treated as stimulus features that "pull for" or provide "resistances" to general stages of social reasoning, and not as important elements of cognitive structures in their own right.

The model of social cognition presented here focuses on how social context is represented in individuals' social cognition. It was argued that understanding how morality is applied in context requires systematic efforts to disentangle the types of concepts (moral, social organizational, and psychological) instantiated in different situations and judgments, the role played by these concepts (as informational assumptions, as evaluations) and the implicit contracts, definitions of situations, and meanings that may operate in diverse settings to influence individuals' social reasoning. The primary developmental focus will therefore be on providing a description and explanation of how individuals distinguish and coordinate the different aspects of the multifaceted contexts experienced in development. A local-structural developmental analysis was proposed, focusing on the development of specific coordinations of delimited social and moral concepts and their applications to diverse social settings. This requires attention to the special properties or features of different types of moral concepts. For example, in the research presented on psychological harm, it was shown how the symbolic or interpretation-bound nature of psychological harm enables this concept to interact with social context in different ways than other moral concepts, like physical harm. The research showed that certain types of conceptual coordinations, namely those involving conflicts between psychological harm and social-conventional meaning systems, can be especially difficult for young children and may contribute to the apparent developmental "regression" found in moral judgments of these situations.

The findings from research on adults' and adolescent's judgments of civil liberties show that rights like freedom of speech and religion are coordinated with different concepts in different ways, exhibiting situational variation and individual differences. The extensive variability in judgment and reasoning obtained in this study did not, however, prevent specific developmental patterns from being isolated. There were clear, age-related patterns in coordinations of rights with law and equality of opportunity. These developmental patterns could only emerge with a more local, contextually sensitive analysis of judgments and reasoning, and would have been lost had a global-structural perspective been taken.

Applications of the freedom of speech and religion rights of adult and child agents to social contexts like the family, school, and society at large showed both general and specific patterns. Developmentally, rights tended to be applied in greater percentages with increasing age, with the exception of the family context, where a large proportion of adult subjects did not extend these rights to children. This appeared to be based, in part, on an understanding of this context as entailing a different set of relationships among the obligations and rights of children versus adults, perhaps implying the operation of an "implicit contract" (Thorkildsen, 1989) setting the family apart from other social contexts. Different psychological assumptions about children's capacity to exercise their rights and freedoms also served to distinguish how these rights were applied to adult and child agents. The picture emerging from these findings is one of important, though nonrandom and interpretable, variation in the application of freedoms and rights in context.

The view of social context and moral development presented here has attempted to chart a middle ground between global stage theory and recently emerging contextualist perspectives. In my view, the role of social context in social cognition can be adequately addressed neither through abstract, decontextualized global structures of reasoning, nor by a narrow contextualism that essentially equates individuals with their environments. In between these two extremes may be a local-structural analysis of development that maintains important distinctions between individuals and environments, between structural and functional processes, and between the types of social concepts and their applications in everyday life. It is hoped that, in this way, an integration of structural and contextual perspectives on social cognitive development, often thought of as contradictory, may yet prove possible.

Note

1. This, of course, is not to deny that interpretation is involved in fairness judgments as well. As the research by Thorkildsen (1989) and others (e.g., Sigelman & Waitzman, 1991) has shown, definitions of situations do have a bearing on individuals' judgments of fairness. The point is that, for issues of fairness, the interpretation of the victim is not the *sole* determinant of the harmful consequence, as in psychological harm. It may be possible, for example, for individuals to be harmed or adversely affected by situations of extreme competition, even when competition constitutes the "implicit contract" accepted by participants. The fundamental difference is that fairness pertains to systems of reciprocity, exchange, and distribution of goods, which may have an "objective" component, while psychological harm pertains to acts of symbolic communication.

References

Anderson, N. H., & Butzin, C. A. (1978). Integration theory applied to children's judgments of equity. *Developmental Psychology, 14,* 593–606.

Asch, S. (1952). *Social psychology.* Englewood Cliffs, NJ: Prentice-Hall.

Beilin, H. (1983). The new functionalism and Piaget's program. In E. K. Scholnick (Ed.), *New trends in conceptual representation: Challenges to Piaget's theory?* (pp. 3–40). Hillsdale, NJ: Lawrence Erlbaum.

Beilin, H. (1987). Current trends in cognitive development research: Towards a new synthesis. In B. Inhelder, D. deCaprona, and A. Cornu-Wells (Eds.), *Piaget Today* (pp. 37–64). Hillsdale, NJ: Lawrence Erlbaum.

Brendemeier, B. J. (1984). *Moral reasoning and the perceived legitimacy of intentionally injurious sports acts.* Unpublished manuscript, University of California, Berkeley.

Bronfenbrenner, U. (1979). *The ecology of human development: Experiments by nature and design.* Cambridge, MA: Harvard University Press.

Bronfenbrenner, U. (1989). Ecological systems theory. In R. Vasta (Ed.), *Annals of child development* (Vol. 6, pp. 187–251). Greenwich, CT: JAI Press.

Bronfenbrenner, U. (1993). The ecology of cognitive development: Research models and fugitive findings. In R. H. Wozniak & K. W. Fischer (Eds.), *Development in context: Acting and thinking in specific environments* (pp. 3–44). Hillsdale, NJ: Lawrence Erlbaum.

Bronfenbrenner, U., & Crouter, A. C. (1983). The evolution of environmental models in developmental research. In P. H. Mussen (Series Ed.) & W. Kessen (Vol. Ed.), *Handbook of child psychology: Vol. 1. History, theory, and methods* (pp. 357–414). New York: Wiley.

Chapman, M. (1988). *Constructive evolution: Origins and development of Piaget's thought.* Cambridge: Cambridge University Press.

Cohen, R., & Siegel, A. W. (1991). A context for context: Toward an analysis of context and development. In R. Cohen & A. W. Siegel (Eds.), *Context and development* (pp. 3–23). Hillsdale, NJ: Lawrence Erlbaum.

Colby, A., & Kohlberg, L. (1987). *The measurement of moral judgment* (Vols. 1–2). Cambridge: Cambridge University Press.

Cole, M. (1985). The zone of proximal development: Where culture and cognition create each other. In J. V. Wertsch (Ed.), *Culture, communication, and cognition: Vygotskian perspectives* (pp. 146–161). Cambridge: Cambridge University Press.

Damon, W. (1975). Early conceptions of positive justice as related to the development of logical operations. *Child Development, 46,* 301–312.

Damon, W. (1977). *The social world of the child.* San Francisco: Jossey-Bass.

Damon, W. (1980). Patterns of change in children's social reasoning: A two-year longitudinal study. *Child Development, 51,* 1010–1017.

Davidson, P. (1992). The role of social interaction in cognitive development: A propaedeutic. In L. T. Winegar & J. Valsiner (Eds.), *Children's development within social context* (Vol. 1, pp. 19–37). Hillsdale, NJ: Lawrence Erlbaum.

Dodsworth-Rugani, K. J. (1982). *The development of concepts of social structure and their relationship to school rules and authority.* Unpublished doctoral dissertation, University of California, Berkeley.

Duncan, B. (1986). *The coordination of moral and social-conventional knowledge: A developmental analysis of children's understanding of multifaceted situations.* Unpublished doctoral dissertation, University of California, Berkeley.

Dworkin, R. (1977). *Taking rights seriously.* Cambridge, MA: Harvard University Press.

Enright, R. D., Bjerstedt, A., Enright, W. F., Levy, V. M., Jr., Lapsley, D. K., Buss, R. R., Harwell, M., & Zindler, M. (1984). Distributive justice development: Cross-cultural, contextual, and longitudinal evaluations. *Child Development, 55,* 1737–1751.

Farnill, D. (1974). The effects of social-judgment set on children's use of intent information. *Journal of Personality, 42,* 276–289.

Fischer, K. W. (1983). Illuminating the processes of moral development. In A. Colby, L. Kohlberg, J. Gibbs, and M. Lieberman. *Monographs of the Society for Research in Child Development, 48* (1–2, Serial No. 200). Chicago: University of Chicago Press.

Gergen, K. J. (1985). The social constructionist movement in modern psychology. *American Psychologist, 40,* 266–275.

Gilligan, C., & Belenky, M. F. (1980). A naturalistic study of abortion decisions. *New Directions for Child Development, 7,* 69–90.

Grueneich, R. (1982). The development of children's integration rules for making moral judgments. *Child Development, 53,* 887–894.

Helwig, C. C. (1993a, March). *The role of social context and agent in the development of abstract rights concepts.* Paper presented at the biennial meeting of the Society for Research in Child Development, New Orleans.

Helwig, C. C. (1993b). Commentary on Moshman's "Adolescent reasoning and adolescent rights." *Human Development, 36*(1), 41–44.

Helwig, C. C. (1995). Adolescents' and young adults' conceptions of civil liberties: Freedom of speech and religion. *Child Development, 66,* 152–166.

Helwig, C. C., Hildebrandt, C., & Turiel, E. (in press). Children's judgments about psychological harm in social context. *Child Development.*

Helwig, C. C., Tisak, M., & Turiel, E. (1990). Children's social reasoning in context. *Child Development, 61,* 2068–2078.

Hoffman, M. (19183). Empathy, guilt, and social cognition. In W. F. Overton (Ed.), *The relationship between social and cognitive development* (pp. 1–51). Hillsdale, NJ: Lawrence Erlbaum.

Inhelder, B., & Piaget, J. (1959/1969). *The early growth of logic in the child* (E. A. Lunzer & D. Papert, Trans.). New York: Norton.

Jancaterino, W. (1982). *The relationship between children's understanding of social influence and their moral evaluations of harm.* Unpublished doctoral dissertation, University of California, Santa Cruz.

Kahn, P. (1993, March). *A culturally sensitive analysis of culture in the context of context: When is enough enough?* Paper presented at the biennial meeting of the Society for Research on Child Development, New Orleans.

Killen, M. (1989). Context, conflict, and coordination in social development. In L. T. Winegar (Ed.), *Social interaction and the development of children's understanding* (pp. 119–146). Norwood, NJ: Ablex.

Killen, M. (1990). Children's evaluations of morality in the context of peer, teacher–child, and familial relations. *Journal of Genetic Psychology, 151,* 395–410.

Killen, M. (1991). Social and moral development in early childhood. In W. M. Kurtines & J. L. Gewirtz (Ed.), *Handbook of moral behavior and development* (Vol. 2, pp. 115–138). Hillsdale, NJ: Lawrence Erlbaum.

Kohlberg, L. (1969). Stage and sequence: The cognitive-developmental approach to socialization. In D. A. Goslin (Ed.), *Handbook of socialization theory and research* (pp. 347–480). Chicago: Rand McNally.

Kohlberg, L. (1971). From is to ought: How to commit the naturalistic fallacy and get away with it in the study of moral development. In T. Mischel (Ed.), *Psychology and genetic epistemology* (pp. 151–235). New York: Academic Press.

Kohlberg, L. (1984). *Essays on moral development: Vol. 2. The psychology of moral development.* San Francisco: Harper and Row.

Kohlberg, L., Levine, C., & Hewer, A. (1983). *Moral stages: A current formulation and a response to critics.* Basel, Switzerland: Karger.

Krebs, D. L., Vermeulen, S. C. A., Carpendale, J. I., & Denton, K. (1991). Structural and situational influences on moral judgment: The interaction between stage and dilemma. In W. M. Kurtines & J. L. Gewirtz (Eds.), *Handbook of moral behavior and development* (Vol. 2, pp. 139–169). Hillsdale, NJ: Lawrence Erlbaum.

Lautrey, J. (1993). Structure and variability: A plea for a pluralistic approach to cognitive development. In R. Case & W. Edelstein (Eds.), *The new structuralism in cognitive development: Theory and research on individual pathways* (Contributions to Human Development, Vol. 23, pp. 101–114). Basil, Switzerland: Karger.

Leming, J. (1978). Intrapersonal variations in stage of moral reasoning among adolescents as a function of situational contexts. *Journal of Youth and Adolescence, 7,* 405–416.

Leon, M. (1980). Coordination of intent and consequence information in children's moral judgment. In F. Wilkening, J. Becker, & T. Trabasso (Eds.), *Information integration by children* (pp. 71–112). Hillsdale, NJ: Lawrence Erlbaum.

Lerner, R. M., & Lerner, J. V. (1989). Organismic and social contextual bases of development: The sample case of adolescence. In W. Damon (Ed.), *Child development today and tomorrow* (pp. 69–85). San Francisco: Jossey-Bass.

Linn, R. (1987). Moral reasoning and behavior of striking physicians in Israel. *Psychological Reports, 60,* 443–453.

Lockhart, K. L., Abrahams, B., & Osherson, D. N. (1977). Children's understanding of uniformity in the environment. *Child Development, 48,* 1521–1531.

McClosky, H., & Brill, A. (1983). *Dimensions of tolerance: What Americans believe about civil liberties.* New York: Oxford University Press.

Moshman, D. (1986). Children's intellectual rights: A First Amendment analysis. In D. Moshman (Ed.), *New Directions in Child Development, 33,* 25–38.

Moshman, D. (1993). Adolescent reasoning and adolescent rights. *Human Development, 36*(1), 27–40.

Much, N., & Shweder, R. A. (1978). Speaking of rules: The analysis of culture in the breach. In W. Damon (Ed.), *New Directions in Child Development, 2,* 19–39.

Nelson, S. A. (1980). Factors influencing young children's use of motives and outcomes as moral criteria. *Child Development, 51,* 823–829.

Nucci, L. P. (1986). Children's conceptions of morality, social conventions, and religious prescription. In C. Harding (Ed.), *Moral dilemmas: Philosophical and psychological reconsiderations of the development of moral reasoning* (pp. 137–174). Chicago: Precedent Press.

Nucci, L. P., & Lee, J. (1993). Morality and personal autonomy. In G. Noam & T. Wren (Eds.), *Morality and the self* (pp. 123–148). Cambridge, MA: MIT Press.

Nucci, L. P., & Nucci, M. S. (1982a). Children's social interactions in the context of moral and conventional transgressions. *Child Development, 53,* 403–412.

Nucci, L. P., & Nucci, M. S. (1982b). Children's responses to moral and social conventional transgressions in free-play settings. *Child Development, 53,* 1337–1342.

Nucci, L. P., & Turiel, E. (1978). Social interactions and the development of social concepts in preschool children. *Child Development, 49,* 400–407.

Nucci, L. P., Turiel, E., & Encarnacion-Gawrych, G. E. (1983). Children's social interactions and social concepts: Analyses of morality and convention in the Virgin Islands. *Journal of Cross-Cultural Psychology, 4,* 469–487.

Nummedal, S. G., & Bass, S. C. (1976). Effects of the salience of intention and consequence on children's moral judgments. *Developmental Psychology, 12,* 475–476.

Overton, W. F. (1984). World views and their influence on psychological theory and research: Kuhn-Lakatos-Laudan. In H. W. Reese (Ed.), *Advances in child development and behavior* (Vol. 18, pp. 191–226). New York: Academic Press.

Overton, W. F. (1994). Contexts of meaning: The computational and the embodied mind. In W. F. Overton & D. S. Palermo (Eds.), *The nature and ontogenesis of meaning* (pp. 1–18). Hillsdale, NJ: Lawrence Erlbaum.

Overton, W. F., & Reese, H. W. (1973). Models of development: Methodological implications. In J. R. Nesselroade & H. W. Reese (Eds.), *Life-span developmental psychology: Methodological issues* (pp. 65–86). New York: Academic Press.

Packer, M. (1992). Toward a postmodern psychology of moral action and moral development. In W. M. Kurtines, M. Azmitia, & J. L. Gewirtz (Eds.), *The role of values in psychology and human development* (pp. 30–59). New York: Wiley.

Packer, M., & Scott, B. (1992). The hermeneutic investigation of peer relations. In L. T. Winegar & J. Valsiner (Eds.), *Children's development within social context: Vol. 2. Research and methodology* (pp. 75–111). Hillsdale, NJ: Lawrence Erlbaum.

Pepper, S. (1942). *World hypotheses.* Berkeley: University of California Press.

Piaget, J. (1947/1960). *The psychology of intelligence* (M. Piercy & D. E. Berlyne, Trans.). Patterson, NJ: Littlefield, Adams.

Piaget, J. (1932/1965). *The moral judgment of the child* (M. Gabain, Trans.). New York: Free Press.

Piaget, J. (1963/1968). Explanation in psychology and psychophysiological parallelism. In P. Fraisse & J. Piaget (Eds.), *Experimental psychology: Its scope and method: Vol. 1. History and Method* (pp. 153–191). (J. Chambers, Trans.). London: Routledge and Kegan Paul.

Piaget, J. (1968/1970). *Structuralism* (C. Maschler, Trans.). New York: Harper and Row.

Piaget, J. (1971). The theory of stages and cognitive development. In D. R. Green, M. P. Ford, & B. George (Eds.), *Measurement and Piaget* (pp. 1–11). New York: McGraw-Hill.

Piaget, J. (1926/1975). *The child's conception of the world* (J. Thomlinson & A. Tomlinson, Trans.). Totowa, NJ: Littlefield, Adams.

Piaget, J., & Garcia, R. (1987/1991). *Toward a logic of meanings* (D. de Caprona & P. M. Davidson, Trans.). Hillsdale, NJ: Lawrence Erlbaum.

Prothro, J. W., & Grigg, C. M. (1960). Fundamental principles of democracy: Bases of agreement and disagreement. *Journal of Politics, 22,* 276–294.

Reese, H. W., & Overton, W. F. (1970). Models of development and theories of development. In L. R. Goulet & P. B. Bates (Eds.), *Life-span developmental psychology: Research and theory* (pp. 115–145). New York: Academic Press.

Rogoff, B. (1990). *Apprenticeship in thinking: Cognitive development in sociocultural activity.* New York: Oxford University Press.

Rogoff, B. (1993). Children's guided participation and participatory appropriation in sociocultural activity. In R. H. Wozniak & K. W. Fischer (Eds.), *Development in context: Thinking and acting in specific environments* (pp. 121–153). Hillsdale, NJ: Lawrence Erlbaum.

Saltzstein, H. D. (1983). Critical issues in Kohlberg's theory of moral reasoning. In A. Colby, L. Kohlberg, J. Gibbs, and M. Lieberman. *Monographs of the Society for Research in Child Development, 48* (1–2, Serial No. 200). Chicago: University of Chicago Press.

Sarat, A. (1975). Reasoning in politics: The social, political, and psychological bases of principled thought. *American Journal of Political Science, 19,* 247–261.

Scribner, S. (1977). Modes of thinking and ways of speaking: Culture and logic reconsidered. In P. N. Johnson-Laird & P. C. Wason (Eds.), *Thinking: Readings in cognitive science* (pp. 483–500). Cambridge: Cambridge University Press.

Searle, J. (1969). *Speech acts.* Cambridge: Cambridge University Press.

Serafica, F. C. (Ed.). (1982). *Social cognitive development in context.* New York: Guilford Press.

Sharfstein, B. (1989). *The dilemma of context.* New York: New York University Press.

Shweder, R. A. (1986). Divergent rationalities. In D. W. Fiske & R. A. Shweder (Eds.), *Metatheory in social science: Pluralism and subjectivities* (pp. 163–196). Chicago: University of Chicago Press.

Shweder, R. A., Mahapatra, M., & Miller, J. G. (1987). Culture and moral development. In J. Kagan & S. Lamb (Eds.), *The emergence of morality in young children* (pp. 1–83). Chicago: University of Chicago Press.

Shweder, R. A., & Miller, J. G. (1985). The social construction of the person: How is it possible? In K. Gergen & K. Davis (Eds.), *The social construction of the person* (pp. 41–69). New York: Springer-Verlag.

Siegel, R., & Cohen, A. W. (1991). Why a house is not a home: Constructing contexts for development. In R. Cohen & A. W. Siegel (Eds.), *Context and development* (pp. 305–316). Hillsdale, NJ: Lawrence Erlbaum.

Sigelman, C. K., & Waitzman, K. A. (1991). The development of distributive justice orientations: Contextual influences on children's resource allocations. *Child Development, 62,* 1367–1378.

Smetana, J. G. (1981). Preschool children's conceptions of moral and social rules. *Child Development, 52,* 1333–1336.

Smetana, J. G. (1984). Toddlers' social interactions regarding moral and conventional transgressions. *Child Development, 55,* 1767–1776.

Smetana, J. G. (1985). Preschool children's conceptions of transgressions: Effects of varying moral and conventional domain-related attributes. *Developmental Psychology, 21,* 715–24.

Smetana, J. G. (1989). Toddler's social interactions in the context of moral and conventional transgressions in the home. *Developmental Psychology, 25,* 499–508.

Smetana, J. G., & Braeges, J. L. (1990). The development of toddlers' moral and conventional judgments. *Merrill-Palmer Quarterly, 36*(3), 329–346.

Smetana, J. G., Kelly, M., & Twentymen, C. T. (1984). Abused, neglected and nonmaltreated children's conceptions of moral and social-conventional transgressions. *Child Development, 55,* 277–287.

Sobesky, W. E. (1983). The effects of situational factors on moral judgments. *Child Development, 54,* 575–584.

Spiro, M. E. (1986). Cultural relativism and the future of anthropology. *Cultural Anthropology, 1,* 259–286.

Stouffer, S. (1955). *Communism, conformity and civil liberties.* New York: Doubleday.

Surber, C. F. (1977). Developmental processes in social inference: Averaging of intentions and consequences in moral judgment. *Developmental Psychology, 13,* 654–665.

Tapp, J., & Kohlberg, L. (1971). Developing senses of law and legal justice. *Journal of Social Issues, 27,* 65–92.

Tappan, M. (1992). Texts and contexts: Language, culture, and the development of moral functioning. In L. T. Winegar & J. Valsiner (Eds.), *Children's development within social context: Vol. 1. Metatheory and theory* (pp. 93–117). Hillsdale, NJ: Lawrence Erlbaum.

Thorkildsen, T. A. (1989). Pluralism in children's reasoning about social justice. *Child Development, 60,* 965–972.

Turiel, E. (1979). Distinct conceptual and developmental domains: Social convention and morality. In C. B. Keasey (Ed.), *Nebraska Symposium on Motivation, 1977: Vol. 25. Social Cognitive Development* (pp. 77–115). Lincoln: University of Nebraska Press.

Turiel, E. (1983). *The development of social knowledge: Morality and convention.* Cambridge: Cambridge University Press.

Turiel, E. (1989). The social construction of social construction. In W. Damon (Ed.), *Child development today and tomorrow* (pp. 86–106). San Francisco: Jossey-Bass.

Turiel, E., & Davidson, P. (1986). Heterogeneity, inconsistency, and asynchrony in the development of cognitive structures. In I. Levin (Ed.), *Stage and structure: Reopening the debate* (pp. 106–143). Norwood, NJ: Ablex.

Turiel, E., Hildebrandt, C., & Wainryb, C. (1991). Judging social issues: Difficulties, inconsistencies and consistencies. *Monographs of the Society for Research in Child Development, 56* (2, Serial No. 224).

Turiel, E., Killen, M., & Helwig, C. C. (1987). Morality: Its structure, functions and vagaries. In J. Kagan & S. Lamb (Eds.), *The emergence of morality in young children* (pp. 155–243). Chicago: University of Chicago Press.

Turiel, E., Smetana, J. G., & Killen, M. (1991). Social contexts in social cognitive development. In W. M. Kurtines & J. L. Gewirtz (Eds.), *Handbook of moral behavior and development* (Vol. 2, pp. 307–332). Hillsdale, NJ: Lawrence Erlbaum.

Wainryb, C. (1991). Understanding differences in moral judgments: The role of informational assumptions. *Child Development, 62,* 840–851.

Weisstub, D. N. (1990). *Enquiry into mental competency: Final report.* Toronto: Queen's Printer for Ontario.

Werner, H., & Kaplan, B. (1963). *Symbol formation.* New York: Wiley.

Wertsch, J. V. (1985). *Vygotsky and the social formation of mind.* Cambridge, MA: Harvard University Press.

Winegar, L. T. & Valsiner, J. (Eds.). (1992). *Children's development within social context* (Vols. 1–2). Hillsdale, NJ: Lawrence Erlbaum.

Wozniak, R. H., & Fischer, K. W. (Eds.). (1993). *Development in context: Acting and thinking in specific environments.* Hillsdale, NJ: Lawrence Erlbaum.

Wringe, C. A. (1981). *Children's rights: A philosophical study.* London: Routledge and Kegan Paul.

Yuill, N. (1984). Young children's coordination of motive and outcome in judgments of satisfaction and morality. *British Journal of Developmental Psychology, 2,* 73–81.

Zellman, G. L., & Sears, D. O. (1971). Childhood origins of tolerance for dissent. *Journal of Social Issues, 27,* 109–136.

6 Psychological and philosophical considerations of prudence and morality

Marvin W. Berkowitz, Jeffrey P. Kahn, Gregg Mulry, and Jeanne Piette

Self-harm is a pressing social issue, especially in adolescence. The most obvious form, suicide, has become the second leading cause of death among adolescents (Cole, 1991). Risk taking in general has become an issue of dire importance to mental health professionals and others concerned with the welfare of adolescents (Dryfoos, 1990; Levitt, Selman, & Richmond, 1991; National Research Council, 1993). Such risk-taking behaviors include substance use (including driving motor vehicles while under the influence of drugs or alcohol), unprotected sex, and use of firearms. One in fifty adolescents has used a weapon at least twice in the past year (Benson, 1993). Less than 50% of adolescents report using a condom at their last time of intercourse (Healthy People 2000, 1990). Twelve percent smoke cigarettes daily and 11 percent drink alcohol frequently (Benson, 1993). Furthermore, even those adolescents who do not directly engage in risky behaviors may nonetheless be negatively affected by those who do. According to a recent report by the Office of the Inspector General (Kusserow, 1992), one-third of youths in long-term penal institutions were under the influence of alcohol at the time of their offenses, nearly one-half of college student crime victims had used drugs or alcohol before the crime occurred, over half of perpetrators and of victims of sexual assault were under the influence of alcohol at the time of the assault, and use of substances is related to earlier onset of sexual behavior and inadequate use of contraceptives. Furthermore, one-third of 12th graders have driven a car after drinking at least twice in the past year, and even 5% of 9th graders have done likewise (Benson, 1993).

Lay analyses of adolescent risk taking usually focus on adolescents'

A portion of this work was funded by a grant from the National Institute on Drug Abuse: Grant Number 5 RO1 DA06331-03.

201

assumed sense of personal invulnerability or immunity and lack of appropriate parental concern and socialization. Other oft-noted factors are cultural
values, poverty, and an inadequate juvenile justice system. Although these
causes are often assumed to be at the root of the problem – even by psychologists (e.g., Elkind, 1974) – they typically either are inaccurate stereotypes
(Quadrel, Fischoff, & Davis, 1993) or account for only a small proportion of
the root causes.

Two critical issues that have been largely ignored in the psychological
literature will be addressed in this chapter. The first issue concerns the moral
nature of self-harm. At least in our culture, self-harm seems to occupy an
unusual prescriptive status. On the one hand, it is considered morally wrong.
That is, one who engages in self-harm acts in a way that ought to be avoided.
On the other hand, it is also often argued that self-harm should not be
subject to social control. That is, society, either formally through legislation
or informally through social sanctioning, should not intervene and has *no
right* to intervene in the way individuals treat themselves. Rather, it is entirely a matter of the actor's prerogative. Examination of legislation regarding drug use gives a sense of the context in which individuals conceptualize
the risk-taking behavior of drug use. Although the use of certain drugs has
been prohibited since 1914, debate about whether the government should
criminalize the use of these drugs continues. Brenner (1992), for example,
suggests that there is an inconsistency in legislating against the use of marijuana while allowing the use of alcohol and nicotine, arguing that the
chances of self-harm are greater for use of alcohol and nicotine than they are
for the use of illegal drugs. Furthermore, Kaplan (1971) notes that secondary
harm to others or to society in general is required to justify laws forbidding
drug use or other types of self-harm. Although it seems that the government
is clear in its intent to prohibit and prevent the use of drugs, it is not apparent
that prohibition is legislated on the basis of preventing self-harm; instead,
drug laws are formulated on the basis of a consideration of the welfare of
others in society and of society in general. So, the moral and legal status of
self-harm in legislation is unclear. Is it morally wrong or an individual's
right? Should society have a say in controlling self-harmful behaviors
whether self-harm is moral or not?

The second central issue to be addressed here is the adolescent's perspective on self-harm – that is, how does the adolescent understand it and how
does he or she evaluate it? Killen, Leviton, and Cahill (1991) raised this
issue in arguing that

Adolescents' lack of knowledge about drugs may be due to the way in which
information about drugs is communicated to adolescents: Such information may be
conveyed in developmentally inappropriate ways. For example, if adolescents con-

sider self-harm to be a personal issue and drug programs do not emphasize the extent to which drug use causes harm to others, then adolescents may not agree with the message that drug use is wrong, as in their view it is a personal issue, one that does not affect others. (p. 337)

Kegan (1994) argues that the failure of many programs aimed at reducing the prevalence of unsafe sexual behaviors in adolescence is directly a product of the failure to understand how adolescents understand sexuality. As these authors suggest, it is of critical importance to understand how adolescents understand self-harm, especially the criteria used to determine its prescriptivity.

In order to address the first issue of the moral status of self-harm, we will examine, first, what psychological theory has to say about the moral status of self-harm and, second, how philosophical ethics views the moral status of self-harm. Finally, in order to address the second issue of adolescents' perspectives on the morality of self-harm, we will explore the empirical literature on adolescent conceptions of drug and alcohol behavior.

Psychological theory and the moral nature of self-harm

Self-harm, from a psychological standpoint, has been largely treated as a clinical issue. Typically, self-harmful behaviors have been discussed from the standpoint of psychotherapeutic practice. Clinicians are predominantly concerned about how to treat a self-harmful or potentially self-harmful patient – for example, how does a therapist respond to suicidal ideation? Any ethical concerns raised are from the point of view of the professional. Such concerns include what ethical obligation a psychotherapist may have to prevent client self-harm or to inform the client's significant others. Little attention has been paid to how the potentially self-harmful individual may evaluate the ethical nature of the self-harmful behavior. If one assumes that how the client makes meaning (including *moral* meaning) of the self-harming behavior affects the ultimate behavior, then this omission can be understood as quite significant.

Recently, however, this issue has come under some scrutiny by developmental psychologists. Cognitive-developmental psychologists in particular are interested in how individuals make meaning of their experiences. For example, Hewer (1985) has employed a stage theory of ego and moral development to differentiate the suicidal reasoning in two case studies. One adolescent, who conceived of his self-worth as derivative of others' evaluations of him, tried to commit suicide because he felt he was letting others down. A second adolescent, whose ego was based on a sense of personal integrity and consistency, tried to commit suicide because he felt he was failing to live up to his own standards. The precipitating reasoning, prescribed therapy, and long-term outcomes for these two adolescents were different and based on their understandings of self and harm to self. This phenomenological orientation dovetails with the issue raised above by Killen et al. (1991).

In a study of high school and college students, Piette (1991) also explored the way in which adolescents understand self-harm. This study examined the extent to which adolescents considered consequences to self and others as they evaluated the morality of self-harming behaviors. All of the subjects in the study considered "intentionally harming yourself" to be morally wrong – although 11% of the subjects indicated that some less severe types of self-harm would instead be a matter of personal choice. In reasoning about why harm to self would be morally wrong, 42% of the subjects incorporated reasons based on secondary harm to others and 77% incorporated reasons based solely on a consideration of the self. Some of the considerations of self included assertion that all people are created equal and so one deserves the same respect as one would give others, consideration of the guilty conscience and harm to future well-being that might result from self-harm, and expression of the obligation not to damage the precious gift of life that one is given. Thus, individuals in this study attended to both harm to self and harm to others in assessing the moral status of self-harm.

Psychologists have begun to apply the theoretical work of Turiel (1983) in exploring the degree to which adolescents and children make moral meaning of self-harm. Turiel (1975, 1978, 1983) first posited the distinction between two domains of social knowledge that had previously been confounded in the psychological literature: morality and social convention.

Social conventions are behavior uniformities that serve to coordinate social interactions and are tied to the contexts of specific social systems. Conventions are based on arbitrary actions that are relative to social contexts. Through their participation in social groups, such as the family, school, or with their peers, children form conceptions about social systems and the conventions, the shared expectations, that coordinate interactions.
. . . The moral domain refers to prescriptive judgments of justice, rights, and welfare pertaining to how people ought to relate to each other. Moral prescriptions are not relative to the social context, nor are they defined by it. Correspondingly, children's moral judgments are not derived directly from social institutional systems but from features inherent to social relationships – including experiences involving harm to persons, violations of rights, and conflicts of competing claims. (Turiel, 1983, p. 3)

Turiel (1978) hinted at a third domain, which he called the domain of psychological knowledge, and which Nucci (1981) explicated and renamed the "personal domain." Nucci defines the personal domain "by actions considered to be outside the realm of societal regulation and moral concern. Personal issues comprise the set of social actions whose import and effects are perceived to be primarily upon the actor" (p. 114). Whereas Shweder, Turiel, and Much (1981) used the term "prudential reasoning" apparently to refer to the personal domain, it was Tisak and Turiel (1984) who eventually applied the term prudential to a subcategory of the personal domain, that is, those acts that affect only the self but are intrinsically harmful or at least potentially harmful to the self. Unfortunately, the defining characteristics of the prudential knowledge domain remain unclear, due both to the conceptual complexity of the issue and the lack of agreement in the literature. We will therefore explore the way self-harmful (prudential) acts are differentiated from other-harmful (moral) acts in the psychological literature.

Shweder et al. (1981) offer a definition of the moral domain, which is consistent with classical deontological ethics (Kant, 1785/1959). They argue that, according to that tradition, morality must consist of issues that are (1) obligatory, (2) generalizable, and (3) important. Furthermore, the obligatory nature of morality presupposes (1) unalterability, (2) ahistoricity, and (3) independence from human judgment (externality). Although they do not fully endorse this position, or clearly define the prudential domain, other researchers have adopted some of these criteria in their empirical analyses of the difference in the way these domains are considered. These data will be examined in a later section of this chapter. Tisak and Turiel (1984) did begin to contribute to the conceptual understanding of this issue with their explication of the domain of "prudential reasoning."

Although moral rules can pertain to acts with negative consequences to persons, this is not sufficient as a defining characteristic. In common with moral rules, prudential rules can also pertain to acts with consequences to persons. Unlike prudential rules, however, moral rules also proscribe features of social relationships. . . . In addition, the consequences of violating a prudential rule are immediate and directly perceptible to the actor (Shweder, Turiel, & Much, 1981), while the consequences of violating a moral rule often are not direct for the actor and require inferences about social relations. (p. 1031)

The distinguishing features invoked in differentiating morality and prudence are therefore (1) the existence of social relational reasoning (cf. Tisak & Tisak, 1990) and (2) the immediacy and obviousness of the consequences to the actor. Interestingly (and unfortunately without any justification), they do not consider the avoidance of punishment to be an example of prudential reasoning.

The only other study to define directly the distinction between prudential and other reasoning, other than further work by Tisak and colleagues using the same definitions (Tisak & Tisak, 1990; Tisak, Tisak, & Rogers, 1993), is an empirical study by Nucci, Guerra, and Lee (1991). These authors agree with Tisak that prudential reasoning is "similar to matters of morality in that they result in harm to persons . . . [but] differ . . . however, in that they do not proscribe features of social relationships" (p. 842).

Three questions arise concerning the social relational distinction between morality and prudence. First, it remains unclear whether moral matters *must* entail social relationships. Can one, for example, discuss the ethical nature of environmental harm without considering the impact on humanity? This raises a second question concerning the distinction between self and other as moral objects. If the self can be construed as an object of one's own action, does the *ethical* distinction between other-harm and self-harm remain meaningful? Hermans, Kempen, and van Loon (1992) argue, for example, that the self can be considered dialogical, such that different components of the self can interact with each other, much like different individuals interact with each other. In this way the self is social, with the object of interaction and dialogue residing inside instead of outside the self. Flanagan (1991) offers a supportive argument that one has a moral obligation to one's own future. Third, it is also unclear whether prudential matters *cannot* entail social relational reasoning. Tisak and Turiel (1984) state that "morality bears upon interactions between people and prudence *may* not" (p. 1030, emphasis added). If the answer to the first two questions is that morality need not entail social relationships, and the answer to the third question is that prudential reasoning may entail social relationships, then the fundamental distinction between the domains, as defined in the psychological literature, is lost. Additionally, if the self can be treated as other, then the meaning of social relationships becomes broad enough to obliterate this defining variable. These three questions will be addressed in detail from the perspective of philosophical ethics in the following section.

Tisak and Turiel's (1984) second variable differentiating the moral from the prudential domain is the immediacy and saliency of the resulting harm. The face validity of this feature of the definition seems questionable. Could not the imprudence of failing to take prescribed medication for a chronic illness or of eating an unhealthy diet result in less immediate and salient harm than, for example, the immorality of physically assaulting another? Given that this distinguishing feature is dropped from subsequent writings (e.g., Nucci et al., 1991; Tisak & Tisak, 1990; Tisak et al., 1993), it will likewise not be further explored here.

It appears then that the theoretical literature concerning the psychology of prudential reasoning has identified the defining features of prudential reasoning as immediate and obvious to the actor and as distinguishable from other harm by its nonsocial relational nature. Furthermore, the former appears to have been subsequently dropped from the definitions and the latter criterion has led to some serious conceptual questions. It behooves us to offer a more satisfactory delineation of the relation of self-harm to moral concerns. We will do so by examining the philosophical nature of self-harm, after which we will explore how adolescents view self-harm by reviewing the empirical psychological literature.

The philosophical problem of self-harm

Societies have long wrestled with the problem of whether self-harm is something that is wrong or an acceptable aspect of personal prerogative. This debate often centers around whether to intervene and how much intervention is acceptable when individuals cause or risk harm to themselves. As the analysis to follow will make clear, the ethical proscription against harming others is based on the dual justification that individuals ought to be protected from unjustified harm and that individuals ought to be free to make autonomous decisions, within certain limits. Both parts of this justification are based in respect for individual autonomy, balanced against the benefits and harms of a particular action.

This discussion is concerned with the special class of actions that cause or risk harm, but specifically in which the actor and the person harmed are one and the same. It is justifiable, then, to protect our autonomy by limiting the autonomy of others. It seems to make little sense, however, to argue that it is also justifiable to protect our autonomy by limiting our own autonomy, as in the case of restricting the liberty to act in ways that cause harm to self. First, we will examine whether acts that harm the self versus acts that harm others are morally distinct. Then we will turn to the question of whether society is justified in acting in ways that literally protect us from ourselves – the question of paternalism.

Morality and imprudence

For philosophers, the term prudence carries a somewhat different connotation than the concept of "self-regarding" as in the earlier discussion of prudence in the psychological literature. In philosophy, prudence is a characteristic leading individuals to act in ways that are self-protecting and "safe," but, as Falk (1978) points out, prudence is only one among many ways of looking after oneself. The dominant philosophical treatment of prudence historically has been from the point of view of virtue ethics, generally traced to the writings of Aristotle. In his *Nicomachean Ethics*, Aristotle (1988) outlines a number of virtues and vices, with the prescriptive analysis that the morally virtuous individual will successfully seek the "golden mean" of the virtue between the extremes of contrasting vices. In the case of prudence, the golden mean must be sought between the extremes of cowardice on one hand and recklessness or rashness on the other – each extreme of which might be viewed as imprudent.

The chief analyses of prudence from the psychological perspective center on the self-relating aspect of actions to distinguish prudent acts from other-affecting actions, which are deemed as moral; or put differently, other-regarding actions are "normative" to self-regarding actions' "prudential" nature (Nucci et al., 1991; Shweder et al., 1981; Tisak & Turiel, 1984). Such a distinction seems dubious from the philosophical perspective on a number of fronts. First, as discussed in previous sections, it is incorrect to claim that a wide array of actions is purely self-regarding. Because even the most private actions have direct or indirect ramifications on others, it is a false distinction to differentiate between self-harming and other actions solely or even largely upon the personal nature of individual actions. Nonetheless, it is conceptually valuable to determine whether even a purely theoretical self-regarding act ought to have a different moral status than an other-regarding act. This is especially important because individual actors often make their decisions based on their own phenomenological analysis of an act, and may construe a self- and other-regarding act as solely a self-regarding act (e.g., "my drinking doesn't hurt anyone but me").

The morality of self- and other-regarding acts

There is a significant history of philosophical perspectives holding that self-regarding acts, such as self-harming, fall outside the realm of morality. On this view, actions that affect only the actor have no moral dimension and are thus inappropriately termed right or wrong. It follows, then, that so long as the act is self-regarding, there is nothing individuals may not do (Baier, 1958). Oddly, although this view has had substantial support from a number of thoughtful philosophers, it is in direct contradiction with all the major Western philosophical perspectives.

From the beginnings of Western philosophy, behavior toward the self has been as much a moral issue as is behavior toward others, with acts that harm the self being perceived on a continuum from gravely wrong to saintly or heroic. For instance, Aristotle's (1988) views on being a person of moral excellence by attaining the "golden mean" include strictly self-regarding virtues and associated vices such as temperance and intemperance; to fall prey to the vice of intemperance is to fail oneself and thus to fail the test of moral excellence. Should a person achieve such virtuous character as to act with such courage as to risk harm to self, they are to be lauded as heroic – though for heroism to be meaningful it must be due to actions that are "above and beyond the call of duty." Self-regarding acts have a distinctly moral nature since they speak to one's (moral) character.

Two other classic Western ethical theories, deontology (Kant, 1785/1959) and utilitarianism (Bentham, 1789/1948; Mill, 1859/1975), further reinforce the moral nature of self-harm. In the case of Immanuel Kant, the duty to respect humanity includes respect for one's own humanity, with failure on this count through acts such as suicide being the worst kind of immoral behavior. Jeremy Bentham's and even Mill's utilitarian views focus on the maximization of "good" to as many in a group as possible. In such a calculation, the benefits and burdens falling to the self cannot be ignored, since self-benefit and self-harm must count in overall utility. The full range of benefits and burdens of an action must be taken into account in establishing the act's overall utility. This must include the benefits and burdens realized by all involved, including the self. Great self-harm, such as suicide, must then be seen as disutility, which must be part of the calculation of overall utility. Whereas utilitarianism can require serious self-harm if it yields an overall increase in utility, it cannot do so without weighing the disutility inherent in the act against the potential benefits of the act in a given circumstance; if self-harm yields an overall balance of burdens over benefits, it is not only *not* required behavior, but can be considered immoral, again due to its inherent disutility to the actor and concerned others. Hence, both deontology and utilitarianism recognize the moral proscription concerning self-harm, although for different reasons and to differing degrees.

Early communitarian thinkers such as David Hume (1772) argued that some acts that harmed the self could be properly seen as benefiting society so much as to be required of individuals, for example, in cases that we would today consider heroic behavior such as risking one's own life to save the lives of many others. Such an approach places so much value on the good of the community that the self is only important to the extent that it makes up a small, though necessary, component of the community. This leads to requirements for actions that most other approaches to morality would consider laudable, though not required (i.e., supererogatory), such as heroic or saintly acts that put one at risk. This focus on community is turned on its head for the general category of egoists, in which we might group philosophers such as Thomas Hobbes (1651). For egoists, the entirety of morality and thus all determinations of what counts as right and wrong ignore other-regarding acts and instead give primacy to self-regarding acts, holding that right action is the action that best serves self-interest.

Given this historical background for philosophical approaches to the morality of self-harm, we can turn to the valid or false distinction between moral (other-regarding) and prudential (self-regarding) acts. The argument centers around the contention presented in the psychological literature that self-regarding acts are amoral or nonmoral, that is outside the realm of morality, since morality entails social relationships. As noted in the preceding section on psychological theory, three issues are raised by this contention. First, the argument requires that we allow that actions without social content are amoral, that is, we have no moral obligations to ourselves; second, that acts can really be purely self-regarding; and third, that the object of actions done to oneself is morally different from the object of actions done to others. As shall now be demonstrated, none of these three bases for the distinction holds up under scrutiny.

Morality as necessarily social. As the preceding synopsis of Western philosophical approaches to self-harm shows, every major tradition treats self-regarding behavior as part of morality, whether lauding it or holding that such behavior is immoral. Although there is a lack of agreement among various traditions about whether self-regarding behavior is morally right or wrong, there is no disagreement that such behavior is a proper part of morality.

Self-harm as inherently social. Even if we allow that purely self-regarding acts fall outside the realm of morality, it is very difficult to defend the claim that any act is truly purely self-regarding, because we can easily point to at least some other-regarding consequences of even the most personal behavior. Take the paradigmatic example of suicide. Few would contend that taking one's own life has no effect on others. Family, friends, co-workers, and others are all affected when a person with whom they shared a relationship dies. When a death is at an individual's own hands, the impact on those left behind is often great. In addition to the very personal act of taking one's own life, it is clear that suicide also severs one's relationship with others. That said, it is also clear that acts such as suicide have different effects and impacts on different people, largely dependent on each person's relationship with the suicidal individual, but none so great as the impact on the individual herself. To try to categorize acts as being exclusively either purely self- or purely other-regarding fails to account for the complexity of our psychological and moral lives.

Moral distinction between self and other as objects of harm. Although it is difficult to find actions that are purely self-regarding, nearly all our actions have some self-regarding aspect. Nearly every moral decision we make must take into account not only its effects on others, but on the actor as well. To act without reference to the ramifications a decision has for oneself qualifies as shortsighted, in poor judgment, or in rare cases, saintly – but never is it generally expected by morality.

A more intuitively palatable approach evolves from the contention that the impact of primarily self-regarding acts on others is recognizable and important, but less morally important than the impact of other-regarding acts on others. So while admitting that self-regarding actions are properly part of morality, this view contends that it is less morally problematic to harm oneself than to harm another. Upon closer scrutiny, this position begins to appear inconsistent. If it is wrong to cause harm to another, why is it not equally wrong to cause harm to oneself? On a consequentialist analysis, harm is harm, no matter to whom it happens. Or as Andre (1987) has put it, "If what is done to me matters, why should it matter who does it?" (p. 157). That answering this question is difficult may be due to a misunderstanding of what is important about self- and other-regarding actions.

As Andre has argued using the example of suicide compared with homicide, what morally distinguishes the two acts is not that one results in different consequences than the other, but that only one has an involuntary victim (Andre, 1987). It is the unwillingness of the person bearing the consequences of the action that makes homicide the moral wrong that it is, on this account. If it is the involuntary nature of the person bearing the consequences of an action that is morally important, then prima facie, self-regarding actions could never be morally wrong but only imprudent. What if, however, there are actions that are morally wrong even if done to *willing* others? If there are such actions, then on grounds of consistency, the same actions that are wrong when done to willing *others* should be wrong if done to one*self.* By symmetry, if actions are morally acceptable when done to willing others, they would also be morally acceptable when done to oneself. This logic can be applied to a current debate, the moral question over the acceptability of voluntary euthanasia. Since voluntary euthanasia is effectively an individual willingly submitting to being killed by another, whether voluntary euthanasia is acceptable will depend on whether suicide (willingly killing oneself) is acceptable, and vice versa.

Two quite different conceptual approaches based on the principle of respect for persons may help clarify this issue and help us come to some conclusions about the morality of self-harm. The first focuses on individual

rights to act autonomously and the role such rights play in the moral acceptability of behavior; the second focuses on the value of continued life and
attempts to assess the claim that in some cases the burdens of continuing
life outweigh its benefits. Both approaches can, in limited cases, support
the conclusion that respect for persons leads to the moral acceptability of
choosing to die.

Reliance on rights has become the dominant justification for individual
behavior in free societies, even if the behavior seems to conflict with the best
interests of the individual, and even in many cases where the behavior
conflicts with community or other group interests (Dworkin, 1978; Feinberg, 1973). The basis for rights and the obligations that flow from them is
out of respect for an individual's interests. For example, citizens may, and
presumably do, have an interest in voting for the candidates of their choice in
an election; and the protection of that interest is realized through the creation or recognition of any citizen's right to vote. Not all interests must or
even should be protected by rights, however. I may have an interest, for
example, in eating fresh strawberries throughout the year. Few would argue
that my interest ought to be protected by a right to eat fresh strawberries year
round, however. Whether there is a right to self-harm will depend both on
whether individuals have an interest in risking harm to self (e.g., through
drug use, driving at excessive speed, or even eating unhealthy foods) and
whether such a potential interest ought to be protected by recognition of a
right. To return to the question that opened this section, whether one has a
right to commit suicide or choose euthanasia depends on whether interests in
undertaking such an act can be identified, and whether such interests are
compelling enough to deserve protection by right. The most persuasive
answer to this question is that individuals have a compelling interest in
controlling their lives and bodies, and that such a basic and compelling
interest ought to be protected through a right to be free to pursue that
interest as individuals see fit. This interest and the right to protect it is often
invoked in the abortion debate as the right to bodily autonomy.

Even such a compelling interest as bodily autonomy is not absolute,
however. An individual requesting assisted suicide for gratuitous reasons
ought to have such a request denied. The principle on which such a refusal
is based is that of weighing the harms and benefits of continued life against
those of death in an attempt to determine (with the individual) what is in
that person's best interests. For the question of suicide and euthanasia,
invoking one's autonomy for the purpose of ending life ought to require
good reasons, both because of the need to assure that autonomous desires
are being expressed in making such a final decision, and because the loss of
human life cannot be taken lightly. This is not to say that there aren't

conceivable situations in which the harms of continued existence are so great as to outweigh its benefits, such that death would be more beneficial than life. Cases of irreversible and severe extreme physical and emotional suffering like the end stages of some cancers, the loss of mental faculties from progressive degenerative diseases such as Alzheimer's disease, or the unrelenting neurological degeneration and self-mutilation characterizing Lesch-Nyhan syndrome all seem to be lives full of harm and offering very little benefit. The prospect of life in these states specifically, or in cases of extreme, intractable pain and/or extreme ongoing loss of cognitive function in general, seems so harmful without compensating benefit that opting for death over continued existence may be a morally acceptable self-harming act (Engelhardt, 1975).

From the preceding discussion, it becomes clear that self-regarding actions do have a role in morality though it is appropriately different from the role of other-regarding actions. Even when actions are not part of a social relationship, but instead are self-regarding, they still may have a moral component, both because of the effect on even distant others of self-regarding actions, and the moral protection we afford self-regarding behavior. The principle at issue is respect for persons, given substance through the right to control one's life and body, and the balancing of the harms and benefits resulting from the action or inaction (Feinberg, 1986). The important difference between self- and other-regarding acts seems to be not that self-regarding actions belong outside the realm of morality, but that only a limited range of self-harming actions ought to be considered morally wrong.

The moral limits of paternalism

The challenge for a society, then, is to square the extent it is willing to grant or deny individuals the liberty to practice voluntary self-regarding, self-harming acts. Although the preceding discussion concluded that self-regarding acts do have moral weight, it does not necessarily follow that a society would or should choose to control such acts through laws and policies. It may well be the view of a society that it is more harmful to the welfare of all to control even immoral self-regarding acts than it is to allow individuals to act in ways that will bring harm to themselves. Society must weigh the relative value of the preservation of individual liberty against the value of preventing individuals from the sometimes moral wrong of causing harm to themselves. This tension is the classic problem raised by societal paternalism.

What is paternalism, and is it ever justified? Paternalism, as its root tells us, is to act as would a father (or, in more egalitarian language, as a parent). Paternalism usually takes the form of one individual acting to substitute one's decision for that of another, under the guise of authority, and often to override the autonomous decision of another, for that person's own benefit. Objections to paternalism can be traced to nineteenth-century England and John Stuart Mill's (1859/1975) essay on political philosophy, *On Liberty*. In it he argues that the only justifiable restriction of individual liberty (the right to be free from interference) by the state is if individual action poses harm to others. Otherwise, Mill argued, no such intervention in the actions of individuals is acceptable, and on this basis he refuted paternalism by the state. Individuals' liberty rights, or rights to be left alone, are stronger than the interests of others or of the community. Put in an overly simplistic way, the only time in which individual liberty interests can be overruled is when the exercise of those interests infringes on the liberty rights of others. This is the philosophical underpinning for the dictum "Your rights end at the tip of your nose" because, so long as one's behavior does not cause harm to others, the liberty to act in whatever way is desired must be respected. This, then, is the historical benchmark for the refutation of paternalism and remains one of the hallmarks of liberal political theory and the basis for our societal presumption that individuals are free to act as they see fit.

Some scholars have made a distinction between paternalism in which clearly autonomous decisions are overridden, calling this variety "strong" paternalism, and paternalism in which apparently nonautonomous decisions are overridden (until such time as it can be ascertained whether the individual is competent and expressing truly autonomous desires), calling the latter "weak" paternalism (Beauchamp & Childress, 1989; Childress, 1982). If the individual is deemed incompetent, then weak paternalism stops being paternalism at all in that the individual's expressed wishes should no longer be deemed autonomous; and by the same token if the individual is deemed competent, then continued weak paternalism becomes the "strong" variety. Once decision-making capacity has been assessed, decisions expressed by competent individuals must be respected or paternalism will remain.

The question then becomes whether strong paternalism can ever be justified. To begin to answer this question, the values in conflict must be illuminated. First, the value of an individual's right to autonomous decision making must be respected. Against the value of respect for individual autonomy, the party in the position of authority must consider what is best for the individual. Thus the value of respect for individual autonomy may come into conflict with what is deemed best for the individual. Paternalism in the strong sense – the only sense we will now mean when the term *paternalism* is used – is therefore only defensible when the value of preserving what is best for the individual, including preventing serious and irreversible harm, is great enough to outweigh the value of respecting individual autonomy. This presumes, of course, that the value of respecting the autonomous decisions of individuals can ever be outweighed. Key to this aspect of the justifiability of paternalism are what counts as autonomous decision making by the competent individual, the value of respect for the autonomous decisions of individuals, the severity of the harm posed by respecting the individual's decision, and the level of the risk of the harm actually occurring. Paternalism, then, can only be justified by showing that acting to protect individuals from harm outweighs the value of respect for autonomy – a justification convincing in only a limited range of circumstances. Self-harm is therefore viewed by philosophical ethics as a legitimately moral issue; however, its weight in a given moral determination is governed by whether the moral value of preventing self-harm is outweighed by the moral right of autonomy in that particular situation.

Adolescent reasoning about the moral nature of self-harm

Whereas substantial research has considered how adolescents make meaning of self-harm, especially suicidal behavior, in general (e.g., Borst & Noam, 1993; Borst, Noam, & Bartok, 1991; Hewer, 1985), only a few studies have examined how adolescents judge, specifically, the prescriptiveness of self-harm – that is, how they make *moral* meaning of self-harm. These studies focus predominantly on the use of alcohol, tobacco, and illegal drugs, but also consider suicide. The issue of drug use has been especially attractive to researchers because it is not clear in what domain of social knowledge it rightly belongs (Berndt & Park, 1986; Power, Higgins, & Kohlberg, 1989; Yussen, 1977). In this section, we will first review these studies and then shed further light on the topic by presenting new data on adolescent considerations of the morality of substance use from Project Decide, a National Institute on Drug Abuse study of adolescent moral reasoning and drug and alcohol use.

The first study to examine the distinction between self-harm and other-harm from a sociomoral developmental perspective was presented by Tisak and Turiel (1984). This study most directly addressed the definitional issues described thus far. The events this study depicted entailed rules governing episodes of physical injury due to unsafe behavior (self-harm; prudence) or physical attack (other-harm; morality), plus loss of property due to theft (other-harm; morality). They asked five questions about these events relevant to the conceptual distinction between prudence and morality: (1) Is the behavior right or wrong? (rightness), (2) Which rule is more important? (importance), (3) Would it be all right to abolish the rule about this behavior? (alterability), (4) Would it be all right to do this if there were no rule about it? (externality), and (5) Would it be all right for another school not to have such a rule? (generalizability). Nearly all of the elementary school children studied considered both types of behavior to be wrong, but the other-harm was considered more wrong than the self-harm. The moral-physical rule was deemed more important than the moral-property rule which in turn was judged more important than the prudential rule. Furthermore, the children indicated that the moral rules were more external and generalizable than the prudential rule. Finally, the prudential rule was judged more alterable than the moral rules. Whereas these data appear to support the distinction between moral and prudential knowledge domains along the conceptual lines hypothesized to define the moral domain (rightness, importance, alterability, externality, generalizability), (1) in most cases the differences were small (e.g., 100% considered violating the moral rules to be wrong and 89% considered violating the prudential rule to be wrong), (2) in all cases the majority applied all five criteria to both moral and prudential rules, and (3) some differences may have been artifacts of the methods used (e.g., the importance judgment was a forced-choice procedure).

Two other studies also directly contrast moral and prudential events (Berndt & Park, 1986; Killen et al., 1991). Berndt and Park interviewed fourth- and eighth-grade children about their own and their peers' transgressions, which were coded as either moral (acts that violate another person), conventional (violations of socially sanctioned rules), personal (acts that do not affect others and are not governed by social norms – although including some self-harmful acts such as recklessness), or drug use. Subject clearly differentiated between the moral and drug use categories in their reasoning about the acts. Moral acts were accompanied by reasoning about retaliation, avoidance of punishment, and peer attitudes toward others, and drug use was accompanied by reasoning about personal choice, concern for approval, and prudence. Whereas Berndt and Park and Tisak and Turiel (1984) preidentified which rules concerned moral or prudential events, Killen et al. presented a list of behaviors and asked the subjects to categorize them as either moral, conventional (rightness derived solely from social regulation), or personal. These authors did not differentiate personal from prudential concerns. Their high school sample judged four acts as predominantly moral matters: killing, stealing, cocaine use, and crack use. (All drug behaviors except caffeine consumption were judged to be as harmful as killing and stealing.) Suicide was judged fairly equally to be in the moral (43%) and personal (40%) domains. Nicotine and caffeine use were considered to be predominantly personal issues and alcohol and marijuana use were more evenly divided between the three categories (the mode for marijuana was moral and the mode for alcohol was personal). The authors also asked subjects why it is wrong or right to use drugs and why it is wrong or right to use drugs if evidence demonstrates that they are harmful. The reasons offered were predominantly moral or a mixture of moral and personal, with many more moral justifications if the drug was demonstrated to be harmful. The vast majority (75%) indicated that one has the right to harm oneself, including 95% of 9th graders. Most 9th graders (85%) but about half of 11th and 12th graders indicated that one has the right to commit suicide, but this number dropped to only 30% if the suicide would harm others. The reasons were predominantly moral and moral/personal for the latter case, but mostly personal and moral/personal for generally defined self-harm. Suicide not specifically identified as harming others was more evenly divided between moral, personal, and moral/personal justifications.

Another interesting question concerns the differential judgments of those more favorably and less favorably disposed toward the potentially self-harmful behavior, in this case drug use. Two studies directly address this issue. Nucci et al. (1991) compared the responses of 9th and 12th graders who were categorized as either low drug users or higher drug users. They reported that low users rated drug use as more wrong and more harmful. Killen et al. (1991) reported that 10th, 11th, and 12th graders who consider drug use to be acceptable were more likely to sanction self-harm and suicide than were those not accepting of drug use. Nucci et al. also reported that high users offered more personal justifications than did low users. For those that used personal justifications, low users were more likely to offer prudential justifications of the unacceptability of drug use and high users were more likely to offer arguments that it is purely a matter of personal choice without reference to harm or prudence.

All of the other studies being reviewed also examined the justifications offered by the subjects. Tisak and Turiel (1984) reported that the justifications for the moral events were largely concerned with the other's welfare and that the justifications for the prudential event were largely concerned with harm to the self. This is not surprising, given that is precisely what the events were about. Nucci et al. (1991) reported that drug use was associated mostly with personal justifications but that within the personal domain, most of the arguments offered concerned the unacceptability of the behavior due to self-harm. Tisak et al. (1993) reported that judgments of the parental prohibition against seeing a particular friend were justified with personal reasoning, but that when the parental prohibition was due to the friend's drug use, the justifications were moral for the 9th graders and moral for the 12th graders only for marijuana use – whereas personal justifications were offered for beer use and cigarette use. (These subjects also judged marijuana use regulation to be more important than beer use regulation, which was also more important than cigarette use regulation.) Interestingly in this study, it is not clear whose point of view the subject is taking. This becomes critical in distinguishing concerns with self-harm from concerns with other-harm. For example, when asking high school students why it is legitimate or illegitimate for parents to prohibit their child from associating with a drug-using peer, the subjects tended to invoke "the child's welfare" as a justification. If they are taking the parental point of view, then the justification is clearly in the moral domain. If, however, they are taking the child's point of view, then what the authors label as a moral reason may indeed be a prototypical prudential reason.

Three studies have examined the issue of legitimate authority over governing drug use, albeit in different ways. Killen et al. (1991) examined who was considered to have legitimate authority over drug use. Parents were considered to have such authority in the home by all subjects, but out of the home by only 80% of the sample. Government was legitimized by 93% of the sample and religious authorities by 60%. Tisak et al. (1993) reported that 9th and 12th graders did not consider parents who do not offer a justification to have legitimate authority to restrict a child's access to a particular friend; however, if the parents justified the prohibitions by alluding to the friend's drug use, then their authority was deemed legitimate by 9th graders, but not legitimate with respect to a friend's beer and cigarette use by 12th graders. Finally, Nucci et al. (1991) reported that the high drug users were more likely than low users to consider the self as the only legitimate authority to govern drug use; low users were more likely than high users to consider parents and the law as legitimate authorities over drug use.

Project Decide

The first, third, and fourth authors of this chapter have all participated in Project Decide, a three-year National Institute on Drug Abuse study of adolescent moral reasoning and drug and alcohol abuse. Project Decide was initially designed to investigate whether moral reasoning is related to adolescent substance use. However, prior research showed little consistent relation between the way adolescents think about right and wrong and whether they use alcohol, nicotine, and/or illicit substances (Berkowitz,

Guerra, & Nucci, 1991). Furthermore, as we have already demonstrated, adolescents often do not consistently consider substance use to be a moral issue. Hence, it was theorized that moral reasoning would only serve as a factor in adolescent decisions about substance use if they considered substance use to be a moral issue (Berkowitz et al., 1991). In order to test this hypothesis, a multimethod assessment of adolescent thinking about morality and substance use was created (Berkowitz et al., 1994) in order to ascertain the degree to which adolescents consider substance use to be a moral issue and the relation of their thinking about right and wrong to their actual behavior. As part of Project Decide, 190 adolescents between the ages of 12 and 19 were asked about 14 drug-related behaviors and 10 nondrug behaviors. They categorized these behaviors as either moral, conventional, or personal, and rated the harmfulness of each behavior both for the actor and for others. Most of the behaviors were clearly more harmful to the self and were rated as such. Interestingly, the 5 behaviors that were clearly more harmful to others (supplying alcohol to a minor, smoking cigarettes when pregnant, selling drugs, stealing, hitting and hurting another) were not clearly rated as such. The three other-harming drug categories were rated as equivalently harmful to the self and other. Stealing and hitting were rated as more harmful to another than to the self only by adolescents older than 14 years of age; 12- to 14-year-olds saw stealing as more harmful to the self and hitting as equally harmful to self and other.

Age was a significant variable in a number of other ways as well. In ratings of harmfulness, three distinct age trends were identified. First, older adolescents rated the *nondrug* behaviors (e.g., stealing, riding a motorcycle without a helmet, hitting, calling a teacher by her first name) as more harmful to oneself than did the younger adolescents (although no age differences were found for ratings of the harmfulness of these acts to others). Second, younger adolescents rated the "softer"-drug behaviors (tobacco, alcohol, marijuana) as more harmful than did the older adolescents. Third, there were no age differences for ratings of behaviors involving "harder" drugs (amphetamines, opiates). This was due to the ceiling effect of all subjects tending to rate such behaviors as very harmful. In a parallel set of findings, the same three trends were observed for age effects in the domain categorizations of the 24 behaviors (i.e., older adolescents considered the nondrug behaviors as moral more than did younger adolescents, younger adolescents considered the soft-drug behaviors moral more often than did older adolescents, and there were no age differences for categorization of the hard-drug behaviors). For all subjects, the drug behaviors tended to be considered issues of morality (i.e., rated as wrong regardless of whether there was a rule or law about it). There are two qualifications to this generalization. First, the harder the drug, the more likely it was to be considered a moral issue. Second, smoking cigarettes and occasional drinking were considered to be matters of personal choice.

Two other findings from the Project Decide data are worth noting here. First, those subjects considering a behavior as a moral issue also tended to rate that behavior as more harmful to self and other. Second, those subjects rating a drug behavior as harmful were less likely to report engaging in use of that substance.

Conclusions are difficult to generate, despite a substantial body of empirical research. The most direct evidence on the phenomenological distinction between self-harmful (prudential) and other-harmful (moral) acts comes from Tisak and Turiel (1984) who studied a preadolescent sample of 6- to 11-year-old children. From their data one can conclude that moral events are indeed differentiated from prudential events by children. The moral events are viewed as more wrong, more important, less alterable, less contingent on explicit rules, and more generalizable. As noted already, however, the differences appear to be more quantitative than qualitative. The rest of the literature, unfortunately, (1) studied older children (especially problematic, given some of the age effects reported) and (2) did not address these five philosophically grounded questions about the criterion for identifying the moral domain. (Tisak et al., 1993, did ask subjects about rightness and importance and Nucci et al., 1991, asked about rightness, but neither contrasted moral and prudential events on these criteria.)

Three other conclusions may be reached from the remaining studies of adolescent reasoning about self-harm. First, the "harder" the drug, the more likely it is to be treated as a moral issue. Interestingly, Killen et al. (1991) found that all drugs (except caffeine) were rated as harmful as were killing or stealing; however, only opiate use was considered a predominantly moral issue, nicotine use was seen largely as a personal issue, and marijuana and alcohol use were considered both moral and personal much the same way suicide was. Nucci et al. (1991) pooled responses across drug categories; however, an earlier report (Nucci et al., 1989) indicated that subjects were more likely to treat harder drugs as an issue of prudence and softer drugs as an issue of personal choice. Project Decide (Berkowitz, Zweben, & Begun, 1992) found that most drug behaviors were considered moral issues, but that behaviors involving harder drugs were more likely to be categorized as moral. Second, external regulation of drug behavior is not uniformly sanctioned. Some reports demonstrated that adolescents do accept control of drug use by legal officials (Killen et al., 1991), whereas others suggested that only the self and those close to the self are legitimate authorities (Nucci et al., 1991). Others indicated that this too varies depending on the drug type (Tisak et al., 1993).

Finally, age and degree of drug use may interact with these judgments. Nucci et al. (1991) reported few age differences between 9th and 12th graders, but Tisak et al. (1993) did find such differences. Many of the age differences found in Project Decide were between 9th, 10th, 11th, and 12th graders as compared with younger adolescents. It is conceivable that Nucci et al. would have found more age trends with a slightly broader age range as studied in Project Decide. Interestingly, the age trends for harmfulness ratings in Project Decide were different for nondrug-related behaviors, soft-drug-related behaviors, and hard-drug-related behaviors. Nucci et al. also found consistent differences between low and high drug users, with the former viewing use as more wrong, more harmful, and more legitimately regulated by parents and legal authorities. Similarly, Project Decide found high drug users to view drug behaviors as less an issue of morality and less harmful than did low drug users.

Whereas a significant body of research has been amassed concerning how adolescents and children view the moral nature of self-harmful acts, it is clear that more research is needed to clarify the inconsistencies in the existing literature and to test more directly the conceptual distinctions between self- and other-harmful behaviors. Such research needs to examine more consistently the variables of age, gender, substance use, type of harmful behavior, and the five defining dimensions of the moral domain.

Conclusions

Self-harm is clearly treated differently by philosophers, psychologists, and adolescents. Philosophers tend to agree that self-harm is a matter of moral concern. They disagree on how to calculate the moral import of self-harm. A reasonable philosophical position is that self-harm is a moral issue, but its moral weight must be calculated relative to other moral claims in a given situation. Most notable are claims of autonomy and the respect for the best interests of persons. A critical issue in these calculations is the degree of consent on the part of the individual, manifested most clearly in the competence to make moral decisions.

Psychologists tend to formally differentiate self-harm and other-harm. They argue that, unlike other-harm, self-harm is not a moral issue. This determination seems to be based principally upon the nonsocial nature of self-harm. As noted in the philosophical analysis, this criterion does not stand up to conceptual scrutiny. By implication, psychological accounts prioritize the principle of autonomy over the best interests of persons and paternalistic concerns for the prevention of harm. Psychological accounts, therefore, are left with a distinction based on an invalid and overly simplistic criterion.

Adolescents also differentiate between self- and other-harm, but on a more quantitative than qualitative basis. These two types of harm are perceived as more different in degree than in kind. This last conclusion must be qualified by the acknowledgment that the research that exists is limited in a variety of ways. It tends to be quite narrow in focus, concentrating largely on issues of substance use. It also often does not directly address the question at hand, deriving conclusions indirectly.

Clearly, more research is needed to ascertain how children and adolescents understand self-harm and, in contrast, other-harm. Studies examining more diverse self-harmful behaviors would also be desirable. In particular, more studies directly asking the defining questions laid out by Tisak and Turiel (1984) are warranted, as are studies specifically examining the ethical criteria of autonomy, respect for and best interests of persons, and prevention of harm. We do not know which ethical considerations are recognized or at what developmental levels they may be salient.

It is clear that there are both age- and structure-related variables at play in the development of sociomoral perspectives on self-harm. Unfortunately, we are only beginning to scratch the surface of these complex relations. Why do adolescents reason more prohibitively about nondrug behaviors but less prohibitively about drug behaviors as they increase in age? Given that adolescents differentiate between their degree of autonomy in decisions about substance use in different contexts (e.g., home vs. school), how does context interact with individual reasoning in such decisions? Why do adolescents argue against the morality of self-harming behaviors yet engage in them so prevalently? How do children and adolescents develop their perspectives on self-harm? How can prevention programs capitalize on the answers to these and related questions?

Self-harm is a prevalent and critical issue for youth today. If we are to respond adequately to the challenge of reducing the waste produced by self-harm, then we must better understand both its ethical status in order to formulate justifiable policy and its phenomenological nature in order to design more effectively prevention and intervention programs (Berkowitz & Begun, in press).

References

Andre, J. (1987). The equal moral weight of self- and other-regarding acts. *Canadian Journal of Philosophy, 17,* 155–166.

Aristotle (1988). *Nicomachean ethics* (M. Oswald, Trans.). New York: Macmillan.

Baier, K. (1958). *The moral point of view.* Ithaca, NY: Cornell University Press.

Beauchamp, T. L., & Childress, J. F. (1989). *Principles of biomedical ethics* (3rd ed.). New York: Oxford University Press.

Benson, P. L. (1993). *The troubled journey: A portrait of 6th–12th grade youth.* Minneapolis: Search Institute.

Bentham, J. (1789/1948). *Introduction to the principles of morals and legislation* (W. Harrison, Ed.). Oxford: Hafner Press.

Berkowitz, M. W., & Begun, A. L. (in press). Designing prevention programs: The developmental perspective. In W. J. Bukoski & Z. Amsel-Sloboda (Eds.), *Drug abuse prevention: Sourcebook on strategies and research* (NIDA Monograph). Rockville, MD: National Institute on Drug Abuse.

Berkowitz, M. W., Begun, A. L., Zweben, A., Giese, J. K., Mulry, G., Horan, C., Wheeler, T., Gimenez, J., & Piette, J. (1994). Assessing how adolescents think about the morality of substance use: A phenomenological-psychological approach. *Drugs and Society, 8,* 111–124.

Berkowitz, M. W., Guerra, N., & Nucci, L. (1991). Sociomoral development and drug and alcohol abuse. In W. M. Kurtines & J. L. Gewirtz (Eds.), *Handbook of moral behavior and development* (Vol. 3, pp. 35–53). Hillsdale, NJ: Lawrence Erlbaum.

Berkowitz, M. W., Zweben, A., & Begun, A. (1992). *Adolescent moral thinking and drug use.* Paper presented at the annual conference of the American Educational Research Association, San Francisco.

Berndt, T. J., & Park, K. A. (1986). *Children's reasoning about morality, conventions, personal issues, and drug use.* Unpublished manuscript, Purdue University.

Borst, S. R., & Noam, G. G. (1993). Developmental psychopathology in suicidal and nonsuicidal adolescent girls. *Journal of the American Academy of Child and Adolescent Psychiatry, 32*(3), 501–508.

Borst, S. R., Noam, G. G., & Bartok, J. A. (1991). Adolescent suicidality: A clinical-developmental approach. *Journal of the American Academy of Child and Adolescent Psychiatry, 30*(5), 796–803.

Brenner, T. A. (1992). The legalization of drugs: Why prolong the inevitable? In R. L. Evans & I. M. Berent (Eds.), *Drug legislation: For and against* (pp. 157–179). LaSalle, IL: Open Court Publishing.

Childress, J. F. (1982). *Who should decide? Paternalism in health care.* New York: Oxford University Press.

Cole, D. A. (1991). Adolescent suicide. In R. M. Lerner, A. C. Petersen, & J. Brooks-Gunn (Eds.), *Encyclopedia of adolescence* (Vol. 2, pp. 1113–1116). New York: Garland.

Dryfoos, J. G. (1990). *Adolescents at risk: Prevention and prevalence.* New York: Oxford University Press.

Dworkin, R. (1978). *Taking rights seriously.* Cambridge, MA: Harvard University Press.

Elkind, D. (1974). *Children and adolescents: Interpretive essays on Jean Piaget* (2nd ed.). New York: Oxford University Press.

Engelhardt, H. T. (1975). Ethical issues in aiding the death of young children. In M. Kohl (Ed.), *Beneficent euthanasia* (pp. 180–192). Buffalo: Prometheus Books.

Falk, W. D. (1978). Morality, self, and others. In J. Feinberg (Ed.), *Reasons and responsibility* (pp. 48–62). Belmont, CA: Dickenson.

Feinberg, J. (1973). *Social philosophy.* Englewood Cliffs, NJ: Prentice-Hall.

Feinberg, J. (1986). *Harm to self.* New York: Oxford University Press.

Flanagan, O. (1991). *Varieties of moral personality: Ethics and psychological realism.* Cambridge, MA: Harvard University Press.

Healthy People 2000 (1990). *Healthy youth 2000: National health promotion and disease prevention objectives for adolescents.* Chicago: American Medical Association.

Hermans, H. J. M., Kempen, H. J. G., & van Loon, R. J. P. (1992). The dialogical self. *American Psychologist, 47,* 23–33.

Hewer, A. (1985). Moral reasoning in the assessment and outcome of suicidal breakdown. In

M. W. Berkowitz & F. Oser (Eds.), *Moral education: Theory and application* (pp. 347–367). Hillsdale, NJ: Lawrence Erlbaum.

Hobbes, T. (1651). *Leviathan.* London.

Hume, D. (1772). *An enquiry concerning the principles of morals.* London.

Kant, I. (1785/1959). *Foundations of the metaphysics of morals* (Lewis White Beck, Trans.). Indianapolis: Bobbs-Merrill.

Kaplan, J. (1971). The role of the law in drug control. *Duke Law Journal, 1971,* 1065–1104.

Kegan, R. (1994). A rationale for guiding adolescents' sexual behavior from the perspective of developmental psychology. *Moral Education Forum, 19*(2), 7–17.

Killen, M., Leviton, M., & Cahill, J. (1991). Adolescent reasoning about drug use. *Journal of Adolescent Research, 6,* 336–356.

Kusserow, R. P. (1992). *Youth and alcohol: Dangerous and deadly consequences.* Office of the Inspector General, Department of Health and Human Services (OEI-09-92-00261).

Levitt, M. Z., Selman, R. L., & Richmond, J. B. (1991). The psychosocial foundations of early adolescents' high-risk behavior: Implications for research and practice. *Journal of Research on Adolescence, 1,* 349–378.

Mill, J. S. (1859/1975). *On liberty* (D. Spitz, Ed.). New York: Norton.

National Research Council (1993). *Losing generations: Adolescents in high-risk settings.* Washington, D.C.: National Academy Press.

Nucci, L. (1981). Conceptions of personal issues: A domain distinct from moral or societal concepts. *Child Development, 52,* 114–121.

Nucci, L., Guerra, N., & Lee, J. (1989). *Adolescent judgments of drug use.* Paper presented at the conference of Society for Research in Child Development, Kansas City.

Nucci, L., Guerra, N., & Lee, J. (1991). Adolescent judgments of the personal, prudential, and normative aspects of drug usage. *Developmental Psychology, 27,* 841–848.

Piette, J. (1991). *Adolescent moral reasoning and reasoning about marijuana use.* Unpublished manuscript, Marquette University, Milwaukee.

Power, F. C., Higgins, A., & Kohlberg, L. (1989). *Lawrence Kohlberg's approach to moral education.* New York: Columbia University Press.

Quadrel, M. J., Fischoff, B., & Davis, W. (1993). Adolescent (in)vulnerability. *American Psychologist, 48,* 102–116.

Shweder, R. A., Turiel, E., & Much, N. C. (1981). The moral intuitions of the child. In J. H. Flavell & L. Ross (Eds.), *Social cognitive development: Frontiers and possible futures* (pp. 288–305). Cambridge: Cambridge University Press.

Tisak, M. S., & Tisak, J. (1990). Children's conceptions of parental authority, friendship, and sibling relations. *Merrill-Palmer Quarterly, 36,* 347–367.

Tisak, M. S., Tisak, J., & Rogers, M. J. (1993). *Adolescents' reasoning about authority and friendship relations in the context of drug usage.* Unpublished manuscript, Bowling Green State University, Ohio.

Tisak, M. S., & Turiel, E. (1984). Children's conceptions of moral and prudential rules. *Child Development, 55,* 1030–1039.

Turiel, E. (1975). The development of social concepts: Mores, customs and conventions. In D. J. DePalma & F. M. Foley (Eds.), *Moral development: Current theory and research.* (Vol. 1, pp. 7–38). Hillsdale, NJ: Lawrence Erlbaum.

Turiel, E. (1978). Social regulations and domains of social concepts. In W. Damon (Ed.), *New directions for child development: Social cognition* (pp. 45–74). San Francisco: Jossey-Bass.

Turiel, E. (1983). *The development of social knowledge: Morality and convention.* Cambridge: Cambridge University Press.

Yussen, S. R. (1977). Characteristics of moral dilemmas written by adolescents. *Developmental Psychology, 13,* 162–163.

7 Context, conflict, and constraint in adolescent–parent authority relationships

Judith G. Smetana

Developmental psychologists have assumed that parent–child authority relations in early childhood are characterized by constraint (on the part of parents) and respect for authority (on the part of the child). With development, relations of constraint are thought to give way to relations involving mutuality, sharing, and cooperation. For instance, in his seminal work on moral development, Piaget (1932/1965) proposed that young children's heteronomous morality entails a view of rules as sacred and unchangeable and a conception of adults as infallible. The morality of the young child is transformed gradually into an autonomous morality or reciprocity based on a mutual respect for rules. More than 50 years later, Youniss and Smollar (1985) echoed this view in describing parent–child relations during adolescence as shifting from unilateral to mutual authority.

The thesis of this chapter is that, although the conclusion that autonomy develops from constraint may be correct, the linear and unidimensional view of development implied by these models is not. More specifically, it is proposed that different forms of adult authority concepts *coexist* during childhood and adolescence. Adolescents' judgments are both unilateral (about some issues) and mutual (about some issues), and shifts in parental authority occur over some types of issues, but not over others. Thus, the development of children's and adolescents' conceptions of authority is not as straightforward as these earlier views of development suggest. The argument to be elaborated here is that authority relations must be considered in terms of the context in which they occur and that autonomy and constraint are both features of childhood and adolescent relations with adults. Furthermore, developmental and contextual variability in judgments are greater in some domains than in others. The chapter begins with a brief description of several

I am grateful to Joan Miller, Larry Nucci, Elliot Turiel, and Cecilia Wainryb for their comments on earlier drafts of this manuscript.

theoretical views of authority relations, followed by the description of an alternative model, based on a domain-specific view of social development.

Theories of parent–child authority relations

Almost all current views of parent–child authority relations have been influenced heavily by Piaget's early work on moral judgment (Piaget, 1932/1965). From his interviews with young children, Piaget (1932/1965) attempted to generalize from children's concepts of game rules to their concepts of moral rules. Piaget proposed that authority-obeying morality does not appear clearly and explicitly until about the age of 6 and that children's moral development is characterized by two progressive stages of reasoning. At the earlier level, labeled heteronomous morality, the right or good is seen as unilateral respect for adult authority and adherence to fixed and externally determined rules. Piaget proposed that relations with authorities, such as parents or teachers, who impose external rules upon the child, are likely to reinforce a heteronomous orientation. Therefore, for development to occur, children must have experiences of cooperation among equals. Through such interactions, children differentiate the self from others and develop the ability to take their perspective. With age and social experiences with peers, children progress from viewing rules as fixed and unalterable to an understanding of rules as changeable by general agreement or mutual consent. The basis for this autonomous morality is the emergence of concepts of reciprocity and equality. At this level, rules are regarded as products of agreement and, therefore, as neither absolute or fixed. Thus, Piaget proposed that conceptions of justice or rights develop out of, or are differentiated from, relations of constraint.

Kohlberg (1969, 1971) also embraced a differentiation model of moral development, although he differed from Piaget in defining the early stages of moral development as based on power and punishment, rather than respect for authority. Nevertheless, he also viewed early moral judgments as based on unilateral conceptions of authority (as entailed, for instance, in the "power and obedience" stage). Through the processes of development, principles of justice are gradually differentiated from nonmoral judgments. Because Kohlberg studied older children and employed more complex dilemmas than the situations studied by Piaget (1932/1965), Kohlberg elaborated Piaget's two-stage theory into a model of six progressively more differentiated and integrated conceptions of justice. In this view, children are not capable of making autonomous moral judgments until young adulthood.

John Rawls (1971), the philosopher whose theory of justice is consistent with Kohlberg's (1969, 1971) theory of moral development, also adopted the notion of early constraint in parent–child relations in accounting for moral development in a just society. His view is consistent with the view underlying many other philosophical accounts of morality (Okin, 1989). Citing Piaget (1932/1965), Rawls described the first stage of moral development, wherein children are first subject to the legitimate authority of their parents, as "the morality of authority."

> It is characteristic of the child's situation that he is not in a position to assess the validity of the precepts and injunctions addressed to him by those in authority, in this case, his parents. He lacks both the knowledge and the understanding on the basis of which their guidance can be challenged. Indeed, the child lacks the concept of justification altogether, this being acquired much later. Therefore he cannot with reason doubt the propriety of parental injunctions. (p. 463)

Rawls viewed the development of autonomous morality of principles of justice as developing through relationships of love, trust, cooperation, reason, and perspective taking.

In contrast to these views, Damon (1977) has argued that theorists of moral development have taken too seriously the child's early subservience to adult authority. He proposed that moral knowledge grows out of children's early reflections on everyday experiences with justice conflicts rather than solely out of experiences with adult constraint. According to his perspective, authority is one of many social relations that children experience rather than the origin of children's social-moral principles. Damon examined age-related changes in two aspects of children's authority knowledge: legitimacy and rationales for obedience.

Damon's account of the development of authority concepts elaborates on the view of development described by Piaget (1932/1965). Like Piaget, Damon described the origins of authority concepts in very young children as a very primitive understanding wherein authority is not yet conceptualized as a force external to the self. Damon found that young children's authority conceptions are based on authority figures' attributes, such as greater physical strength or power. With age, children recognize other attributes that legitimate authority, such as talents or abilities, prior training, or experience. By early adolescence, children are able to coordinate all these attributes with specific situational factors, and authority is viewed as a shared, consensual relation between parties adopted for the welfare of all.

Although parent–child relations are not a central focus of his work, Selman's (1980) developmental analysis of parent–child relations, and particularly children's thinking about punishment, closely parallels Damon's description. According to Selman, early conceptions of parent–child rela-

tions, and particularly children's thinking about punishment, closely parallels Damon's description. According to Selman, early conceptions of
parent–child relations are generally unreflective and are based on parents'
greater physical ability, which enables them to literally direct the child's
behavior or to force compliance. These notions are gradually transformed to
increasingly more benevolent conceptions that entail increasing recognition
of parents' child-rearing goals and modes of communication and a mutual
coordination of perspectives that include tolerance, respect, and recognition
of parents' and children's psychological needs. Although observed in only
fragmentary form in his data, Selman proposed a final developmental level
where parent–child relations are seen "as an ongoing changing system,
unique in human experience, in which autonomy and interdependence are
established, but fluctuate through the life cycle" (p. 151).

Thus, Damon (1977) and Selman (1980) replaced the differentiation
model of moral development espoused by Piaget (1932/1965), Rawls
(1971), and Kohlberg (1969, 1971) with an alternative conception in which
moral development and authority concepts are seen as following separate
developmental trajectories. This separation of morality from other types of
social relations is consistent with a great deal of research, discussed in the
following section, that suggests that differentiation views of moral development such as those espoused by Piaget (1932/1965) and Kohlberg (1969,
1971) underestimate children's ability to make "autonomous" moral judgments. Even very young children treat a set of acts, referred to as moral, as
prescriptive and obligatory, regardless of the demands of authority.

The argument for treating authority relations as a separate developmental system is based on the significance of the parent–child relationship in
children's lives and its difference, on a number of dimensions such as
power and reciprocity, from other relationships children experience, such
as friendships (Damon, 1977; Selman, 1980). These distinctions between
the more hierarchical parent–child relationship and more reciprocal peer
relationships are consistent with much research and theory in developmental psychology (Hunter & Youniss, 1982; Piaget, 1932/1965; Sullivan, 1953;
Youniss & Smollar, 1985) and have become particularly prevalent in recent
theorizing about the role of close relationships in development (e.g., Collins & Laursen, 1992; Hartup, 1989).

Whereas the decision to treat parent–child authority relations as a developmental system may be solidly grounded from a relational perspective, it
may be more problematic from an epistemological standpoint. That is, it is
not clear whether the topic is a well-formulated one, comprising an organized system of thought that is structurally transformed in ontogenesis.
Turiel (1983b) has questioned whether children and adolescents form sys-

tems of knowledge about issues such as authority relations that are not part of other domains to which relations with authority might pertain.

Concepts of authority might be subsumed under other conceptual domains, and the meaning ascribed to authority may depend on the types of authority relations described. For instance, children encounter a number of authority relations during childhood. It is not clear whether developmental changes in authority concepts pertain uniquely to children's thinking about parent–child relationships or whether they describe children's thinking about other authority relationships as well. Thus, the attributes that endow parents with legitimate authority, the boundaries that restrict their authority, and differentiations from other forms of adult authority need to be specified. Furthermore, in these models, authority concepts are typically depicted as decontextualized. However, parents assert their authority or demand compliance in a variety of contexts (e.g., at home, in school, at their grandparents' houses, or at summer camp), and parents may not be seen as legitimate authority in all contexts. Finally, developmental models of authority concepts must consider the acts to which authority relations are directed. Parents' assertions of authority, demands for compliance, or punishments are almost always in reference to specific acts. Damon (1977) found that children rejected the legitimacy of parental requests to steal. He noted that these responses did not yield systematic age variations that could be analyzed from the perspective of developmental levels, but the implications of this finding were not pursued in his work. The boundaries of authority in relation to the acts regulated by adult authority need to be specified.

Authority relations may not be separated so cleanly from concepts of justice. As the previous example illustrates, parents may command behaviors that are unfair or unjust, they may punish acts that cause harm to others, or they may set rules or demand compliance with regulations intended to protect children's welfare or rights. Thus, parental authority is not always separable from issues of morality. At the same time, parental authority need not be specifically concerned with these issues at all. As will be discussed later in the chapter, the types of issues that provide challenges to parental authority during adolescence often have little to do with justice, rights, or others' welfare.

The work of Youniss and his colleagues (Hunter & Youniss, 1982; Youniss & Smollar, 1985), unlike the research described previously, described developmental changes in the parent–child relationship itself (rather than in children's and adolescents' authority concepts). Through several interview studies with adolescents at different ages, Youniss and Smollar (1985) obtained a great deal of descriptive information on the different dimensions of parents' and adolescents' relationships. They found that adolescents described their parents as retaining unilateral authority over issues involving objective performance (defined as academic performance and adherence to rules) or areas in which parents keep their role as validators. In other areas, they found that unilateral authority was transformed into cooperative decision making and negotiation. And for some topics, Youniss and Smollar found that parents have little authority, notably over areas in which parents are unaware of what their sons and daughters are doing or thinking about, or areas in which adolescents are allowed to act without their parents' intervention. Thus, Youniss and Smollar (1985) found that parental authority varies during adolescence. Although rich in descriptive detail, their analysis lacks a conceptual framework for characterizing the boundaries of legitimate parental authority. In the next section, a distinct domain model of social knowledge that provides such a conceptual framework is described, and then the relation of the model to authority concepts is elaborated.

The domain model: Morality, social convention, and personal issues

A great deal of recent research has indicated that children's understanding of morality, or their prescriptive judgments regarding how to behave, forms an organized system of thought that is developmentally and conceptually distinct from their concepts of social organization and social conventions (Davidson, Turiel, & Black, 1983; Nucci, 1981; Smetana, 1981, 1983, 1985; Turiel, 1979, 1983a; Turiel & Davidson, 1986). Even very young children have been found to view the wrongness of moral issues as stemming from the intrinsic consequences of acts for others (e.g., their effects on others' rights and welfare), rather than from the power of parental or adult authority. According to this view, children across a wide age range are able to distinguish a set of issues pertaining to others' welfare, trust, or the equitable distribution of resources as prescriptive, generalizable, and obligatory. Moreover, across ages, children have been found to judge moral events to be generalizable, independent of authority dictates, and wrong in the absence of rules.

In contrast, the heteronomy described by Piaget as characterizing young children's view of morality is more consistent with the research findings on children's judgments regarding social conventions. Social conventions have been defined as one aspect of children's reasoning about social organization and social systems (Turiel, 1979, 1983a). Conventions are arbitrary, consensually determined behavioral uniformities that coordinate the interactions of individuals within social systems by providing individuals with a set of expectations regarding appropriate behavior. They are relative to the social context in that in different social systems, conventional uniformities may differ and yet serve the same symbolic function (Smetana, 1983; Turiel, 1983a). Children across a wide range have been found consistently to judge social conventions to be relative to the social context, alterable, subject to authority jurisdiction, and contingent on rules.

In turn, concepts of morality and social convention have been distinguished from children's psychological understanding, and more specifically from concepts of personal issues (see Nucci, 1977, 1981, in press; Nucci & Lee, 1993; Smetana, 1982, 1995, for a more extended discussion). Personal issues have been defined as issues that pertain only to the actor, and therefore, are considered to be outside of the realm of conventional regulation and moral concern (Nucci, 1977, 1981, in press; Nucci & Lee, 1993; Smetana, 1982, 1983; Turiel, 1983a; Turiel & Davidson, 1986). Issues of personal choice comprise the private aspects of one's life and entail issues of preference and choice pertaining to friends or activities, the state of one's body, and privacy. It has been proposed that the inclusion of actions within the personal domain may represent an important aspect of the individual's autonomy or distinctiveness from others (Nucci, 1981; Smetana, 1989a).

Claims regarding individual autonomy may appear, at first glance, to represent moral (rather than personal) judgments. The view of personal issues described here is consistent, however, with that of other researchers (Dworkin, 1978; Gewirth, 1978, 1982; Nucci, in press; Nucci & Lee, 1993), who have argued that the notion of rights is grounded in the establishment and maintenance of personal agency. In this view, personal concepts are those aspects of the psychological domain that identify "freedom" as being necessary for maintaining agency and uniqueness. The content of the personal domain thus becomes the content of the individual's identified freedoms. Thus, appeals to personal jurisdiction can be seen as the source of rights claims.

Extensive studies have been conducted with preschool and school-age children and adolescents that indicate that children consistently distinguish between moral and conventional acts, and to a lesser extent, concepts of personal jurisdiction in their judgments and justifications (for reviews of this research, see Helwig, Tisak, and Turiel, 1990; Turiel, Killen, & Helwig, 1987). Thus, rather than forming a developmental sequence, heteronomy, moral autonomy, and autonomy from moral and societal constraint are found throughout development in children's judgments of social convention, morality, and personal issues, respectively.

Judgments of authority in the moral domain

The research reviewed in the previous section indicates that children across a wide age range make autonomous judgments about moral acts and rules and reason about moral transgressions and rules in terms of fairness, rights, or others' welfare. In this research, the criteria for distinguishing morality from social convention have included one frequently used dimension explicitly pertaining to authority; children have been asked to evaluate whether the wrongness of transgressions is independent of authority (e.g., moral) or contingent on authority (e.g., conventional).

However, another body of research emerging from the domain-specificity framework has focused more directly on children's conceptions of adult authority. Children's and adolescents' judgments and justifications have been examined along several other authority-related dimensions, including authorities' legitimacy to make rules, children's obligation to obey authority, adult authorities' obligation to regulate acts, and authority justifications.

Several studies have examined children's and adolescents' judgments regarding the legitimacy of parental authority (Smetana, 1988a, 1993; Smetana & Asquith, 1994; Tisak, 1986) and teachers' and principals' authority (Laupa, 1991; Laupa & Turiel, 1986, 1993; Smetana & Bitz, 1994) to make rules about hypothetical moral acts. The findings from these studies are highly consistent: Children ranging in age from 1st graders to 12th graders have been found to view morality as legitimately regulated by adults (except, as described later, when they are asked to evaluate "immoral" requests, for instance, to steal, or the adults are depicted as lacking in authority on one of several dimensions). Responses affirming the legitimacy of adult authority range from 85% to 100% across studies. When authority is legitimated, responses also do not vary by type of authority (e.g., teachers vs. parents) or family structure. Although married families have been described as more hierarchical and less egalitarian than divorced families (Hetherington, 1989; Weiss, 1979), adolescents who experience different forms of parental authority by virtue of living in different family structures do not differ in their judgments of parents' legitimacy to regulate moral conduct in the family (Smetana, 1993a). In addition, several studies have demonstrated that adolescents' and parents' judgments of the legitimacy of parental authority regarding moral issues do not differ (Smetana, 1988a, 1993b; Smetana & Asquith, 1994), nor do the studies reveal significant age variation from early childhood to late adolescence in judgments of adults' legitimate authority to make moral rules.

Laupa and colleagues (1991; Laupa & Turiel, 1986, 1993) have demonstrated that there are boundaries to legitimate authority, however. In her studies, judgments of legitimacy varied as a function of social position of the authority (e.g., teachers vs. former teachers), knowledge (competent vs. incompetent teachers), and adult status (peer vs. adult authorities). Social position and knowledge both were more important in determining the legitimacy of authority than was adult status, and an awareness of competence and knowledge as criteria for determining the legitimacy of authority increased in middle childhood. Moreover, these findings were replicated in a sample of Korean children in Seoul, Korea (Kim & Turiel, 1993). Several studies also have indicated that adult authority does not legitimately extend to causing harm, prescribing immoral acts, or being unjust or unfair (Damon, 1977; Emler, Ohana, & Moscovici, 1987; Kim & Turiel, 1993; Laupa & Turiel, 1986, 1993; Weston & Turiel, 1980).

Furthermore, the results of several studies indicate that authority is contextually bounded. Laupa and Turiel (1993) found that in general, young children (kindergartners through sixth graders) rejected school principals' authority outside of the jurisdiction of the school. Likewise, in data from Smetana and Asquith (1994), only parents were nearly unanimously endorsed by adolescents as having authority to regulate moral transgressions in the family. In contrast, in another study, the majority of adolescents endorsed teachers and school principals as having the legitimate authority to regulate moral behavior in school (Smetana & Bitz, 1994). As might be expected, however, adolescents overwhelmingly rejected friends as having legitimate moral authority in either the family or school, and teachers were unanimously rejected as having legitimate authority to regulate moral conduct at home. Consistent with the notion of moral autonomy, a significant proportion of adolescents viewed themselves as legitimate moral authorities both at home and in school. However, a small but significant proportion (over a third) of adolescents also endorsed parents and the law as having legitimate authority to regulate morality in school (Smetana & Bitz, 1994) and religious institutions and the law as having the legitimate authority to regulate moral conduct in the family (Smetana & Asquith, 1994). Unfortunately, the reasons for these judgments were not probed. Nevertheless, these findings suggest that adult authority is viewed as shared with those most closely responsible for protecting adolescents' welfare (e.g., parents) and with societal institutions when individuals' welfare or rights are endangered.

Research also indicates that adolescents uniformly view parents (Smetana & Asquith, 1994) as having a duty or obligation to regulate moral conduct. This is consistent with the definition of morality as prescriptive and obligatory (Turiel, 1983a). Moreover, the findings from another study (Tisak, 1986) indicate that children are consistently viewed as having an obligation to respond to moral transgressions, even if there is no explicit rule requiring them to do so. In these studies, the transgressions were depicted as contextually appropriate – that is, adolescents were asked whether parents have an obligation to regulate moral issues at home. We do not know whether judgments of obligation extend to other authority sources in different contexts or how younger children evaluate rule obligation.

Across studies, children are nearly unanimous in endorsing their obligation to obey parental (Braine, Pomerantz, Lorber, & Krantz, 1991; Damon, 1977; Smetana & Asquith, 1994; Tisak, 1986), and teacher (Kim & Turiel, 1993; Laupa, 1991; Laupa & Turiel, 1986) moral rules, once instituted. When the individual giving the command is depicted as having an appropriate social position, children are nearly unanimous in endorsing obedience, with no significant variations according to age. As with judgments of legitimacy, judgments of obedience were seen as bounded; children did not endorse obedience highly when the individual was depicted as lacking the appropriate social position (Laupa, 1991) or knowledge (Kim & Turiel, 1993).

In several studies, children have been asked to justify either why adults can enforce moral rules, or why children need to follow moral rules (Laupa, 1991; Laupa & Turiel, 1986, 1993; Tisak, 1986). Tisak (1986) reported that children primarily justified the legitimacy of adult authority with reference to characteristics of the acts (e.g., the act's effect on others' welfare), and to a lesser extent, on punishment avoidance. Laupa and Turiel (1986, 1993) reported that children's justifications for the legitimacy of adult authority were primarily oriented toward authority and only minimally toward punishment or characteristics of the act, whereas Laupa (1991) reported that for individuals depicted as having both social position and knowledge, justifications primarily focused on authority attributes. Finally, Laupa and Turiel (1993) found that responses entailed a mixture of act-oriented justifications and authority justifications.

Summary. The results of these studies are illuminating when considered in relation to previous findings on authority concepts (Damon, 1977; Piaget, 1932/1965; Selman, 1980; Youniss & Smollar, 1985). At first glance, the findings seem to confirm Piaget's (1932/1965) notion of heteronomy – but, in contrast to Piaget's results, for children of all ages. Children and adolescents were found to respect adults' moral authority to regulate acts revolving around fairness, welfare, and justice. Adults were seen as having legitimate authority to regulate conduct in the moral domain, and children viewed moral regulation as obligatory, both in terms of rule making and obedience to rules. Moreover, there appear to be few generational, contextual, or developmental variations in these findings. This is consistent with Much and Shweder's (1978) description of children's accounts and excuses in naturally occurring "situations of accountability" in nursery schools and kindergartens. They concluded that children's accounts of moral transgressions "suggest that the force or validity of moral breaches is not readily negotiable . . . a strategy in keeping with the perception of moral rules as unalterable and intrinsically valid and worthy of respect" (p. 37).

The findings differ from Piaget (1932/1965), however, in indicating that children draw boundaries to adult authority to regulate morality based on the characteristics of the acts and the contextual appropriateness and attributes of the authority issuing commands. Adults are not seen as having the authority to prescribe immoral acts, and adult authority has to be legitimated by appropriate social position and knowledge. Adolescents also view themselves as sharing legitimate authority with adults, providing further evidence for autonomy in adolescents' moral judgments. At the same time, adolescents view the regulation of moral conduct in the family as within the legitimate jurisdiction of societal institutions such as religious institutions and the law. Thus, children and adolescents appear to have a sophisticated conception of moral authority that entails a recognition that protection of others' rights and welfare transcends particularized relationships in specific contexts.

Moral reasoning in adolescent–parent conflict

The previous studies were designed to reveal distinctions in children's conceptual development and focus on children's and adolescents' reflective judgments regarding hypothetical situations. Another strategy is to examine children's understanding in real-life situations or their judgments about such situations to determine how their social knowledge is reflected in their daily lives. The former type of analysis has been characterized as a "formal analysis" of children's developing concepts, whereas the latter has been called a "functional analysis" (Flavell & Wohlwill, 1969). As others have noted (Dunn & Slomkowski, 1992), within this latter approach, studies of conflict are particularly illuminating. Studies of children's or adolescents' conflicts with their parents provide valuable information on how authority relations in different conceptual domains are negotiated in everyday interaction.

The conclusion that, in general, adolescents view adults as retaining authority over moral issues is supported by recent research on adolescents' and parents' reasoning about actual family conflict (Smetana, 1989a; Smetana, Braeges, & Yau, 1991; Smetana, Yau, Restrepo, & Braeges, 1991). This research indicates that moral issues are infrequent sources of conflict in adolescent–parent relationships. In these studies, only 10% of adolescents' reasoning about actual family conflicts in both individual interviews and family interactions pertained to moral issues, and only a slightly higher percentage of mothers' and fathers' reasoning (approximately 15% in both individual interviews and family interactions) entailed moral justifications. Moreover, adolescents' moral reasoning about conflicts declined with age from preadolescence to adolescence.

Moral reasoning pertained primarily to conflicts over interpersonal relations, and conflicts were described by adolescents as originating in their relationships with siblings or friends. They became problematic in adolescent–parent relationships because parents were drawn in as third parties in moral disputes. That is, the following examples illustrate that adolescents often viewed the outcome of parental intervention in interpersonal conflicts as unfair or unjust or they felt that parents were not properly impartial (or not sufficiently partial in the desired direction!) in settling disputes or distributing resources. Moral conflicts rarely were described as originating in the parent–adolescent relationship itself.

"It's just that they [the parents] feel, you're so much bigger, you're so much stronger, don't pick on him [the brother]. And I sit there and I get so mad sometimes, you know. . . . He's allowed to sit here and take his little plastic men, or whatever, and throw them at me and hit them at me, and chase me. I'm supposed to sit there and turn the other cheek and walk away. And it just seems to me, it's like – They see me standing there big, and they see him standing there smaller, and they never see the situation where he picks up something which could possibly do some destructive damage. They don't see that part. They see the end of it where he swings and misses and I go – WHAM – and hit him or push him, and they hear the end result. So that's what bugs them. . . . But they have to hear my story too! . . . I'm not going to say that beating on your little brother is a healthy release of nervous energy. I think there's better ways you can get rid of it. I just think there's some times when it's justified. So, I mean, it's like [they're] expecting too much."

"Well, my sister and I have disagreements often and my Mom sort of acts like a referee, so she sometimes picks sides. Sometimes because of the facts of what she hears, and it's really about 50% of the time she's on my side and 50% she's on my sister's side. SO WHY IS THAT A CONFLICT? Well, I feel I've always got to be right. I always want my mom to be on my side."

"And he [the brother] usually gets more privileges in the house, and I don't think it's because he's older, it's just because he's braver than I am. He stands up to them. . . . But they usually just say, 'I want you to do this.' And I usually end up doing whatever they want. . . . They'll just say, 'you're wrong,' and they'll accuse me of being wrong, even though they don't know what we're fighting about. Or they'll say, 'You have no right to say anything like that,' and they don't even know what I said!"

These examples are interesting in several respects. First, they are consistent with observational studies of young children, which indicate that although adults may intervene in moral conflicts, the conflicts themselves occur primarily between children (Dunn & Munn, 1985, 1987; Nucci & Nucci, 1982a, 1982b; Nucci & Turiel, 1978; Smetana, 1984, 1989b). In turn, this provides indirect support for the contention (Damon, 1977; Piaget, 1932/1965) that morality develops out of reciprocity between peers rather than from the more hierarchical parent–child relationship.

The examples also are of interest with respect to the issue of sex differences in moral judgments. It has been hypothesized that prevailing theories of moral development are biased against women because they undervalue or ignore women's distinctive voice (Gilligan, 1982; Gilligan & Attanucci, 1988). More specifically, Gilligan has proposed that morality in males is dominated by concerns with justice or fairness abstracted from relationships, whereas morality in females is oriented toward responsibility and care embedded in a web of interpersonal relationships. Although the dichotomous view of development espoused by Gilligan has not withstood empirical scrutiny well (e.g., Walker, 1984, 1991), some sex differences in reasoning have been observed. As Walker (1991) has argued in his careful analysis, few sex differences are observed when children and adolescents are asked to reason about hypothetical moral dilemmas. However, sex differences do emerge when adolescents are asked to reason about self-generated moral dilemmas, but the differences can be attributed primarily to differences in dilemma content. Females' self-generated moral dilemmas focus more on personal moral conflicts (involving a specific person or group of people with whom the subject has an ongoing and significant relationship), which in turn, are more likely to generate a care orientation. In contrast, males' moral dilemmas are more likely to focus on impersonal content (involving institutions, a person, or group of people whom the subject does not know well, or a generalized group, such as students), which in turn, are more likely to reflect a justice orientation. With dilemma content controlled, few sex differences in reasoning are found.

The relevance of the findings on adolescent–parent conflict just discussed to the issue of sex differences in moral reasoning is that when moral conflicts were examined in the context of the family, the conflicts were inherently interpersonal and relational – and thus reflecting a care perspective – for both boys and girls. No sex differences in the frequency of interpersonal moral family conflicts were observed. However, both adolescent males *and* females reasoned about these interpersonal moral conflicts in terms of justice, fairness, and rights, reflecting a justice orientation in their reasoning. No sex differences in reasoning were observed. In contrast to Gilligan, then, these responses indicate that real-life moral conflicts in the family involve contextualized judgments about particular relationships, which are then constructed in terms of justice and rights.

Finally, the findings are consistent with the findings of the research on concepts of adult authority. They suggest that moral issues are not contentious in parent–adolescent relations because parents' moral authority in the family is rarely challenged. Parents are seen as retaining moral authority in the family, at least throughout adolescence. Further research needs to determine if and when parents' moral authority wanes. If adolescent–parent conflict rarely pertains to moral issues, then what kinds of issues cause conflict?

Adolescent–parent conflict: The boundaries of autonomy

In the studies of adolescent–parent conflict described previously (Smetana, 1989a; Smetana, Braeges, et al., 1991; Smetana, Yau, et al,. 1991), parents justified their perspectives on disputes by referring to family rules, parental authority, the adolescent's responsibility in the family, the need for social coordination in dividing labor, and the perceived social costs of adolescents' social nonconformity (e.g., the mother's embarrassment, concern about others' misperceptions of the adolescent, and adolescents' fear of ridicule from peers), and, finally, to contrasting social norms and standards. All of these are examples of social conventional justifications. Conventional justifications were the modal response among parents in these samples; nearly half of all justifications pertained to social conventions, with the remaining justifications divided among prudential reasons (pertaining to health or comfort), pragmatics, psychological justifications, and, as noted previously, moral justifications (see Smetana, 1988b, 1989a; Smetana, Braeges, et al., 1991, for more detail).

In contrast, adolescent appeals to social convention were relatively infrequent and accounted for approximately 13% of their total justifications in both individual interviews and family interactions. Moreover, adolescents' conventional reasoning typically referred to peer group conventions, which were seen as contrary to parental or societal conventions. When asked to provide counterarguments, adolescents clearly understood their parents' conventional perspectives on disputes, but this perspective was explicitly rejected.

Rather, adolescents appealed to exercising or maintaining personal jurisdiction. Appeals to personal jurisdiction were the most frequent type of justification offered by adolescents, accounting for nearly half (49%) of their justifications in individual interviews and more than a third (37%) of their justifications in family interactions. Adolescents' appeals to personal jurisdiction may represent a social-cognitive component of adolescents' developing autonomy or distinctiveness from others (Smetana, 1988a, 1994).

Several empirical studies have indicated that children identify a set of issues as under their personal jurisdiction from early childhood on (Nucci, 1977, 1981; Nucci & Herman, 1982; Smetana, 1986; Tisak, 1993). Moreover, recent research on lower- and middle-class mothers' views of the behaviors that 4- to 6-year-old children should be able to decide for themselves and the issues that mothers are willing to negotiate with their children (Nucci & Smetana, in preparation) suggests that there is considerable continuity from early childhood to adolescence in the types of issues that are contested between mothers and children. In both early childhood and adolescence, conflicts were over schedules, routines, bedtimes (in adolescence, this issue was expressed as conflicts over curfew), chores (typically depicted as "picking up" in the early years), appearances, and regulating activities. Of course, there are some differences between the content of parent–child conflicts in early childhood and adolescence. Conflicts over homework were rare among mothers with young children but occurred with some frequency during adolescence, whereas conflicts over what the child eats were prevalent in early childhood but virtually nonexistent in adolescence. Nevertheless, these issues – preferences, activities, the state of one's body – are prototypically personal issues in this culture.

Notably, the issues that mothers mentioned as sources of conflict with their young children were the same issues that they viewed in another part of the interview as up to the child to determine, which also were consistent with the issues identified by mothers of even younger children in another study (Gralinski & Kopp, 1993). Their justifications for why these issues should be left up to the child indicated an awareness of young children's developing competence, self-esteem, agency, and autonomy. Likewise, when asked to provide counterarguments, or to reason from their adolescent's perspectives, parents also referred to their adolescents' need for personal jurisdiction. However, parents also rejected these reasons as having validity in the context of disputes. These findings are somewhat puzzling. They suggest that parents may have forgotten what they acknowledged as parents a decade earlier! To understand these findings better, we return to studies of children's and adolescents' judgments of adult authority regarding conventional and personal issues.

Judgments of authority in the conventional domain

Compared with the number of studies of adult authority to regulate morality reviewed previously, relatively few studies have investigated children and adolescents' concepts of adult authority regarding acts in the conventional domain.

The available research indicates that children (Damon, 1977; Tisak, 1986) and adolescents (Smetana, 1988a, 1993; Smetana & Asquith, 1994) agree that parents have the legitimate authority to regulate family conventions such as doing the chores, using appropriate manners, and addressing parents appropriately. Several studies also indicate that students acknowledge that school authorities may legitimately establish and enforce school-based norms pertaining to appropriate conventional behavior such as forms of address, dress codes, or talking in class, as well as the rules and procedures for academic activity (e.g., doing homework on time, writing legibly, or the form for doing math problems; Blumenfeld, Pintrich, & Hamilton, 1987; Dodsworth-Rugani, 1982; Smetana & Bitz, 1994; Weston & Turiel, 1980). The majority of children and adolescents in these studies judged adult authority regarding social conventions as legitimate based on concerns with social coordination and punishment avoidance (Tisak, 1986), although studies directly comparing judgments regarding morality and convention indicate that adult authority is seen as less legitimate for conventional than for moral issues (Smetana & Asquith, 1994; Smetana & Bitz, 1994; Tisak, 1986). Moreover, few differences between parents' and adolescents' judgments of the legitimacy of parental authority regarding conventional issues have been observed; both parents and adolescents agreed that parents should retain authority over these issues (Smetana, 1988a, 1993; Smetana & Asquith, 1994). Thus, in general, the findings reveal little variation in judgments of the legitimacy of authority to regulate conventional acts as a function of context (e.g., home or school), family structure (Smetana, 1993a), generation, or age.

The studies also indicate that as in the moral domain, parental authority in the conventional domain is contextually bounded. Adolescents consistently endorse parents' authority to regulate familial social conventions, and they clearly reject the legitimacy of other authorities or institutions to regulate social conventions in the family (Smetana & Asquith, 1994). They were more equivocal about their own authority to regulate conventional conduct; half of the adolescents studied in Smetana and Asquith (1994) viewed themselves as having legitimate authority to regulate family social conventions.

Several studies also indicate that teacher and school authority is contextually bounded and restricted to certain types of acts. A majority of adolescents in one study viewed teachers as having the right to regulate conventional behavior in school (Smetana & Bitz, 1994), but teachers were seen as having significantly more authority than school principals, perhaps because the acts depicted primarily pertained to classroom transgressions. In contrast, adolescents clearly rejected parents, friends, or the law as having legitimate authority to regulate school social conventions, although more than a third of the adolescents in this study viewed themselves as legitimate authorities over conventional issues in the school context (Smetana & Bitz, 1994). Furthermore, recent research (Raviv, Bar-Tal, Raviv, & Houminer, 1990; Raviv, Bar-Tal, Raviv, & Peleg, 1990) indicated that children's views of teachers as "epistemic" authorities differ according to the type of expertise considered. Their research indicates that teachers are generally regarded as authorities regarding formal knowledge (e.g., knowledge pertaining to school studies, politics, and science), but with age, children are less likely to view teachers as experts regarding children's pastimes, physical appearances, and choice of friends.

Adolescents typically viewed parents as having a duty or obligation to regulate conventional acts in the family (Smetana & Asquith, 1994), although they viewed parents as having significantly less of an obligation to regulate conventional than moral rules. Moreover, children endorsed the notion that they have an obligation to respond to witnessed conventional transgressions, although such a response is seen as less obligatory than for moral transgressions (Tisak, 1986). Finally, both children (Tisak, 1986) and adolescents (Smetana & Asquith, 1994) view themselves as having an obligation to obey parents' conventional rules, once formalized. However, in contrast to judgments regarding moral transgressions, the endorsement of obedience appears to decline with age. The nearly unanimous responses endorsing obedience in middle childhood (Tisak, 1986) appear to decline to a strong but not unanimous majority (69%) in adolescence (Smetana & Asquith, 1994).

Summary. The results of these studies indicate that children and adolescents view adults as having legitimate jurisdiction over social conventions. Given that social conventions are defined as contextually relative, adults' authority is perceived by adolescents as bounded by the social context: Parents are seen to have legitimate jurisdiction over social conventions in the family, and teachers are seen to have legitimate jurisdiction over the social conventions of the classroom. Moreover, the finding that principals are seen as having less authority to regulate classroom conventions than do teachers suggests that adolescents draw the boundaries of conventional authority very narrowly, indeed! Moreover, the results of these studies suggest that authorities are not seen as having an obligation to regulate social conventions, but children do see themselves as having an obligation to comply with conventional rules, once instituted.

However, judgments that children are obligated to comply with conventional authority decline with age from childhood to adolescence. More-over, adolescents view themselves as having the legitimate authority to regulate social conventions both at home and in school. Thus, they view conventional authority as shared with adults. These findings are of interest in relation to the challenges to parental conventional authority observed in studies of adolescent–parent conflict (Smetana, 1989a, 1993a).

Adult authority regarding personal issues

There have been few studies examining children's and adolescents' concepts of parental authority regarding acts in the personal domain (Smetana, 1988a, 1993; Smetana & Asquith, 1994). In the available studies, hypotheti-cal personal items have pertained to preferences (e.g., for television pro-grams or music); spending decisions (what to buy for lunch at school, whether to spend allowance money on games), appearances (dress, makeup, or hairstyle), activities (talking on the phone), control over one's body (e.g., bedtimes), and friendship preferences. There has been even less systematic research examining children's and adolescents' conceptions of legitimate school authority regarding personal issues in the school context. One recent study examined adolescents' judgments about personal issues in school, such as what students can keep in their lockers, the privacy of their communica-tions, and choices and preferences regarding appearances, friendship choices, and activities (Smetana & Bitz, 1994).

The findings from these studies are highly consistent: Children uniformly view personal issues as beyond the bounds of legitimate adult jurisdiction. Most adolescents reject parents or teachers as having legitimate authority to regulate hypothetical acts in the personal domain (Smetana, 1988a, 1993; Smetana & Asquith, 1994; Smetana & Bitz, 1994). Moreover, adoles-cents were nearly unanimous in endorsing their legitimate jurisdiction over personal issues and in rejecting friends, teachers, religious institutions, or the law as having legitimate authority over personal issues in the context of the family. Interestingly, adolescents also overwhelmingly endorsed their legitimate jurisdiction over personal issues in school, but they were more equivocal in rejecting friends' and parents' authority regarding these issues. Only the law was unanimously rejected as having legitimate jurisdiction over personal choices in school (Smetana & Bitz, 1994).

Furthermore, a recent study revealed that most adolescent subjects judged that schools, friends, or religious institutions do not have the legiti-mate authority to regulate drug use, which was treated as a personal or prudential issue that is primarily under personal discretion. (Prudential issues have been defined as a nonsocial issue pertaining to the self, including health, comfort, and safety; Tisak, 1993; Tisak & Turiel, 1984.) Only a minority of subjects judged that parents legitimately have the authority to regulate drug use (Nucci, Guerra, & Lee, 1991). Although adolescents in this study clearly recognized that drugs may cause harm to the self, a significant percentage of adolescents endorsed themselves as legitimate authorities with regard to drug use, and high-drug-using adolescents were nearly twice as likely to endorse themselves as authorities regarding drug use than their low-drug-using counterparts (Nucci et al., 1991). (Arguments can be made that self-harm is a moral issue; see Berkowitz et al., Chapter 6, this volume, for elaborations of this argument.)

Adolescents and their parents consistently have been found to differ in their judgments of personal issues (Smetana, 1988a, 1993; Smetana & Asquith, 1994). Across studies, more than half of all parents endorse the view that they have legitimate jurisdiction over actions that adolescents view as within their personal domain. Moreover, judgments that parents have legitimate authority over personal issues consistently have been found to decline with age from preadolescence to late adolescence (Smetana, 1988a; Smetana & Asquith, 1994).

Adolescents uniformly rejected the notion that parents have an obligation to regulate acts in the personal domain (Smetana & Asquith, 1994). Parents also do not view rules regarding personal issues as obligatory, but they view regulation of the personal domain as more obligatory than do adolescents (Smetana & Asquith, 1994). Furthermore, adolescents generally do not see themselves as obligated to comply with rules governing the personal domain, once they are formalized, and judgments of rule obedience declined with age during adolescence (Smetana & Asquith, 1994).

Summary. The findings demonstrate rather conclusively that adolescents draw boundaries to legitimate parental authority and that personal issues are seen as beyond those boundaries. Adolescents consistently viewed personal issues as not legitimately regulated by parents and nonobligatory, both in terms of parental rule making and adolescent compliance. These findings are not surprising, given that personal issues are, by definition, considered to be beyond the bounds of societal regulation and moral concern. But the findings also reveal that the boundaries of the personal domain are permeable: they increase with age during adolescence and are contested by parents. Parents of adolescents – like the mothers of 4- and 6-year-olds studied by Nucci and myself – clearly believe that there are boundaries to parental authority and acknowledge that some actions are legitimately subject to adolescents' personal jurisdiction. But their acknowledgment of adolescents' personal jurisdiction appears to lag behind adolescents'.

Boundaries of parental authority and adolescent–parent conflict

The findings reviewed in the previous sections indicate that although the boundaries of personal jurisdiction are enlarged or expanded during adolescence, personal jurisdiction does not develop de novo during adolescence, nor is conventional regulation shed completely in adulthood. Children and adolescents accept parents' legitimate authority to regulate social conventions in the family, although there appears to be a decline from childhood to adolescence in the extent to which they view compliance with parental conventions as obligatory. At the same time, the studies indicate that parents of children across a wide age range acknowledge the validity of at least some of children's appeals to personal jurisdiction. Thus, the shifts from unilateral to mutual authority noted by other researchers (Damon, 1977; Youniss & Smollar, 1985) appear to occur primarily at the intersection between conventional authority and personal jurisdiction, and adolescent–parent conflict occurs over where these boundaries should be drawn.

This hypothesis was tested explicitly in several of the studies of adolescents' conceptions of parental and teacher authority reviewed earlier. In these studies, adolescents (and parents in the studies of parental authority) evaluated an additional category of items, referred to as multifaceted. Multifaceted items were defined as issues containing both personal and conventional components and that thus overlap domain boundaries. For instance, issues such as the adolescent cleaning her room, a frequent source of conflict in adolescent–parent relations (Smetana, 1989a), can be seen as personal to the extent that the room is seen as part of the house. Furthermore, schools regulate a variety of issues that are considered to be personal prerogatives in other contexts. The results of one study examining children's positive and negative feelings about various classroom rules (Arsenio, 1984) indicated that a majority of the negative rule evaluations provided by fifth grade boys involved undue teacher control of such nonacademic activities as restrictions on free-time activities and bathroom procedures. A more recent study (Smetana & Bitz, 1994) examined students' judgments about school regulation of similar multifaceted issues (e.g., when students can use the bathroom, when and where they can have intimate interactions such as kissing boyfriends and girlfriends, when they can see their friends, and keeping communications between friends private; Smetana & Bitz, 1994).

The findings from these studies suggest that multifaceted issues comprise the zone where shifts from unilateral to mutual authority occur (Smetana, 1988a, 1993; Smetana & Asquith, 1994; Smetana & Bitz, 1994). Multifaceted issues, like the "zone of proximal development" described by Vygotsky (Rogoff, 1990; Vygotsky, 1978; Wertsch, 1979), may constitute the dynamic

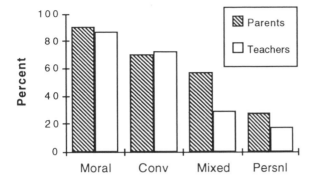

Figure 7.1. Judgments of legitimacy of parental and teacher authority. From Smetana and Asquith (1994) and Smetana and Bitz (1994).

region where the development of autonomy proceeds. This view differs from Vygotsky, however, in at least one crucial respect: Development is not seen as proceeding through children's guided participation in activities slightly beyond their competence. Rather, children's active assertions of competence provoke development and may guide parents!

The assertion that multifaceted issues constitute a dynamic region of development implies that judgments regarding these concepts should be developmentally and contextually variable and that parents and children should differ in their judgments regarding these issues. The findings from research on judgments of multifaceted issues in the family and at school are consistent with these predictions. First, the results of several studies indicate that the extent to which these issues are seen as personal and beyond the bounds of adult authority increases with age during adolescence (Smetana, 1988a, 1993; Smetana & Asquith, 1994). Also, as Figure 7.1 illustrates, judgments of multifaceted issues appear to be more sensitive to contextual variation than are other issues. For instance, parental rules regarding multifaceted issues are seen to be more legitimate than school rules (Smetana & Asquith, 1994; Smetana & Bitz, 1994). Furthermore, across studies, parents consistently viewed multifaceted issues as legitimately regulated by parents and contingent on parental authority, based on concerns with social convention, whereas adolescents consistently viewed these issues as under their personal jurisdiction, based on personal reasons (Smetana, 1988a, 1993; Smetana & Asquith, 1994). Finally, adolescents and parents reported more frequent conflicts over actual multifaceted issues than over moral, conventional, or personal issues (Smetana & Asquith, 1994). Together these findings provide evidence that shifts from unilateral to mutual authority during adolescence

(Youniss & Smollar, 1985) and from dependence to individuation occur primarily over the boundaries of adolescents' personal jurisdiction and that adolescent–parent conflict provides one mechanism for enlarging those boundaries.

Adolescents and parents have different interpretations of conflicts because the rules, expectations, or events that cause conflict are multifaceted, and adolescents' and parents' competing goals in social situations lead them to focus on, or subordinate, different concerns (Smetana, 1988b). Parents' appeals to social conventions (either societal laws, such as those pertaining to drug use, cultural norms or conventions, or more idiosyncratic family rules and expectations) serve to maintain social order, facilitate social interaction, and facilitate adolescents' effective participation in society. Thus, parents' appeals to social convention can be seen to serve a socializing function in adolescent development.

In contrast, adolescents' appeals to personal jurisdiction serve to increase adolescents' agency, or enlarge their sphere of personal action, and thus can be seen to serve an individuating function in development. The conflict between adolescents' appeals to personal jurisdiction over issues that parents consider to be social-conventional entails the renegotiation of the boundaries between parental authority and individual authority over the self and, as such, mirrors the fundamental tension between the individual and society. There may be little disagreement between parents and children during middle childhood on the conventionality of a variety of family issues, but adolescents view themselves as becoming increasingly emancipated from these parental perspectives.

Several factors may account for the increased conflict in parent–child relationships found during adolescence (Collins & Laursen, 1992; Montemayor, 1986; Steinberg, 1990). Several researchers have argued that conflict is more likely during developmental transitions, when parents' expectancies are violated (Collins, 1990; Emery, 1992), but this explanation does not specify the developmental processes that account for conflict. Adolescents' developing understanding of conventions as normative regulation within hierarchical systems (Turiel, 1979, 1983a) leads to the recognition that adult conventions can be changed, perhaps provoking the challenges to parental authority that are instantiated in adolescent–parent conflict. The decline in children's orientations toward compliance with adult conventional authority noted previously may be one aspect of children's developing understanding of conventions. Adolescents' rejection of parental convention also may be an aspect of their developing understanding of self and personal issues. Nucci and Lee (1993) have asserted that children are not able to individuate until early adolescence, when the personal domain is conceptualized in psychological terms, and children are able to view their personal sphere as fully beyond the legitimate intrusion of their parents. Changes in children's developing psychological understanding of parents during adolescence also may lead to increased questioning of parental authority. For instance, research utilitizing a questionnaire measure has demonstrated that, during adolescence, children begin to perceive their parents as people and deidealize them (Steinberg & Silverberg, 1986). It is possible that this realization and accompanying recognition of their parents' fallibility lead adolescents to question the validity of parental rules and authority.

Conflict thus entails adolescents' and parents' inability to coordinate conflicting social-cognitive perspectives and provides a context for parents and children to articulate and discuss divergent perspectives. This, in turn, leads to changes in those perspectives. That is, conflict forces parents to reevaluate the limits of their authority and the boundaries of adolescents' personal jurisdiction. Thus, parents' appeals to social convention, adolescents' rejection of their parents' perspective, and their reinterpretation of conventions as legitimately under their personal jurisdiction form a continual dialectic in which the boundaries of parental authority are subtly transformed. Parents shift from viewing a variety of conflicts as conventional and legitimately subject to their authority to granting the adolescent increasing personal jurisdiction over these issues.

Autonomy and conflict in a cultural context

Recently, it has been argued that American culture (and more broadly, Western cultures) are individualistic and stress self-sufficiency, personal goals, autonomy, and detachment from others (e.g., Kessen, 1979; Markus & Kitayama, 1991; Sampson, 1977; Shweder, 1986; Shweder & Bourne, 1984; Triandis, 1989, 1990). This description typically is contrasted to other cultures that are oriented toward authority, tradition, duty, collectivism, and harmony in interpersonal relations (but for a critique of this view, see Turiel, 1994; Turiel & Wainryb, 1994; Wainryb & Turiel, Chapter 9, this volume). If autonomy develops from constraint and adolescent–parent conflict provides one mechanism for the development of adolescent autonomy, as has been maintained here, then this characterization of cultural differences raises inevitable questions about the meaning and cross-cultural generality of the picture of parent–child authority relations and adolescent–parent conflict described here.

Although there are variations in how personhood is defined across cultures (Geertz, 1975; Markus & Kitayama, 1991; Shweder & Bourne, 1984), it has been asserted that notions of self and personhood are basic human concepts (Damon & Hart, 1988; Geertz, 1975). Support for this proposition comes from surveys of the anthropological literature, which indicate that concepts of the self and person are universal (LeVine & White, 1986). This suggests that although there may be cultural variations in the boundaries that constrain or define the personal domain (Nucci, in press; Nucci & Lee, 1993), and thus, what is considered to be under the individual's personal jurisdiction, all cultures must treat some issues as fundamentally within the boundaries of personal control and necessary for the establishment of the self.

In turn, this suggests that variations in the conceptual boundaries between the personal and the conventional domains may be directly related to the occurrence of adolescent–parent conflict. That is, conflict may be greater in cultures (such as ours) that view the individual as exercising personal jurisdiction over a broad range of issues – as having what Goffman (1971) terms numerous "territories of the self." Conflict also may be greater in cultures (such as ours) where adolescents clearly have transitional status in society (Benedict, 1938) and where the boundaries between the personal and the conventional are sometimes ambiguously defined. For instance, research has indicated that American children and adults treat social rules that have low social utility (e.g., rules of etiquette) as conventional in private contexts such as the family, but as personal in public contexts (Miller & Bersoff, 1988). In contrast, adolescent–parent conflict may be more muted in cultures where the boundaries of the personal domain are drawn both more clearly and more restrictively and where issues that in this culture are considered to be under personal jurisdiction are seen as regulated by society and social convention. A recent analysis of anthropological descriptions of over 160 cultures suggests that adolescent–parent conflict is widespread, even in more traditional or collectivistic cultures (Schlegel & Barry, 1991). Their societal-structural analysis is consistent with this hypothesis. That is, although they focus on the social organization of society – the means of production, the structure of the household, and control over property – to account for variations in adolescent–parent conflict, these features are seen as determining the extent to which adolescents are required to become independent from their families.

More direct evidence for this hypothesis comes from a recent study of adolescent–parent conflict among lower-class Chinese adolescents in Hong Kong (Yau & Smetana, 1995). As in the Smetana (1989a) study discussed previously, adolescents were interviewed extensively about self-generated conflicts. Adolescents did report having conflicts with their parents, although the conflicts were reported to be less frequent, less severe, and fewer in number than among primarily white, middle-class American adolescents. However, conflicts were over the same types of issues as found in the American sample (although conflicts about homework and academic achievement were more prevalent among Hong Kong adolescents than among American adolescents), and Chinese adolescents, like their American counterparts, reasoned about conflicts primarily as issues of maintaining or exercising personal jurisdiction. These findings suggest that even in a culture that is considered to be collectivistic and oriented toward interpersonal obligations, conflict may serve the same individuating function in development.

Although the content of the personal domain may be canalized by culture (Nucci, in press; Nucci & Lee, 1993), how cultures draw the boundaries between individuals' personal jurisdiction and societal convention and social order appears to be continually renegotiated during adolescence within the context of the family and also may, in turn, provide a mechanism for change in those cultural boundaries. There is some evidence in support of this hypothesis. For instance, Feldman and Rosenthal (1990) found that Western-acculturated Chinese adolescents expected greater behavioral autonomy at earlier ages than their less acculturated counterparts. Thus, to paraphrase Cole (1985), adolescent–parent conflict and relationships may be the crucible of development *and* culture.

Conclusions

The studies reviewed here generally support the view that autonomy develops from adult constraint, but they suggest that this development is more complex and circuitous than has been depicted in earlier accounts. Children of all ages are morally autonomous and demonstrate respect for adults' authority to regulate morality and social convention in different contexts. They display a willingness to comply with adult regulation in the moral and conventional domains – as long as the authority is legitimated and the context is appropriate. Rather than reflecting an immature orientation toward the greater power and authority of adults, children's judgments reflect an awareness of the features of the acts that are regulated, the contextual boundaries of authority, and the attributes that endow the authority with legitimacy.

In the view outlined here, autonomy (in the personal domain) develops from constraint (in the conventional domain), as the boundaries of personal jurisdiction are continually redrawn and renegotiated in dialectical relations with parents in ontogenesis. Adolescent–parent conflict provides one mechanism for challenging parental authority and for redefining conventional issues as under adolescents' personal jurisdiction.

It should be noted that this account of the conceptual development of personal autonomy is inherently social, relational, and affective. That is, the content of the personal domain – what is considered to be personal – and how broadly or narrowly the boundaries of the personal domain are drawn are seen as varying across cultural contexts. Moreover, within cultural contexts, evidence suggests that there is considerable contextual and developmental variability in judgments of personal jurisdiction. This view of development is also relational in that within cultural contexts, concepts of autonomy and the boundaries of adult authority are seen as constructed, elaborated, and negotiated in interactions with parents and other agents of society. In describing reasoning about conflict and conceptions of authority, I have characterized these issues in primarily cognitive terms. But the concepts that are constructed are inseparable from the affective context in which they develop. As parents and their adolescents surely will attest, these conflicts can be hotly debated and deeply felt. In contrast to the social constructivists (e.g., Shweder & Bourne, 1984), who view the development of self as merely recapitulating societal constructs, this suggests that conceptions of personal autonomy are socially constructed but not socially determined (Nucci, in press; Nucci & Lee, 1993). In negotiating, challenging, and resisting adult authority, children and adolescents reconstruct the social and moral order and thereby construct the self.

References

Arsenio, W. (1984). *The affective atmosphere of the classroom: Children's conceptions of teachers and social rules.* Paper presented at the annual meeting of the American Educational Research Association, New Orleans.

Benedict, R. (1938). Continuities and discontinuities in cultural conditioning. *Psychiatry, 1,* 161–167.

Blumenfeld, P. C., Pintrich, P. R., & Hamilton, V. L. (1987). Teacher talk and students' reasoning about morals, conventions, and achievement. *Child Development, 58,* 1389–1401.

Braine, L. G., Pomerantz, E., Lorber, D., & Krantz, D. H. (1991). Conflicts with authority: Children's feelings, actions, and justifications. *Developmental Psychology, 27,* 829–840.

Cole, M. (1985). The zone of proximal development: Where culture and cognition create each other. In J. V. Wertsch (Ed.), *Culture, communication, and cognition: Vygotskian perspectives* (pp. 146–161). Cambridge: Cambridge University Press.

Collins, W. A. (1990). Parent–child relationships in the transition to adolescence: Continuity and change in interaction, affect, and cognition. In R. Montemayor, G. R. Adams, & T. P. Gulotta (Eds.), *From childhood to adolescence: A transitional period?* (pp. 85–106). Newbury Park, CA: Sage.

Collins, W. A., & Laursen, B. (1992). Conflict and relationships during adolescence. In C. U. Shantz, & W. W. Hartup (Eds.), *Conflict in child and adolescent development* (pp. 216–241). Cambridge: Cambridge University Press.

Damon, W. (1977). *The social world of the child.* San Francisco: Jossey-Bass.

Damon, W., & Hart, D. (1988). *Self-understanding in childhood and adolescence.* Cambridge: Cambridge University Press.

Davidson, P., Turiel, E., & Black, A. (1983). The effect of stimulus familiarity on the use of criteria and justifications in children's social reasoning. *British Journal of Developmental Psychology, 1,* 49–65.

Dodsworth-Rugani, K. J. (1982). *The development of concepts of social structure and their relationship to school rules and authority.* Unpublished doctoral dissertation, University of California, Berkeley.

Dunn, J., & Munn, P. (1985). Becoming a family member: Family conflict and the development of social understanding in the second year. *Child Development, 56,* 764–774.

Dunn, J., & Munn, P. (1987). The development of justifications in disputes. *Developmental Psychology, 23,* 781–798.

Dunn, J., & Slomkowski, C. (1992). Conflict and the development of social understanding. In C. U. Shantz & W. W. Hartup (Eds.), *Conflict in child and adolescent development* (pp. 70–92). Cambridge: Cambridge University Press.

Dworkin, R. (1978). *Taking rights seriously.* Cambridge, MA: Harvard University Press.

Emery, R. E. (1992). Family conflicts and their developmental implications: A conceptual analysis of meanings for the structure of relationships. In C. U. Shantz & W. W. Hartup (Eds.), *Conflict in child and adolescent development* (pp. 270–298). Cambridge: Cambridge University Press.

Emler, N., Ohana, J., & Moscovici, S. (1987). Children's beliefs about institutional roles: A cross-national study of representations of the teachers' role. *British Journal of Educational Psychology, 57,* 26–37.

Feldman, S. S., & Rosenthal, D. A. (1990). The acculturation of autonomy expectations in Chinese high schoolers residing in two Western nations. *International Journal of Psychology, 25,* 259–281.

Flavell, J. H., & Wohlwill, J. F. (1969). Formal and functional aspects of cognitive development. In D. Elkind & J. H. Flavell (Eds.), *Studies in cognitive development: Essays in honor of Jean Piaget* (pp. 67–120). Oxford: Oxford University Press.

Geertz, C. (1975). On the nature of anthropological understanding. *American Scientist, 63,* 47–53.

Gewirth, A. (1978). *Reason and morality.* Chicago: University of Chicago Press.

Gewirth, A. (1982). *Human rights: Essays on justification and applications.* Chicago: University of Chicago Press.

Gilligan, C. (1982). *In a different voice.* Cambridge, MA: Harvard University Press.

Gilligan, C., & Attanucci, J. (1988). Two moral orientations: Gender differences and similarities. *Merrill-Palmer Quarterly, 34,* 223–237.

Goffman, E. (1971). *Relations in public.* New York: Harper and Row.

Gralinski, J. H., & Kopp, C. B. (1993). Everyday rules for behavior: Mothers' requests to young children. *Developmental Psychology, 29,* 573–584.

Hartup, W. W. (1989). Social relationships and their developmental significance. *American Psychologist, 44,* 120–126.

Helwig, C. C., Tisak, M. S., & Turiel, E. (1990). Children's social reasoning in context: Reply to Gabennesch. *Child Development, 61,* 2068–2078.

Hetherington, E. M. (1989). Coping with family transitions: Winners, losers, and survivors. *Child Development, 60,* 1–14.

Hunter, F., & Youniss, J. (1982). Changes in functions of three relations during adolescence. *Developmental Psychology, 18,* 806–811.

Kessen, W. (1979). The American child and other cultural inventions. *American Psychologist, 34,* 815–820.

Kim, J. M., & Turiel, E. (1993). *Korean children's concepts of adult and peer authority.* Unpublished manuscript, University of California, Berkeley.

Kohlberg, L. (1969). Stage and sequence: The cognitive-developmental approach to socialization. In D. Goslin (Ed.), *Handbook of socialization theory and research* (pp. 347–480). Skokie, IL: Rand McNally.

Kohlberg, L. (1971). From is to ought: How to commit the naturalistic fallacy and get away with it in the study of moral development. In T. Mischel (Ed.), *Cognitive development and epistemology* (pp. 151–235). New York: Academic Press.

Laupa, M. (1991). Children's reasoning about three authority attributes: Adult status, knowledge, and social position. *Developmental Psychology, 27,* 321–329.

Laupa, M., & Turiel, E. (1986). Children's conceptions of adult and peer authority. *Child Development, 57,* 405–412.

Laupa, M., & Turiel, E. (1993). Children's concepts of authority and social context. *Journal of Educational Psychology, 85,* 191–197.

LeVine, R., & White, M. (1986). *Human conditions: The cultural basis for educational development.* New York: Routledge and Kegan Paul.

Markus, H. R., & Kitayama, S. (1991). Culture and the self: Implications for cognition, emotion, and motivation. *Psychological Bulletin, 98,* 224–253.

Miller, J. G., & Bersoff, D. M. (1988). When do American children and adults reason in social conventional terms? *Developmental Psychology, 24,* 366–375.

Montemayor, R. (1986). Family variation in storm and stress. *Journal of Adolescent Research, 1,* 15–31.

Much, N., & Shweder, R. A. (1978). Speaking of rules: The analysis of culture in breach. In W. Damon (Ed.), *New directions for child development: Vol. 2. Moral development* (pp. 19–40). San Francisco: Jossey-Bass.

Nucci, L. P. (1977). *Social development: Personal, conventional, and moral concepts.* Unpublished Ph.D. dissertation, University of California, Santa Cruz.

Nucci, L. P. (1981). The development of personal concepts: A domain distinct from moral or societal concepts. *Child Development, 52,* 114–121.

Nucci, L. P. (in press). Morality and the sphere of personal actions. In T. Brown, E. Turiel, & E. Reed (Eds.), *Knowledge and values.* Hillsdale, NJ: Lawrence Erlbaum.

Nucci, L. P., Guerra, N., & Lee, J. (1991). Adolescent judgments of the personal, prudential, and normative aspects of drug usage. *Developmental Psychology, 27,* 841–848.

Nucci, L. P., & Herman, S. (1982). Behavioral disordered children's conceptions of moral, conventional, and personal issues. *Jorunal of Abnormal Child Psychology, 10,* 411–426.

Nucci, L. P., & Lee, J. (1993). Morality and personal autonomy. In G. G. Noam & T. Wren (Eds.), *The moral self: Building a better paradigm* (pp. 123–148). Cambridge, MA: MIT Press.

Nucci, L. P., & Nucci, M. S. (1982a). Children's social interactions in the context of moral and conventional transgressions. *Child Development, 53,* 403–412.

Nucci, L. P., & Nucci, M. S. (1982b). Children's responses to moral and social-conventional transgressions in free-play settings. *Child Development, 53,* 1337–1342.

Nucci, L. P., & Smetana, J. G. (in preparation). *Mothers' reasoning about their children's personal autonomy.* Unpublished manuscript, University of Illinois at Chicago.

Nucci, L.P., & Turiel, E. (1978). Social interactions and the development of social concepts in preschool children. *Child Development, 49,* 400–407.

Okin, S. M. (1989). *Justice, gender, and the family.* New York: Basic Books.

Piaget, J. (1932/1965). *The moral judgment of the child.* New York: Free Press.

Raviv, A., Bar-Tal, D., Raviv. A., & Houminer, D. (1990). Development in children's perceptions of epistemic authorities. *British Journal of Developmental Psychology, 8,* 157–169.

Raviv, A., Bar-Tal, D., Raviv, A., & Peleg, D. (1990). Perceptions of epistemic authority by children and adolescents. *Journal of Youth and Adolescence, 19,* 495–509.

Rawls, J. (1971). *A theory of justice.* Cambridge: Cambridge University Press.

Rogoff, B. (1990). *Apprenticeship in thinking: Cognitive development in social context.* Oxford: Oxford University Press.

Sampson, E. E. (1977). Psychology and the American ideal. *Journal of Personality and Social Psychology, 35,* 767–782.

Schlegel, A., & Barry, H., 3rd. (1991). *Adolescence: An anthropological inquiry.* New York: Free Press.

Selman, R. L. (1980). *The growth of interpersonal understanding: Developmental and clinical analyses.* New York: Academic Press.

Shweder, R. A. (1986). Divergent rationalities: In D. W. Fiske & R. A. Shweder (Eds.), *Metatheory in social science: Pluralisms and subjectivities* (pp. 163–196). Chicago: University of Chicago Press.

Shweder, R. A., & Bourne, E. J. (1984). Does the concept of the person vary cross-culturally? In R. A. Shweder & R. A. Levine (Eds.), *Culture theory: Essays on mind, self, and emotion* (pp. 158–199). Cambridge: Cambridge University Press.

Smetana, J. G. (1981). Preschool children's conceptions of moral and social rules. *Child Development, 52,* 1333–1336.

Smetana, J. G. (1982). *Concepts of self and morality: Women's reasoning about abortion.* New York: Praeger.

Smetana, J. G. (1983). Social-cognitive development: Domain distinctions and coordinations. *Developmental Review, 3,* 131–147.

Smetana, J. G. (1984). Toddlers' social interactions regarding moral and conventional transgressions. *Child Development, 55,* 1767–1776.

Smetana, J. G. (1985). Preschool children's conceptions of transgressions: The effects of varying moral and conventional domain-related attributes. *Developmental Psychology, 21,* 18–29.

Smetana, J. G. (1986). Preschool children's conceptions of sex-role transgressions. *Child Development, 57,* 862–871.

Smetana, J. G. (1988a). Adolescents' and parents' conceptions of parental authority. *Child Development, 59,* 321–335.

Smetana, J. G. (1988b). Concepts of self and social convention: Adolescents' and parents' reasoning about hypothetical and actual family conflicts. In M. R. Gunnar & W. A. Collins (Eds.), *21st Minnesota Symposium on Child Psychology: Development during the transition to adolescence* (pp. 79–122). Hillsdale, NJ: Lawrence Erlbaum.

Smetana, J. G. (1989a). Adolescents' and parents' reasoning about actual family conflicts. *Child Development, 60,* 1052–1067.

Smetana, J. G. (1989b). Toddlers' social interactions in the context of moral and conventional transgressions in the home. *Developmental Psychology, 25,* 499–508.

Smetana, J. G. (1993). Conceptions of parental authority in divorced and married mothers and their adolescents. *Journal of Research in Adolescence, 3,* 19–40.

Smetana, J. G. (1994). Conflict and coordination in adolescent-parent relationships. In S. Shulman (Ed.), *Close relationships and socioemotional development* (pp. 155–184). Norwood, NJ: Ablex.

Smetana, J. G. (1995). Parenting styles and conceptions of parental authority during adolescence. *Child Development, 66,* 299–316.

Smetana, J. G., & Asquith, P. (1994). Adolescents' and parents' conceptions of parental authority and adolescent autonomy. *Child Development, 65,* 1147–1162.

Smetana, J. G., & Bitz, B. (1994). *Adolescents' conceptions of teachers' authority and their relation to rule violations in school.* Unpublished manuscript, University of Rochester.

Smetana, J. G., Braeges, J. L., & Yau, J. (1991). Doing what you say and saying what you do: Reasoning about adolescent–parent conflict in interviews and interactions. *Journal of Adolescent Research, 6,* 276–295.

Smetana, J. G., Yau, J., Restrepo, A., & Braeges, J. (1991). Adolescent–parent conflict in married and divorced families. *Developmental Psychology, 27,* 1000–1010.

Steinberg, L. (1990). Interdependency in the family: Autonomy, conflict, and harmony in the parent–adolescent relationship. In S. S. Feldman & G. R. Elliot (Eds.), *At the threshhold: The developing adolescent* (pp. 255–276). Cambridge, MA: Harvard University Press.

Steinberg, L., & Silverberg, S. B. (1986). The vicissitudes of autonomy in early adolescence. *Child Development, 57,* 841–851.

Sullivan, H. S. (1953). *The interpersonal theory of psychiatry.* New York: Norton.

Tisak, M. (1986). Children's conceptions of parental authority. *Child Development, 57,* 166–176.

Tisak, M. (1993). Preschool children's judgments of moral and personal events involving physical harm and property damage. *Merrill-Palmer Quarterly, 39,* 375–390.

Tisak, M., & Turiel E. (1984). Children's conceptions of moral and prudential rules. *Child Development, 55,* 1030–1039.

Triandis, H. C. (1989). The self and social behavior in differing cultural contexts. *Psychological Review, 96,* 508–520.

Triandis, H. C. (1990). Cross-cultural studies of individualism and collectivism. In J. J. Berman (Eds.), *Nebraska Symposium on Motivation, 1989: Vol. 37. Cross cultural perspectives* (pp. 41–133). Lincoln: University of Nebraska Press.

Turiel, E. (1979). Distinct conceptual and developmental domains: Social convention and morality. In C. B. Keasey (Ed.), *Nebraska Symposium on Motivation, 1977: Vol. 25. Social cognitive development* (pp. 77–116). Lincoln: University of Nebraska Press.

Turiel, E. (1983a). *The development of social knowledge: Morality and convention.* Cambridge: Cambridge University Press.

Turiel, E. (1983b). Domains and categories in social-cognitive development. In W. F. Overton (Ed.), *The relationship between social and cognitive development* (pp. 53–89). Hillsdale, NJ: Lawrence Erlbaum.

Turiel, E. (1994). Morality, authoritarianism, and personal agency in cultural contexts. In R. J. Sternberg & P. Ruzgis (Eds.), *Personality and intelligence* (pp. 271–302). Cambridge: Cambridge University Press.

Turiel, E., & Davidson, P. (1986). Heterogeneity, inconsistency, and asynchrony in the development of cognitive structures. In I. Levin (Ed.), *Stage and structure: Reopening the debate* (pp. 106–143). Norwood, NJ: Ablex.

Turiel, E., Killen, M., & Helwig, C. (1987). Morality: Its structure, functions, and vagaries. In J. Kagan & S. Lamb (Eds.), *The emergence of morality in young children* (pp. 155–243). Chicago: University of Chicago Press.

Turiel, E., & Wainryb, C. (1994). Social reasoning and the varieties of social experiences in cultural contexts. In H. W. Reese (Ed.), *Advances in child development and behavior (Vol. 25).* New York: Academic Press.

Vygotsky, L. S. (1978). *Mind in society: The development of higher psychological processes.* Cambridge, MA: Harvard University Press.

Walker, L. J. (1984). Sex differences in the development of moral reasoning: A critical review. *Child Development, 55,* 677–691.

Walker, L. J. (1991). Sex differences in moral reasoning. In W. M. Kurtines & J. L. Gewirtz (Eds.), *Handbook of moral behavior and development* (Vol. 2, pp. 333–364). Hillsdale, NJ: Lawrence Erlbaum.

Weiss, R. S. (1979). Growing up a little faster: The experience of growing up in a single-parent household. *Journal of Social Issues, 35,* 71–111.

Wertsch, J. V. (1979). From social interaction to higher cognitive processes. *Human Development, 22,* 1–22.

Weston, D., & Turiel, E. (1980). Act–rule relations: Children's concepts of social rules. *Developmental Psychology, 16,* 417–424.

Yau, J., & Smetana, J. G. (1995). *Adolescent-parent conflict among Chinese adolescents in Hong Kong.* Unpublished manuscript, Hong Kong University.

Youniss, J., & Smollar, J. (1985). *Adolescents' relations with mothers, fathers, and friends.* Chicago: University of Chicago Press.

Part III

Social judgment in different cultures

8   Development in the context of everyday family relationships: Culture, interpersonal morality, and adaptation

Joan G. Miller and David M. Bersoff

In recent years, there has been considerable theoretical debate concerning the influence of contextual factors on the ontogenetic development of morality (e.g., Gilligan, 1977, 1982; Kohlberg, 1981; Shweder, 1982; Turiel, 1983). Although all theories of moral development accord some weight to contextual influences, they differ markedly in whether exposure to different contexts of socialization is seen as having a formative influence on the type of moral orientation developed.

The present chapter will focus specifically on understanding contextual influences on the development of interpersonal morality. Discussion will begin with a critical review of the morality-of-caring framework of Gilligan (1977, 1982), a model in which it is posited that contrasting socialization experiences give rise to divergent views of self and morality as well as to contrasting tensions in adaptation. While underscoring the contribution of this model in enhancing current understanding of contextual influences on development, we argue that the approach does not give sufficient weight to cultural factors. Based on results from a cross-cultural investigation comparing Americans' and Hindu Indians' conceptions of family relationships, evidence will be presented to show that, whereas morality needs to be seen as integrally related to the development of self and to problems in adaptation, this development also must be recognized to be culturally influenced and culturally variable. Finally, more general conclusions will be drawn regarding the place of cultural considerations in a contextually sensitive theory of moral development.

The research program described was supported by grants to the first author from the National Institute of Mental Health (MH42940) and the National Science Foundation (DBS-9108924).

259

Gilligan's view of interpersonal moral development

Although the morality-of-caring framework developed by Gilligan is widely known for its identification of a previously unrecognized type of morality and for its claim of gender differences in this morality (Gilligan, 1977, 1982), it also has made major contributions toward understanding contextual influences on development. In contrast to the cognitive developmental or distinct domain perspectives on moral development, which have tended to focus on the child's deductive or inductive processing of information provided in everyday social interaction (e.g., Kohlberg, 1981; Turiel, 1983), the morality-of-caring perspective asserts that the development of morality must also be understood in the context of the development of self and of more general problems in adaptation (Gilligan, 1982; Gilligan & Wiggins, 1987). In addition, whereas these previous models have portrayed moral development as occurring independently of cultural learning, the morality-of-caring perspective portrays such development as affected, in part, by the normative beliefs and practices of the culture related to gender. Finally, in challenging the assumption that universal features of the contexts of development give rise to universal moral codes, the morality-of-caring perspective maintains that individuals are exposed to qualitatively distinct socialization experiences, which are associated with qualitatively distinct moralities.

Drawing on psychodynamic and attachment formulations (e.g., Ainsworth, 1973; Bowlby, 1969; Chodorow, 1979), Gilligan offers a model that explains the emergence of morality in terms of experiences in early socialization contexts. In identifying with their mothers and in having experiences in family interaction that emphasize interpersonal responsiveness, girls are seen as developing a connected self and an associated morality of caring (Gilligan & Wiggins, 1987). These orientations are viewed as becoming problematic only in adolescence, when girls find that they conflict with the emphasis on autonomy in the larger culture. In contrast, in identifying with their fathers and in desiring to overcome the inequality they experience in relation to them, boys develop an autonomous sense of self and an associated morality of justice – orientations that are supported by and congruent with the values of the larger culture.

Although acknowledging the existence of both a morality of justice and a morality of caring, rather than of only one type of morality, the model nonetheless remains universalistic. It is claimed that the moralities of caring and of justice assume the same form regardless of cultural context and reflect opposite poles of a universal tension in adaptation:

The different dynamics of early childhood inequality and attachment lay the ground-work for two moral visions – one of justice and one of care. . . . Although the nature of the attachment between child and parent varies across individual and cultural settings and although inequality can be heightened or muted by familial or societal arrangements, all people are born into a situation of inequality and no child survives in the absence of adult connection. Since everyone is vulnerable both to oppression and to abandonment, two stories about morality recur in human experience. (Gilligan & Wiggins, 1987, p. 281)

A cultural critique

Whereas the framework developed by Gilligan has made a major contribution to current understanding of contextual influences on development, it has also been subject to various criticisms. For example, concerns have been raised about the weak support existing for the claim of gender differences in morality, about whether a caring orientation is sufficient to respond to impersonal justice issues, and about the inadequate attention given to the relationship between caring and justice orientations (e.g., Flanagan, 1991; Mednick, 1989; Nails, 1983; Walker, 1984, 1991). The limitation of the model to be raised here is its downplaying of the impact of cultural considerations on moral development.

In Gilligan's approach, the only aspects of culture that are seen as impacting on the development of a morality of caring are the commonalities in beliefs, values, and practices related to gender differentiation (Miller, 1991, 1994a). As reflected in the passage just cited, these commonalities are identified by a reductionist process that dismisses, as unimportant, aspects of culture that transcend gender issues or reflect cross-cultural differences in how gender differences are interpreted or experienced. No attention is paid to the many nongender based differences in cultural meaning systems and practices that have been shown to affect individual views of self, morality, emotion and even attachment (e.g., Harwood, 1992; Harwood & Miller, 1991; Markus & Kitayama, 1991; Triandis, 1989).

As a consequence of this neglect of aspects of culture that are not linked to gender inequality, Gilligan's perspective is ill-equipped to explain the development of morality cross-culturally (Miller, 1991, 1994a). The framework leads to the implausible prediction that concepts of self and morality will be more similar among individuals of the same gender from divergent cultural contexts (e.g., a secular American woman vs. a traditional Hindu Indian woman) as compared with among individuals of different genders from similar cultural backgrounds (e.g., a traditional Hindu Indian man vs. a traditional Hindu Indian woman).

Even when applied to explain development only among the types of American populations on which it was originally formulated, the theory may be criticized for treating the meaning of females' early socialization experiences as self-evident rather than as dependent on cultural meanings. In particular, preadolescent girls are portrayed as constructing their views of self and morality from their experiences in close relationships, with the characteristics of their early views of self and morality standing only as counterpoints to the individualistic beliefs and values of the larger culture, rather than as reflections of these cultural views. It cannot be assumed, however, that whereas American males' views of self and morality are both supported by and consonant with the individualism of American culture, American females' views of self and morality are not also influenced by this individualism.

As portrayed in Gilligan's account, the connected self and the morality of caring, in fact, may be seen to be related to the beliefs and values of the larger culture. For example, individuals who maintain a connected self conceptualize their identity as apart from social role expectations (Gilligan, 1982) – a view of self that anthropological theorists have linked to modern Western individualistic cultural views and documented to be deemphasized in many non-Western cultures (Balagangadhara, 1988; Dumont, 1965, 1970; Rosaldo, 1984). In turn, individuals who maintain a morality of caring seek to balance responsiveness to self with responsiveness to other – a stance that is associated with individualism and tends to be deemphasized in collectivist cultures with their stress on giving priority to the require-ments of the social whole (Dumont, 1970; Triandis, 1989). In sum, the present critique raises the possibility that the model offered by Gilligan may be closely associated with modern Western individualistic beliefs and values and be less applicable in contrasting cultural contexts (see also Miller & Bersoff, 1992; Miller, Bersoff, & Harwood, 1990).

The cultural context of interpersonal moral development

A program of research we have been conducting over the past few years takes into account both Gilligan's insight that conceptions of morality re-flect views of self and problems in adaptation and the anthropological insight that views of self and problems in adaptation are culturally variable. Our focus is on the ways in which conceptions of morality are influenced by cultural meanings and practices. Like Gilligan, we assume that experience in early socialization contexts is important for the development of views of self and morality and is related to everyday adaptive concerns. However, in contrast to Gilligan, we assume that the meaning accorded to these experiences is, in part, culturally constituted and thus differs in cultures emphasizing alternative views of the self and associated cultural practices.

In our approach, consonant with other recent work from a cultural psychology perspective (Miller, 1994b; Shweder, 1990; Shweder & Sullivan, 1993), culture is viewed as providing criteria for what constitutes objective knowledge in a given setting (Hamlyn, 1971). However, in contrast to assumptions within learning theory traditions, it is maintained that individuals do not merely passively receive, in unchanged form, cultural understandings (for a critique of cultural determinism, see D'Andrade, 1984; Turiel, 1983; Turiel, Killen, & Helwig, 1987). Rather, enculturation is viewed as a bidirectional process of influence, in which meanings are negotiated, transformed, and created, not merely preserved. It thus is expected that whereas children's understandings are always constructed within a given cultural context, they will not merely mirror those of adults but may differ qualitatively from those of adults in ways that reflect the child's experiences and developmentally related ways of interpreting the world (e.g., Miller, 1986; Shweder & LeVine, 1975).

Our studies have focused specifically on identifying the conceptions of interpersonal morality that develop among American populations emphasizing highly individualistic cultural views of the self (Bellah, Madsen, Sullivan, Swidler, & Tipton, 1985; Dumont, 1965; Lukes, 1973), as contrasted with conceptions among traditional Hindu Indian populations, emphasizing more relational or interdependent cultural views of the self (Dumont, 1970; Kakar, 1978; Markus & Kitayama, 1991; Marriott, 1990). The samples in our research have included American children and adults from New Haven, Connecticut, and Hindu Indian children and adults from Mysore City in southern India.

Our work has demonstrated that as compared with Americans, Indians tend to treat interpersonal responsibilities as socially enforceable moral duties rather than as matters for personal decision making (Miller & Luthar, 1989; Miller et al., 1990) and as applying across a wider range of need and role situations (Miller et al., 1990). Interpersonal responsibilities, however, are not merely perceived to be more obligatory among Indians than among Americans but are also interpreted in contrasting ways relative to the self. In particular, Indians tend to treat individual inclinations as consonant with interpersonal social expectations, whereas Americans tend to treat them as opposed (Miller & Bersoff, 1994). Finally, we find that Indians, like Americans, recognize a domain of moral issues centered around issues of justice (see also Shweder, Mahapahtra, & Miller, 1987). However, in contrast to Americans, Indians tend to give greater priority to interpersonal responsibilities relative to competing justice expectations

(Miller & Bersoff, 1992) and are more prone to make contextual exceptions in applying justice rules (Bersoff & Miller, 1993; Miller & Luthar,
1989). The cross-cultural differences observed in these various studies have
been shown to be unrelated to gender and to bear little or no relationship
to socioeconomic status.

In terms of developmental trends, our past studies reveal both cross-
cultural similarities and differences in childrens' interpretations of interpersonal responsibilities. Consonant with past research in the distinct domain
tradition that has shown marked agreement in childrens' and adults' social
domain categorizations (e.g., Turiel, 1983; Turiel et al., 1987), our studies
generally reveal that American and Hindu Indian children's interpretations
of interpersonal responsibilities more closely resemble those of adults from
their own culture than those of children from the comparison culture
(Bersoff & Miller, 1993; Miller & Bersoff, 1992; Millet et al., 1990). However, we have found certain commonalities in young children's interpretations of interpersonal responsibilities, which suggest that they are not
merely passively absorbing information provided by adults. For example,
in both cultures, there is some tendency for young children to treat interpersonal responsibilities in more obligatory terms than do adults (Miller et al.,
1990), as well as to be more prone than are adults to absolve agents of
accountability for justice breaches performed under specific types of emotional duress (Bersoff & Miller, 1993).

We interpret our results as implying that qualitatively distinct types of
interpersonal moral codes develop in American and Hindu Indian cultures,
reflecting the contrasting cultural views of the self emphasized in each
setting. Consonant with the highly individualistic cultural views of the self
stressed in the United States, Americans tend to adopt what we have
termed an "individually oriented" perspective (Miller, 1994a). Conforming
in select ways to both the superrogatory view of interpersonal responsibilities, maintained by Kohlberg and others (e.g., Gert, 1988; Higgins, Power,
& Kohlberg, 1984; Kohlberg, Levine, & Hewer, 1983; Nunner-Winkler,
1984) and the morality-of-caring orientation held by Gilligan and her associates (Gilligan, 1982; Gilligan, Ward, & Taylor, 1988), this moral orientation emphasizes individual freedom of choice, balancing one's own needs
and desires against those of others as well as maintaining personal responsibility for conduct. In contrast, consonant with the more relational cultural
views of the self emphasized in Hindu Indian culture, Hindu Indians tend
to hold what we have labeled a "duty-based" perspective – an orientation
that does not conform to the pattern identified within the morality-of-
caring framework. Emphasis is placed on social duties that are viewed as

intrinsic to individual nature as well as on the importance of interpersonal interdependence and contextual sensitivity.

Whereas our studies support Gilligan's claim that concepts of morality must be understood in relation to concepts of self, they demonstrate that interpersonal morality develops in qualitatively distinct ways in cultures emphasizing alternative views of the self. In our work to date, however, little explicit attention has been paid to the link drawn by Gilligan between conceptions of morality and problems in adaptation. It appears likely, however, that just as the interpersonal moral code that is emphasized among Americans differs qualitatively from that emphasized among Hindu Indians, the perceived adaptive stresses associated with this code differ qualitatively as well.

A cross-cultural examination of conception of family relationships

In this section, we report on a two-part cross-cultural investigation that was designed to explore some of the implications for adaptation of the individually oriented as contrasted with duty-based interpersonal moral codes that we have identified. Focusing on conceptions of exemplary family behavior, the research examines the types of interpersonal concerns that Americans and Hindu Indians consider salient in everyday family interaction. As a secondary aim, the investigation sought to determine whether the cross-cultural differences observed in our past studies obtain when subjects assess behaviors in their personal experiences rather than hypothetical behaviors.

Study 1: Evaluations of exemplary family behavior in our own experience

The first study required subjects to generate examples of real-life behaviors that they considered exemplary for family members in particular roles to display. Balanced by gender, the sample included 40 middle-aged Americans and 40 middle-aged Hindu Indians, recruited from the same types of middle-class populations employed in our past studies ($M = 37.1$ years). Middle-aged adults were interviewed in order to tap individuals who had considerable experience in adult family roles. The decision was made not to include a child sample, since the study focused on certain adult family relationships, about which children tend to have limited knowledge. However, based on our past cross-cultural developmental research, it may be expected that young children tend, in general, to resemble adults in their interpretations of interpersonal responsibilities within family relationships (Miller et al., 1990).

Interviews with Americans were conducted in English by Yale University research assistants, whereas interviews with Indians were conducted in the local language of Kannada by researchers from the Mysore area who were native Kannada speakers. Interviews were divided into two sessions, scheduled one day apart. In the first session, subjects were asked to recall an example of a behavior they considered exemplary that had been performed in the context of a specific family role by a person whom they knew. They were then asked to explain why they evaluated the behavior in this way. For example, in the case of the mother role, subjects were asked: "Please tell me something a mother you know well did for her children that you thought was a very good thing for a mother to have done." After narrating this example, the subject was asked: "In your opinion, why was this a good thing for the mother to have done?" In a randomized order, these questions were repeated for the six different family roles of: husband, wife, father, mother, adult son, and adult daughter. Subjects' responses were tape-recorded and later transcribed.

In the second session, subjects were reminded of the behavior they had generated for each role and asked to respond to criterion probes assessing their moral appraisals of this behavior. As undertaken in assessment of moral reasoning in our past related research (e.g., Miller & Bersoff, 1992), the probes included a question assessing whether subjects feel that the behavior is governed by an objective obligation as well as a question assessing whether they feel that it is legitimate to regulate the behavior. These questions were personalized to fit each particular case. For example, one subject narrated a case in which a wife, who became pregnant shortly after marriage and wanted to have the baby, agreed to have an abortion after her husband became extremely upset about the pregnancy and asked her to do this. To tap perceived obligation, this subject was asked: "If a wife does not want to have an abortion under these circumstances, do you think that she still has an obligation to do this anyway? We mean here more than an obligation that exists just because of a rule or law." In turn, to tap perceived legitimacy of regulation, this subject was asked: "In your opinion, is it alright for other people to try to make a wife, who really doesn't want to, have an abortion under these circumstances or is it the wife's own business whether or not she does this?" It was explained to subjects that the question referred to nonphysical efforts to change the agent's behavior – such as shunning or snubbing.

In conformity with current theoretical definitions (Miller et al., 1990; Nucci, 1981; Shweder, 1982; Turiel, 1983), responses to these two probes were used to code subjects' characterizations of the behaviors into various social domains: (A) Behaviors regarded both as governed by an objective obligation and as legitimately regulated were considered moral issues. (B) Behaviors regarded as governed by an objective obligation but not as subject to social regulation were considered personal-moral issues. (C) Behaviors regarded as neither governed by an objective obligation nor as legitimately regulated were considered matters of personal choice. (D) Behaviors regarded as legitimately regulated but not as governed by an objective obligation were considered social conventions.

A four-category coding scheme was constructed for classifying the behaviors narrated, with each behavior scored in only one category. This scheme was based both on the nature of interpersonal responsibilities as well as on differences in the types of behaviors expected to be emphasized by Hindu Indians, with their duty-based interpersonal moral code, as contrasted with those emphasized by Americans, with their individually oriented interpersonal moral code: (A) Reflecting the centrality of the needs of others in defining interpersonal responsibilities, the category *basic needs* included cases in which an agent responded to a family member's needs in situations that did not involve high cost to the agent. Examples of responses scored in this category included a grown daughter driving her mother to the hospital to receive chemotherapy, a mother disciplining her young child in an effective manner, and a husband, who had a serious heart attack, showing his wife how to take over the family business after his death. (B) Reflecting the types of concerns expected to be valued in a culture emphasizing the performance of broad and stringent duties, the category *selflessness* included cases in which an agent fulfilled responsibilities of care in the face of extreme personal hardship or risk or in which an agent forgave personal insult or harm suffered from a family member. Examples of responses scored in this category included a father taking on a full-time second job and giving up any luxuries for himself in order to send his children to a private school where they would receive a better education than was available at the local public school, a son agreeing to his father's wish that he join the family business even though it meant abandoning his personal ambition to become an engineer, and a wife standing by her husband despite his alcoholism and gambling. (C) Reflecting the types of concerns expected to be emphasized in a culture treating interpersonal responsibilities as voluntaristic commitments, the category *psychological support and affection* included cases in which an agent expressed affection, caring, gratitude, or psychological acceptance to a family member or otherwise acted to enhance the quality of his or her interpersonal relationship with a family member. Examples of responses scored in this category included a son holding a surprise anniversary party for his parents, a father taking his son fishing, and a wife telling her husband that she would like him to be more affectionate with her. (D) Finally, a residual category of *miscellaneous* responses was used to score behaviors that did not fit into any of the other categories. A high level of reliability was obtained in applying the coding scheme.

Statistical analyses were conducted utilizing MANOVA and ANOVA techniques, with the Tukey procedure employed for post hoc comparisons. Data that consisted of proportions summing to one were subjected to a log-ratio transformation, in order to correct the problems of nonindependence of variation associated with data of this type. No significant effects of gender were observed in any of the analyses.

Replicating trends observed in our past experimentally oriented research, Indians were observed more frequently to categorize the behaviors in moral terms than did Americans (India: $M = 67\%$; United States: $M = 10\%$). In contrast, Americans more frequently categorized the behaviors as matters for personal decision making than did Indians – that is, they viewed them either in personal-moral terms (United States = 38%; India = 0%) or as matters of personal choice (United States = 51%; India = 32%).

Analyses performed on the types of behaviors narrated revealed that as compared with Indians, Americans more frequently narrated behaviors that involved psychological support and affection (United States: $M = 49\%$; India: $M = 4\%$) and less frequently narrated behaviors that involved selflessness (United States: $M = 17\%$; India: $M = 72\%$). No cross-cultural differences were observed in narration of behaviors that involved basic needs ($M = 28\%$).

Examination of the American responses revealed that Americans tended to emphasize psychological support and affection because such behavior was seen as strengthening interpersonal ties, reducing the perceived sense of isolation between persons and building self-esteem. As seen in the following responses generated by American subjects, small gifts or gestures took on importance as acts that communicated caring for the other and indicated a willingness to include the other in one's life:

A daughter sent her mother a card and told her how much she loves her.
(Why do you feel that this behavior is desirable?)
Because it allowed the daughter to express some love that she never had and maybe to let the mother know that there was some love there that she never knew of.

Affection and psychological support were also regarded as valuable in reducing the other's fear of abandonment and in building his or her sense of self-worth. For example, in the parent–child relationship, acts of this type served to communicate that the child was deserving of attention:

A mother would sit her child on her lap and they would sing a song together.
(Why do you feel that this is desirable?)
Because it makes the child feel that you really care for them, that you're interested in them, that you like the contact of just being with them versus making the child feel that you want them just to kind of go away and play by themselves. It makes the daughter feel like something special – and she grows up with a greater feeling of security. Children need to know that they're worth their parents' time – that they're worth somebody's time.

As seen in the following example, even at older ages, affection and psychological support were valued as growth-producing – with the psychological backing provided by others seen as boosting the agent's self-confidence and ability to function autonomously:

A husband has been supportive of his wife getting into writing. He encouraged her to do newspaper writing. She was getting really discouraged doing computer programming and felt that it was really drying her out. The husband kept on encouraging her to take classes – giving all kinds of different suggestions.
(Why do you feel that this behavior is desirable?)
Because his confidence gave her more confidence. If you know somebody has confidence in you, you're better able to go along a little better. It gives you a little extra push. I think that works with just about any relationship.

In turn, examination of the Indian responses suggested that Indians tended to emphasize selflessness because they considered such behavior as important in maintaining harmonious interpersonal relationships. Such a concern is reflected, for example, in the following narrative offered by an Indian adult:

There was this friend of mine. He was an engineer. After three or four years of his marriage, his wife had a severe attack of paralysis. This man would come back from work and take good care of his wife. He had employed a nurse to take care of her. He was spending a lot to get her full treatments. It couldn't be possible for them to live as man and wife in her condition; yet they are very happy together.
(Why do you feel that this behavior is desirable?)
This depends upon the mind and behavior of a man. Human relations depend on this. It is a mental stability. If a man cannot adjust to this, it is his foolishness. Putting her in a nursing home for full-time care is not advisable. So I feel that it was good of the husband to have taken care of her by himself at home and to have made her happy by not putting her in a nursing home.

The subject, it may be seen, considers the husband's behavior exemplary because it shows that he possesses sufficient mental control to be able flexibly to adjust to the changing circumstances of his marriage rather than to give in to personal stresses that might otherwise lead him to fail to meet his responsibilities to his wife. Whereas in this case, the husband's forbearance results in happiness for both himself and his wife, selfless behavior is valued even in situations in which it results in personal ambitions or desires being thwarted. For example, in the following case, the Indian subject asserts that interpersonal harmony requires that a wife give up her career:

A lady had a masters degree in science and was a lecturer at the university. She married a chartered accountant who worked in a far off place. Upon his request, she left her job immediately. If she wanted, she could have gotten a job there also because she had seven to eight years' teaching experience. However, he did not want her to work because he was earning very well. Even though she was very interested in teaching – rather than just in earning money – she sacrificed her interest.

(Why do you feel that this behavior is desirable?)

Always, the husband or the wife should not be stubborn. They should be acceptable to the ideas of each other – give-and-take policy. Sometimes you may have to sacrifice, sometimes she has to sacrifice – then only can family life go well.

The subject, it may be seen, does not conceptualize the family as a unit that exists primarily to satisfy the needs and desires of the individuals involved – a view of the family linked to modern Western views of the self (Schneider, 1985) and expressed in some of the responses of Gilligans' informants (e.g., Gilligan, 1982, p. 54). Rather, in considering the family as a unit that has intrinsic value beyond the personal interests of the individual members, the subject considers the wife's behavior in relation to the welfare of the family as a whole. In particular, the subject argues that it is undesirable for a woman to give priority to her personal career at the expense of her husband's feelings since such behavior disrupts smooth family relations.

Study 2: Evaluations of exemplary family behavior narrated by others

A follow-up investigation was performed to provide additional information about the meaning of the family behaviors under consideration as well as to clarify certain ambiguities in interpretation of the results. Based on the findings of the first study, it is unclear whether behaviors involving psychological support and affection, as contrasted with selflessness, are mentioned more frequently in one culture relative to the other because they are considered to have contrasting importance or merely because they differ in salience. With subjects in each culture only evaluating incidents that they generated themselves, it also remains unclear whether cross-cultural differences exist in how the two types of issues are evaluated.

To address these questions, a second sample of middle-aged adults was asked to reason about a common set of incidents involving these two culturally variable issues – psychological support and affection as well as selflessness. Drawn from the same populations as in the first study and balanced by gender, subjects included 20 middle-class American adults and 20 middle-class Hindu Indian adults ($M = 39.0$ years). For comparative purposes, 20 lower-class Hindu Indian adults of the same age were also interviewed, with separate comparisons undertaken between their responses and those of the middle-class Hindu Indian adults.

A set of 12 incidents was compiled to be presented to subjects for their common appraisals (see appendix). This was achieved by sampling, for each of the six roles, one representative psychological support and affection incident that had been originally generated by an American subject and one representative selflessness incident that had been originally generated by an Indian subject.

Moral judgment was assessed using the same types of criterion probe measures employed in the first study. In addition, the perceived importance of undertaking the action was examined by having subjects rate each behavior on a 6-point scale ranging from (0) "not important" to (5) "extremely important," as well as, at the end of the interview, rank order the 12 behaviors from the one considered most important for a family member to undertake to the one considered least important for a family member to undertake. Perceived satisfaction was measured by having subjects evaluate how much satisfaction the agent experienced in undertaking the behavior on a 9-point scale ranging from (0) "no satisfaction" to (8) "extremely much satisfaction," as well as explain the basis for their satisfaction ratings. Finally, to assess the comparability of subjects' understandings of the behaviors, subjects were asked, in each case, to indicate how much effort or sacrifice it was for the agent involved to undertake the specific behavior under consideration. This rating was undertaken on a 5-point scale ranging from (0) "no effort or sacrifice" to (4) "very much effort or sacrifice."

Subjects' open-ended explanations for their satisfaction ratings were scored in terms of five categories, which were empirically derived based on the specific types of issues mentioned.[1] These categories were: (A) *Satisfaction from fulfilling duty* included cases in which it was judged that the agent experienced satisfaction in meeting his or her perceived obligations to a family member; (B) *Satisfaction from the well-being of others* included cases in which it was judged that the agent experienced satisfaction in knowing that a family member's needs were being met; (C) *Satisfaction from relationship enhancement* included cases in which it was judged that the agent experienced satisfaction from improving his or her relationship with a family member or from the opportunity for interaction with a family

Table 8.1. *Percentage of social domain categorizations*

	India	United States
Affection/psychological support		
Moral	33.3	7.5
Personal-moral	41.7	41.7
Personal choice	21.7	48.3
Selflessness		
Moral	47.5	2.5
Personal-moral	32.5	23.3
Personal choice	17.5	74.2

member that the behavior allowed; (D) *Unfulfilled desires* included cases in which it was judged that the agent regretted the personal sacrifice entailed in the action; and (E) *Miscellaneous* included responses that did not fit into any of the other categories. A high level of reliability was attained in applying the coding scheme.

The ratings of effort and sacrifice made by subjects demonstrated that they interpreted the two types of behaviors in similar ways. In both cultures, the selflessness behaviors were seen as entailing more effort or sacrifice to perform ($M = 3.41$) than did the affection/psychological support behaviors ($M = 1.70$). No significant differences occurred in the amount of effort or sacrifice associated with the selflessness behaviors, although Indians saw greater effort or sacrifice entailed in the affection/psychological support behaviors than did Americans (India: $M = 1.94$; United States: $M = 1.46$).

Analyses performed on subjects' social domain categorizations indicated that Indians categorized both types of behaviors more frequently in moral terms and less frequently in personal-choice terms than did Americans (see Table 8.1). Personal choice categorizations were made more frequently of selflessness than of psychological support and affection among Americans, with personal-moral categorizations made more frequently of psychological support and affection than of selflessness among all subjects.

The present trends are similar to those observed in the first study. Although Indians were observed to place less weight on moral categorizations and more weight on personal-moral categorizations when evaluating the scenarios generated by others as compared with the scenarios that they generated themselves, their responses still differed markedly from those of Americans: In both studies, Indians made greater use of moral categorizations and lesser use of personal-choice categorizations than did Americans.

Table 8.2. *Mean evaluations of importance of behavior and of agent satisfaction*

	Affection/support		Selflessness	
	India	United States	India	United States
Rating of importance of behavior	3.92	4.03	4.10	2.76
Ranking of importance of behavior	7.88	5.34	5.12	7.66
Rating of agent satisfaction	6.43	6.34	5.43	4.05

Note: A higher rating score and a lower ranking score mean greater importance.

The findings imply, then, that the cross-cultural differences observed in judgment of everyday family behaviors in the first investigation did not arise merely because individuals spontaneously mentioned different types of concerns.

Analyses undertaken on subjects' ratings and rankings of importance revealed that Indians considered selfless behavior as more important than did Americans on both the rating and ranking measures, whereas Americans considered affection and psychological support as more important than did Indians only on the ranking procedure. In terms of within-culture effects, Americans treated affection and psychological support as more important than selflessness on both the rating and ranking measures, whereas Indians treated selflessness as more important than affection and psychological support only on the ranking measure (see Table 8.2).

These findings indicate that Americans maintain an interpersonal moral code that tends to place greater importance on affection and psychological support than on selflessness both in absolute and relative terms. In contrast, they reveal that Indians maintain an interpersonal moral code in which selflessness tends to be considered relatively more important than affections and psychological support, but both are valued.

Analyses of subjects' ratings of the satisfaction experienced by the agent revealed that Indians associated more satisfaction with selflessness than did Americans. Individuals in both cultures were also found to associate more satisfaction with affection and psychological support than with selflessness (see bottom portion of Table 8.2).[2]

In examining the reasons subjects gave for their satisfaction ratings, focus centered on the proportion of the responses that were coded into each of the four main content categories, as calculated by dividing the

Table 8.3. *Percentage of different types of justifications offered for agent satisfaction ratings*

	Affection/support		Selflessness	
	India	United States	India	United States
Satisfaction from fulfilling duty	18.8	21.2	37.8	44.2
Satisfaction from others' well-being	60.1	37.5	47.1	18.7
Satisfaction from enhancement of relationship	15.6	36.0	1.5	1.9
Unfulfilled desires	0.0	2.1	8.2	34.6

number of times a particular reason was cited in a given case by the number of all reasons cited in that case. Results indicated that, as compared with Indians, Americans placed greater emphasis on satisfaction from relationship enhancement when evaluating psychological support and affection as well as greater emphasis on satisfaction from fulfilling duty and on unfulfilled desires when evaluating selflessness. Indians placed greater emphasis than did Americans on satisfaction associated with the well-being of others in both cases. In terms of within-culture trends, all subjects mentioned satisfaction from duty more frequently in relation to selflessness than in relation to psychological support and affection. Americans also mentioned unfulfilled desires more frequently in relation to selflessness than in relation to psychological support and affection (Table 8.3).

The results reveal that psychological support and affection as compared with selflessness are accorded contrasting meanings in each culture. As compared with Indians, Americans place more weight on the relationship-enhancing aspects of affection and psychological support, rather than merely the satisfaction associated with promoting the other's well-being. Also, although Americans maintain that there is satisfaction associated with fulfilling one's duty through selfless behavior, they are more prone than are Indians to assume that agents regret such behaviors because they result in unfulfilled personal desires. These cross-cultural differences in the meaning of the two types of behaviors are illustrated in sample responses.

In the case of the affection and psychological support incident for the son role, Americans and Indians were asked to evaluate the following behavior:

Because of his job, a married son had to live in a city that was a four-hour drive from his parents' home. The son made a point of keeping in touch with his parents by either visiting, calling, or writing them on a regular basis.

An American subject portrayed the son's behavior as satisfying in that it enabled him to enhance his relationship with his parents, while still retaining a sense of individual autonomy:

Lets them know he cares. He must know they appreciate it and will feel better about himself. He can be his own person and still remember what his relationship with his parents has done for him.

In contrast, an Indian subject focused on the satisfaction associated with fulfilling the obligations of care toward one's parents and of knowing that their welfare needs are being met:

He will get satisfaction by knowing of the well-being of his parents. Even if they live far away, the son must think of the well-being of his parents.

In another example, the following behavior was presented to subjects as the selfless incident for the wife role:

A year after their marriage, a woman's husband was injured in a motorcycle accident and became paralyzed from the waist down. The wife found that many of her expectations for marriage were disappointed. For the rest of his life, her husband would require a lot of care and would be depressed and inactive. But even though the wife felt very unfulfilled by her marriage, she decided not to leave him because she felt that if she did, his life would be even worse.

Interpreting the importance of a family member's behavior as that of ensuring the smooth functioning of the family as a whole, an Indian subject focused on the satisfaction she expected the wife would experience in being responsive to her husband's welfare and fulfilling her duty as a wife:

She will have the satisfaction of having fulfilled her duty. She helped her husband during difficulty. If difficulties and happiness are both viewed as equal, only then will the family life be smooth.

In contrast, in maintaining that it is important that personal needs and ambitions are met in the context of family relationships, an American subject focused on the dissatisfaction she expected that the wife would experience in giving insufficient attention to her personal desires:

She is acting out of obligation – not other reasons like love. She has a sense of duty, but little satisfaction for her own happiness.

Implications

The results of this two-part study lend support to the claim that views of self and morality are culturally grounded. Consonant with the individualistic values of American culture, Americans were observed to treat the self as an agent with distinctive individual interests and goals, whose commitments to others should be balanced against these personal motives. This was reflected, for example, in Americans' negative evaluations of selflessness, as interfering with the realization of an agent's personal desires. Reflecting their maintenance of an individually oriented interpersonal moral code, Americans were also observed to treat interpersonal responsibilities within the family predominately in terms of a private morality – that is, as matters for personal decision making rather than as socially enforceable obligations.

With their more relational cultural views of the self, Indians, in contrast, tended to conceptualize the self as part of an interdependent social body, with interpersonal responsibilities seen as requiring in some cases that personal ambitions be subordinated to the requirements of this social whole. Notably, the finding that Indians considered affection and psychological support to be just as important in absolute terms as did Americans demonstrates that even in a duty-based interpersonal moral system, family relationships involve close affective ties. However, the results imply that, in such a system, affective ties tend to be viewed as arising from role-related responsibilities, rather than, as is the case among Americans, viewed as a primary basis of these responsibilities (see also Gilligan, 1982; Gilligan & Wiggins, 1987). Thus, among Indians even the communication of affection and psychological support was observed to be treated as amenable to social enforcement.

More generally, the results point to contrasting problems for the self in the two cultural traditions, with these problems explaining, at least in part, the differential emphasis that Americans and Indians place on affection and psychological support as compared with selflessness. A central problem for Americans was found to be that of balancing connection and individuality. Among Americans, connection cannot be taken for granted, in that it is seen as primarily a matter for personal decision making, rather than a socially enforceable expectation. Equally, individual autonomy cannot be taken for granted, in that it may be threatened by the perceived loss of self associated with extreme selfless behavior. Acts involving the communication of affection and psychological support appear to be particularly valued in this type of system as responses to these dual stresses. In particular, the present evidence reveals that displaying affection and psychological support is viewed by Americans as a means of solidifying social ties and reassuring others that they can expect support and will not be isolated. Equally, such behavior is viewed as a way of fortifying the recipient's sense of self-esteem so that he or she is better able to function autonomously, as the system requires.

In turn, the tension between individuality and connection, though present to some degree among Indians, does not appear as salient or central a stress as among Americans. Among Indians, connection, for the most part, can be taken for granted since interpersonal responsiveness tends to be considered a social enforceable duty rather than a matter for personal decision making. As reflected in Indians' views that it is desirable to subordinate personal ambitions and desires to the requirements of social duty, Indians also do not tend to value the development of an independent self who pursues his or her own goals autonomously from other's expectations.

Rather, the present results suggest that a central problem for the self among Indians is that of regulating self-serving ambitions that interfere with responsiveness to the social whole and with harmonious transactions and exchanges with others. As observed, among Indians interpersonal duties are considered wide-ranging and potentially extremely high in personal cost. Acts of selflessness appear to be particularly valued in such a system in demonstrating that agents are able to master personal strivings that could otherwise lead them to neglect these duties. Such behavior is also valued in indicating that agents are able to display the accommodation and equanimity necessary to function well as part of a social whole.

In sum, the present study has supported Gilligan's claim that morality needs to be viewed in relation both to concepts of self and to problems in adaptation, while also showing that the various components of this model are, in part, culturally patterned. Just as it cannot be assumed that there is only one morality of caring or one view of self linked to caring, it equally cannot be assumed that problems for the self are only of one type. Rather, the present findings underscore the importance of recognizing that models of adaptation are grounded in variable cultural contexts. Although the view of adaptation as reflecting a tension between autonomy and connection has proved to be a powerful model in psychological theory, informing not only Gilligan's work but attachment theory more generally (e.g., Ainsworth, Blehar, Waters, & Wall, 1978), the results suggest that it needs to be viewed as, at least somewhat, culturally bound: The findings imply that this tension may be more likely to occur in individualistic cultures, which place considerable value and stress on the development of individual autonomy, than in relational cultures, which place greater value and stress on interpersonal interdependence (see also Harwood, 1992; Harwood & Miller, 1991).

Conclusion

The present demonstration of the impact of culture in affecting perceived problems in adaptation highlights the need to reevaluate the role accorded to cultural context in theories of social cognitive development. Culture, the results imply, is not only a background in which psychological processes develop and are displayed but a source of powerful regularities in social cognition, which must be taken into account to explain the course of development as well as to evaluate the adequacy of any developmental end points attained.

The results challenge the adequacy of the developmental constructivist viewpoint, reflected in the theories of Kohlberg (1981) and Gilligan (1982), which portrays development as proceeding independently of cultural learning – with such learning affecting only the rate but not the path of development. In the present case, for example, such an interpretation would lead to interpreting the Indian pattern of responses as merely a less developed version of the American pattern rather than as a qualitatively distinct developmental outcome.

To understand the responses displayed by Americans and Indians, it may be argued, requires adopting an indigenous perspective in which responses are understood in terms of local normative frameworks – that is, as based on culturally specific presuppositions. In this effort, as theorists have noted (Turiel, Hildebrandt, & Wainryb, 1991; Wainryb, 1991), attention must be paid not only to the contrasting values in different cultural communities but also to their contrasting natural-order presuppositions. In the present case, for example, understanding the Indian system from the perspective of American cultural values would lead to a focus only on the limited opportunities the Indian system allows for individual freedom of choice. However, such an interpretation may be seen to be ethnocentric, in that it fails to take into account the Indian view of interdependence as both natural and normatively desirable and thus fails to anticipate the greater satisfaction that Indians, as compared with Americans, associate with selfless behavior. Conversely, to understand the American system of interpersonal morality from the perspective of Hindu Indian culture would also be inadequate in that it would lead to a focus exclusively on the stresses associated with the greater likelihood of experiencing social isolation. It is only when recognition is given to the American cultural view of self-determination and autonomy as basic to human nature and as of fundamental value that the unique satisfactions associated with the American system of interpersonal morality become apparent.

In conclusion, a cultural perspective needs to be regarded not as an alternative to a developmental constructivist approach, but as a perspective that may valuably be integrated with such an approach (Miller, in press). Culture must be considered not only as a distinct context of development, in that it represents shared meanings and practices that cannot be reduced to individual psychology (Miller, 1994b), but also as a mediator of all other contexts of development. Thus, it must be recognized that experiences in the family as well as in other everyday socialization contexts are always, in part, constituted by culturally shared norms, values, and conceptual presuppositions. The constructivist insight that development involves an active agent who constructs meaning from experiences needs to be combined with the insight of cultural perspectives that humans inhabit worlds that are public and socially shared (Bruner, 1990; Shweder, 1990). From such an integrated perspective, social-cognitive development would be understood to represent an open process in which individuals draw on historically and culturally grounded presuppositions in actively interpreting, modifying, and constructing socially constituted worlds.

Appendix: Summary of common set of family behaviors

Affection/psychological support

1. A father uses his free time to play with his children and talk with them about things they care about.
2. A mother interacts with her children in an affectionate way, which shows the children that she loves them.
3. A husband provides encouragement to his wife to pursue her interest in becoming a writer.
4. A wife gives her husband extra emotional support during a period when he is feeling anxious about a job change.
5. A grown son keeps in touch with his parents by visiting, writing, or calling them on a regular basis.
6. A grown daughter, who had won free airline tickets to vacation in England, presents the tickets to her parents as a gift.

Selflessness

1. A father, who has been widowed for over 10 years and finally finds a woman that he very much loves and wants to marry, declines to marry this woman because she is not very friendly to his teenage son.
2. A mother gives up her job as a professor and takes on a less desirable higher-paying job in order to raise enough money for her son to complete college.
3. A husband remains loyal to his wife who developed diabetes and a severe mental problem after the birth of their son, resulting in her

no longer making him feel content in his marriage and being unable to fulfill his dream of having a large family.

4. A wife does not abandon her husband after he becomes paralyzed in an accident and requires extensive personal care.

5. A son resigns from his job as an officer in the air force in order to settle near his elderly parents and be available to look after them personally.

6. A daughter postpones her dream of getting married for many years until after her parents have died, in order to be available to help her parents with family responsibilities, which they cannot manage due to their failing health. The daughter does this because she judges that she lacks the time and energy needed simultaneously to have a husband and children and to help her elderly parents.

Notes

1. No subjects were observed to mention issues involving individual rights or justice and thus no category was created to encompass these types of concerns.

2. Comparisons of the responses of the middle-class and lower-class Indians revealed that lower-class Indian subjects ($M = 6.45$) rated selflessness as significantly more satisfying than did middle-class Indians. Also, in contrast to middle-class Indians, lower-class Indians rated selflessness as just as satisfying as affection and psychological support ($M = 6.52$). No significant effects of socioeconomic status occurred in analyses undertaken on all of the other dependent measures in the study.

References

Ainsworth, M. D. S. (1973). The development of infant–mother attachment. In B. M. Caldwell & H. N. Ricciuti (Eds.), *Review of child development research* (Vol. 3, pp. 1–94). Chicago: University of Chicago Press.

Ainsworth, M. D. S., Blehar, M. C., Waters, E., & Wall, S. (1978). *Patterns of attachment: A psychological study of the Strange Situation.* Hillsdale, NJ: Lawrence Erlbaum.

Balagangadhara, S. N. (1988). Comparative anthropology and moral domains: An essay on selfless morality and the moral self. *Cultural Dynamics, 1,* 98–128.

Bellah, R. N., Madsen, R., Sullivan, W. M., Swidler, A., & Tipton, S. M. (1985). *Habits of the heart: Individualism and commitment in American life.* Berkeley: University of California Press.

Bersoff, D. M., & Miller, J. G. (1993). Culture, context and the development of moral accountability judgments. *Developmental Psychology, 29,* 664–676.

Bowlby, J. (1969). *Attachment and loss.* New York: Basic Books.

Bruner, J. S. (1990). *Acts of meaning.* Cambridge, MA: Harvard University Press.

Chodorow, N. (1979). *The reproduction of mothering.* Berkeley: University of California Press.

D'Andrade, R. G. (1984). Cultural meaning systems. In R. A. Shweder & R. A. Levine (Eds.), *Culture theory: Essays on mind, self, and emotion* (pp. 88–119). Cambridge: Cambridge University Press.

Dumont, L. (1965). The modern conception of the individual: Notes on its genesis. *Contributions to Indian Sociology, 66,* 13–61.

Dumont, L. (1970). *Homo hierarchicus.* Chicago: University of Chicago Press.

Flanagan, O. (1991). *Varieties of moral personality: Ethics and psychological realism.* Cambridge, MA: Harvard University Press.

Gert, B. (1988). *Morality: A new justification of the moral rules.* New York: Oxford University Press.

Gilligan, C. (1977). In a different voice: Women's conceptions of the self and of morality. *Harvard Educational Review, 47,* 481–517.

Gilligan, C. (1982). *In a different voice: Psychological theory and women's development.* Cambridge, MA: Harvard University Press.

Gilligan, C., Ward, J., & Taylor, J. (Eds.). (1988). *Mapping the moral domain: A contribution of women's thinking to psychological theory and education.* Cambridge, MA: Harvard University Press.

Gilligan, C., & Wiggins, G. (1987). The origins of morality in early childhood relationships. In J. Kagan & S. Lamb (Eds.), *The emergence of morality in young children* (pp. 277–305). Chicago: University of Chicago Press.

Hamlyn, D. W. (1971). Epistemology and conceptual development. In T. Mischel (Ed.), *Cognitive development and epistemology* (pp. 3–24). New York: Academic Press.

Harwood, R. L. (1992). The influence of culturally derived values on Anglo and Puerto Rican mothers' perceptions of attachment behavior. *Child Development, 63,* 822–839.

Harwood, R. L., & Miller, J. G. (1991). Perceptions of attachment behavior: A comparison of Anglo and Puerto Rican mothers. *Merrill-Palmer Quarterly, 37,* 583–599.

Higgins, A., Power, F. C., & Kohlberg, L. (1984). The relationship of moral atmosphere to judgments of responsibility. In W. M. Kurtines & J. L. Gewirtz (Eds.), *Morality, moral behavior and moral development* (pp. 74–106). New York: Wiley.

Kakar, S. (1978). *The inner world: A psychoanalytic study of childhood and society in India.* Oxford: Oxford University Press.

Kohlberg, L. (1981). *Essays on moral development: Vol. 1. The philosophy of moral development.* New York: Harper and Row.

Kohlberg, L., Levine, C., & Hewer, A. (1983). Moral stages: A current formulation and a response to critics. In J. A. Meacham (Ed.), *Contributions to human development* (Vol. 10, pp. 1–178). Basel, Switzerland: Karger.

Lukes, S. (1973). *Individualism.* Oxford: Blackwell.

Markus, H., & Kitayama, S. (1991). Culture and the self: Implications for cognition, emotion and motivation. *Psychological Review, 98,* 224–253.

Marriott, M. (Ed.), (1990). *India through Hindu categories.* New Delhi: Sage.

Mednick, M. T. (1989). On the politics of psychological constructs: Stop the bandwagon, I want to get off. *American Psychologist, 44,* 1118–1123.

Miller, J. G. (1986). Early cross-cultural commonalities in social explanation. *Developmental Psychology, 22,* 514–520.

Miller, J. G. (1991). A cultural perspective on the morality of beneficence and interpersonal responsibility. *International and Intercultural Communication Annual, 15,* 11–23.

Miller, J. G. (1994a). Cultural diversity in the morality of caring: Individually oriented versus duty-based interpersonal moral codes. *Cross-cultural research, 28,* 3–39.

Miller, J. G. (1994b). Cultural psychology: Bridging disciplinary boundaries in understanding the cultural grounding of self. In P. K. Bock (Ed.), *Handbook of psychological anthropology* (pp. 139–170). Westport, CT: Greenwood.

Miller, J. G. (in press). Taking culture into account in social cognitive development. In G. Misra (Eds.), *Socialization and social development in India.* Newbury Park, CA: Sage.

Miller, J. G., & Bersoff, D. M. (1992). Culture and moral judgment: How are conflicts between justice and friendship resolved? *Journal of Personality and Social Psychology, 62*, 541–554.

Miller, J. G., & Bersoff, D. M. (1994). Cultural influences on the moral status of reciprocity and the discounting of endogenous motivation. *Personality and Social Psychology Bulletin.* Special issue on "The self and the collective: Groups within individuals," *20*, 592–602.

Miller, J. G., Bersoff, D. M., & Harwood, R. L. (1990). Perceptions of social responsibilities in India and in the United States: Moral imperatives or personal decisions? *Journal of Personality and Social Psychology, 58*, 33–47.

Miller, J. G., & Luthar, S. (1989). Issues of interpersonal responsibility and accountability: A comparison of Indians' and Americans' moral judgments. *Social Cognition, 3*, 237–261.

Nails, D. (1983). Social-scientific sexism: Gilligan's mismeasure of man. *Social Research, 50*, 643–664.

Nucci, L. P. (1981). Conceptions of personal concepts: A domain distinct from moral or societal concepts. *Child Development, 52*, 114–121.

Nunner-Winkler, G. (1984). Two moralities? A critical discussion of an ethic of care and responsibility versus an ethic of rights and justice. In W. M. Kurtines & J. L. Gewirtz (Eds.), *Morality, moral behavior and moral development* (pp. 348–361). New York: Wiley.

Rosaldo, M. Z. (1984). Toward an anthropology of self and feeling. In R. A. Shweder & R. A. LeVine (Eds.), *Culture theory: Essays on mind, self, and emotion* (pp. 137–157). Cambridge: Cambridge University Press.

Schneider, C. E. (1985). Moral discourse and the transformation of American family law. *Michigan Law Review, 83*, 1803–1879.

Shweder, R. A. (1982). Beyond self-constructed knowledge: The study of culture and morality. *Merrill-Palmer Quarterly, 28*, 41–69.

Shweder, R. A. (1990). Cultural psychology – What is it? In J. W. Stigler, R. A. Shweder, & G. Herdt (Eds.), *Cultural psychology: Essays on comparative human development* (pp. 1–43). Cambridge: Cambridge University Press.

Shweder, R. A., & Levine, R. A. (1975). Dream concepts of Hausa children: A critique of the "Doctrine of Invariant Sequence" in cognitive development. *Ethos, 3*, 209–230.

Shweder, R. A., Mahapahtra, M., & Miller, J. G. (1987). Cultural and moral development in India and the United States. In J. Kagan & S. Lamb (Eds.), *The emergence of morality in young children* (pp. 1–89). Chicago: University of Chicago Press.

Shweder, R. A., & Sullivan, M. A. (1993). Cultural psychology: Who needs it? *Annual Review of Psychology, 44*, 497–527.

Triandis, H. C. (1989). The self and social behavior in differing cultural contexts. *Psychological Review, 96*, 506–520.

Turiel, E. (1983). *The development of social knowledge: Morality and convention.* Cambridge: Cambridge University Press.

Turiel, E., Hildebrandt, C., & Wainryb, C. (1991). Judging social issues. *Monographs of the Society for Research in Child Development, 56* (2, Serial No. 224). Chicago: University of Chicago Press.

Turiel, E., Killen, M., & Helwig, C. (1987). Morality: Its structure, functions and vagaries. In J. Kagan & S. Lamb (Eds.), *The emergence of morality in young children* (pp. 155–243). Chicago: University of Chicago Press.

Wainryb, C. (1991). Understanding the differences in moral judgments: The role of informational assumptions. *Child Development, 62*, 840–851.

Walker, J. L. (1984). Sex differences in the development of moral reasoning. *Child Development, 53*, 677–691.

Walker, J. L. (1991). Sex differences in moral reasoning. In W. M. Kurtines & J. L. Gewirtz (Eds.), *Handbook of moral behavior and development* (Vol. 2, pp. 333–364). Hillsdale, NJ: Lawrence Erlbaum.

9   Diversity in social development: Between or within cultures?

Cecilia Wainryb and Elliot Turiel

In early August 1992, Mosbah Halaby, a 48-year-old journalist and writer, native of the Druze village of Dalyat-el-Carmel, in Israel, rejoiced in the imminent publication of his seventh book *Diary of a Druze Girl*. As reported in various local newspapers, the book was to include stories dealing with everyday life in the Druze community, with customs and traditions, family life, love, and sexuality. Some of the stories reportedly depicted extramarital affairs and sexual relationships with non-Druze.

The Druze are a small Arab community which was formed in the early 11th century and has since functioned as an inbred society. Druze society is hierarchically organized. Within the social structure, there are traditions requiring adherence by everyone; there are specific duties assigned to people in different roles, and there are strong sanctions associated with transgressions of behaviors prescribed by traditions and duties. The Druze family is patrilineal and patriarchal, and many restrictions are placed on the activities of women and girls. The relations between the sexes are also strictly regulated; marriages are arranged and Western-type dating never occurs. The Druze religion was founded upon Islam, and remains still today a central focus and regulating social force. Druze society is divided into the Uqqal ("sages") and Juhhal ("ignorant"). The Uqqal are the spiritual elite, the select few who are initiated into the truth of the faith; they are considered the guardians of the faith, and are the only ones allowed to read and interpret the Scriptures. As such, these spiritual leaders exercise considerable influence in Druze society, supervising and regulating social practices and interactions. The Juhhal, who constitute the majority of the community, are not versed in the Scriptures but are nevertheless expected to follow the more literal or outward aspects of religion and to conform to the patterns of behavior as dictated by the religious leaders.

Halaby's plans for his new book were suddenly thwarted by the reactions

283

of the Druze elders and spiritual leaders, who publicly disqualified the book as injurious. Halaby and his family were immediately excommunicated, barred from joining religious festivals and cut off from contact with other Druze. The whole Druze community was enjoined to avoid contact with the excommunicated family. After a number of days of voluntary confinement in his home, where he reportedly received threatening and offensive phone calls, Halaby gave in to the collective pressure. In a bid for reconciliation, he publicly apologized and symbolically burned "Diary of a Druze girl" in front of his home; subsequently, he ordered his publisher to destroy all copies of the recently printed book. "Diary of a Druze Girl" never made it to the shelves of libraries or bookstores.

The Druze culture, with its strict social hierarchy as well as traditions and duties, is a classic example of the types of social arrangements and moral requirements often contrasted with Western cultures, which are arranged in less hierarchical ways, and in which individual prerogatives and rights are said to be the organizing principles for morality. The suppression of Halaby's book may, indeed, be regarded by many as a clear example of the irrelevance of rights, like freedom of speech, to members of traditional, hierarchically organized cultures. In this chapter, we consider in some detail the role of cultural contexts in the development of concepts of self and morality, with special emphasis on the structure of such concepts in traditional societies like that of the Druze. This includes analyses of concepts of personal prerogatives and individual rights that go beyond the mere enumeration of examples, like the suppression of Halaby's book, which seem to reflect divergent moral codes and cultural practices in different cultures. We begin with a review and critique of the dominant approaches to culture and social development – approaches that focus on homogeneity within cultures and divergences in concepts of self and morality between cultures.

Diversity between cultures

The idea that social contexts play a central role in development has recently gained much popularity in psychology (as attested by the growing number of volumes dealing with these issues, e.g., Bolger, Caspi, Downey, & Moorehouse, 1988; Lockman & Hazen, 1989; Rogoff, 1990; Rogoff & Lave, 1984; Serafica, 1982; Stigler, Shweder, & Herdt, 1990; Valsiner, 1988; Winegar & Valsiner, 1992; Wozniak & Fischer, 1993; as well as the present volume). In an important sense, the idea is not new. The social environment was an essential component in theoretical formulations as diverse as those put forward by Skinner (1948), N. Miller and Dollard

(1941), Baldwin (1897), Piaget (1936/1952), Werner (1948), Vygotsky (1962), and Freud (1923/1962). What has always been and still remains a more difficult and controversial aspect of this issue is to define precisely particular social environments and to specify how social contexts affect the development of individuals.

In recent years there has been an increasing tendency to identify social environments and social contexts with "culture." A number of different conceptions of culture have been put forth. Some definitions are primarily behavioral; culture is conceptualized as a complex of behavioral patterns of customs, practices, and traditions acquired by the individual from the group (e.g., Benedict, 1934). Other definitions tend to be more cognitive and semiotic; culture is seen as an interwoven structure or system of symbols. This type of conception is best exemplified in Geertz's formulation (1973, p. 89) of culture as "an historically transmitted pattern of meanings embodied in symbols, a system of inherited conceptions expressed in symbolic forms by means of which men communicate, perpetuate, and develop their knowledge about and attitudes towards life." Underlying this formulation is a conception of human action as symbolic; culture is thus viewed as the context within which social events, relations, and institutions acquire their meaning, and as the only intelligible framework within which they can be interpreted. An alternative formulation of culture as a structure of symbols and meanings – perhaps a more subjectivistic or psychologistic one – defines culture as an intentional or constituted world that does not exist independently of the individual's involvement with and interpretation of it (e.g., Bruner, 1990; D'Andrade, 1981, 1984; LeVine, 1984; Shweder, 1990). In this context, culture is thought to be "real, factual, and forceful, but only as long as there exists a community of persons whose beliefs, desires, emotions, purposes, and other mental representations are directed at it, and are thereby influenced by it" (Shweder, 1990, p. 2). Culture, thus, does not have an "objective" reality, separate from the individuals' understandings and activities; culture lies in people's minds. Culture can (and does) affect and determine people's attitudes, judgments, and emotions, but only by virtue of the person's mental representations of it.

In spite of the multiplicity of meanings attributed to the concept of culture, there are a number of key common assumptions uniting these formulations, which entail consequences of importance to the study of diversity in social development. First, most conceptions of culture reject the idea of the constant or the universal, or what has come to be known as the assumption of psychic unity of humankind (Bruner, 1990; Geertz, 1973; Shweder, 1990). Although, in most cases, proponents of "cultural psychology" (as it has been labeled recently) have recognized that certain commonalities in psychological functioning are found across cultures, it is agreed that they do not reflect the existence of central or general mechanisms; the idea itself of a constant human nature is deemed impossible. Shweder (1990) went as far as to reject the entire intellectual enterprise of psychology (and what he regards as its Platonist philosophic underpinnings) in its endeavor to uncover general or universal features of psychological functioning, which he compared to notions such as "placeless space, eventless time, and squared circles" (p. 8).

As opposed to the notions of general and transcendent properties of human functioning and development, most treatments of culture have focused on the particular, the variable, and the diverse among cultures. Their conceptualization of culture is premised on the idea that social environments have a dominant focus, identity, or configuration, which serves to distinguish cultures from each other. The idea of cultures exhibiting different patterns of organization was shared by many American anthropologists in the early part of the 20th century (e.g., Benedict, 1934; Boas, 1908, 1938; Herskovits, 1947, 1955). Ruth Benedict (1934, p. 206), for example, asserted that cultures "are oriented as wholes in different directions. They are travelling along different roads in pursuit of different ends." Similar notions about cultural patterns with distinct generalized orientations and value systems have recently resurfaced in the writings of psychologists and anthropologists (e.g., Geertz, 1973; Markus & Kitayama, 1991; Shweder, 1986, 1990; Triandis, 1989, 1990).

A second commonly held assumption is that culture structures subjective experience, and shapes the thoughts, emotions, and behaviors of individuals. The means by which cultures achieve this have been described in a variety of ways. Although the process of cultural transmission has not been specified in much detail, the most common belief is that by participating in a culture, persons acquire its particular features. Herskovits (1947, 1955) coined the term *enculturation* to describe the process by which persons acquire the particular contents and perspectives of their cultural milieu without any direct or deliberate teaching. Another version of this explanation, referred to as social communication or social construction (Shweder, 1986; Shweder, Mahapatra, & Miller, 1987; Shweder & Miller, 1985), purports that conceptions of self, society, and morality are transmitted to children by the "local guardians of the moral order" (in particular, parents), through communications of cultural judgments and standards in the context of routine practices (e.g., within the family). Such practices convey the organization of the family and the society at large, and reflect the moral and social order. A somewhat different version of the process by which the socio-cultural environment affects human experience (e.g., Goodnow, 1980; Rogoff, 1990) is that a culture provides distinctive definitions of the valued or adaptive goals and means of development and, by such means, shapes the thoughts and actions of individuals. An alternative process, described as one of cultural meaning creation (e.g., Bruner, 1990), posits that culture steers individuals' beliefs and actions by giving them meaning and situating them within culturally shaped interpretive systems. This is achieved by imposing culturally derived symbolic systems, mainly in the form of language and discourse patterns. Beginning with the acquisition of language, the culturally determined narrative thinking organizes the persons' experiences and their concepts of self and the social world. Regardless of the process of acquisition posited, there is a broad agreement that culture is central in the social development of individuals. In Geertz's words, "undirected by culture patterns . . . man's behavior would be virtually ungovernable, a mere chaos of pointless acts and exploding emotions, his experience virtually shapeless" (1973, p. 46).

Furthermore, irrespective of other differences among them, proponents of the notion that culture has a central role in development converge on the idea that it is the *particular forms of culture* that steer and regulate people's beliefs and acts. It is the dominant focus or configuration, or the more or less homogeneous and integrated patterns around which cultures are organized, that are explicitly or tacitly communicated to, and acquired by, the members of the culture. Such cultural patterns shape individuals' conceptions of the self, as well as their emotions, morality, and strategies for problem solving. Notably, even in the context of formulations of culture as intentional worlds that exist only in the person's interpretations, the content of such interpretations is thought to be common enough to determine the development of individuals within a culture in the same direction.

These shared postulates result in the proposition that members of a culture reflect – in their thoughts, emotions, and social practices – the overarching orientation of their culture. This is why, time and again, cultures and their members have been typified according to a given dominant focus or orientation, such as cultures oriented to shame or guilt, as conformist or autonomous, as aggressive or pacifist, as sociocentric or egocentric. Currently, the most commonly used categories for distinguishing among cultures are those of individualism and collectivism (Sampson, 1977; Shweder, 1990; Triandis, 1989, 1990). Individualistic cultures are said to emphasize personal interests and goals, whereas collectivistic cultures focus on maintaining the social order and interdependence among persons in different roles. Persons in so-called individualistic and collectivistic cultures are thought to hold markedly divergent construals of the self. Persons in individualistic cultures are said to construe the self as independent and empha-size the uniqueness of individuals; sociocentric concepts of self, which emphasize the fundamental relatedness and interdependence of individu-als, are said to be common in collectivistic cultures (Cousins, 1989; Geertz, 1984; Markus & Kitayama, 1991; Shweder & Bourne, 1982; Triandis, 1989, 1990). Similarly, individualistic and collectivistic orientations are said to be reflected in the morality of individuals. Whereas a morality focused on personal rights, individual freedoms, and liberties is said to characterize individualistic cultures, the morality of members of collectivistic cultures is said to be focused on fulfilling role-related duties and obligations, and maintaining social harmony and interdependence (Haidt, Koller, & Dias, 1993; Shweder, Mahapatra, & Miller, 1987; Triandis, 1989).

By postulating such general and homogeneous cultural orientations, these theorists actually produce a view that limits the scope of social diver-sity. To be sure, there is a concern with diversity, since the stated goal of those relying on the notion of culture is to study "the way cultural tradi-tions and social practices regulate, express, transform, and permute the human psyche, resulting . . . in ethnic divergences in mind, self, and emo-tion" (Shweder, 1990, p. 1). Shweder and Sullivan (1993) further described the goal of cultural psychology as developing "a credible theory of multicul-turalism" (p. 498) and asserted that the current popularity of such an endeavor "is a measure of the culture-sensitive intellectual climate of our times" (p. 503). Although in a somewhat more dispassionate fashion, com-parable claims about the importance of developing an appropriate under-standing of cross-cultural diversity, multiculturalism, and local and variable processes are found in the writings of many others (Bruner, 1990; Cole, 1990, 1992; Geertz, 1973; Jahoda, 1993; Triandis, 1989). All agree that culture is the best parameter for comprehending and explaining diversity in moral, social, and emotional functioning.

However, the focus on differences between cultures brings with it the idea of uniformity and homogeneity within cultures. Cultures are por-trayed through a particular ethos or orientation, rendering each of them nondiverse. Such within-culture homogeneity encompasses both the unifor-mity of the thinking of an individual, as well as commonalities among persons. Hindu Indians, as an example, are said to be concerned with fulfilling social duties and obligations, with little regard for personal choice, individual entitlements, or rights. Furthermore, most members of a culture, irrespective of their social position or status in society or even in more circumscribed social systems (such as their positions within the fam-ily) are said to share the same orientation to social issues and values.

Consequently, the construct of culture often results in propositions of two kinds of generalities. One is a (seemingly unintended) strong assertion of a psychological law or mechanism – namely, that through participation in a culture the individual acquires the culture's particular orientation to morality and self (no other developmental processes are considered). The second is that cultures are described as consisting of uniform perspectives on morality and self. Accordingly, a diversity of perspectives is not accorded to a given culture or to its individual members. There is a failure to consider the possibility of a multiplicity of concerns and a plurality of social orientations coexisting in the social and moral judgments and practices of members of a culture. Whereas the importance of diverse local cultural symbols, practices, and roles is recognized, the possibility that individuals within a culture may construe or interpret such cultural symbols, practices, or roles in different ways is not acknowledged.

The limitations of a homogeneous rendering of cultures were considered as far back as the 1920s. Writing about Melanesian society in the Trobriand Archipelago, Malinowski (1926) dissented with the prevailing characterization of primitive cultures in terms of homogeneous systems. He argued that individuals in such societies are not "completely dominated by the group" (p. 3), or driven solely by reverence for tradition and custom, and an automatic acquiescence to their biddings. In his classic ethnography, Malinowski described the Melanesian social system as including legal, moral, social, religious, economic, political, and personal considerations. In turn, he rejected the idea that Trobrianders are motivated by an instinctive submission to tradition and, instead, attributed to them a complex system of psychological and social considerations (including needs, self-interest, ambition, reciprocal relations, interpersonal obligations, and social cohesion). Their social life includes not only connections to the social order and obedience to rules and authority, but the pursual of personal goals, cooperation, conflict, and compromise. The Trobriander, Malinowski concluded, "is neither an extreme collectivist nor an intransigent individualist – he is, like man in general, a mixture of both" (p. 56).

In Malinowski's time, the trend may have been to classify those considered "primitive" in homogeneous terms, as contrasted with the supposedly nonprimitive whose cultures are heterogeneous and complex. In the more recent approaches to cultural contrasts we have considered, most cultures are characterized as homogeneous. Those cultures that in the past would have been classified as nonprimitive are said actually to contain a coherence around concepts of self and morality that usually represent an overriding orientation to individualism, autonomy, and independence (and, in that sense, resemble the coherence of so-called primitive cultures). Malinowski's point, however, was that all cultures are heterogeneous and include a mixture of both orientations. We are in agreement with Malinowski's position and with a number of anthropologists who recently have called for a reevaluation of the ways the concept of culture has been used to characterize people in one-dimensional terms and to highlight differences among cultures (e.g., Abu-Lughod, 1991, 1993; Appadurai, 1988, 1991; Clifford, 1986, 1988; Fox, 1991; Ortner, 1991). Many have expressed a concern that the concept of culture depends on distinguishing "self" from "other," and thus inevitably carries with it a sense of inequalities and hierarchy, and leads to establishing and freezing differences among people. According to Clifford (1986, p. 10), "cultures do not hold still for their portraits. Attempts to make them do so always involve simplification and exclusion, selection of a temporal focus, the construction of a particular self-other relationship, and the imposition or negotiation of a power relationship." Abu-Lughod further argues that the concept of culture, with its built-in generalization and typification, over-emphasizes coherence and homogeneity. She asserts that the complexity of "other" people's lives is overlooked, and stresses that "other" people in "other" cultures are also "confronted with choices, struggle with others, make conflicting statements, argue about points of view on the same events, undergo ups and downs in various relationships and changes in their circumstances and desires, face new pressures, and fail to predict what will happen to them or those around them" (1991, p. 154). By overlooking the complexity of their lives, the generalized concept of culture contributes to the perception of groups as bounded entities "populated by generic cultural beings" (1993, p. 9) or as "robots programmed with cultural rules" (1991, p. 158).

Contexts of diversity

Social contexts do have an influence on the development of social judgments and actions. As discussed elsewhere (Turiel, 1994; Turiel, Smetana, & Killen, 1991; Turiel & Wainryb, 1994a), this is clearly demonstrated by findings from disparate perspectives, including social-psychological research on conformity (Asch, 1956), obedience (Milgram, 1963, 1974), and prosocial behavior (Darley & Latane, 1968; Latane & Darley, 1970), large scale public-opinion surveys dealing with attitudes toward personal freedoms and rights (McClosky & Brill, 1983; Stouffer, 1955), and behavioristic studies dealing with learning and conditioning (Gewirtz, 1972). The shifts in judgments and actions associated with contextual variations are inconsistent with the proposition that individuals in Western society primarily manifest a particular type of cultural orientation. As a whole, these findings indicate, instead, that the judgments and behaviors of individuals reflect not only a concern with individual rights and personal choice, but also with justice and others' well-being, with interpersonal considerations and friendships, and with obedience, authority, and tradition.

As an example, large-scale opinion surveys (McClosky & Brill, 1983; Stouffer, 1955) have consistently shown that in some situations large majorities of Americans endorse freedoms of speech and religion, freedom of assembly, the right to privacy and to divergent life-styles. However, many of these same individuals do not endorse those rights and freedoms when they are in conflict with considerations of tradition, the maintenance of public order, or the general welfare. Similarly, in bystander intervention studies (Darley & Latane, 1968; Latane & Darley, 1970), in which subjects were presented with opportunities to help strangers in distress, manipulations in the situational context were associated with variations in social responses. Whereas in some experimental conditions (typically when a number of individuals witness a call for help), most subjects did not respond to the needs of others, in other experimental situations (typically when the subject was the only witness), most subjects did intervene to help a stranger in distress. The former type of response could be seen as a detached or individualistic tendency, and the latter type could be seen as reflecting a sense of interdependence and altruism.

By our interpretation, these research findings cast doubt on the proposition that the social and moral practices and judgments of individuals within a culture are determined by broad and overarching cultural orientations. However, alternative interpretations to ours are possible. It could be argued, for instance, that the variations found within a culture are much less significant than differences existing between cultures. It could also be maintained that the variations uncovered within modern Western societies, especially the United States, do not constitute a contradiction of the expected cultural homogeneity hypothesis because such societies include a conglomerate of cultural and ethnic groups – each holding and transmitting its own cultural patterns of values. But, the argument follows, homogeneous cultural orientations with a single dominant feature or focus would characterize other (simpler and more traditional) societies.

Our position is, first, that traditional societies are not homogeneous (research conducted in traditional societies is discussed later). Second, we consider the variations uncovered by the experiments and surveys to constitute a central part of social life and of social development in most societies (and the specific findings as inconsistent with characterizations of individualism). We view social development as resulting from individuals' interpretations of social interactions, which are not uniform. Within most cultures, individuals observe and participate in social interactions entailing harm and injustice, the enactment of social roles and duties, opportunities for personal expression and the persual of personal entitlements, as well as interpersonal obligations and friendship. Furthermore, social interactions and social systems are dynamic and provide individuals with a variety of perspectives. Social interactions are, thus, not all of one kind. Portrayals of a global context – such as that of culture – that identify only certain dominant characteristics of social reasoning and behavior (such as individualism or collectivism) would necessarily overlook the complexity in reasoning and behavior ensuing from interacting within such multifaceted social environments. Our alternative view of social development defines a number of sources that result in diversity within cultures. One source of variation is the different (and often opposing and contradictory) types of concepts stemming from the individual's varied interactions with the environment. A second source of variations stems from multifaceted social situations requiring the coordination of conflicting concerns or considerations. A third source of variation lies in the informational beliefs or assumptions about various aspects of reality that are applied in interpreting social events.

Extensive research carried out mostly in the United States (for reviews, see Helwig, Tisak, & Turiel, 1990; Turiel, Killen, & Helwig, 1987) has demonstrated that children begin to form differentiated social concepts at an early age. Children, for example, develop concepts about the self, personal choice, personal entitlements, and individual rights – concepts that could be categorized under the rubric of individualistic concerns. At the same time, however, young children also form concepts concerning the well-being of others, justice, and fairness. These prescriptive moral concepts are inconsistent with the individualistic characterization of Western society. Moreover, children also develop collectivistic-like concerns with authority, obedience, social roles, and conventions, as well as with interpersonal considerations. Thus, children (as well as adults) simultaneously display multiple (and often contradictory) concerns with individualistic-like and collectivistic-like considerations.

Matters are more complicated, though. Often social situations and social interactions are complex and combine two or more considerations in conflict with each other (Duncan, 1986; Killen, 1990; Smetana, Killen, & Turiel, 1991). Children as young as 6 years old have been found to take into account and coordinate competing concerns. Research has shown that considerable variation in responses ensues from attempts at coordinating more than one consideration in complex social situations. Children, for example, have been shown to give precedence to justice in some situations, whereas in other situations they override such considerations and give precedence to other concerns; sometimes they give priority to social considerations such as group cohesion or obedience, sometimes they give precedence to interpersonal considerations such as friendship, and sometimes to personal goals and preferences.

One additional source of variation is that of the substantial informational diversity existing within culture. As individuals attempt to make sense of situations they face, they bring to bear informational assumptions or beliefs about relevant aspects of reality. Such beliefs affect their interpretation of social events, and, ultimately, their evaluation. In other words, people who hold different informational assumptions to be true may differ in their construal of an event and, thus, differ in its judgment. Evidence for this process comes from recent developmental studies (Turiel, Hildebrandt, & Wainryb, 1991; Wainryb, 1991) showing that the evaluation of issues such as corporal punishment, age discrimination, and more complex and controversial issues such as abortion and pornography, are contingent on informational assumptions. As an example, different evaluations of corporal punishment were associated with informational beliefs held about the ways young children learn. Similarly, differences in evaluations of abortion were found to be associated with differing assumptions about the beginning of life or of personhood.

Although little research has been done on the acquisition of informational assumptions, it seems likely that more than one source for such beliefs exists within cultures (Wainryb & Turiel, 1993). Science and religion, for example, are likely sources from which laypeople derive their informational beliefs about diverse aspects of reality. To use the same example again, accepted beliefs about whether physical punishment is an effective means for teaching children may be seen as having a scientific source (e.g., experts, such as Dr. Spock). Similarly, "facts" believed to be true about the causes and spread of a disease, which could affect moral and social decisions (about, e.g., whether it would be right to prevent children with AIDS from participating in school activities) may also be seen as grounded on scientific sources. Another source likely to be important in the acquisition of informational assumptions is religion. Religion-based beliefs about such issues as the normal functions of human sexuality, the beginning of life, or the nature of the afterlife may all serve as grounds for moral and social decisions regarding issues such as pornography, homosexuality, contraception and abortion, or special requirements on the behavior of widows. Both scientific and religious beliefs may be acquired through incorporating or learning of knowledge and information not derived firsthand (e.g., knowledge acquired from Dr. Spock, or from the pope), or may be constructed as parts of systems of explanation of diverse realms of reality. Children, for example, have been said to be incipient scientists constructing concepts in the realms of the biological (S. Carey, 1985), the psychological (Ross, 1981), and the societal (Turiel, 1983). Along with other cultural sources, science and religion clearly account for some of the variation seen in the information accepted by people within a culture. First, science and religion often provide different accounts of reality. Classic examples are the different accounts of human origins (evolution vs. creationism), and different accounts of the sources of disease (viruses and germs vs. spirits and moral transgressions). Furthermore, religions may differ in their accounts, as do different schools of scientific thought. An additional source of variation in the assumptions maintained has been documented by research in cognitive and social psychology demonstrating that substantial and systematic biases and errors in the perception and processing of information lead individuals to form (informational) beliefs about themselves and others that are inaccurate (Ross & Nisbett, 1991). Although we can only speculate about the acquisition of informational assumptions, the distinction between moral concepts and informational assumptions is well documented. Findings clearly indicate that subjects distinguish between moral concepts and informational assumptions, and that much of the diversity observed in reasoning about concrete social situations reflects differing assumptions about what is believed to be true (Wainryb, 1991).

The evidence discussed thus far suggests that the variations in social judgments and actions constitute a significant part of social life within cultures. Furthermore, the evidence reviewed suggests that such variations are not mechanically elicited by variations in context. Instead, they reflect distinct, systematic, and organized ways of thinking about the social world. Since individuals develop several organized and systematic ways of approaching the social world, there is a need for a shift from overgeneralized, overarching constructs (such as culture) to more differentiated contexts within cultures. In addition, this evidence has implications for processes of development. As shown, young children make distinctions among different types of social concepts (e.g., moral concepts, conventional concepts, personal concepts) and social functions (e.g., functions of justice, functions of social organization), which they use to organize and think about the social world (Turiel, 1983). Although the processes of acquisition of informational assumptions have not been investigated in much detail, it has been suggested (Wainryb & Turiel, 1993) that their development differs from that of moral and social concepts, and that it involves a number of sources or contexts within culture, such as religious belief systems and scientific belief systems. Overall, then, the findings discussed thus far do not point to the incorporation or internalization of a set of rules, values, or social communications. The findings are also incompatible with the proposition that development entails changes in a general structure. Instead, the findings of variation and heterogeneity are consistent with an alternative view of development, which posits organized and systematic changes within domains of thinking and within the realm of informational assumptions, stemming from the individual's varied social interactions, observations, and interpretations of different types of social contexts, events, and communications.

Diversity in cultures

The research considered thus far was conducted mainly in the United States, where it is evident that there is a fair amount of variation in the social judgments of individuals (this includes variations in the judgments maintained by individuals and variations between persons). Given the possibility that such variations are a product of a society composed of diverse cultural groups, it is informative to consider whether societies with less diversity of that kind would show homogeneity or heterogeneity in their social orientations. Therefore, we turn now to research conducted among people in traditional, relatively isolated societies (at least in comparison to the United States).

One of the settings for the research was the Druze community, described at the beginning of this chapter, with its social hierarchy and sanctions over maintenance of traditions and duties. Along with Malinowski, we hold the view that members of traditional societies, like the Druze, hold diverse social and moral judgments – including a mixture of "collectivistic" and "individualistic" ones. As noted earlier, the Druze community constitutes a good example of the type of culture contrasted with individualistic Western cultures. Hierarchically organized social systems of a traditional type have been identified as collectivistic because it is thought that people's judgments are oriented to the social order, to roles in the system, and to interdependence. The focus of the social life of persons in this type of society is said to be the fulfillment of fixed duties and role expectations, and obedience to authority. Furthermore, concepts of personal agency and independence of self are said to be social constructions of individualistic cultures; since in traditional collectivistic settings persons are supposedly defined by their status in the hierarchy and by their role relations, the ideas of personal agency, personal choice, and self-interest are thought to be absent or irrelevant. As put by Triandis (1990, p. 52), "In the case of extreme collectivism individuals do not have personal goals, attitudes, beliefs, or values, but only reflect those of the ingroup. One's behavior is totally predictable from social roles." Another attribute of traditional cultures, stemming from the emphasis on interdependence rather than independence, is that interpersonal obligations are regarded as fixed duties. Individualistic cultures, by contrast, are said to give more credence to personal choices over obligations to others. In turn, individualism produces concepts of conventionality in ways not apparent in traditional cultures. The concept of autonomous agents who engage in voluntary social arrangements produces the idea of conventionality – a set of social practices viewed as alterable by consensus and contingent on specific social contexts. Given the absence of the idea of persons with autonomy (and its concomitant freedom to alter social practices), traditional cultures are said to lack concepts of alterable and contingent conventional practices.

These propositions regarding traditional, collectivistic cultures rest on the idea that persons are not autonomous agents, with personal choices or entitlements or with a sense of independence. Even though traditional, hierarchically organized cultures differ in important respects from Western cultures with different (and in certain respects, lesser) hierarchical arrangements, research shows that people in traditional cultures do form a mixture of judgments on the dimensions of authority, interpersonal obligations, and social conventions. After considering research bearing on each of these issues, we focus on research bearing on a central proposition in the characterization of collectivism, namely, that persons in collectivistic societies do not maintain concepts of persons as autonomous, independent agents with choices and entitlements.

Deference to authority

One study that directly addressed whether children in traditional and hierarchically organized cultures are primarily oriented to authority dictates was conducted in Korea (Kim & Turiel, 1993). Although Korea has become industrialized in recent years, much of the traditional and authority orientation remains (Kalton, 1989). The concepts of Korean children (ages 6 through 11 years) were assessed in much the same way as in studies by Laupa and her colleagues, which were originally done with American children (see Laupa, Turiel, & Cowan, Chapter 4, this volume, for an extensive discussion). The findings showed that Korean children do not uncritically accept authority commands; instead, they evaluate the legitimacy of the commands. First, Korean children, like American children, rejected the legitimacy of an authority (a teacher) who gives commands that would result in a child harming another. In their way of reasoning, deference to authority does not include rendering legitimate commands pertaining to acts they consider wrong from a moral viewpoint. As has been found with

American children, Koreans evaluate the commands of authorities in conjunction with their evaluations of the acts themselves – thus setting boundaries to the legitimacy of persons in positions of authority.

Furthermore, Korean children also made differentiations between authority, per se, and attributes of the authority figure, even with regard to commands pertaining to nonmoral issues. The Kim and Turiel study examined children's evaluations of the legitimacy of authorities in resolving disputes among children in a game context. The attributes of persons giving commands (e.g., age, social position, knowledge) were varied as a means of ascertaining the features that children consider most important in granting legitimacy to authority commands (see Laupa et al., Chapter 4, this volume). Again, children did not display an undifferentiated or absolutistic concept of authority; instead, even at young ages they displayed understandings of the various attributes affecting the legitimacy of an authority, including the person's age, the person's social position, and the person's knowledge of the problem at hand. Notably, in justifying the legitimacy of authorities' commands, children referred more often to the knowledge possessed by the authority figure than to the person's age or social position. This means that – even within this traditional culture – a person's position or role in the social hierarchy was given less credence in legitimizing an authority's command than the knowledge to solve a problem competently.

Research conducted with the Druze, who could be said to be part of a culture more clearly traditional and hierarchically organized than Koreans, also evidenced that people have differentiated concepts of authority. In one study (Wainryb, 1995), children (ages 8 through 17 years) were presented with a number of situations posing conflicts between two social considerations (e.g., between interpersonal and personal considerations, or between interpersonal considerations and justice), and were asked to choose which of the two considerations should be given priority by the character in the story. Of particular interest in this context are children's judgments about situations of conflict between obedience and justice (e.g., a father requests his son or daughter to steal or destroy another person's property). Whereas considerable variation was found in the ways subjects resolved many conflict situations, a majority (at all ages) agreed in their resolution of the conflict between authority and justice: 96% of subjects rejected the parental command and said that the child should not commit such an act even at the expense of disobeying the father's order. Furthermore, when asked to rate each behavioral alternative, children at all ages rated obedience in this context very negatively and the alternative very positively.

Another study, also conducted among the Druze (Wainryb & Turiel, 1994) provides further information regarding how members of traditional

cultures think about authority and obedience. In this research, which was
designed mainly to examine concepts of personal agency and entitlements
in the context of hierarchical social arrangements, adolescents and adults
were presented with conflict situations in which a person in a position of
authority (husband, father) objects to the choices of activities by another
family member (wife, daughter, or son). The activities involved choices
with regard to occupation, education, and recreation. At all ages, subjects
judged that men have decision-making authority over their wives and
daughters; thus, when wives or daughters wished to engage in an activity
against the man's will, most subjects judged that the conflict should be
resolved by the female acquiescing to the man's wishes. However, a variety
of attributes were used to justify the legitimacy of the authority – including
the person's social position in the hierarchy and the person's competence
and knowledge. In addition, Druze females described potentially serious
negative consequences to a woman's welfare if she failed to acquiesce to
her husband's or father's wishes. As examples, the husband might divorce
the wife, force her out of her home, or cause her physical harm. These
additional reasons as to why females need to obey the males in dominant
positions demonstrate that persons in subordinate positions do not solely
accept an overriding cultural ethos nor do they identify with the hierarchical arrangements of the system. Women, who are in clearly subordinate
positions in this type of society, reflect on their assessments of the legitimacy of the authority and the reasons for obeying. It should also be noted
that the Druze did not regard men's authority over wives and daughters to
extend in the same ways to their sons. On the contrary, the Druze accorded
decision-making authority to sons, even when fathers objected.

Interpersonal obligations

The claim that traditional collectivistic and Western individualistic societies
maintain essentially different types of interpersonal codes is based, empirically, on comparisons of Hindu Indians and Americans. For example, research shows that Americans regard breaches of role-related interpersonal
responsibilities (such as caring for, helping, or supporting a family member
or friend) as a matter of personal choice, whereas Indians tend to think of
them as entailing a sense of objective obligation and within the scope of
legitimate social regulation (J. Miller, Bersoff, & Harwood, 1990; J. Miller
& Luthar, 1989). On the basis of these data it has been posited that Americans maintain an "individually centered" interpersonal code, as they view
interpersonal responsibilities as discretionary matters of personal choice

and desire. By contrast, Indians are said to maintain a "duty-based" inter-personal code, as they view interpersonal commitments as mandatory and closely associated to one's position or role in the system (J. Miller, 1994).

However, certain findings cast doubt on how generalized such interpersonal codes are and how uniformly they are held across social contexts within cultures. In one study (J. Miller & Bersoff, 1993), the role of personal liking or affinity in the evaluation of interpersonal responsibilities was assessed. Since persons in individualistic cultures are said to emphasize the role of personal choice and individual discretion in interpersonal obligations, it was expected by Miller and Bersoff that the American's assessments of interpersonal responsibilities would be considerably affected by the emotional close-ness of the relationship. Reflecting the emphasis on the duty-based nature of interpersonal commitments held in collectivistic settings, it was expected that the Indians' assessments of interpersonal obligations would remain relatively unaffected by the closeness of the relationship. On the whole, the findings indicated that Americans' evaluations of interpersonal responsibili-ties were more affected by emotional considerations than those of Indians. Nevertheless, variations were also found within both groups. Among Ameri-cans, parent–child relationships were judged to entail obligatory responsi-bilities regardless of the affective closeness of the relationship. Among Indi-ans, relationships between adult colleagues were regarded as entailing less of an obligatory status if the adults in the relationship felt distant and did not like each other. In another study, also comparing Americans and Hindu Indians (J. Miller & Bersoff, 1992), interpersonal obligations were presented in conflict situations with issues of justice. Although, overall, Indians gave priority to interpersonal over justice considerations more often than Ameri-cans, the findings also indicated that decisions in both groups were affected by the features of the events, in such a way that even Indians favored interper-sonal considerations less frequently as the seriousness of the moral transgres-sion increased.

In one of the studies with the Druze (Wainryb, 1995), children and adolescents were presented (among others) with conflicts between interper-sonal considerations and justice considerations (e.g., a child has to choose between giving special consideration to a sibling or treating all children in a group equally), and between interpersonal and personal considerations (e.g., a child has to choose between being responsive to a sibling's request and pursuing a personal goal as planned). Although the majority of chil-dren (82%) gave priority to justice over interpersonal commitments, the same subjects were divided in their judgments regarding the conflict be-tween personal and interpersonal concerns: 56% gave precedence to the personal and 44% to the interpersonal. Clearly, within this context, neither consideration was systematically subordinated to the other. When asked to rate the behavioral alternatives in each conflict, subjects viewed the justice solution as extremely good and the interpersonal solution as extremely bad. By contrast, with regard to the conflict between interpersonal and personal considerations, subjects judged that fulfilling a personal goal at the expense of an interpersonal responsibility, and fulfilling an interpersonal responsibility at the expense of a personal goal are both neither entirely good nor entirely bad solutions (mean ratings were at about the middle of the scale). Interpersonal obligations, thus, do not seem to be determined entirely by overriding cultural orientations. Instead, they appear to vary within cultures (even within "collectivistic" cultures) as a function of other dimensions, such as closeness in the relationship, the type of social concern they come in conflict with, or the seriousness of the violation incurred to fulfill the interpersonal expectation.

Social conventions

The question of conventionality is a complex one. Numerous studies conducted in the United States have documented that by a young age children distinguish between morality and convention. They judge conventions as alterable, contingent, and nongeneralizable (the research has been extensively reviewed [e.g., Helwig et al., 1990] and is considered in other chapters in this volume [e.g., Smetana, Chapter 7]). Several studies obtaining findings consistent with those in the United States were also conducted in non-Western cultures (Bersoff & Miller, 1993; N. Carey & Ford, 1983; Hollos, Leis, & Turiel, 1986; Song, Smetana, & Kim, 1987; Zimba, 1987). We interpret findings on distinctions between moral and conventional issues to support two basic propositions, guiding our perspective, regarding social development and culture. One is that individuals interpret social events and, thereby, make discriminations among practices embedded in their culture. (This is detailed elsewhere [e.g., Turiel, 1983; Turiel et al., 1987]). To give one example, children interpret practices regarding prohibitions on persons harming each other differently from practices dictating uniformities in dress.) The second proposition, which follows from the first, is that within a culture there is a variety of concepts of social practices.

This position has been challenged (Haidt et al., 1993; Nisan, 1987; Shweder et al., 1987) with the argument that the distinction between morality and convention is itself culturally specific, in that it is based on the supposedly individualistic cultural orientation to freedom of choice and individual discretion informing social practices (thus, certain practices are considered alterable and based on a consensus among persons). The proposition is that, since traditional cultures are oriented to maintaining fixed duties and fulfilling social roles, the ideas of alterable social practices based on consensus do not exist. Furthermore, morality encompasses the duties and roles in the social order (and it is not based on individuals' judgments of justice and rights).

In order to demonstrate empirically that the concept of convention is not relevant to traditional, hierarchically organized cultures, Shweder et al. (1987) studied mainly the judgments of members of a Hindu temple town in India. They assessed judgments regarding a series of social prohibitions, found in India, pertaining to matters like food or dress; examples are prohibitions on a widow wearing jewelry and bright clothing, a widow eating fish, and a son eating chicken after his father's death. It was presumed that these kinds of prohibitions should be part of the system of conventionality because their content dealt with uniformities in outward behavior, and not matters like inflicting harm or violating rights. Among the Indian subjects, it was indeed found that the infractions of the "conventional" prohibitions were judged similarly to "moral" infractions (e.g., harming persons, breaking promises). Both types of prohibitions were judged as unalterable and their violation as universally wrong (in some cases, as unalterable but wrong only in India).

There are three major issues overlooked in the Shweder et al. analysis that serve to seriously question their interpretation of their results. First, the social prohibitions pertaining to matters like dress and food were linked to a religious system with informational assumptions about an afterlife and the transmigration of souls (Turiel et al., 1987; Turiel & Wainryb, 1994a). Second, Shweder et al. failed to elicit from subjects reasons or justifications for their judgments. Third, the sample of subjects was restricted with regard to Indian Hindu culture (only members of the temple town and a group of "Untouchables" were included).

As part of the religious system, the social prohibitions are linked to informational assumptions regarding the effects of earthly events on persons in the afterlife. As examples, it is believed that if a widow eats fish she will offend her dead husband's spirit, or that if a man eats chicken after his father's death the father's soul will not receive salvation. Most of these assumptions entail experiences or phenomena that, though not directly observable, entail specific causal relations between earthly events and unobserved entities (such as souls). It is likely that if people in other places (e.g., in the United States) were to hold the same informational assumptions regarding the afterlife or the harm that can result to souls, they too would judge issues such as a widow eating fish as a moral transgression. It is also likely that if Indians were to be convinced that the opposite information was true (e.g., that souls are not affected by earthly actions) they would, in turn, cease to judge such matters in moral terms.

The role of informational assumptions in evaluating the practices of others was demonstrated by a study conducted in the United States (Wainryb, 1993). Children and adolescents were asked to evaluate acts performed in hypothetical societies where different informational assumptions were held. For example, a culture was described in which parents hit their children because it is believed that children who misbehave are possessed by an evil spirit that can only be exorcised by spanking. Another culture was described in which retarded children are put in special schools and prevented from all interaction with nonretarded children because it is believed that mental retardation can be transmitted during contact through play. For the most part subjects at all ages recognized that, given such different informational beliefs, people in those countries may construe a harmless act as a harmful one, and vice versa. Subjects were thus accepting of acts based on such informational assumptions (even if different from their own) and attached no blame to those people, because they perceive them as acting out of ignorance, misinformation, or alternative world views. These findings (along with findings by Wainryb, 1991) demonstrate the influence of informational beliefs on the application of moral and conventional concepts within cultures. Social practices – moral and conventional – are embedded in contexts that include informational beliefs; informational beliefs add to the context of an event in such a way that an event like a widow eating fish can be perceived as causing harm, and an event such as hitting a child can be construed as harmless. Claims about the absence of conventional thinking in collectivistic settings have been made, however, without accounting for the mediating effect of informational beliefs.

Research by Madden (1992), conducted in the same area in India where the Shweder et al. study was conducted, addressed the role of conventional judgments in ways that accounted for the shortcomings of the original research noted earlier. In Madden's study, judgments were assessed regarding prohibitions linked to religion and unobservable events in the afterlife (which we refer to as "belief-mediated events") as well as transgressions of conventions unrelated to those events (e.g., a husband cooking dinner for his wife and her friends; a wife kissing her husband in public). Madden assessed justifications as well as judgments about the alterability and generalizability of the acts; he also examined the role of informational assumptions. Furthermore, Madden's study included not only a group of priests from the temple town, but also a group of students engaged in graduate studies at a local college.

Madden found that the priests distinguished between the conventional transgressions and moral issues entailing harm and injustice. Conventional transgressions were judged less negatively than moral transgressions, more contingent on existing practices, more alterable, and more relative to cultural contexts. Furthermore, justifications of judgments that it is wrong to violate a convention differed from justifications for the moral transgressions. Moral transgressions were judged wrong because of their harmful consequences to others; conventional transgressions were mostly discussed in terms of societal customs and traditions, the coordination of social interactions, and, to some extent, religious rituals and codes.

The transgressions of belief-mediated prohibitions linked to the religion (e.g., the widow eating fish) were, interestingly, judged by the priests to be as wrong as the moral transgressions. However, on the dimensions of contingency on existing practices, alterability, and relativity, the priests distinguished between belief-mediated and moral issues, and judged the belief-mediated events in ways similar to their judgments of conventional issues (i.e., more contingent, alterable, and relative than the moral issues). The justifications for belief-mediated issues were also strikingly similar to those given in the context of conventional issues. The priests did not "moralize" all types of issues; rather, they displayed different types of judgments, including conventional thinking.

In an attempt to ascertain how informational assumptions influence judgments about the belief-mediated issues, Madden asked his subjects to consider the possibility that informational assumptions opposite to their own were true (e.g., that no harmful effects to souls ensue from earthly practices), and to make judgments on that basis. This turned out to be a difficult procedure to implement since the majority of priests (66%) refused to entertain the hypothetical (which, in itself, is an interesting issue that needs to be explored further). Nevertheless, the majority of those willing to entertain the alternative assumptions shifted their judgments about the transgressions and judged them as acceptable.

Further evidence that "Indian" culture cannot be characterized as absent of the concept of convention comes from Madden's data with the students (see also Bersoff & Miller, 1993). These data were clear-cut (and more clear-cut than with the priests). On the dimensions of contingency, alterability, and relativity, and in their justifications, students unequivocally responded to conventional and belief-mediated events in conventional terms, and distinguished them from moral events. It is important to note that the students were indeed part of Indian culture. They lived in the area, went to school there, and had not traveled abroad. This demonstrates that the use of a restricted sample, as the one in the Shweder et al. study, may fail to account for differences in judgments and reasoning among people of the same culture.

These findings are not restricted to India. Similar results were obtained with another sample of Druze children and adolescents in Israel (Wainryb & Turiel, in preparation). Although some of these data still await analysis, preliminary findings indicate that the Druze judged negatively both events entailing harm and injustice (e.g., hitting) and events mediated by informational beliefs about females' attributes and roles (e.g., girls wearing "immodest" clothes), and judged less negatively transgressions of conventions (e.g., failing to wear a uniform to school). Furthermore, as was the case with Indian subjects, they judged moral transgressions to be unalterable, generalizable, and nonrelative, but judged belief-mediated and conventional transgressions as more contingent and relative.

Concepts of persons and rights

If members of traditional, hierarchically organized cultures do have concepts of social conventions, as distinguished from moral concepts, then some doubt is cast on the idea that such cultures fundamentally differ from Western cultures in their conceptualization (or lack thereof) of persons as autonomous agents. However, the connection between autonomy and conventions, proposed by Shweder et al. (1987), is one we do not fully accept. The question of the conceptualization of persons as autonomous agents, with personal jurisdiction, personal choices, entitlements, and rights must be addressed directly. Such direct analyses of concepts of personal choices and entitlements in traditional cultures are important because the proposition that members of such cultures form sociocentric, interdependent concepts (overriding personal autonomy and independence) is central to characterizations of individualism and collectivism (Cousins, 1989; Markus & Kitayama, 1991; Shweder & Bourne, 1982; Triandis, 1989).

Analyses of personal autonomy are also necessary in order to have a better understanding of traditional cultures. We propose that personal goals, entitlements, and individual rights are part of the thinking of members of hierarchically organized societies, even though they may take a different form in the context of other types of social arrangements. In our view, children develop concepts of personal agency, including a sense of self, of personal goals and interests, as well as an understanding that other persons also have personal goals and interests. We propose that irrespective of the type of social arrangements – of the type of hierarchical relationships – interpersonal relationships are multifaceted and dynamic, and involve mutual expectations, conflicts, and negotiations over issues of personal preference, rights, and fairness. All relationships, however authoritarian, involve more than just the fulfillment of established or fixed duties and obligations. Relationships, even in hierarchical and authoritarian contexts, involve instances in which certain individuals (those in dominant positions, e.g.) impose their own personal choices and decisions on others, as well as instances in which certain individuals (those in subordinate positions, e.g.) attempt to pursue their own personal goals and desires, try to assert their rights and entitlements, and arrive at compromises.

Support for these propositions comes from two studies conducted among the Druze. In one study (part of which we reviewed in this section), adolescents and adults were presented with conflict situations in the context of family relations (Wainryb & Turiel, 1994). In one type of situation, the father or husband (normally occupying the dominant position) objects to the activities of his wife, daughter, or son (who occupy subordinate positions); in the other type of situation, the usual expectation was reversed and it was the person in the subordinate position who objected to the activities of the one in the dominant position (e.g., the wife objects to the activities of her husband). In general, subjects – both males and females – attributed a great deal of power and authority to husbands in relation to their wives, and to fathers in relation to their daughters (as stated earlier, less power was attributed to fathers with respect to their sons). The most frequent justification for their views that husbands and fathers can make decisions for their wives and daughters hinged on issues of status, roles, and duties. In some cases, these were straightforward assertions of the person's position in the hierarchy (e.g., "he gets to decide because he's the head of the family"; "she must obey him because she's his wife"). In other cases, statements referred to role-related obligations and competencies (e.g., "the father gets to decide because he's responsible for the family"; "he knows what's best for his daughter"). In many situations, however, justifications reflected also a concern with personal autonomy. As an example, personal choice and rights were most frequently used as reasons for why fathers could not impose their views on their sons (to a much lesser extent, such concepts were applied to daughters and wives). Notably, personal choice, personal needs, and individual jurisdiction were given as reasons for why the husbands and fathers could impose their views on wives and daughters (e.g., "the daughter should do it because her father wants it done now"; "he can tell her what to do because he owns her"). In addition (as also reviewed earlier), females in this study referred to the serious consequences of disobedience (for the females) as yet another reason for justifying the power and authority of the males. While accepting, to a very large extent, the legitimacy of man's authority and his own personal autonomy, females also had a critical perspective on the existing social arrangements. On direct probing, the majority of girls and women stated that the father's or husband's demands were unfair and violated the rights and entitlements of wives and daughters.

Taken as a whole, these responses show a mixture of social orientations, and a juxtaposition of roles and duties in the social hierarchy with concerns for personal jurisdiction and autonomy, and the pursual of personal entitlements. Other findings made this point even more clearly. In another type of situation presented to subjects, it was the person in the subordinate position who objected to the activities of the person in the dominant position. Almost all of the subjects – males and females – rejected such interference and judged that the decision should be made by the person in the dominant position, the man. The justifications overwhelmingly revolved around the husband's or father's personal autonomy, personal choice, wishes, needs, preferences, or jurisdiction.

Clearly, inequalities associated with the hierarchical arrangements (such as the patriarchy in the context of families) are both acknowledged and accepted within hierarchically organized societies. Nevertheless, the findings of this study indicate that along with the adherence to the duties and restrictions imposed by such hierarchical arrangements, personal entitlements and personal autonomy constitute a prevalent aspect of social relationships in these contexts. The very assertion of inequalities and restrictions within the hierarchical arrangement includes the assertion of personal entitlements and personal autonomy by those in dominant positions. Furthermore, the findings demonstrated that, from the viewpoint of those in subordinate positions, there is not just an acceptance or an identification with the restrictions imposed on them by the system. On the contrary, the data from the females in this study showed that they recognize the serious consequences of disobedience, and the unequal and vulnerable position that hierarchical relations imply for those in subordinate positions. Furthermore, females judge these inequalities to be a violation of their own personal rights.

The Wainryb and Turiel study confirms our hypothesis that embedded in social hierarchies is a strong sense of personal entitlements and independence, especially for those in dominant positions. What about concepts of rights among the Druze, who, as discussed at the outset, prevented author Mosbah Halaby from exercising his freedom of speech by forcing him to cease publication of his book? Many Westerners would regard this event as a breach of a fundamental right and as a strong indication that concepts of rights are not considered important in the Druze community. In our view, however, restrictions on certain activities should not be generalized to encompass all concepts of freedoms and rights in a society. Since the Druze do attribute autonomy and personal entitlements to persons, they may also judge that individuals should have certain freedoms and rights. We tested this proposition in a different study, also conducted in the Druze community (Turiel & Wainryb, 1994b). In this study, Druze adolescents and adults were posed with general questions about freedoms of speech, religion, and reproduction, and were also presented with a set of contextualized situations. In these situations, each freedom was pitted in conflict with one of three competing moral or social considerations: avoiding harm to persons, community interests, or directives from family authority; "weak" and "strong" competing considerations were presented. As examples, in the situations pitting freedom of speech against harm, hypothetical stories depicted a man giving a speech in front of the government building. In the "weak condition," the speaker blamed immigrants for the economic and social difficulties facing the nation and said that immigration should be stopped and all recently arrived immigrants should be thrown out of the country. The "strong condition" described a man giving a similar speech very near election time in front of a large group of people, including immigrants, who were very agitated, argued excitedly, and shouted. In the situations pitting freedom of speech against community interests, hypothetical stories described situations in which the government made laws restricting public speeches critical of the government. In the "weak condition" the restriction was on the grounds that criticism of the government is detrimental to the smooth and efficient running of the country. In the "strong condition" the restriction was justified on the grounds that criticism weakens the standing of the government in the eyes of enemy countries and thus decreases its ability to defend the country. In the conflicts between speech and directives from family authority, the hypothetical stories described a young man who wanted to attend a town meeting in the city hall to argue against the mayor's plan to build a new road. In the "weak condition" his father objects to this on the grounds that publicly speaking against the mayor would shame the family; the father thus tells the son that he cannot speak at the meeting. In the "strong condition" the father objects to the son's action on the grounds that it will upset the mayor, who would subsequently cause trouble for the whole family; the father thus tells his son that he cannot speak at the meeting. Subjects were also asked about weak and strong conditions in which a daughter or a wife was told by a father or husband that she should not speak at the public meeting. (Comparable conflict situations were presented for freedoms of religion and of reproduction in weak and strong conditions.)

The findings of this study indicated that the large majority of subjects (over 90%), irrespective of sex or age, maintains that freedoms of speech, religion, and reproduction are basic human rights that are not contingent on existing laws, generate obligations of noninterference on the part of the government, and are, for the most part, generalizable to other countries. Subjects' judgments about the conflict situations revealed considerable heterogeneity. The type of freedom, the type of conflict, and the strength of the conflicting consideration, all affected subjects' judgments as to whether the freedom should be upheld in the context of the given conflict situation; while in some conditions virtually all subjects upheld the freedom, in other conditions the large majority gave priority to the competing consideration. Across all conditions, freedom of religion was upheld more often than freedoms of speech or reproduction; considerations of harm to persons were given priority over freedoms more often than family authority, which, in turn, was given priority more often than community interests; strong competing considerations were given priority more often than weak considerations, except in the case of freedom of religion, which was affirmed in the face of weak and strong competing considerations.

Overall, this pattern of results demonstrates that individuals in hierarchical settings – even in a community that pressures an author to censor his work – form general concepts of civil liberties and individual rights, which they hold to be prescriptive and generalizable. Not unlike persons in Western cultures (Helwig, 1995; McClosky & Brill, 1983), individuals in these settings were also shown to judge these rights not as absolute or inviolate, but as freedoms that are weighed against and, at times, subordinated to competing moral and social concerns.

Conclusions

The research we have considered in this chapter supports two conclusions. One is that social context has a central role in the social judgments and actions of individuals. The second is that within cultural settings, differentiations need to be made among social contexts and, correspondingly, in persons' social judgments. Broad and overarching conceptualizations or identifications of the social environment, such as those implied in the concept of culture, overlook important aspects of diversity in development. The research shows that individuals in traditional, hierarchical cultures (supposedly duty-oriented and sociocentric) do judge in accord with roles, duties, and traditions in the social system. At the same time, they are cognizant of consensual issues of conventionality, draw boundaries on the jurisdiction of authority commands, and are aware of personal choice, entitlements, and rights as components of their social interactions.

These findings are inconsistent with the proposition that the social and moral development of persons is primarily determined by a homogeneous cultural orientation. Moreover, within a culture or society, morality is not adequately defined as based either on duties and the maintenance of social roles, or on rights and justice. Morality encompasses both types of concerns, which can produce moral conflicts of varying kinds in varying social contexts. To comprehend the heterogeneity in social and moral judgments or actions, it is necessary to delineate more specific contexts within cultures, in interaction with domains of thought, the role of informational beliefs, and the differing perspectives and roles in the social system.

We are not proposing that cultures are all the same, nor do we minimize the implications of cultural differences for the lives of individuals. Nontrivial differences exist in the social arrangements of cultures. In some cultures, there are sharp status distinctions between men and women within the family, and strong sanctions associated with disobedience or transgressions. As we have seen, however, in such traditional cultures several other types of social considerations apply – including concepts of self as independent, a sense of personal autonomy, and conflicts between people of different status and roles. Moreover, nontraditional (i.e., Western) cultures are not free of status distinctions or roles producing inequalities between men and women (Okin, 1989). We propose that characterizing societies or entire groups by means of unidimensional labels or categories (such as collectivistic or duty-bound) misses the richness and complexity of social life of members of such groups. Solely relying on a globally defined context, such as culture, is insufficient. A broader perspective on culture is needed – one that accounts for the multifaceted nature of social experiences *within* cultures.

Note

1. Recently, there have been attempts to deal with the question of specificity and complexity of individuals. Shweder & Sullivan (1993), for example, proposed that individuals may be innately equipped with a complex and heterogeneous array of differentiated interpretive schemes. Nevertheless, they still claim that any inherited potential for complexity and sophistication that individuals may have at birth is refashioned through their participation in the practices of the local culture and is ultimately overriden by cultural acquisitions (see also J. Miller, in press; Shweder, 1990).

References

Abu-Lughod, L. (1991). Writing against culture. In R. G. Fox (Ed.), *Recapturing anthropology* (pp. 137–162). Santa Fe: School of American Research Press.
Abu-Lughod, L. (1993). *Writing women's worlds: Bedouin stories.* Berkeley: University of California Press.
Appadurai, A. (1988). Putting hierarchy in its place. *Cultural Anthropology, 3,* 36–49.
Appadurai, A. (1991). Global ethnoscapes: Notes and queries for a transnational anthropol-

ogy. In R. G. Fox (Ed.), *Recapturing anthropology* (pp. 191–210). Santa Fe: School of American Research Press.

Asch, S. E. (1956). Studies of independence and conformity: A minority of one against a unanimous majority. *Psychological Monographs, 70* (No. 9).

Baldwin, J. M. (1897). *Social and ethical interpretations in mental development.* New York: Macmillan.

Benedict, R. (1934). *Patterns of culture.* Boston: Houghton Mifflin.

Bersoff, D. M., & Miller, J. G. (1993). Culture, context, and the development of moral accountability judgments. *Developmental Psychology, 29,* 664–676.

Boas, F. (1908). *Anthropology.* New York: Columbia University Press.

Boas, F. (1938). *The mind of primitive man.* New York: Free Press.

Bolger, N., Caspi, A., Downey, G., & Moorehouse, M. (Eds). (1988). *Persons in context: Developmental processes.* Cambridge: Cambridge University Press.

Bruner, J. (1990) *Acts of meaning.* Cambridge, MA: Harvard University Press.

Carey, N., & Ford, M. (1983, August). *Domains of social and self-regulation: An Indonesian study.* Paper presented at the meeting of the American Psychological Association, Los Angeles.

Carey, S. (1985). *Conceptual change in childhood.* Cambridge, MA: MIT Press.

Clifford, J. (1986). Introduction: Partial truths. In J. Clifford & G. Marcus (Eds.), *Writing culture: The poetics and politics of ethnography* (pp. 1–26). Berkeley: University of California Press.

Clifford, J. (1988). *The predicament of culture: Twentieth-century ethnography, literature, and art.* Cambridge, MA: Harvard University Press.

Cole, M. (1990). Cultural psychology: A once and future discipline? In J. J. Berman (Ed.), *Nebraska Symposium on Motivation, 1989: Vol. 37. Cross-cultural perspectives* (pp. 279–336). Lincoln: University of Nebraska Press.

Cole, M. (1992). Context, modularity, and the cultural constitution of development. In L. T. Winegar & J. Valsiner (Eds.), *Children's development within social context: Vol. 2. Research and methodology* (pp. 5–31). Hillsdale, NJ: Lawrence Erlbaum.

Cousins, S. (1989). Culture and selfhood in Japan and the U.S. *Journal of Personality and Social Psychology, 56,* 124–131.

D'Andrade, R. G. (1981). The cultural part of cognition. *Cognitive Science, 5,* 179–195.

D'Andrade, R. G. (1984). Cultural meaning systems. In R. A. Shweder & R. A. LeVine (Eds.), *Culture theory: Essays on mind, self and emotion* (pp. 88–119). Cambridge: Cambridge University Press.

Darley, J. M., & Latane, B. (1968). Bystander intervention in emergencies: Diffusion of responsibility. *Journal of Personality and Social Psychology, 8,* 377–383.

Duncan, B. B. (1986). *The coordination of moral and social conventional knowledge: A developmental analysis of children's understanding of multifaceted stories.* Unpublished doctoral dissertation, University of California, Berkeley.

Fox, R. G. (1991). For a nearly new culture history. In R. G. Fox (Ed.), *Recapturing anthropology* (pp. 93–114). Santa Fe: School of American Research Press.

Freud, S. (1923/1962). *The ego and the id.* New York: Norton.

Geertz, C. (1973). *The interpretation of cultures.* New York: Basic Books.

Geertz, C. (1984). "From the native's point of view": On the nature of anthropological understanding. In R. A. Shweder & R. A. LeVine (Eds.), *Culture theory: Essays on mind, self, and emotion* (pp. 123–136). Cambridge: Cambridge University Press.

Gewirtz, J. L. (1972). Some contextual determinants of stimulus potency. In R. D. Parke (Ed.), *Recent trends in social learning theory* (pp. 7–33). New York: Academic Press.

Goodnow, J. J. (1980). Everyday concepts of intelligence and its development. In N. Warren (Ed.), *Studies in cross-cultural psychology* (Vol. 2). London: Academic Press.

Haidt, J., Koller, S. H., & Dias, M. G. (1993). Affect, culture, and morality, or is it wrong to eat your dog? *Journal of Personality and Social Psychology, 65,* 613–628.

Helwig, C. C. (1995). Adolescents' and young adults' conceptions of civil liberties: Freedom of speech and religion. *Child Development, 66,* 152–166.

Helwig, C. C., Tisak, M., & Turiel, E. (1990). Children's social reasoning in context. *Child Development, 61,* 2068–2078.

Herskovits, M. J. (1947). *Man and his work: The science of cultural anthropology.* New York: Alfred Knopf.

Herskovits, M. J. (1955). *Cultural anthropology.* New York: Alfred A. Knopf.

Hollos, M., Leis, P. E., & Turiel, E. (1986). Social reasoning in Ijo children and adolescents in Nigerian communities. *Journal of Cross-Cultural Psychology, 17,* 352–374.

Jahoda, G. (1993). *Crossroads between culture and mind.* Cambridge, MA: Harvard University Press.

Kalton, M. C. (1989). *Korean ideas and values. The Korea Papers: Profiles in Educational Exchange.* NAFSA Field Service Working Paper No. 10. Washington, DC: NAFSA Publication Department.

Killen, M. (1990). Children's evaluations of morality in the context of peer, teacher-child, and familial relations. *Journal of Genetic Psychology, 151,* 395–410.

Kim, J. M., & Turiel, E. (1993). *Korean children's concepts of adult and peer authority.* Unpublished manuscript, University of California, Berkeley.

Latane, B., & Darley, J. M. (1970). *The unresponsive bystander: Why doesn't he help?* New York: Appleton-Crofts.

LeVine, R. A. (1984). Properties of culture: An ethnographic view. In R. A. Shweder & R. A. LeVine (Eds.), *Culture theory: Essays on mind, self and emotion* (pp. 67–87). Cambridge: Cambridge University Press.

Lockman, J., & Hazen, N. (Eds.). (1989). *Action in social context: Perspectives on early development.* New York: Plenum.

Madden, T. (1992). *Cultural factors and assumptions in social reasoning in India.* Unpublished doctoral dissertation, University of California, Berkeley.

Malinowski, B. (1926). *Crime and custom in savage society.* Totowa, NJ: Littlefield, Adams.

McClosky, H., & Brill, A. (1983). *Dimensions of tolerance: What Americans believe about civil liberties.* New York: Russell Sage Foundation.

Markus, H. R., & Kitayama, S. (1991). Culture and the self: Implications for cognition, emotion and motivation. *Psychological Review, 98,* 224–253.

Milgram, S. (1963). Behavioral study of obedience. *Journal of Abnormal Social Psychology, 67,* 371–378.

Milgram, S. (1974). *Obedience to authority.* New York: Harper and Row.

Miller, J. G. (1994). Cultural diversity in the morality of caring: Individually-oriented versus duty-based interpersonal moral codes. *Cross-cultural Research, 28,* 3–39.

Miller, J. G. (in press). Taking culture into account in social cognitive development. In G. Misra, (Ed.), *Socialization and social development in India.* Newbury Park, CA: Sage.

Miller, J. G., & Bersoff, D. M. (1992). Culture and judgment: How are the conflicts between justice and interpersonal responsibilities resolved? *Journal of Personality and Social Psychology, 62,* 541–554.

Miller, J. G., & Bersoff, D. M. (1993). *Culture and affective closeness in the morality of caring.* Paper presented at the Biennial meeting of the Society for Research in Child Development, New Orleans.

Miller, J. G., Bersoff, D. M., & Harwood, R. L. (1990). Perceptions of social responsibilities in India and the United States: Moral imperatives or personal decisions? *Journal of Personality and Social Psychology, 58,* 33–47.

Miller, J. G., & Luthar, S. (1989). Issues of interpersonal responsibility and accountability:

A comparison of Indians' and Americans' moral judgments. *Social Cognition, 7,* 237–261.

Miller, N. E., & Dollard, J. (1941). *Social learning and imitation.* New Haven, CT: Yale University Press.

Nisan, M. (1987). Moral norms and social conventions: A cross-cultural comparison. *Developmental Psychology, 23,* 719–725.

Okin, S. M. (1989). *Justice, gender, and the family.* New York: Basic Books.

Ortner, S. B. (1991). Reading America: Preliminary notes on class and culture. In R. G. Fox (Ed.), *Recapturing anthropology* (pp. 163–190). Santa Fe: School of American Research Press.

Piaget, J. (1936/1952). *The origins of intelligence.* New York: International Universities Press.

Rogoff, B. (1990). *Apprenticeship in thinking.* New York: Oxford University Press.

Rogoff, B., & Lave, J. (Eds.). (1984). *Everyday cognition: Its development in social context.* Cambridge, MA: Harvard University Press.

Ross, L. (1981). The "intuitive scientist" formulation and its developmental implications. In J. H. Flavell & L. Ross (Eds.), *Social cognitive development: Frontiers and possible futures* (pp. 1–42). Cambridge: Cambridge University Press.

Ross, L., & Nisbett, R. E. (1991). *The person and the situation: Perspectives on social psychology.* Philadelphia: Temple University Press.

Sampson, E. E. (1977). Psychology and the American ideal. *Journal of Personality and Social Psychology, 35,* 767–782.

Serafica, F. C. (Ed.). (1982). *Social cognitive development in context.* New York: Guilford.

Shweder, R. A. (1986). Divergent rationalities. In D. W. Fiske & R. A. Shweder (Eds.), *Metatheory in social science: Pluralisms and subjectivities* (pp. 163–196). Chicago: University of Chicago Press.

Shweder, R. A. (1990). Cultural psychology – what is it? In J. W. Stigler, R. A. Shweder, & G. Herdt (Eds.), *Cultural psychology: Essays on comparative human development* (pp. 1–43). Cambridge: Cambridge University Press.

Shweder, R. A., & Bourne, E. J. (1982). Does the concept of person vary cross-culturally? In A. J. Marsella & G. M. White (Eds.), *Cultural conceptions of mental health and therapy* (pp. 97–137). Boston: Reidel.

Shweder, R. A., Mahapatra, M., & Miller, J. G. (1987). Culture and moral development. In J. Kagan & S. Lamb (Eds.), *The emergence of morality in young children* (pp. 1–83). Chicago: University of Chicago Press.

Shweder, R. A., & Miller, J. G. (1985). The social construction of the person: How is it possible? In K. J. Gergen & K. E. Davis (Eds.), *The social construction of the person* (pp. 41–69). New York: Springer Verlag.

Shweder, R. A., & Sullivan, M. A. (1993). Cultural psychology: Who needs it? *Annual Review of Psychology, 44,* 497–523.

Skinner, B. F. (1948). *Walden two.* New York: Macmillan.

Smetana, J. G., Killen, M., & Turiel, E. (1991). Children's reasoning about interpersonal and moral conflicts. *Child Development, 62,* 629–644.

Song, M. J., Smetana, J. G., & Kim, S. Y. (1987). Korean children's conceptions of moral and conventional transgressions. *Developmental Psychology, 23,* 577–582.

Stigler, J. W., Shweder, R. A., & Herdt, G. (Eds.). (1990). *Cultural psychology: Essays on comparative human development.* Cambridge: Cambridge University Press.

Stouffer, S. (1955). *Communism, conformity and civil liberties.* New York: Doubleday.

Triandis, H. C. (1989). The self and social behavior in differing cultural contexts. *Psychological Review, 96,* 508–520.

Triandis, H. C. (1990). Cross-cultural studies of individualism and collectivism. In J. J. Berman

(Ed.), *Nebraska Symposium on Motivation, 1989: Vol. 37. Cross-cultural perspectives* (pp. 41–133). Lincoln: University of Nebraska Press.

Turiel, E. (1983). *The development of social knowledge: Morality and convention.* Cambridge: Cambridge University Press.

Turiel, E. (1994). Morality, authoritarianism, and personal agency in cultural contexts. In R. J. Sternberg & P. Ruzgis (Eds.), *Personality and intelligence* (pp. 271–299). Cambridge: Cambridge University Press.

Turiel, E., Hildebrandt, C., & Wainryb, C. (1991). Judging social issues: Difficulties, inconsistencies and consistencies. *Monographs of the Society for Research in Child Development, 56,* (2, Serial No. 224).

Turiel, E., Killen, M., & Helwig, C. C. (1987). Morality: Its structure, functions, and vagaries. In J. Kagan & S. Lamb (Eds.), *The emergence of morality in young children* (pp. 155–243). Chicago: University of Chicago Press.

Turiel, E., Smetana, J. G., & Killen, M. (1991). Social contexts in social cognitive development. In W. M. Kurtines & J. L. Gewirtz (Eds.), *Handbook of moral behavior and development: Vol. 2. Research* (pp. 307–332). Hillsdale, NJ: Lawrence Erlbaum.

Turiel, E., & Wainryb, C. (1994a). Social reasoning and the varieties of social experiences in cultural contexts. In H. W. Reese (Ed.), *Advances in child development and behavior* (Vol. 5, pp. 289–326). New York: Academic Press.

Turiel, E., & Wainryb, C. (1994b). *Concepts of rights in a hierarchical society.* Unpublished manuscript, University of California, Berkeley.

Valsiner, J. (Ed.). (1988). *Child development within culturally structured environments.* Norwood, NJ: Ablex.

Vygotsky, L. (1962). *Thought and language.* Cambridge, MA: MIT Press.

Wainryb, C. (1991). Understanding differences in moral judgments: The role of informational assumptions. *Child Development, 62,* 840–851.

Wainryb, C. (1993). The application of moral judgments to other cultures: Relativism and universality. *Child Development, 64,* 924–933.

Wainryb, C. (1995). Reasoning about social conflicts in different cultures: Druze and Jewish children in Israel. *Child Development, 66,* 390–401.

Wainryb, C., & Turiel, E. (1993). Conceptual and informational features in moral decision making. *Educational Psychologist, 28,* 205–218.

Wainryb, C., & Turiel, E. (1994). Dominance, subordination, and concepts of personal entitlements in cultural contexts. *Child Development, 65,* 1701–1722.

Wainryb, C., & Turiel, E. (in preparation). *Heterogeneity in social reasoning within cultural contexts.* University of Utah.

Werner, H. (1948). *Comparative psychology of mental development.* New York: International Universities Press.

Winegar, L. T., & Valsiner, J. (Eds.). (1991). *Children's development within social context.* Hillsdale, NJ: Lawrence Erlbaum.

Wozniak, R. H., & Fischer, K. W. (Eds.). (1993). *Development in context: Acting and thinking in specific environments.* Hillsdale, NJ: Lawrence Erlbaum.

Zimba, R. F. (1987). *A study on forms of social knowledge in Zambia.* Unpublished doctoral dissertation, Purdue University.

Part IV

Moral integration and character

10   Moral commitment in inner-city adolescents

Daniel Hart, Miranda Yates, Suzanne Fegley, and
Gerry Wilson

Committed, meaningful moral action fascinates and frequently astounds us: Why is it that some persons are willing to work on behalf of the welfare of others, even at the cost of their own? In this chapter we try to answer this question, focusing particularly on the sustained moral commitments of adolescents living in poor urban areas in the United States. This is a work of "practical anthropology" (Kant, 1785/1958) or descriptive psychology. That is, our efforts are not directed toward defining what is considered moral by these adolescents. Indeed, we put aside this issue (which despite its significance cannot be considered here because of space restrictions) and proceed with the assumption that their activities, which benefit others and which have no obvious instrumental reward, are genuinely moral in nature and are considered by the adolescents to be so. The goal will be to elucidate the ways in which sustained action is realized in the psychology of American adolescents embedded in a specific culture.

"Inner-city adolescents" in "poor urban areas in the United States" suggest a marginalized population, on the periphery of the middle-class sample so frequently studied by psychologists and thought by them to constitute the population. It is worth noting that "inner-city adolescents" are a large fraction of the American populace. In 1990, there were 7,744,943 children living in the 26 largest cities of the United States (with no breakdown available for the age group from 12 to 18; Children's Defense Fund, 1992). In 1989, an average of 23.5% of this population was classified as poor with the percentage ranging from 46.4% in Detroit to 12.6% in San Jose. Twenty-five percent of the 117,092 children in Washington, D.C., were poor. Moreover, many inner-city adolescents are African Americans and

The research described in this chapter was supported by the Lilly Endowment and by the Dean's Office of the College of Arts and Sciences, Rutgers University. We are grateful for their support. Address correspondence to : Daniel Hart, Department of Psychology, Rutgers University, Camden, NJ 08102.

Latinos. In Washington, for example, 65.8% of the children are African American and 5.4 are Latino. In other cities, the percent of children who are Latino reaches 69% (El Paso). Adolescents from these ethnic backgrounds have frequently been overlooked by psychologists, and surprisingly little is known about their development. When psychologists have studied African American and Latino adolescents, frequently it is in the study of juvenile delinquency, academic failure, and psychopathology. Consequently, the study of moral commitment in adolescents of the inner-city can offer insights into the psychology of a thick stratum of American life that has been ignored or pathologized by researchers.

Moreover, understanding moral commitment in adolescence can be an essential component of a full account of moral commitment in adulthood. One illustration of this is found in the life of Paul Robeson, one of the most gifted Americans of his generation. Robeson achieved success and national acclaim in a number of roles, including All-American football player, singer, actor, and civil rights activist (see Duberman, 1989, for an excellent biography). He was raised in a family with high standards for moral behavior and high expectations for success, a context that allowed the full range of his talents to emerge. Robeson's academic, artistic, and athletic skills brought him acclaim as an adolescent. The fiery commitment to justice that was an important theme of his adulthood was also developing. Under the guidance of his father, Robeson began to explore issues of social justice, particularly as it pertained to African Americans in early twentieth-century America. His growing awareness of the plight of African Americans and his commitment to improving their lives became a central theme of Robeson's life. Indeed, much of his life – his support of trade unions, the campaigns for equal rights, the visits to communist countries – can be understood as the story of the transformations in his moral vision over the course of adolescence and adulthood. Robeson's life probably could not be fully understood without an account of the roots of his moral awareness in adolescence.

How is it that some persons like Robeson strive to synthesize the moral ideals of adolescence with the realities of adult life? While some persons change the directions of their lives in adulthood and develop moral goals at this point (see Colby & Damon, Chapter 11, this volume, for a description), we believe that for many others adolescence can be a crucial period for the formation of moral commitment.

The psychology of moral commitment

Any number of different theories and methods might shed light on the underpinnings of moral commitment and exceptionally altruistic behavior.

Because there is little research on the topic, a variety of quite different, competing explanations could be used to guide the selection of methods. For instance, one might posit that the commitment to care reflects a broad personality disposition such as agreeableness (see Graziano & Eisenberg, in press, for a discussion of this trait), or defensiveness in the form of altruistic surrender (e.g., Vaillant, 1977), or social learning; each hypothesis could be examined with a range of methodologies appropriate for the paradigm.

Our own view is that one particularly promising approach toward understanding sustained moral action focuses on persons' conceptions of themselves and of others. In part, this view reflects our intuition that moral commitment can be best understood by soliciting from the involved individual his or her view of the self and the world. We do not believe that sustained moral action can ever be satisfactorily explained by research traditions that reject or minimize the individual's own interpretations and meanings (i.e., some streams of personality theory and social psychology). The self is such an important facet of social understanding in the Western world that we are led to assume that its study may shed light on moral commitment.

This view derives considerable support from recent philosophical work emphasizing the importance of the sense of self as a component of the moral domain. For instance, Flanagan claims:

> the connection with either or both social peace, harmony, and welfare, on the one hand, and self-esteem and personal identity, on the other, is probably a necessary condition for something – a value, a virtue, a kind of action, a principle, or a problem – to fall under the concept of "morality." (1991, p. 18)

Moral judgments are intimately tied with strong judgments of the self's worth and value; to act morally is associated with self-esteem, whereas immoral actions elicit self-condemnation (Kohlberg, 1981).

Psychological theory also suggests the importance of the understanding of self and identity in sustained moral action (Damon & Hart, 1992; Keller & Edelstein, 1993; Wegner, 1980). To some social critics, such an argument seems wrong: an articulated self-concept and the individualism that may give rise to it are viewed as phenomena that oppose moral behavior and support only self-seeking instrumentalism. However, the available research does not support such an objection. Snyder and Omoto (1992), for instance, studied the motivations of persons volunteering their services on behalf of persons with AIDS. A range of motivations was identified, including service to the community, understanding the epidemic, personal esteem, and so on. More important, Snyder and Omoto found that the motivation of the volunteer predicted the length of involvement in public service to persons with AIDS. Their results indicated that "volunteer attrition seemed not to be associated with the relatively 'self-less' or other-focused motivations"; instead, those who were motivated with "more 'selfish' desires of feeling good about one-self and acquiring knowledge and skills" (p. 115) were likely to continue with volunteer service, whereas those without this motivation dropped out. This type of finding, in combination with similar ones (Hayes & Lipset, 1994; Ladd, 1994), suggests that an awareness and concern for one's own identity can be supportive of moral action.

Even stronger evidence for the role of the sense of self in committed moral action has been described by Colby and Damon (1992; Chapter 11, this volume). In their recent study of unusually altruistic adults, Colby and Damon report that a characteristic shared by all their subjects was the alignment of personal goals with moral ones.

In this chapter, then, we shall focus on the synthesis of moral commit-ment with the construction of the sense of self by adolescents living in poor urban areas.

Youth in Camden, New Jersey, and Washington, D.C.

Two groups of adolescents are considered in this chapter. The first, and the focus of much of the chapter, is formed of 15 morally exemplary youth drawn from Camden, New Jersey. This group has been extensively studied using a variety of techniques (see Hart & Fegley, in press a). We also occasionally draw upon data from a study of 150 African American adolescents from Washington, D.C., who are participants in a school-based community ser-vice program (Yates, 1995). These students attend a nonelitest parochial school and come from middle and lower socioeconomic backgrounds. In this chapter, we explore some of the findings from these two studies, seeking to place the results within a matrix of previous research, psychological theory, and the context of daily life as experienced by these adolescents.

Camden, New Jersey, as a context for development

Camden's history is unusual: not because it has suffered a general decline over the past 50 years that characterizes many eastern cities, but because this decline has continued unremittingly, leaving the city destitute. Up through World War II, Camden was a thriving industrial city, home to the Campbell Soups, RCA-Victor, New York Shipyards, and an Easterbrook pen factory, to name only the larger companies employing thousands of blue-collar workers. Although it was never a city with the finish of neighboring Philadelphia, it did have its own middle-class, cultural activities, and a sense of future prosperity.

This has all changed. Campbell Soups maintains its corporate headquarters in Camden, but has moved its manufacturing plants elsewhere; RCA has only a fraction of the jobs in Camden that it once had; New York Shipyards and Easterbrook have left the city altogether. Essentially, these jobs have not been replaced. The population has declined from 114,000 during the 1940s to 80,000 today. More important than the decline in numbers, however, has been the change in the composition of the city's populace. Once, Camden was home to a predominantly white population; now the city's population is, except for a few neighborhoods, African American and Latino (primarily Puerto Rican). Where once there was a thriving middle-class, now there is essentially none. Fewer than 100 *households* in the entire city have annual incomes of $50,000 or more. This means that Camden is virtually bereft of professionals. Camden once was home to a large population of persons drawing good salaries from manufacturing jobs; now, most persons in the city receive some form of public support. Over 60% of the children in Camden live in families with household incomes placing them below the poverty line. It is not surprising, therefore, that the 1989 U.S. Mayors' Report rated Camden as the poorest urban area in the country.

The economic distress of the city has led to a flourishing drug trade, an escalating AIDS epidemic, a distressingly high infant mortality rate, and rampant educational failures. One estimate is that more than half of the adolescents who enter ninth grade never graduate from high school.

By most measures, then, coming of age in Camden is difficult and stressful. Becoming a success in adulthood (and, tragically, even reaching it) is much more difficult in the city than it is for most adolescents living elsewhere. Stress combined with exposure to violence – a mixture found in Camden as in many other cities – endangers the development of children; Garbarino, Kostelny, and Dubrow (1991) in their international study of children living in five war zones argue that this brew may be particularly detrimental to moral development.

Yet, despite the hardships and stress that characterize life in Camden, there is a large group of talented, smart, caring adolescents. Our interest has been in the adolescents in Camden who have demonstrated unusual commitments to care for others. These adolescents (who, we should note, are easy to find in Camden, New Jersey, and Washington D.C., belying common stereotypes of these urban areas) have not only survived the challenge of growing up in a stressful environment, but have flourished in it. Their lives, to varying degrees, reflect creativity in the incorporation of dedicated, sustained moral action. We have sought to understand how such commitments are made and sustained.

To study sustained moral action, it was of course necessary to identify a group in whom it was evident. A group of adolescents who had demonstrated unusually admirable commitments to care for others, or as we shall call them, *care exemplars,* was identified by soliciting community nominations. Church groups, schools, and social agencies in Camden were sent letters asking for nominations of adolescents who had demonstrated sustained and dedicated caring activities that benefited others. These institutions were then contacted by one of the authors to elicit nominations and to learn more about those adolescents who were nominated. From the large pool of nominees, 15 were selected as best representing the diversity of caring occurring in the city. A group of comparison adolescents was formed by matching each of the care exemplars with an adolescent of the same age and ethnic background, and usually from the same neighborhood.

The care exemplars were engaged in a wide range of activities: Some were involved in providing direct service (working in soup kitchens and shelters for the homeless, leading counseling groups for young teenagers, caring for community gardens, helping the elderly in nursing homes, coaching mentally retarded children for the Special Olympics), while others focused their efforts on community leadership (organizing neighborhoods for political action, serving on city boards, recruiting students for school service activities).

The sense of self in the care exemplars

A case example

A useful way to enter into a discussion of the sense of self in committed moral action is by considering briefly the activities and thoughts of one 17-year-old African American care exemplar, whom we shall call David Street. David was the most remarkable adolescent in our study. He was an outstanding student, occupied several prominent leadership positions in his school, and sat as a youth representative on the boards of several important city organizations. He had been deeply involved in volunteer activities over the course of 4 years, spending many afternoons in a public service agency in the city working with young adolescents. His commitment to helping others resulted in national recognition for his efforts.

When asked to describe himself, David Street mentioned that a defining characteristic of himself is his goal of involvement in the community. He explained the personal importance of this involvement:

I just had this complex, I call it, where people think of Camden as being a bad place, which bothered me. Every city has its own bad places you know. I just want to work with people, work to change that image that people have of Camden. You can't start with adults because they don't change. But if you can get into the minds of young children, show them what's wrong and let them know that you don't want them to be this way, then it could work because they're more persuadable.

What led to David's commitment to improve the city by protecting its youth? A partial answer to this question emerged in his responses to one of the moral dilemmas that was posed to all the subjects. The dilemma (Kohlberg's famous Heinz Dilemma) pits the value of saving life against the importance of obeying the law, by asking whether it is ever right to steal in order to save a life. A particularly difficult question following the presentation of the dilemma asks the subject if there exists a genuinely correct decision, given the choices. David Street responds not with an answer, but with a poignant memory from his own life.

IS THERE REALLY ONE CORRECT SOLUTION TO MORAL PROBLEMS LIKE THIS ONE? Basically, it's like I said before. You're supposed to try to help save a life. HOW DO YOU KNOW? Well it's just I mean if how could you live with yourself? Say that I could help save this person's life; could I just let that person die? I mean I couldn't live with myself if that happened. A few years ago my sister was killed and um I was um the night she was killed I was over at her house, earlier that day. And a few days before I was at her house too. I have said to myself, well maybe if I had spent the night at her house that day, maybe this wouldn't have happened.

His sister's death led him to reconsider the direction of his own life, which at the time also seemed headed toward trouble and eventual disaster. This period of reflection led to the conclusion that his goals for life would not be realized if he continued down the same path. Consequently, he redirected his energies into his education and public service.

By the time we interviewed David Street, he had been involved in public service for much of his adolescence. There was an urgency in his view of his involvement with children and young adolescents, a sense that he could make a real contribution to his community despite what many might view as a low-status position as a high school student. Not only was David Street sure about what he wanted to do, but he had a clear notion of how his actions fit with his views of himself and society. A glimpse of his commitment and personal philosophy is evident in the following interview excerpt, in which he was asked to explain the relevance of "not a bad influence on others," another term he used to describe himself:

OKAY. YOU SAID THAT YOU'RE NOT A BAD INFLUENCE ON OTHERS. WHY IS THAT IMPORTANT? Well I try not to be um, a bad role model. All of us have bad qualities of course; still, you have to be a role model even if you're a person walking down the street. You know we have a society today where there are criminals and crooks. There's drug users. Kids look to those people. If they see a drug dealer with a lot of money, they want money too; and then they're going to do drugs. So it's important that you try not to be a bad influence because that can go a long way. Even if you say oh wow, you tell your little sister or brother to be quiet so mom and dad won't wake so you won't have to go to school. And they get in the habit of being quiet (laugh), you're not going to school, things like that. So when you're a bad influence, it always travels very far. WHY DON'T YOU WANT THAT TO HAPPEN? Because in today's society there's just really too much crime, too much violence. I mean everywhere. And um I've even experienced violence because my sister was murdered. You know, we need not to have that in future years; so we need to teach our children otherwise.

David's accomplishments and insightful self-reflection are remarkable by any standard. We have encountered few 17-year-olds anywhere who have done as much or are as articulate and thoughtful about themselves. He becomes all the more remarkable when the obstacles to his success are remembered: an adolescence spent in a city where high school graduation puts one in the minority of one's peers, the traumatic death of his sister, the temptations of easy money through involvement with drugs. David Street was able to avoid being swept by these influences off the path to moral commitment. Like any accomplishment, there were costs incurred. One cannot excel in academics and donate hundreds of hours to public service without spending less time with one's friends and peers than typical adolescents. And, if we had looked more closely, other costs might have been evident as well. Yet David Street did not regret his choice to pursue public service, realizing, perhaps, that some loss was inevitable.

It would be inaccurate to suggest that David Street – and his interview excerpts that are presented here – is representative of our sample of care exemplars. The depth and sincerity of his commitment surpassed those of all the others. Yet, many of the themes revealed in David's life are present, if in somewhat muted forms, in the lives of the other care exemplars. We turn now to a discussion of the consistent differences between the care exemplars and the comparison adolescents.

Group comparisons

Each care exemplar and matched comparison adolescent (matching was done for age, gender, ethnicity, and neighborhood) was intensively interviewed in several sessions for a total of 4 to 6 hours. The interviews elicited four qualities and aspects of the sense of self that previous research has suggested are important: (1) self-attributions, (2) integration of representations of parents and ideals into the self-concept, (3) theories of self, and (4) the understanding of the self from the past into the future.

Attributions to the self. One way in which the care exemplars were expected to differ from the comparison adolescents was in the characteristics that were ascribed to the self. From childhood on, persons are able to describe themselves with a range of features (for reviews, see Damon & Hart, 1988, 1992; Hart & Fegley, in press b). These include characterizations of the self's physical appearance, activities and capabilities, relationships, personality, thoughts, and emotions. Research has demonstrated that those characteristics which are spontaneously offered in descriptions of self are cognitively *accessible* (Higgins, King, & Mavin, 1982), and consequently are more likely to influence one's interpretation of the social world; characteristics that persons can use to judge themselves, but which are not offered spontaneously, are less accessible and therefore much less important in influencing thought and behavior. It is for this reason that we have relied heavily on free-description methods. Exactly which characteristics are spontaneously offered to describe the self varies considerably from person to person, according to age, personality, and context (see Damon & Hart, 1988, 1992, for reviews).

Each care exemplar and comparison adolescent was asked to offer descriptions of his or her general self, goals, emotions, and personality. Our expectation was that the care exemplars would offer at least some types of characteristics in their self-descriptions that would be rarely offered by the comparison adolescents. David Street, for instance, described one of his goals as "being involved in the community" and, as an important feature of himself, the fact that he "wasn't a bad influence." Specifically, the hypothesis was that the care exemplars would be more likely than the comparison adolescents to ascribe to themselves moral personality traits (e.g., "honest," "moral," "trustworthy"), moral, caring typical activities (e.g., "helping others"), and moral goals ("community involvement," "I want to help others," "be a fair person"). Two of these predictions were confirmed: The care exemplars were indeed more likely to describe themselves in terms of moral personality traits and moral goals (accounting for 7% of the total ascriptions) than were the comparison adolescents (for whom these types of characteristics accounted for less than 2% of the total).

What does this difference mean? And what gives rise to it? It is worth noting that even among the care exemplars self-ascriptions related to moral personality and moral goals are relatively rare. Most of the characteristics offered in this self-description task referred to nonmoral activities ("bowl a lot"), general social traits ("shy," "friendly"), or psychological qualities ("smart," "happy"). These findings, then, suggest a slight difference in orientation between the care exemplars and the comparison adolescents. As Flanagan (1991) notes in a review of saintliness, no person's identity is constituted of a commitment to a single goal or principle; certainly this is true with the care exemplars.

How do these differences emerge? Laboratory research might be used to justify either the position that involvement in moral action precedes the attributions or, alternatively, that the attributions lead to the moral commitments. Supportive of the first position is a long line of investigation focusing on *self-perception*. As Bem (1978) pointed out, persons often infer what kind of persons they are from the actions they are involved in; self-attributions in many situations, then, follow from, rather than precede, actions. Providing further support for this finding, research on community service programs suggests that students expect that the involvement will lead to changes in the sense of self (Newmann & Rutter, 1983). Although experimental studies have not as yet included measures of self-ascriptions, there is some evidence to indicate that self-esteem and the sense of competence do change from pretest to posttest following involvement in community service (Hamilton & Fenzel, 1988; Newmann & Rutter, 1983).

But there is experimental evidence that attributions can lead to altruistic behavior as well as follow from it. For instance, laboratory research has demonstrated that making such attributions concerning moral character salient for children increases the probability that children will behave altruistically (Grusec & Redler, 1980).

In our view, both processes – self-attributions following from actions and self-attributions leading to moral commitments – are likely to work in tandem. The adolescent with a moral commitment is neither a purposeless automaton who "discovers" the meaning of the behavior only upon its completion nor is his or her behavior determined by reflection on an abstract set of a priori self-attributions. Attributions to the self change and their meaning to the self develops as the adolescent attempts to understand behavior, morality, and the connections of the self to these two spheres. Consequently, action and attribution interact: Action may lead to self-attributions, which then change the meaning of the action that was performed; in turn, the new attributions and construals can lead to new patterns of behavior.

Integration of parents and ideals into the self-concept. Not only were the care exemplars hypothesized to differ from the comparison adolescents in the types of ascriptions made to the self, but in the organization of these ascriptions as well. One way to look at the organization has been suggested by Rosenberg and his colleagues (Rosenberg, 1988; Rosenberg & Gara, 1985). Rosenberg has suggested that it is possible to imagine the self-concept as consisting of a variety of specific representations of self and other. For instance, persons may have ideal selves (representations of what they would ideally be), undesired selves (images of what they do not wish to be; see Ogilvie, 1987), future or possible selves (Hart, Fegley, & Brengelman, 1993; Markus & Nurius, 1986), expected or ought selves (what other people think the self should be like; Strauman & Higgins, 1988), and social selves (what the self is like with specific other persons – e.g. self-with-mother; Hart, 1988a). Additionally, persons may have conceptions of important persons (mother, father, etc.). Rosenberg argues that these various representations of self and other are arranged in a hierarchical structure, with the location of representations in this structure revealing the ways in which the representations influence each other. The hierarchical arrangement of these representations is inferred from the characteristics that are ascribed to each representation (consequently, subjects were asked to describe each of these in the interviews). According to Rosenberg, between any two representations one of three types of relations might exist: (1) The two representations are thought of in essentially the same ways, described in nearly identical terms, and consequently can be imagined to be in the same set; (2) the two representations are thought of in fundamentally different ways, described in very different terms, and therefore the two representations are in different sets; or (3) one representation may incorporate the other representation as a subset of itself – have all the characteristics of the subset representation, but a number of others as well. In research, the set relationships among all the representations for a subject are inferred simultaneously, using a computer program to analyze the patterns of descriptions (DeBoeck & Rosenberg, 1988).

In the study of Camden youth, several predictions were made. We believed that the most important relations to examine in the hierarchical structure involved the actual self (what the person believes the self actually is), representations involving parents (subjects were asked to describe what the mother and father are like; what the self is like with mother and father; what mother and father expect the self to be like) and best friend (subjects were asked to describe what the best friend is like, what the self is like with my best friend, and what person the best friend expects the self to be), and the ideal self. Our hypothesis was that the care exemplars would differ from the comparison adolescents in the representations that are either identical with, or a subset of, the actual self as determined by the arrangement of subselves and representations in a hierarchy. Specifically, the care exemplars were expected to be more likely to have actual selves that incorporate (are superordinate to) their ideal selves. Most persons have ideal selves. As Rawls notes, "an individual says who he is by describing his purposes and causes, what he intends to do with his life" (1971, p. 408). Yet, it seems likely that these purposes and causes are more central to the lives of the care exemplars. In set terms, those persons or selves which are subsumed by the actual self are presumed to be more central to one's current identity than persons or selves that are in different sets (Rosenberg, 1988). The actions of the care exemplars suggests that they were driven by their ideals in ways not true for most adolescents.

The analyses supported this prediction. The care exemplars tended to describe their actual selves with a broad range of terms, a subset of which was also used to describe the ideal self. In contrast, the comparison adolescents described their actual selves in ways that indicated little connection to their ideal selves. In set terms, for 66% of the exemplars, but only for 27% of the comparisons, the actual self incorporated the ideal self. This finding demonstrates that, like the morally admirable adults studied by Colby and Damon (Chapter 11, this volume), the care exemplars were expected to experience their values and ideals, which together constitute their ideal selves as central to their identities.

The care exemplars were also expected to have actual selves that were more likely than the actual selves of the comparison adolescents to incorporate parentally related representations (what my mother is like; what my father is like; what I am like with my mother; what I am like with my father; what my mother expects me to be; what my father expects me to be). One reason to hypothesize that parents are more influential in a positive way in the lives of the care exemplars than in the lives of the comparison adolescents has to do simply with the challenges of growing up in a city with all the problems of Camden. It is possible to view the moral creativity evidenced by the care exemplars – adolescents who successfully grow up in very difficult contexts – as a special case of resilience. Studies of adolescent resilience (e.g., Losel & Bliesener, 1990) demonstrate the importance of solid relationships with parents as factors that protect adolescents from risks.

There is now a substantial body of work to indicate that parents do affect their children's moral development in a variety of ways. Hart (1988b) found that boys who identified with their fathers, and who had fathers who were emotionally involved with them, reached substantially higher stages of moral judgment in adulthood than boys with uninvolved fathers with whom they could not identify. Studies of community service and moral action converge on the conclusion that parents – through both their styles of interacting with their children and the actions they model – are important factors in their children's lives. Fitch (1987) and Tierney and Branch (1992) and other researchers have found that college students who perform community service are more likely than nonvolunteer students to have parents who themselves perform community service.

Research on persons whose commitments to helping others pose hardships and even risks to themselves frequently finds that these persons were inspired and shaped by their parents. Rosenhan (1970), for instance, found that one important way persons who were fully committed to the early civil rights movement in the United States differed from those whose involvement was less substantial involved parents: Those who were fully committed "formed and maintained a positive cordial, warm, and respecting relationship with their parent (and often both parents)" (p. 261), whereas the less committed tended "to describe their parent (or both parents) in negative or ambivalent terms" (p. 262). Moreover, Rosenhan reports that the parents of those fully committed to the civil rights struggle were likely to have modeled sustained altruistic action when their sons and daughters were children.

Much the same pattern has been reported by London (1970) and by Oliner and Oliner (1988). Both studies focused on Christians who risked their lives to save Jews from death during World War II. London (1970) found that the Christians who saved Jews from the Nazis tended to express an intense identification with at least one parent, who was seen to have been a model of moral conduct. In a much more extensive study, the Oliners (1988) reached the same conclusion with a similar sample of persons who had acted to save Jews from the Holocaust.

The analyses of the descriptions of the adolescents in the study of Camden youth confirmed the predictions. All but one of the care exemplars had actual selves that incorporated parentally related selves or representations; this was true for only 60% of the comparison adolescents. These findings confirm the importance of parents in the moral commitment and altruistic action.

A final prediction concerning the hierarchical organization of the self-concept involved representations of, or related to (self with best friend, self expected by the best friend), the best friend. Previous research (Hart, 1988a) had shown that as adolescents get older, and spend increasingly large spans of time with their peers, they are likely to see their actual selves as incorporating best friend–related representations. However, because the activities of the care exemplars reduce the time they can spend with their peers, we predicted that they would be less likely than the comparison adolescents to incorporate representations related to the best friend into their actual selves. This prediction was confirmed; for 80% of the comparison adolescents, but for only 47% of the exemplars, the actual self was either a superordinate set to, or in the same set with, a representation related to the best friend.

This finding should not be taken to imply that friends and peers necessarily inhibit moral commitment. As we noted earlier, interactions with peers are rich contexts in which to learn the intricacies and dangers of helping others (Krappmann & Oswald, 1991) and to develop principles by which to judge when one does and does not have a moral obligation (e.g., Piaget, 1932/1965). Moreover, many adolescents report that their friends support their involvement in community service (Youniss, 1993). Indeed, a sense of connection to fellow participants may encourage those without autonomous moral commitment to continue in community service (Clary & Miller, 1986).

However, in Camden as in other Western cultural contexts, deep, sustained, moral commitment is done at the risk of at least some isolation, and perhaps alienation, from one's friends and peers. For instance McAdam (1988) found that young adults who participated in the civil rights movement both (1) continued to be deeply involved with social movements through middle adulthood, and (2) experienced difficulty with close interpersonal relationships (e.g., marriage) throughout their lives. Indeed, McAdam concludes from his interviews that the dedicated volunteerism of his subjects resulted in "social isolation and marginality" (p. 223) for many of them. The results of our study of Camden youth and McAdam's study of civil rights volunteers suggest that it may be difficult for adolescents and adults to balance moral commitment to community action and interpersonal relationships.

Theories of self. A third way the sense of self was expected to differ between the care exemplars and comparison adolescents concerned the sorts of theories persons have about themselves. In previous sections, we considered the specific attributes the adolescents held about themselves, and the ways in which their descriptions of their actual selves were related to descriptions of their ideals, parents, and best friends; theories of self refer to the principles persons rely on to organize and to make sense of the self's characteristics.

In previous studies, Damon and Hart (Damon & Hart, 1988; Hart, 1992) have described three types of theories adolescents and young adults hold about themselves, with each type of theory corresponding to a developmental level. At a Level 2 theory of self (Level 1 theories are typically only found among young children), the organizing principles are normative physical or social standards. A person at Level 2 is likely to explain the significance of each characteristic of self through comparison with others; for instance, being "good at basketball" may be important because the self is "better than everyone else at school." Level 3 theories of self link the meaning of different characteristics of self to both social acceptance and differentiation from the social context. Being "smart," for instance, may be important to an individual with a Level 3 theory because "my friends don't like stupid people, and wouldn't like me if I were stupid." Finally, at Level 4, theories of self are based on systematic beliefs and life plans. Persons relate the different characteristics of self to these personal philosophies. David Street revealed his Level 4 theory of self in his explanations of the personal importance of "not being a bad influence" in order to avoid transmitting the violence and danger he saw in his neighborhood into future generations.

Level 4 theories are quite rare in adolescence (Damon & Hart, 1988) and are found in only a minority of adults (Hart, 1992). Nonetheless, we expected that the care exemplars – like David Street – would be more likely than the comparison adolescents to have or at least to be developing Level 4 theories. There are several reasons for this hypothesis. First, theory (Hart & Fegley, in press b) suggests that persons whose actions, ethnicity, or geographic location puts them at the edges of their culture or at the intersection of different cultures are frequently called upon to articulate and to defend their beliefs and behavior. For both the care exemplars and the comparison group, the experience of growing up as a member of an ethnic minority group may have pushed the development of their theories of self. The care exemplars' theories of self, however, may have been driven to develop even further than the comparison adolescents because the exemplars' actions remove them to some degree from the network of their neighborhood peers. They may need to identify for themselves the principles that can subsume their moral activities and the costs associated with them.

A second reason that the care exemplars might be expected to be more advanced in their theories of self than the comparison adolescents is that their actions are likely to occur in contexts in which issues and principles are discussed. Garbarino et al. (1991) argue that moral development – particularly among children and adolescents living in stressful environments – "seems to reflect the degree to which children are supported in engaging in issue-focused discussions and social interactions" (p. 379). These same sorts of discussions are likely to support the development of Level 4 theories of self as well. We believe that these sorts of discussions are more likely to occur in community service activities of the sorts that the care exemplars were involved in than in the athletic and academic pursuits of the comparison adolescents.

One purpose of the research currently underway in Washington, D.C., is to investigate the ways in which such discussions are opportunities for the collective construction of moral and political understanding (Youniss, 1981; Youniss & Yates, 1994). An opportunity to discuss the issues and conflicts arising from community service with peers and adults can lead to a deepened appreciation of the complexities of moral issues, and as well to a clearer understanding of self. Below is an excerpt from a group discussion in which an adolescent who is volunteering in a soup kitchen explores the meaning of her contact with a person who has come to the kitchen for a meal:

One lady I was talking to she told me that she worked at McDonald's and she came down to the soup kitchen for meals. And she was saying how she lived with four different people and I just listened to her story. And one day, I was downtown. I was in McDonald's and I saw her there, and I, and I saw her. It's like, you know, your friends go to McDonald's and see an older person work there and tend to say, "this person is not doing anything with their lives, 'cause they work at McDonald's" or whatever. A lot of people who work in the fast food jobs and stuff like that they, you know, it's not like it's where they want to be. It's just what happened to them. A lot of people tease them. WHAT DID IT TEACH YOU? It helped me to understand that housing in the District is expensive and while I was talking to the lady, she was telling me how much her rent was. I think she said it was $700 a month, and that what she was making at McDonald's just wasn't enough for rent, her children, and food and stuff. It's just that talking to her made me realize that there are a lot of people who need a lot of help and how we need to get them better housing and stuff like that.

Certainly there is no assurance that such remarks in the context of a discussion group composed of peers will lead to consolidated changes in the understanding of social issues or the understanding of self. However, it may be the case that these new insights – "made me realize that there are a lot of people who need a lot of help" – will become consolidated into moral goals ("we need to get them better housing and stuff"), which in turn become articulated with theories of self in which values and personal philosophies are central.

Preliminary evidence for the consolidation of these types of insights into theories of self is emerging in interviews with alumni from the Washington community service program. These alumni have been identified as demonstrating exceptional moral commitment in adolescence by the teacher who began the service program in conjunction with a social justice class. For example, Chris participated in the program 7 years ago and now works as a special education teacher in a poor neighborhood in Washington, D.C. In the following excerpt, he recalls how the experience of working in a soup kitchen and discussing issues of social justice led to new behavior, which then led to an insight:

One day I was getting off the bus and this guy said, "you got any money?" and I was like, "No." I said "do you want a sandwich or something." He said, "yeah." So I went in the house and made him a sandwich and brought it back and I talked to him for about a half an hour. And I never would have done that before the class. But I sat and talked with him. I learned that he had two kids, and a wife, and he'd lost his job and they were all living in a shelter. I never would have done that [made him a sandwich and talked to him] before the class. And, I stopped seeing color, to a certain degree. I learned that you take things, for, you know, what they are.

This insight gradually became elaborated into a theory of self and a career in special education. The process was slow, perhaps because Chris as the oldest child was the first person to attend college from his family and his parents thought he might enter a profession that would be prestigious and lucrative. But, as he entered college, Chris realized that his interests were no longer focused on potential income:

Up until that day when I changed my major [to psychology], my goal was to be an accountant and get a job, family, blah, blah, blah. Then, I changed I wanted to work with people like I am now. . . . It was building up and then one day, I decided "I'm going to do it." . . . I like where I am now [in special education] because I like seeing that I can make a difference. And I always try to tell my kids that they can make a difference in somebody's life. I moved into teaching so maybe I can give these kids the things that they need to know to survive.

Chris's experience as an adolescent working in community service and discussing issues of social justice fostered the development of this theory of self in which a sense of responsibility to others became central.

Connections to past and future selves. A final difference between the care exemplars and the comparison adolescents emerged from analyses (see Hart & Fegley, in press a, for details) of the ways in which the actual self and past and future selves (e.g., "what were you like four years ago? two years ago?" or "what will you be like in two years? four years? as an adult?") were described. The actual selves of the care exemplars, in comparison to those of the comparison adolescents, were found to be closer conceptually to past and future selves. Apparently, the care exemplars see greater continuity and connection in the temporal flow of their lives than do other adolescents.

One way this finding can be interpreted is in the terms of identity offered by Erikson (1968). The comparison adolescents might be described as seeing themselves in a period of moratorium: The persons they are at present are transient, reflecting neither the persons they were in the past nor the persons they will become in the future. There may be a sense in these adolescents that making commitments and following through on them is difficult, because identifying the self's real goals and desires in a period of transition is difficult. The care exemplars, in contrast, have a sense of urgency about them; they believe that the persons they are in the present are closely connected to who they have been and who they will be. As a consequence, they appear more inclined to pursue their goals, which are viewed as enduring facets of themselves. One example of this urgency can be seen in the comments of Shari, a Washington student talking about her frustration resulting from the sense that her social justice is too much talk and too little action:

This class, this class has really pissed me off. I'm telling you. I'm about to go out there and do something. Like that man with AIDS on the street corner near the soup kitchen. If I ever see that man again, I'm taking him right to Providence Hospital and getting him some help. . . . I mean we're sitting here talking about issues, but what are any of us really doing?

One of Shari's classmates objects:

We ourselves are only sixteen or seventeen years old, and we don't necessarily have to do something right now, because we don't have any power. . . . Adults are not going to listen to us.

Although this objection is greeted with approval by Shari's peers, she denies it, and argues for the possibility and effectiveness of local action:

I'm talking about that man sitting on the corner, Tamika. It doesn't kill me to help him, say to take a dollar out of my pocket and hand it to him [Shari actually takes a dollar out of her pocket, and hands it to a classmate]. See, that doesn't kill me. That doesn't make or break what I do. But for that man and others, a dollar makes or breaks them. . . . I do have power at age sixteen.

The sense that one's goals can be effectively pursued may be one source for the binding of the actual self with the future and past selves. Our study of lives also suggests that *transforming events* may play a role. For David Street, one such transformation event was the death of his sister; his reflection on her murder led him to realize that the pattern of his behavior at the time would result in serious problems in his life in later adolescence. The consequence of this perception of continuity between present and future was the revision of his actual self in order to align it with his ideals and a more desirable future self.

Stability and generalizability of commitments

What has been learned about moral commitment from the study of inner-city adolescents? In a narrow sense this question is easy to answer. African American and Latino adolescents in urban areas like Camden and Washington, between the ages of 12 and 17, who are committed to sustained moral action see themselves in very different ways than do other adolescents. In particular, those who have moral commitments are more likely than other adolescents to (1) attribute moral goals and moral personality traits to themselves, (2) have actual selves that incorporate both their ideal selves and representations related to their parents, (3) construct theories of themselves in which systematic beliefs serve to generate coherence among the qualities of the self, and (4) perceive continuity in their lives remembered from the past and projected into the future.

However, addressing only the narrowly construed question leaves unexplored two issues of considerable interest: continuity of committed moral action across developmental transitions and the relevance of the findings presented here to the daily contexts of other adolescents.

Continuity across transitions

There is abundant evidence that sustained moral commitments are possible *within* broad development periods. This is especially clear with adults: Persons are capable of pursuing particular moral goals for their entire adult lives (see Colby & Damon, Chapter 11, this volume, for a discussion of two such lives). The study of Camden youth revealed that some adolescents were involved in their caring activities for years at a time, demonstrating that relatively long-term commitments are possible in this era as well.

Our own view is that sustained moral commitment of the sort considered here is likely to be rare in childhood; consequently the issue of its stability across the transition into adolescence is probably moot. Children have neither the psychological resources nor the environmental support to initiate and remain committed to paths of moral action. The foundation may be built – children may have the opportunity to participate in service activities, receive good parenting which encourages exploration, and observe parents behaving altruistically and reflect upon its significance and meaning – but there are no childhood caring prodigies (at least to our knowledge).

From adolescence into adulthood is a transition across which the retention of commitments can be considered. So many changes occur in the United States as the adolescent moves across into adulthood that there is good reason to expect that many of the care exemplars will abandon the caring activities that led them to the study: High school graduation, the flowering of romantic relationships, entry into college, and financial imperatives to find a job are but a few of the obstacles to carrying adolescent commitments into adulthood. Camden and Washington pose additional roadblocks to continued commitment. To the extent to which the actions of the care exemplars reflect one type of highly developed resiliency and talent, it seems probable that these adolescents are particularly likely to earn opportunities to leave behind them the stresses of inner-city life: scholarships to elite colleges in distant cities, high paying jobs which allow them to live in more comfortable neighborhoods, and so on.

These sorts of tensions are evident in the life of David Street, who was considered earlier in the chapter. David was reinterviewed 3 years after his initial participation in the study. He was still deeply involved in caring activities, working by his estimate 40 to 50 hours a week with children in the social service agency, which had nominated him three years previously. During the intervening 3 years, David had graduated from high school and had attended a local community college. His decision to attend the community college was made in part so that he could continue his community service. He was, however, planning to leave Camden in order to complete his college education at a small school quite distant from the city. When he is asked what has changed about himself since he was last interviewed, David's response reveals an awareness of the difficulty in synthesizing his community work with the opportunities and structures of adult life:

WHAT HAVE YOU LEARNED SINCE YOU WERE LAST INTERVIEWED?
Basically, I think balancing. Balancing my work with the community and my realization that I'm a young adult and need to go to school and get a job.

The felt conflict between community involvement and the realities of adult life has not stripped his work of personal significance, however. Indeed, it is evident that David Street found ways to grow within his commitment during the 3 intervening years. He has been fortunate enough to work in a context where his growing competence is rewarded with new opportunities:

My former boss has encouraged me the most. She wanted to get a program started and then have someone from the community take it over. Which is exactly what I've done. She told me that you might see failures – which I do. Some kids in my program have already been in jail. But you also see successes. And it is the successes – even if it is only one kid – that matter and make it all worthwhile. If you can help make just a few lives better, it's worth all the work.

Because David Street has been able to develop his caring talents in a setting that provided both support (his former boss) and an opportunity to exercise responsibility and initiative, we expect that he will carry his commitment to community service across the transition into adulthood. However, this combination of social support and increasing responsibility is probably rare in the settings in which the other care exemplars worked, which may make it more difficult for them to remain committed into adulthood. This is unfortunate, particularly in the contexts of our studies, Camden, New Jersey, and Washington, D.C. Certainly communities like these could benefit from a constant crop of new leaders committed to moral action, and losing adolescents who could become these leaders because of inadequate support and opportunity is a terrible waste.

Generalizations across contexts

As our efforts to embed our findings in a network of previous research on other samples attests, our belief is that the psychology of moral commitment as presented here does characterize moral commitment in a range of cultural contexts throughout the Western world. For daily life as it is experienced in many Western cultures, attributions to self of moral goals and personality, exposure to good parenting and parents who model altruistic behavior, and the alignment of self with moral ideals may all contribute to sustained moral commitment. This conclusion is consistent with the findings from the study of Camden youth and with other studies as well (e.g., Colby & Damon, Chapter 11, this volume; London, 1970; Oliner & Oliner, 1988; Rosenhan, 1970).

Other characteristics of the care exemplars may be specific to their particular context. Earlier, we described how the care exemplars were less likely than the comparison adolescents to incorporate into their actual selves representations of best friends and best friend–related selves. There is little reason to suppose that this necessarily must be so in order for moral commitment to occur. It is possible to imagine that in a culture in which nearly all adolescents are involved in altruistic activity, incorporating representations related to one's friends into the self would support and deepen moral commitment; however, this is not the nature of Camden or most locations in the United States.

Similarly, theories of self in which the characteristics of self are given coherence by reference to personal philosophies are not essential to the nature of moral commitment. Persons need not be especially insightful about themselves in order to behave ethically (Flanagan, 1991). Yet in contexts in which sustained moral action in the form of dedicated caring for others is unusual, it may be useful to understand clearly how one's behavior is related to a systematic patterning of beliefs that organize the sense of self.

Providing a context for development for adolescents in urban environments

We wish to conclude with a few suggestions for promoting moral commitment of the types we have studied in inner-city adolescents. First, we have suggested that the sense of self is inextricably intertwined with moral commitment in urban contexts like Camden, New Jersey, and Washington, D.C. More research is needed, of course, but nonetheless it seems wise to assume that facilitating the development of moral commitment requires a context in which the sense of self can develop along the lines that we have suggested earlier.

In our view, there is no "cheap" or "quick" way to provide such an environment. Our results and previous research suggest that the factors that allow for the development of a sense of self that would support moral commitment are not simple manipulations: Rewarding helping behavior in the classroom, showing children filmstrips, and so on may be too little, too weak, and just ineffective.

Instead, we suggest that a context that will facilitate moral commitment is best characterized by (1) warm relationships with persons who themselves evidence moral character, (2) opportunities to form and test moral commitments, (3) discussions of commitments and their meaning for the individual, and (4) experiences that facilitate the sense of effectiveness and connection to the future.

Relationships with parents appear in our research and that of others to be fundamental to the development of exemplary moral character. Parents of our exemplars appear to set such good examples that the adolescents subsume their images of the parents within their actual selves. This process may be close to Rosenhan's (1970) description of the parenting of fully committed civil rights workers. He suggests that the parents of fully committed civil rights workers demonstrated consistency between their articulated moral principles and their actions. Through this consistency, parents offered their adolescents a context within which they could both develop the same sort of integrity and be protected (at least to some extent) from the immobilizing ambivalence experienced by many adolescents who view their parents – and by extension the world of adulthood – as hypocritical and untrustworthy. Our experience suggests that an adult other than a parent can fulfill the role of setting a standard of moral conduct to which the adolescent aspires, but this adult must have an emotional bond to, and a relationship with, the adolescent.

In Camden, New Jersey, moral commitment also appears to be associated with a relative lack of closeness to best friends. We hesitate to conclude that this is necessarily bad; one might argue that distance between self and friends suggests an increase in psychological autonomy. Moreover, our research cannot prove that declining closeness between self and best friend follows from, and does not precede, the onset of moral commitment. Nonetheless, the findings from this research and that of McAdam (1988) suggest that deep moral commitments may pose special challenges to interpersonal relationships with friends and peers. It seems wise to be concerned with this issue in the development of programs to foster moral development.

Second, adolescents need opportunities to explore various sorts of moral commitments. In Washington, D.C., and Camden, New Jersey, churches have been particularly effective in offering these experiences to adolescents. But other social institutions can (and, in our opinion, should) fulfill this role as well: Schools, clubs, social organizations of all sorts can include as part of their missions providing adolescents with a range of experiences in helping and caring for others. Providing opportunities to perform actions that "help" or "care" for others is not enough; adolescents need as well discussion and reflection in order to understand for themselves the meaning of moral commitment and action.

Finally, moral commitment in adolescence needs to be supported in developmentally appropriate ways in order for it to be carried forward into adulthood. Although it may be useful for young adolescents to be involved in activities that are fully structured by adults, older adolescents require opportunities to form and to explore moral commitments of their own. It is through this sort of self-initiated action that adolescents can develop the sense of effectiveness that can deepen their commitments. Moreover, self-initiated moral action and exploration enables the adolescent to view the developing moral commitment as a clearer reflection of his or her own talents and interests. In this respect, the construction of one's own moral "niche" allows the adolescent to envision a future in which this "niche" can be an important component of the life structure.

Summary

Moral commitment among inner-city adolescents is common and sincere. Under very difficult circumstances, the African American and Latino adolescents we have studied have fashioned lives in which caring for others and their communities is prominent. Their lives and their achievements deserve both further investigation and our admiration.

References

Bem, D. (1978). Self-perception theory. In L. Berkowitz (Ed.), *Cognitive theories in social psychology* (pp. 1–62). New York: Academic Press.

Children's Defense Fund. (1992). *The state of America's children, 1992.* Washington, DC: Children's Defense Fund.

Clary, G. E., & Miller, J. (1986). Socialization and situational influences on sustained altruism. *Child Development, 57,* 1358–1369.

Colby, A., & Damon, W. (1992). *Some do care: Contemporary lives of moral commitment.* New York: Free Press.

Damon, W., & Hart, D. (1988). *Self-understanding in childhood and adolescence.* Cambridge: Cambridge University Press.

Damon, W., & Hart, D. (1992). Social understanding, self-understanding, and morality. In M. Bornstein & M. E. Lamb (Eds.), *Developmental psychology: An advanced textbook* (3rd ed., pp. 421–464). Hillsdale, NJ: Lawrence Erlbaum.

DeBoeck, P., & Rosenberg, S. (1988). Hierarchical classes: Models and data analysis. *Psychometrika, 53,* 361–381.

Duberman, M. (1989). *Paul Robeson.* New York: Ballantine Books.

Erikson, E. (1968). *Identity: Youth and crisis.* New York: Norton.

Fitch, R. T. (1987). Characteristics and motivations of college students volunteering for community service. *Journal of College Student Personnel, 28,* 424–431.

Flanagan, O. (1991). *Varieties of moral personality.* Cambridge: Harvard University Press.

Garborino, J., Kostelny, K., & Dubrow, N. (1991). What children can tell us about living in danger. *American Psychologist, 46,* 376–383.

Graziano, W. & Eisenberg, N. (in press). Agreeableness: A dimension of personality. In S. Briggs, R. Hogan, & W. Jones (Eds.), *Handbook of personality psychology.* San Diego: Academic Press.

Grusec, J. & Redler, E. (1980). Attribution, reenforcement, and altruism. *Developmental Psychology, 16,* 525–534.

Hamilton, S., & Fenzel, M. (1988). The impact of volunteer experience on adolescent social development. *Journal of Adolescent Research, 3,* 65–80.

Hart, D. (1988a). A longitudinal study of adolescents' socialization and identification as predictors of adult moral judgment development. *Merrill-Palmer Quarterly, 34,* 245–260.

Hart, D. (1988b). Self-concept in the social context of the adolescent. In D. Lapsey & F. Power (Eds.), *Self, ego, and identity: Integrative approaches* (pp. 71–90). New York: Springer-Verlag.

Hart, D. (1992). *Becoming men: The development of aspirations, values, and adaptational styles.* New York: Plenum.

Hart, D., & Fegley, S. (in press a). Prosocial behavior and caring in adolescence: Relations to self-understanding and social judgment. *Child Development.*

Hart, D., & Fegley, S. (in press b). The development of self-awareness and self-understanding in cultural context. In U. Neisser & D. Jopling (Eds.), *Culture, experience, and the conceptual self.*

Hart, D., Fegley, S., & Brengelman, D. (1993). Perceptions of past, present, and future selves among children and adolescents. *British Journal of Developmental Psychology, 11,* 265–282.

Hayes, J. W., & Lipsett, S. M. (1994). Individualism: A double-edged sword. *Responsive Community, 4,* 69–80.

Higgins, E. T., King, G. A., & Mavin, G. H. (1982). Individual construct accessibility and subjective impressions and recall. *Journal of Personality and Social Psychology, 43,* 35–47.

Kant, I. (1785/1958). *Groundwork of the metaphysics of morals* (H. J. Paton, Trans.). New York: Harper and Row.

Keller, M., & Edelstein, W. (1993). The development of a moral self from childhood to adolescence. In G. Noam & T. Wren (Eds.), *The moral self* (pp. 310–336). Cambridge, MA: MIT Press.

Kohlberg, L. (1981). *The philosophy of moral development.* New York: Harper and Row.

Krappmann, L., & Oswald, H. (1991). Problems of helping among ten-year-old children: Results of a qualitative study in naturalistic settings. In L. Montada & H. W. Bierhoff (Eds.), *Altruism in social systems* (pp. 142–158). Toronto: Hogrefe and Huber.

Ladd, E. (1994). The myth of moral decline. *Responsive Community, 4,* 52–68.

London, P. (1970). The rescuers: Motivational hypotheses about Christians who saved Jews from the Nazis. In J. Macaulay & L. Berkowitz (Eds.), *Altruism and helping behavior* (pp. 241–250). New York: Academic Press.

Losel, F., & Bliesener, T. (1990). Resilience in adolescence: A study on the generalizability of protective factors. In K. Hurrelman & F. Losel (Eds.), *Health hazards in adolescence* (pp. 299–320). Berlin: W. de Gruyter.

McAdam, D. (1988). *Freedom summer.* New York: Oxford University Press.

Markus, H. R., & Nurius, P. (1986). Possible selves. *American Psychologist, 41,* 954–969.

Newmann, F. M., & Rutter, R. A. (1983). *The effects of high school and community service programs on students' social development.* Madison: Wisconsin Center for Education Research.

Ogilvie, D. (1987). The undesired self: A neglected variable in personality research. *Journal of Personality and Social Psychology, 52,* 379–385.

Oliner, S., & Oliner, P. (1988). *The altruistic personality.* New York: Free Press.

Piaget, J. (1932/1965). *The moral judgment of the child.* New York: Free Press.

Rawls, J. (1971). *A theory of justice.* Cambridge, MA: Harvard University Press.

Rosenberg, S. (1988). Self and others: Studies in social personality and autobiography. In L. Berkowitz (Ed.), *Advances in experimental social psychology* (Vol. 24, pp. 57–95). New York: Academic Press.

Rosenberg, S., & Gara, M. A. (1985). The multiplicity of personal identity. In P. Shaver (Ed.), *Review of personality and social psychology* (Vol. 6, pp. 87–113). Beverly Hills, CA: Sage.

Rosenhan, D. (1970). The natural socialization of altruistic autonomy. In J. Macaulay & L. Berkowitz (Eds.), *Altruism and helping behavior* (pp. 251–268). New York: Academic Press.

Snyder, M., & Omoto, A. M. (1992). Volunteerism and society's response to the HIV epidemic. *Current Directions in Psychological Science, 1,* 113–116.

Strauman, T., & Higgins, E. T. (1988). Self-discrepancies as predictors of vulnerability to distinct syndromes of chronic emotional distress. *Journal of Personality, 56,* 685–707.

Tierney, T. P., & Branch, A. Y. (1992). *College students as mentors for at-risk youths.* Philadelphia: Public/Private Ventures.

Vaillant, G. (1977). *Adaptation to life.* Boston: Little, Brown.

Wegner, D. (1980). The self in prosocial action. In D. Wegner & R. Vallacher (Eds.), *The self in social psychology* (pp. 131–157). New York: Oxford University Press.

Weiner, B. (1980). A cognitive (attribution)-emotion-action model of motivated behavior: An analysis of judgments of help-giving. *Journal of Personality and Social Psychology, 39,* 186–200.

Yates, M. (1995). *Community service among adolescents as a developmental process.* Unpublished doctoral dissertation, The Catholic University of America.

Youniss, J. (1981). An analysis of moral development through a theory of social construction. *Merrill-Palmer Quarterly, 27,* 385–403.

Youniss, J. (1993). Integrating culture and religion into developmental psychology. *Family Perspective, 26,* 171–188.

Youniss, J., & Yates, M. (1994, February 10–13). *Community service and political-moral awakening.* Paper presented at the biennial meeting of the Society for Research on Adolescence, San Diego, CA.

11 The development of extraordinary moral commitment

Anne Colby and William Damon

The work that we will discuss in this chapter is a study of morality in everyday life, but not a study of morality in everyday lives. The study focuses on a group of people who are extraordinary from the moral point of view and on their everyday morality (the morality that they sustain, day in and day out over many decades of their lives). Our aim has been to learn more about the nature, development, and expression of exceptional moral commitment, including the conditions and contexts that foster and sustain it.

We have not yet compared the characteristics and processes we identified in this exceptional sample with a sample of less highly dedicated people. We expect, however, that the differences between the two groups will be a matter of degree and that we will find essentially the same developmental processes operating in the lives of more morally ordinary people. With some extrapolation, we ought to be able to extend the insights derived from the study of exceptional lives to contribute to our understanding of morality in everyday life (and lives) more generally.

The two themes of this book are morality understood as part of social context within which it occurs and transformations and continuities in morality during different periods of life. In this chapter, we will describe and illustrate a mechanism or process that we believe is especially important for development in adulthood, although no doubt it operates, along with other important processes, in childhood as well. We will trace the process by which two individuals' central life goals become more fully informed by and integrated with their deepest values and how their values and goals become broader and more intensely focused on others' welfare and the common good.[1]

In the process we describe, the transformation of goals through social influence, experiences in social relationships and other social contexts interact with the individual's current goals, beliefs, and propensities to yield a gradual transformation leading toward deeper engagement with and commitment to the common good. In interaction with *particular* social contexts – relationships, cultural settings, institutions, and organizations – individuals develop adaptations that constitute their unique configuration of moral values, beliefs, ideologies, personality characteristics, and behavioral patterns.

One purpose of our study of moral exemplars was to describe an array of such unique adaptations, showing how different values may operate in different social contexts and in pursuit of different moral goals. A second purpose was to identify commonalities that cut across the unique adaptations, both shared characteristics and common developmental processes. Thus, we look at a process common to all of the people we studied that led both to unique adaptations in each and to some qualities that all shared, however different they were in other ways.

The central notion behind the transformation of goals is that development in a person's beliefs and conduct is brought about through social influence processes that gradually transform the person's goals. The conditions for developmental change are set when social influence coordinates with individual goals in a manner that triggers a reformulation of the person's goals. We consider this process – the *transformation of goals through social influence* – to be a critical instigator of moral development during much of the life course. In order to support development, social influence processes must trigger reevaluation of a person's current capacities and must provide guidance for the further elaboration of these capacities. In the moral realm, such social influence results in a gradual transformation of moral goals, along with a transformation of strategies to achieve these goals. Most significantly, this means that social influence plays a key role in the formation of major moral commitments.

The process of transformation of goals is not limited to the domain of moral development. It can apply to any area in which the individual formulates and reformulates central life goals within the context of continuing social experience. In the area of career development, for example, a young elementary education teacher might take a position working with intellectually normal dyslexic children simply because she needed a job and that was the only position she was offered. In the course of working with these children she might develop skills and interests that lead her toward other areas of special education, moving next into work with other learning disabilities, then with brain-damaged and developmentally delayed children. Her career goals are transformed in a way that she would not have predicted at the start through the experiences she encounters as a result of each choice she makes.

To complicate matters further, the transformation of goals need not always be morally positive or even neutral in direction. In many cases, individuals follow paths that are better described as corruption than development. Social pressures are complex and multidirectional. Which of the various pressures are most salient and the nature of their influence depend very much on the individual's cognitive framework for interpreting morality and on his or her character and values. The difference between corruption and moral growth is not to be found in the transformation process or in the external circumstances individuals encounter, but in the particular interactions between the values, beliefs, and personality characteristics people bring to the situations they encounter and the nature of their experiences in those situations.

This kind of interaction is exemplified well by the first case we will discuss in this chapter, that of Virginia Durr. Durr's cognitive moral framework (which was a classic Stage 5 understanding of law and justice in Kohlberg's sense) predisposed her to be more susceptible to some influences than others and led her to construe a given experience differently than would someone with a different cognitive moral framework. Virginia Durr's life also illustrates the way in which an individual's identity can be structured around certain values. For Durr, the values of respect, justice, and truth were so central to her self-identity that she could not allow herself to draw back from the challenges she encountered, regardless of the personal costs they entailed.

Despite its importance, we do not believe that transformation of goals is the primary condition for all types of psychological growth, or even for all types of moral growth, at all ages. In the early years of life, for example, natural emotional responses such as empathy do not require goal transformation for their elaboration (Damon, 1988). Goal transformation becomes a key process when a person communicates regularly with others about moral values. For those who continually immerse themselves in moral concerns, and in social networks absorbed by such concerns, goal transformation remains the central architect of progressive change throughout life. A central goal of the study reported here was to elaborate the nature of this kind of transformation within people who made exceptional contributions to the common good.

In order to illustrate the transformation of goals, we will describe, in abbreviated form, the lives of two women from a sample of 23 "moral exemplars" about whom we have written more fully in our book *Some Do Care: Contemporary Lives of Moral Commitment* (Colby & Damon, 1992). The sample was selected according to criteria elaborated in Colby and Damon (1992). It included 12 women and 11 men and was diverse in regard to race, ethnicity, religion, and socioeconomic status. The exemplars we studied made significant contributions in many areas including poverty, civil rights and civil liberties, peace, the sanctuary movement, and religious freedom. We conducted in-depth interviews with the participants and also drew on autobiographies, oral histories, other documents, and interviews with coworkers.

This chapter will center on the lives of two women in the study – Virginia Foster Durr and Suzie Valadez. Virginia Durr was for many years a leader in the American civil rights movement, fighting for voting rights for African Americans and racial integration. Suzie Valadez has devoted much of her adult life to providing services to the poor of Juarez, Mexico. The two women are different in many ways, including social class, religious orientation, the problems their work addresses, their political ideologies, and their understanding of what they are trying to accomplish. Durr is a college-educated white woman from a socially elite background. Her world view is secular, politically left-liberal, and she sees her work as guided toward social and political reform. Suzie Valadez is from a working-class Mexican American background, did not complete high school, is deeply religious in a fundamentalist sect, and sees her work as following a spiritual calling to minister to the poor. In these two women we can see common processes operating to yield both unique adaptations that must be understood idiographically and common characteristics shared by the two in spite of their differences.

Virginia Foster Durr

Virginia Foster Durr was 84 when we first interviewed her, 87 at the last interview. Mrs. Durr comes from an aristocratic white family and grew up in Alabama surrounded by people who believed that black people were innately inferior to whites. Yet, Virginia later became a central figure in the fight for civil rights for African Americans.

Virginia Durr spent over 30 years leading the struggle to outlaw the poll tax, which had been used for many years in the southern United States to prevent women, blacks, and poor people from voting. She worked to desegregate the restaurants and hotels in Washington, D.C., and all of the public facilities, including schools, in Alabama. Because of the principled stands on race and civil liberties that they took, she and her husband, Clifford, lived for most of their adult lives with very little money, sometimes so little that they could not afford to maintain an independent household. For more than twenty years, Virginia worked in Clifford's law office, the two of them serving primarily poor, black clients who were fighting discrimination, segregation, and other forms of exploitation.

How did this happen? How did a woman born to such privilege in a segregated and pervasively racist society end up spending her life fighting for the rights of the outcasts of that society? In order to understand this, we traced the origins of Virginia Durr's commitment to equal justice and the formation and subsequent transformation of her life goals (Colby & Damon, 1992). As we saw in all of our exemplars, Virginia Durr was open to moral change and exhibited a broadening and ennobling of her goals as she engaged with the experiences and people she encountered. We can trace the resulting changes across the course of her life, including important transformations that occurred in middle adulthood and beyond. In addition to tracing the transformations in Durr's life, we looked to see how she sustained her commitment through some trying times, including material hardship, social stigma, and physical danger, all the while drawing upon a deep sense of certainty in the rightness of her cause.

An incident when Virginia was a college student illustrates how successfully she was educated in racial prejudice by the culture in which she grew up. On entering her sophomore year at Wellesley College, Virginia moved into the dormitory and went down to the dining room that evening for dinner. "The first night, I went to the dining room and a Negro girl was sitting at my table. My God, I nearly fell over dead. I couldn't believe it. I just absolutely couldn't believe it. . . . I promptly got up, marched out of the room, went upstairs, and waiting for the head of the house to come. . . . I told her I couldn't possibly eat at the table with a Negro girl. I was from Alabama and my father would have a fit."

The head of the house calmly explained that the rules of the college required her to eat at that table for a month and if she did not comply, she would have to withdraw from college. This was the first time that Virginia's values had ever been seriously challenged and she stayed awake all night worrying about the dilemma. She was afraid of angering her father, yet she enjoyed Wellesley and very much wanted to stay. "Now I was having the time of my life at Wellesley. I had never had such a good time. I was in love with a Harvard law student, the first captain of Virgina Military Institute, and life was just a bed of roses. But I had been taught that if I ate at the table of a Negro girl I would be committing a terrible sin against society. About dawn, I realized that if nobody told Daddy, it might be all right. That was the only conclusion I came to. I didn't have any great feeling of principle. I had not wrestled with my soul." Virginia stayed at Wellesley and spent a month eating at the table with the black girl, whom she came to like and respect. "That was the first time I became aware that my attitude was considered foolish by some people and that Wellesley College wasn't going to stand for it. That experience had a tremendous effect on me."

This incident illustrates the transformation of goals as it applies to Virginia's development, a process that we consider to be central to moral development, especially in adulthood. By transformation of goals, we are referring to a process in which development occurs as a result of the interaction of the goals, motives, values, and beliefs that a person brings to a situation and the social influences she encounters when she engages with the situation and the activities it entails. People enter situations in order to meet a particular set of goals and then by engaging with the situation and the people in it, their goals are changed; in the case of people who are developing morally, the goals are becoming elevated and broadened.

Virginia's goal in agreeing to sit at the dining table with the black student was very clearly to be allowed to remain at Wellesley, in large part so that she could continue her active and entertaining social life. The result was not an immediate awakening to a new perspective on race relations and civil rights. The incident did move Virginia along a perceptible step in that direction, however. She was forced to interact with an educated, middle-class black girl for the first time and realized that the girl was intelligent and civilized. She became aware of the fact that her views on segregation were not shared by the community she had joined, a community she prized very highly. Although this incident did not change Virginia's racial views overnight, it did sow the seeds of doubt about the beliefs she was raised with. Thus, a particular social context, Wellesley College, with its integrated student body and antisegregationist rules, played an early role in Virginia's transformation.

Later, after living in Alabama again for several years, Virginia married a lawyer from a well-to-do Alabama family, Clifford Durr. The Durrs moved to Washington in 1933 in order for Clifford to take a position in Roosevelt's New Deal Administration. They settled in the genteel suburb of Seminary Hill, right outside Alexandria, Virginia, and began an important new period in their lives.

As she came to know more about the New Deal and the people who were making it happen, Virginia Durr began to want a role in it herself. "I lived in a lovely, quiet neighborhood that I adored. But I also wanted to be in Washington in the midst of all the excitement, because to me the New Deal was perfectly thrilling. Cliff was saving the banks and the telephone was ringing all the time. It was an exciting time to be there." She had met Eleanor Roosevelt and admired her greatly, so she decided to volunteer for the Women's Division of the National Democratic Committee, since she had heard that Mrs. Roosevelt worked closely with that group.

Eleanor Roosevelt did come in to the office quite often, along with a number of other interesting women, and Virginia loved the work. One of the primary goals of the Women's Division at that time was to get rid of the poll tax so that white southern women could vote. Virginia had long resented the sex-stereotyped roles that southern women had to play, and she "plunged into the fight to get rid of the poll tax with greatest gusto." She soon began going to the headquarters every day, answering the phone, putting out literature against the poll tax, and trying to persuade someone in Congress to introduce a bill to abolish the poll tax.

This was the beginning of what would be for Virginia Durr a 30-year campaign to abolish the poll tax in the southern United States. From the very beginning, however, the anti–poll tax work encountered serious political opposition. The Women's Division was forced to stop its work on this issue, but Virginia maintained her commitment to it and soon resumed the struggle within the framework of another organization, the Southern Conference for Human Welfare, as president of the anti–poll tax committee. The fact that the committee was a part of the Southern Conference gave her a sense that the anti–poll tax work was part of a larger movement and provided a very powerful feeling of support for the work.

Many southerners, however, including close friends from Virginia's childhood, were opposed to the liberal movement represented by the Southern Conference, and Virginia encountered intense pressure to step back from her involvement. But, despite this pressure, the fight against the poll tax was an obsession for Virginia for many years, even though she had three and then four children at home.

The anti–poll tax struggle was a very difficult one, which occurred over several decades. Eventually, however, the struggle was won. A bill passed abolishing the poll tax for military personnel only, and then in 1964 a constitutional amendment abolished it for federal elections. In 1965 Lyndon Johnson signed the Voting Rights Act, which abolished the tax for state elections.

The poll tax fight provides an especially illuminating example of the transformation of goals, because it took place over such an extended period of time. Virginia Durr's goal in joining the Women's Division of the Democratic Party was to have some part to play in the excitement of New Deal Washington, to have an opportunity to work with Eleanor Roosevelt, and to meet some interesting women. She soon became intensely involved in the fight for women's right to vote, but was not at first sympathetic to blacks' struggle for equal rights.

Mrs. Durr herself sees the influence of personal relationships as critical to the shift in her racial views. When she began working with the National Democratic Committee in Washington, Virginia was still, from her own subsequent point of view, "an absolute Alabama racist." Although she admired very much Mrs. Roosevelt and the other women on the committee, she initially disagreed with them completely on the race issue. She worked closely with these more liberal white women over an extended period, and also became acquainted with such important black women leaders as Mary McLeod Bethune and Mary Church Terrell. "And I'm absolutely positive that the reason I changed is because I was working with all these women in the Democratic Committee and women whom I admired. And I was, all of a sudden, you know, here I was working with women who thought my whole tradition was wrong. I admired Mrs. Roosevelt tremendously, and she thought I was wrong."

We also see the importance of the institutional contexts within which she worked, especially the Democratic National Committee and the Southern Conference for Human Welfare, which put her into a visible leadership role as chair of the anti–poll tax committee and propelled her into desegregation as well as voting rights.

Because of the coalitions that formed around the voting rights issue, Mrs. Durr soon began to work closely with black organizations and distinguished black women such as Mrs. Bethune. The activities of the committee itself violated segregation laws, because the committee held integrated meetings in cities that outlawed them, held meetings in hotels reserved for whites only, and the like. In part, through her association with the leaders of these organizations, Mrs. Durr became very much involved not only with voting rights but other civil rights issues as well, especially the issue of desegregation.

Combined with an intellectual awakening on these issues stimulated by her more liberal friends in Washington, the opportunity and need to work closely with black people on the poll tax issue led to a transformation of Virginia Durr's goals that changed her life dramatically, indeed changed fundamentally who she was.

After this initial very exciting period in Washington, the Durrs went through a very difficult period that cannot be described in this brief report. The difficulties concerned primarily their efforts to stand up against Senator Joseph McCarthy's anticommunist purges. Eventually, they moved back to Alabama, where Clifford opened a law office and Virginia worked as his secretary.

Although during the early 1950s Virginia devoted most of her energy to her work in the law office and her family, she remained involved with civil rights issues and was active in the very early efforts to integrate Montgomery. This activity picked up dramatically when the *Brown v. the Board of Education* decision on desegregation came down and, as Virginia put it, "all hell broke loose. There was no choice. You had to stand up and be counted or move. We didn't move."

The Durrs remained very active in the civil rights movement throughout the 1960s. Among other things, they housed and fed dozens of students and other protesters who passed through Montgomery on their way to Selma and other protests. During this period, Virginia felt she was living "in the middle of a storm." But in spite of the violence and turbulence of the times, the overriding feeling was that the battle for civil rights was slowly being won. Most of the important segregation cases that Clifford tried were eventually won. Virginia was left with a profound respect for the law, "when it works," and to her it seemed that by and large the law was working.

Clearly, Virginia Durr had come a long way from her plantation heritage. Her moral development occurred gradually over the course of her life, with noteworthy changes occurring as late as her 30s and beyond. A history of openness to moral changes leads some individuals to continue developing in the moral area while others do not progress much after early adulthood. Although Virginia's emerging new values were not entirely self-initiated, they do reflect what we might call an "active receptiveness" to social influence of particular sorts.

Durr's openness to change was not a blanket receptiveness toward just any sort of influence. For example, she resisted strenuously the pressures to give in to the anticommunists or to go along with the prevailing racial views of her friends in Alabama. When she arrived in Washington, Virginia already had some liberal ideas in the economic and political areas, had a real concern for equality and respect for others, deeply valued honesty, and had already had the Wellesley experience with the black classmate. These things no doubt contributed to her receptiveness to new ideas about racial equality when contradictions were pointed out between her views on race and her values and ideologies in other areas. The fact that some of the people she admired most, for example, Eleanor Roosevelt, disapproved of her views on race also helped motivate her to rethink her beliefs.

This excerpt from the interview with Mrs. Durr illustrates her perception of the process of change.

AC: Now, before I start asking the questions that I came with, I would like to hear a little bit more about your experience of not having made choices, as you put it. Maybe you could just talk about that a little bit. You've mentioned that a couple of times . . .

VD: You make, I suppose you make choices every day of your life. But the thing is, as far as the decisions I made concerning my part say in the racial struggle in the South, it wasn't a decision, it was something that grew over a period of years and one thing led to another. But I never (like Paul on the road to Damascus, was it?) thought that I saw a revealing light and just all of a sudden saw the light. But it was over a period of a number of years that I began to change my feelings. And the same thing was true really about – well in a way, it was true about so many things. I changed as things happened. Rather, things happened and I changed because they happened.

Social influences played a central role in both transforming Virginia Durr's beliefs and goals and in sustaining her motivation and energy. Although acting according to what she believed in often required standing up against intense social and political pressure, Virginia did not experience herself as a lonely hero or nonconformist. She felt very keenly not only her links with others fighting for the same causes but also saw the positions she took as unremarkable and taken for granted by the majority of people elsewhere. "And actually, you see, I never have felt – it's only due to the circumstances of the U.S. that what I did ever seemed to be of any historic value. In other words, integration and the right to vote, which were the two things that I especially worked on, were commonplace in almost every other civilized country which didn't have segregation and certainly gave everybody the right to vote. So I really was identified with an extremely small part even of the United States, which was the South. And therefore, I have never felt that I myself was any great radical. Although I seemed radical to other people, and was considered radical, I never thought of myself as being radical because I was simply doing what was common everywhere else. So I always felt that I was the one that belonged to the majority, that I was the one that was going by the laws of the United States, I was the one that was conforming to the majority."

Mrs. Durr was energized and sustained by her sense that she was fighting a critical battle and that she was fighting alongside powerful and admirable people. She compares the role of people in her life with the role often played for others by religion. "I've gone to church all my life and I am religious in a way in that I believe in a power in the universe beyond my comprehension, but I never have been able yet to feel, as some people do, the intimate power of God. I've had people tell me they felt that God was there. I've never been able to feel that. Well, I've felt always it's more people being with me, supporting me. People – I'm a great people person. I like to be around people, and I like to be with people, and I believe in that. I think it's the people that stick together who can accomplish great things. The difficulty is getting them to stick together."

Without a doubt the most important influence in Virginia Durr's adult life was that of her husband, Clifford Durr. She deeply respected, even revered, her husband, seeing him as a figure of absolute integrity. Clifford's and Virginia's racial views evolved in synchrony, and they supported each other fully at each step of their deepening commitment to civil rights and opposition to the anticommunist movement. Clifford and Virginia shared equally the conviction that one does not go back on one's word or compromise one's principles for the sake of expediency.

During the most turbulent times of the fight to integrate Alabama, it was most often Clifford who insisted that they stay in Alabama and fight rather than retreating to the North. No doubt Clifford and Virginia learned a lot from each other at every point in their long relationship. Clifford's biographer speaks of Virginia's influence on Clifford's political beliefs during the early years of their marriage as Virginia struggled to make sense of the terrible poverty of the Depression. Virginia tells of the long talks the couple had about their work and the moral and political issues with which they were struggling. For example, Clifford would "wrestle over (legal) cases tremendously" with Virginia as they lay in bed at night. These conversations must have stimulated Virginia to think through the moral and political assumptions of her own work as well. Clearly, in the 49-year marriage of Clifford and Virginia Durr, the moral influence was mutual and positive, with each reinforcing and supporting the other's highest values.

It is important to note that the social influences that shaped and motivated Virginia Durr came not only from her supporters but also from her opponents. She talks often about the importance of working closely with like-minded people in her poll tax and desegregation work. Also evident, though less explicit, is the energizing effect of mobilizing against their opponents. Virginia often felt intense anger toward those who sought to preserve the racial status quo in the South and those who violated civil liberties in the name of anticommunism. She felt their pressure to conform in a very personal way, and this pressure strengthened her will to resist.

During our interviews with the 23 moral exemplars, we asked them many questions about how they had formed their personal and moral goals. In the exemplars' answers to these questions, we received numerous accounts of goal transformation through social influence. Some of the accounts focused on early social influences, during childhood or adolescence, deriving from a relationship with a parent or other respected adult. Other accounts focused more on the present influence of close friends, colleagues, organizations, or other valued associations. Some described oppositional forms, brought about through their resistance to social pressures that they considered illegitimate – such resistance providing them with a chance to crystallize their nascent values. Through all the various accounts, the general features of the goal formations and transformations had much in common, despite whether the developmental social influence came early or late in the exemplars' lives.

In Virginia Durr's life, as in all of our exemplars' lives, development did not occur in isolation. For Durr, the active social agents included political associates, friends, people she worked with, and people whom she fought against. As we have said, Durr's most frequent collaborator and source of influence was her husband Clifford. In addition, many black colleagues that Durr worked with over the years made her aware of their painful experiences in ways that resonated with Durr's own sense of humanity. On many occasions Mrs. Durr was drawn into new causes by someone's impassioned testimony or compelling argument. There also were turns of events that unexpectedly engaged her in modes of personal resistance. All of these social experiences – the positive as well as the negative – were developmental crucibles for Virginia Durr. They gave her opportunities to reaffirm her long-standing values, reexamine her beliefs, and develop new goals and strategies that would serve her long-standing commitment to social justice. Usually the crucible was formed by collaborative interchanges with trusted colleagues who challenged and inspired her. But at certain trying times, it was formed by oppositional interchanges with persons trying to pressure her into positions that she considered morally illegitimate. We have seen similar kinds of social influence processes at work in the moral development of all 23 exemplars.

In this kind of case study, as in life, social context and individual factors are inseparable. One might wonder in Virginia Durr's case whether she would have led a life of such notable moral dedication had she not lived in the North for a while, at Wellesley College and New Deal Washington, had she not married a man who also cared passionately about moral issues, had she and Clifford moved to New England after leaving Washington rather than returning to Alabama, had she not lived in the particular historical era of the struggle for blacks' civil rights. Although we can trace the impact of each of these experiences, we cannot say whether any particular experience was critical in her personal development. It does seem clear, though, that her life path represents a genuine interaction of person and context. That is, Virginia Durr might well have led a more ordinary life in another, less turbulent historical era, but many people in her situation in the South at the time of the civil rights struggle failed to rise to the occasion as she did.

Bandura (1982) and others (Laub & Sampson, 1993) have argued that chance encounters play an important role in shaping life paths. This seems especially true when we consider a figure such as Oscar Schindler, the German industrialist who risked his life and spent much of his fortune saving Jews from concentration camps during World War II (Keneally, 1982). If he had not lived during the war, it is very unlikely that Schindler would have become a moral hero. On the other hand, many other people failed to achieve moral heroism when faced with the same opportunities and circumstances.

Over the course of her life, the changes that Virginia Durr went through were gradual, though dramatic. This pattern of change was typical of most of the exemplars. Some, however, showed more abrupt life changes. Haste and Locke (1983) found that the lives of many dedicated people are affected by "triggering events" – sudden, unexpected occurrences that create powerful emotional responses that "trigger" a reexamination of one's life choices. This in turn can lead the way to a new moral perspective and new sense of social responsibility. To a large extent, the life of Suzie Valadez fits this pattern.

Suzie Valadez

Suzie Valadez, age 66 at the time we interviewed her, is known in South Texas as the "Queen of the Dump." She came by this title after years spent feeding, clothing, and providing medical care to thousands of poor Mexicans living in the surroundings of the huge Ciudad Juarez garbage dump. Her operation is run through Christ for Mexico Mission, a charitable religious organization based in El Paso, Texas, that she started in 1963 and now manages along with three of her four children.

Suzie's achievements are especially remarkable because when she moved from California to Texas to start the mission she was a single mother of four young children with no money, a 10-grade education, only slight knowledge of Spanish, and almost no work experience.

The key to understanding Suzie's transformation from a private citizen with personal virtues but no involvement on the community level to the dedicated and passionate leader of a thriving social service organization is her conviction that she was "reborn" in adulthood by her conversion to the fundamentalist Assembly of God branch of Pentecostal Christianity.

Suzie sees her religious conversion as the origin of her missionary work. She believes that it is also the source of her stamina over the difficult years, and that it is the means by which she has been able to accomplish her work. Her sense of personal responsibility for the poor of Mexico also derives directly from this religious belief. The sense that she has been called by God to serve the people of Mexico is the basis of her unwavering certainty about what she is doing. As she puts it, "I didn't know how I was doing it or why, but I know the Holy Spirit was leading me, saying, 'You *have* to help them, you *have* to help them.'"

In both Virginia Durr and Suzie Valadez, we can see both continuities and transformations in their lives. In Virginia, a strong will, independent mind, and willingness to take a stand are themes that begin early in her life and play important roles throughout as other things change. Closely tied with Suzie's religious faith are the personal qualities that most vividly represent her approach to life. In Suzie's case we see evidence of early and consistent compassion, love, and a sense of the holy preciousness of all people. It is clear from her recollections that her love for children and her generous spirit predate her religious conversion, but she prefers to discuss their meaning in the context of her current religious beliefs. "These are precious people. But I love everybody, I mean love. The Lord had given me a love for these people that I myself don't understand."

In seeking an understanding of Suzie's lifelong moral development, we must look to the continuities in her character and to the transformations she has undergone. The most important transformation, of course, is the religious conversion that led to and sustained her call to missionary work.

Suzie began life in very modest material circumstances but within a strong family which provided the context within which she developed the religious convictions and love for people that form the basis of her missionary work. At age 21, Suzie married and began a family. While her children were still very young, her husband deserted her, leaving Suzie a single mother with four children, very little money, a 10-grade education, and virtually no job skills.

At age 26, less than a year after her husband left, Suzie underwent the spiritual conversion from Catholicism to Pentecostalism that was to affect the direction of her life profoundly from that point on. The conversion was triggered by an experience that Suzie considered to be a miracle. When her youngest child Danny was an infant, he developed serious, chronic asthma. By the age of 8 months he was having life-threatening episodes in which he was unable to breathe. At that time, the doctors recommended a radical and painful treatment that frightened Suzie and her parents, so they decided against it. "I fell on my knees by his little bed where he was having a spell. I said, 'Okay, they say there is a God.' So I just fell on my knees and I said, 'Okay God, if there's a God, I want to know right now.' So I lay him there, eight months old, and to this day he has never had another spell. See I was desperate, I was desperate because I was by myself with the four children . . . so I didn't know what to do. But at that time, I rejoiced."

Following this episode, the minister from the local Assembly of God church visited Suzie. Someone had told him about the miracle and he wanted Suzie to come to his church to talk about it. She did so, and soon thereafter, "surrendered her life to Christ and was baptized with the Holy Spirit." "It was a big, big auditorium, and I was there when the minister made an altar call. I went and surrendered myself. If I'm a sinner, I confess all my sins and just gave them to you. And the Lord filled me with the Holy Spirit."

Within a few months of joining the church, Suzie was asked to teach Sunday school. In her view, the minister saw her special talent with children before she did. "He knew, I didn't know, but he knew that there was a gift in me with children. And he said, 'You're very good with children. Children love you.' " Suzie was a great success as a Sunday school teacher, and the class grew from 8 to 32 children in a period of 2 or 3 months.

Thus, the church gave Suzie an opportunity to develop her first exceptional talent. While teaching Sunday school in California, Suzie discovered her gift as a minister and proselytizer to young children. She attributes this to an inherent magnetism of personality that goes back to her childhood and is linked to her love for all people, especially children. "With the love of Jesus in me, I feel like a magnet." Later, the children of Juarez were strongly drawn to her, even before she had any food or clothing to give them. Her initial mission work in Juarez grew directly out of this new discovery of her special attraction for children. She began there with a Sunday school, modeled on her recent California work. This soon led Suzie to pursue a far broader range of charitable activities.

Before she moved from being a Sunday school teacher in California to a missionary in Texas and Mexico, however, a life-changing incident was to occur. One day, while sitting in church with her Sunday school class, Suzie saw a vision of a line of dirty, barefoot children carrying a banner saying "Ciudad Juarez." She described the vision to the pastor, and he told her that it meant she had a calling to Mexico. Suzie felt unprepared to move to Mexico with her four small children and at first resisted the call. The pastor replied by saying, "Don't say no. Let's wait for the confirmation." When Suzie asked him what he meant by confirmation, the pastor replied, "If it's from the Lord, He'll give us some more signs." The first sign was in fact followed by two more, and after the third Suzie decided to go to Mexico. The second sign was a nighttime dream with the same vision. Suzie describes the third and final sign in the following way:

I was in Sunday school again and somebody came running, running and he said, 'Sister Suzie, your house is on fire." All my house totally, totally got burned – clothing, food, everything. So we didn't have nothing left. So the following day our pastor came in and I said, "Pastor, what does this mean?" He said, "The Lord wants you to come to Mexico." So I said, "But I don't have any money, I don't have a car." He said, "Well, don't worry, we're going to have a shower for all of you, your family, and we're going to give you clothes." So I said okay. So my daddy said, "You're not going to go alone. The children are very, very small for you to handle them and then to minister whatever you're going to do." He said, "We'll go with you. Your mom and I will go." So he had a station wagon, and he rented a trailer, and maybe three weeks to the day after my house got burned we got ready, and they had some furniture, and so we came, we came to El Paso.

The "triggering event" that marked the time of dramatic change in Suzie Valadez's life came in the form of the signs (or "calls") that she received when she envisioned Mexican children holding a "Ciudad Juarez" banner and soon thereafter witnessed the total destruction of all her belongings. Without question these occurrences changed her life radically and permanently.

But such events do not happen in isolation. They occur amid a continuing interplay of personal and social forces that can become, in some individuals, agents for progressive moral change. It is the process of transformation of moral goals that gives triggering events their moral meaning and their dynamic effect on a person's life. In Suzie's case, as in any transformation of moral goals, there was a necessary component of social influence. For Suzie, this took the form of guidance and support from those close to her in California.

Suzie's immediate source of guidance during the "three calls" episode was her pastor, who urged her to pack her family and move her home to become a missionary in Mexico. One might even see his advice as a form of rather aggressive recruitment of Suzie into a missionary role. The Assembly of God denomination is, in fact, known for its evangelistic zeal and is the fastest growing church among American Latinos. Other people also played a part by offering crucial social support for the pastor's advice. Members of the church rallied when the house burned, holding showers at which they donated clothes and other household goods *for the explicit purpose* of helping Suzie move to Mexico.

Perhaps most critical was the extraordinary cooperation of Suzie's family. Her parents not only supported the move in principle; they offered to go along with her and join her in her missionary work. In the early years, they provided desperately needed financial help and took care of her children while she worked at the hospital or with the children in Juarez. They later became Suzie's first volunteers in the mission.

Suzie's children, too, went along with remarkably little fuss. They did not grow bitter about the time and energy their mother gave to her work. One very important reason for this is that Suzie's parents lived with them and cared for them while Suzie worked. Later, Suzie's children joined in the missionary work with enthusiasm.

Suzie's pastor, parents, children, and friends all offered her a network of social support and guidance leading in the same direction: Ciudad Juarez. But neither the triggering event nor the social network that supported it would have meant much if Suzie herself had not been prepared to recognize the moral message and follow its dictates. She was ready for a morally significant life change. The sources of her readiness were both personal and religious. They included her awareness that she was in desperate life circumstances, her intense spiritual awakening, her talent for teaching Sunday school, and her love of children. Her religious fervor permeated all of this, providing its own source of longing for a more devoted life. Suzie's visions, of course, were her own. But their meaning and effect upon her came entirely from her sense that they were the word of God.

Suzie's early family life had oriented her toward a love and concern for others as well as toward a commitment to honesty and other moral values. This was important; but by no means was it the whole determinant of Suzie's remarkable story. Her attraction to spiritual values, her passionate religiosity, her interest in helping children, and her deep sense of personal responsibility owe at least as much to events and people later in her life as to her early family experience. Most telling of the later influences was the church that Suzie joined in a spirit of charismatic conversion. The church offered her support, direction, and inspiration. It provided the interpretive context through which Suzie's "three signs" could take on the significance of a true triggering event. Suzie brought her own history, interests, and values to the event. But it was the church that acted as the instrument of change, providing the critical social guidance leading to the transformation and elevation of Suzie's moral goals.

Hispanic Pentecostalism, within which the Assembly of God Church is included, is well suited to provide just this kind of guidance. It is known as the church of the poor, with a particular commitment to outcasts, the poor and oppressed of inner-city barrios. The church not only seeks out the poor and uneducated as members, but welcomes them to leadership positions as well. The doctrines and practices of the church are egalitarian, in the sense that anyone can experience a spiritual awakening or rebirth and thus become a highly valued member or leader of the church community (Villafane, 1989).

In the evangelism or missionary work that strongly characterizes Pentecostalism, women have played a significant role, in spite of the tradition of "machismo" within the Latino culture. Villafane argues that, "Indigenous Pentecostalism could not have survived without the leadership of women, especially 'la misionera' (the local church missionary) ever present in the visitation of homes and hospitals" (p. 242). Within the Latino community, the Pentecostal Church is an important source of social services, and many of these services are provided by women in the context of their missionary work. Thus, Suzie's work can be seen as following a long-standing tradition within the church.

Within Pentecostalism, a conversion experience such as Suzie Valadez underwent is not unusual. Such a conversion provides for believers a clear break from their past lives, identifies them with other participants in the movement, sets them apart from the larger social context, and provides strong motivation for personal change (Gerlach & Hine, 1970, quoted by Villafane, p. 269). As Villafane notes, "the paramount commitment experience in Pentecostalism is personal conversion to Jesus Christ as Lord and Savior. It is a life transforming experience" (p. 270). This was certainly the case with Suzie Valadez. Her initial experience with the "miraculous" healing of her son (while she was still a Catholic) was picked up by the Pentecostal pastor, who encouraged her to come to his church to speak about the miracle. She was then given responsibility for teaching Sunday school, which served to draw her more fully into the church. Her vision of the ragged children was interpreted for her as a call to missionary work in Mexico and the pastor, along with members of the congregation, kept this idea alive until she eventually accepted the call herself. This kind of dramatic life transformation involving "burning one's bridges" and devoting oneself fully to a new way of life was not especially unusual or strange within Suzie's social context. Evangelism was expected, social service was highly valued, and movement into a leadership role by a poor relatively uneducated woman was acceptable, if not commonplace.

Suzie's belief that she has direct personal access to God, that she is striving to fulfill the will of an omnipotent God, and that she will be protected by God's transcendent power are central features of the Pentecostal doctrine. A belief in the power of God to heal the sick is typical of this ideology. It is not unusual for these beliefs to result in a greater willingness to take risks and a paradoxical simultaneous increase in both sense of control over personal destiny and fatalism toward personal and world events (Villafane, p. 274). Insofar as she remains within the context of like-minded believers, she is fully supported in these interpretations, which have been so critical in determining and maintaining the direction of her life.

Although recently some Pentecostal scholars have called for a more politically situated and radical vision, by and large Hispanic Pentecostalism, like African American Pentecostalism, is apolitical, offering a spiritual and personal solution to the problems of poverty and oppression.

Thus, the work that Suzie does with the poor of Juarez focuses on giving them the means to realign their lives according to the values of evangelical Christianity.

Religion was a critical shaping force in the lives and moral development of the majority of exemplars in our study, but the nature of their religious beliefs varied a great deal, with different implications for moral life. The Quakers in the sample, for example, drew on a long tradition of social action and social reform, in contrast to the apolitical quality of Pentecostalism.

During her early years as a missionary, Suzie gradually and with a strong sense of continuity shifted the primary focus of her activities from Sunday school teaching to healing, clothing, and feeding the poor. This transition is a clear instance of goal transformation. Like the other goal transformations that we have seen, the changes were induced by new activities that introduced Suzie to an ever broadening set of social concerns. The new activities followed directly from her original goals, thereby preserving her sense of continuity; but they required Suzie to consider new goals as well. As long as Suzie looked and listened, she found new obstacles to overcome, new miseries to remedy, new children to save, new "ways to serve the Lord." Her receptiveness to these new problems – her willingness to consider them challenges rather than frustrating defeats – explains a great deal about her enduring capacity for moral growth. She did not go looking for unending pressures to do more, but she was willing to take them on when they arose.

It was inevitable that running a large Sunday school for desperately poor children would lead to an open-ended barrage of demands. The mark of Suzie's response was that she invariably welcomed the demands rather than retreating from them. The children were hungry and looked to her for food. To the best of her ability, she fed them. The children were ragged and barefoot and looked to her for clothes. Once again, she responded with whatever she could get her hands on. Once begun, Suzie's work with the poor engaged her more deeply than she had ever expected.

Many social scientists have observed that depersonalizing the poor is an effective way to disengage from them, and hence, deny responsibility for helping them. In contrast, Suzie's mode of operation could almost have been calculated to hook her in more deeply at every step. She regularly formed personal connections with the people she was helping. Her involvement increased her awareness of their problems, and she took on these problems as her own. No sooner was 1 child fed than 30 more sprang up in her place. No sooner was there enough food than a disease would strike, making the lack of medical care painfully evident. Each of her engagements led to a further engagement. She was always pressed to do more, to move ahead to the next level of commitment. For many people, these ever expanding demands, this inexhaustible need, would lead to discouragement and a sense of futility. But the pressure to do more increased Suzie's energy and enthusiasm rather than draining it because of her deep conviction that she had to help and the joy she took in the work.

As in the case of Virginia Durr, Suzie Valadez's remarkable achievements can be seen as tied to specific life circumstances or even chance events. Had she not been abandoned by her husband, had she not been supported by the Pentecostal community, she might have been a kind and generous person within her private sphere but probably would not have gone on to the missionary work that brought her to our attention. On the other hand, most poor, religious single mothers do not respond to their situations as she did. What we see in her life is truly an interaction of the particular circumstances and contexts of her life and the personal characteristics through which she interpreted and responded to those circumstances and contexts.

It is also important to note that the personal qualities our exemplars brought to the crucial experiences of their lives were not the same from one person to the next. Virginia Durr's defiance and strong will served her well in the fight for civil rights but would not have led her to be especially effective as a missionary. Suzie Valadez's generosity and love for children interacted with her experience as a Sunday school teacher to move her along toward her later work in Juarez, but probably could not have resulted in an ever deepening involvement in a struggle for political change. A sense of effectiveness in their efforts was important for sustaining all of the exemplars, but the qualities that contributed to this effectiveness differed depending on the nature of their work.

Common characteristics of exemplars

We have seen in these two cases that the interaction of particular personal qualities with particular kinds of social contexts leads to lifelong moral commitments based on very different ideologies and values and embodying very different goals. In spite of the differences between these two and the other 21 people we studied, we also identified some striking commonalities among them.

We found three characteristics to be dramatically evident across all or almost all of the exemplars. They are *certainty,* which refers to the exemplars' exceptional clarity about what they believe is right and about their own personal responsibility to act on those beliefs; *positivity,* which refers to the exemplars' positive approach to life, enjoyment of their work, and optimism; and *unity of self and moral goals*, which refers to the central place of the exemplars' moral goals in their conceptions of their own identity and the integration of their personal and moral goals.

It is the third of these, the relation of self and morality, that we believe provides the most central key to understanding the unwavering commitment shown by the moral exemplars. This is consistent with Hart and his colleague's findings about highly altruistic adolescents (Chapter 10, this volume). Recall that in their study, adolescents who do a great deal of volunteer work were found to differ from a matched comparison group primarily in that moral concerns were more likely to be central to their sense of self and in the extent to which their ideal selves and the selves that relate to their parents (as opposed to peers) were incorporated into their actual selves.

The close relationship of personal and moral goals that we saw in our exemplars means that they do not see their moral choices as an exercise in self-sacrifice. To the contrary, they see their moral goals as a means of attaining their personal ones, and vice versa. This can only be possible when moral goals and personal goals are in synchrony, perhaps even identical. Our exemplars have been invulnerable to the debilitating psychological effects of privation because all they have needed for personal success is the productive pursuit of their moral mission. Their hopes for themselves and their own destinies are largely defined by their moral goals. In the end, it is this unity between self and morality that makes them exceptional.

We believe that this exceptionality is one of degree rather than kind. It is an extreme version of a developmental process that accounts for self formation and moral growth in every normal individual. Moral commitment, fortunately, is not a bizarre or even unusual part of human life. Almost everyone takes on moral commitments of some sort. These commitments become defining components of self in almost every case. Extraordinary moral commitments of the sort that we have examined, no matter how profound their social importance, function developmentally in a parallel manner to more ordinary ones. In our exemplars, we have seen processes of integration between self and morality that have much in common with those that all of us experience. Moral exemplars do not form their self-identities in a wholly different manner from other people.

The unusual feature of our exemplars' personal development is the strength of this integration and the extensivity of the moral engagements. The result of this strength and extensivity is a true uniting of self and morality. The unity that the exemplars achieve goes far beyond the imagination of those who try to live a typically moral life. It lies at the heart of the exemplars' inspirational effect on others. This is indeed unusual and admirable, but it still does not set moral exemplars wholly apart from other people.

Most incidents of moral commitment are so common that they go unremarked. They may even be hard to recognize as examples of morality at all. A mother vigilantly holds her child's hand while crossing the street; a teacher cuts short her lunch break to assist a struggling student; a person tells a painful truth to a friend. Such examples are commonplace in everyday social behavior. Although the ordinariness of such actions often makes us take them for granted, they nevertheless reveal a well of moral commitment available to most mature members of society.

Even acts of omission may reveal an undiscerned sense of moral commitment. A man walks past a blind beggar on the street, never harboring a thought of grabbing the blind man's coins, despite how easy it would be to get away with. Every indication we have is that most people do so reflexively, not even tempted by the prospect of easy gain.

As Davidson and Youniss (1991) have discussed, these ordinary examples of moral commitment reveal something about the nature of morality as it is played out in everyday social life. Perhaps the most noteworthy thing about these behaviors is their very unnoteworthiness. They are performed habitually, as a matter of course. They do not come about through a logical application of well-worked-out belief systems. They are accomplished almost habitually, as if on automatic pilot. They are experienced with little doubt, hesitation, or inner struggle.

The parallels between these ordinary examples of morality and the extraordinary actions that we have studied are striking. Time and again, we found our moral exemplars acting spontaneously, out of great certainty, with little fear, doubt, or agonized reflection. The moral exemplars performed their moral actions spontaneously, as if they had no choice in the matter. In fact, the sense that they lacked a choice is precisely what many of the exemplars reported.

But the parallels are not complete. By pointing out commonalities between normal and extraordinary moral commitment, we do not wish to blur the special characteristics of the exemplars or their commitments. The great difference between moral exemplars and most people is that exemplars act without equivocation about matters that go well beyond the boundaries of everyday moral engagement. They drop everything not just to see their own children across the street but to feed the poor children of the world, to comfort the dying, to heal the ailing, or to campaign for human rights. It is not so much that the exemplars' orientation to moral concerns is unusual as it is the range of their concerns and the extensiveness of their engagement is exceptionally broad.

We have described in this paper the developmental processes that help exemplars acquire an extraordinary sense of mission. We have suggested that these are not a wholly different species of process than those that shape most persons' moral selves. All people experience social influence; and to the extent that a person acquires moral commitment at all, it is brought about through some developmental transformation in that person's goals. It is not that the exemplars have undergone a qualitatively different process of change. Rather, they have experienced, deeply and intensively, many moral goal transformations over long stretches of their lives. In this regard, they are unusual.

Here we would make the same point again, but in a broader context. The exemplars' expansive moral concerns, and the exemplars' steadfast moral commitments, are extensions *in scope, intensity, and breadth* of normal moral experiences. The exemplars' moral concerns and commitments are continuous with most people's moral concerns and commitments but greater in degree. It is the remarkable extensiveness of the exemplars concerns and commitments that must be explained.

What, then, are the reasons behind the remarkable extensiveness? We believe that a central reason lies in the close relation between self and morality that exemplars establish. Over the course of their lives, there is a progressive uniting of self and morality. Exemplars come to see morality and self as inextricably intertwined, so that concerns of the self become defined by their moral sensibilities. The exemplars' moral identities become tightly integrated, almost fused, with their self-identities. Businessman Cabell Brand, who established and has headed for 30 years a program called Total Action against Poverty, expressed this sense of fusion during an interchange in one of our interviews with him:

WHEN YOU THINK ABOUT THESE (MORAL) GOALS AND VALUES AND SO ON, HOW DO THESE RELATE TO YOUR SENSE OF WHO YOU ARE AS A PERSON AND YOUR IDENTITY? Well, it's one and the same. Who I am is what I'm able to do and how I feel all the time – each day, each moment. . . . It's hard for me to separate who I am from what I want to do and what I am doing.

Blasi (1984) has argued that a person's sense of responsibility to act morally is a conceptual system that is distinct from the person's conception of what is the moral thing to do (i.e., the person's moral judgment, as traditionally defined by Kohlberg and others). In most people, the sense of responsibility is more directly linked to the self-identity than is the conception of the moral. The sense of responsibility is also the primary operative agent in determining the person's actual moral conduct.

This is not to claim that the nature of one's moral conceptions is unimportant for self-identity, one's sense of responsibility, or moral conduct. Certainly there are conceptual moral positions from which it becomes practically impossible to deny one's personal responsibility on critical occasions. For example, a sincere moral belief in the sanctity of life makes it very difficult for a person to ignore the pleas of a person whose life is being threatened. Many moral positions resist separation from a sense of responsibility: They can be segregated from the self (or separated from their action implications) only through rationalization and/or distortion of the facts in the case.

Nevertheless, even though the nature of one's moral beliefs may place limits on how one places morality within the frame of one's personal life, there is still considerable variation possible within these limits. In the end, moral behavior depends on something beyond the moral beliefs in and of themselves. It depends on how and to what extent the individuals' moral concerns are important to their sense of themselves as persons. For some strongly committed people, these concerns are of absolute and undeniable importance to their sense of who they are. But the reason for this lies less in the nature of their moral concerns than in the way they integrate these concerns with their sense of self.

Many of our exemplars drew on religious faith for such a unifying belief. In fact, this was the case for a far larger number of our exemplars than we originally expected. But even those who had no formal religion often looked to a transcendent ideal of a personal sort: a faith in the forces of good, a sustaining hope in a power greater than oneself, a larger meaning for one's life than personal achievement or gain.

We believe that it is accurate to say that, among the 23 exemplars, there was a common sense of faith in the human potential to realize its ideals. Although the substance of the faith and its ideals was too varied and too elusive to be captured in a final generalization, it can perhaps best be described as an intimation of transcendence: a faith in something above and beyond the self. A paradox of our study is that the exemplars' unity of self was realized through their faith in a meaning greater than the self.

Moral judgment stage

In addition to the personal interview schedule that we developed for this study, we also used two standard dilemmas to assess Kohlberg's stages of moral judgment (Dilemmas III and III'). As discussed elsewhere (e.g., Colby & Kohlberg, 1987), the Kohlberg measure provides an assessment of the maturity or sophistication of an individual's moral reasoning about hypothetical moral conflicts.

We knew that we had in our 23 moral exemplars a group of people who had demonstrated high levels of moral commitment in their everyday behavior. We were curious to see whether this clear commitment to moral conduct would be reflected in high scores on the Kohlberg measure. Many populations of adults have been assessed with the Kohlberg interview: Our intention was to compare the 23 exemplars with a more ordinary group of people. In this way, we hoped to learn something about our moral exemplars as well as about the strengths and limitations of the Kohlberg measure. In fact, we did not expect that the scores would be consistently high, since many of the actions taken by the exemplars – for example, helping the poor – do not represent difficult moral conflicts and do not require sophisticated moral judgment.

The moral judgment interviews (MJI) were scored blind to their participation in the study, sex, education, age, and other information about the respondent, and the other rater's scores, by two highly experienced raters using the Standard Issue Scoring System (Colby & Kohlberg, 1987). One interview was judged to be unscorable. The two raters agreed completely on the scores for 77% of the cases. They assigned scores within one-half stage of each other on the remaining cases.

As we expected, the scores on the MJI were not clustered at the high end of Kohlberg's scale, but instead ranged from Stage 3 to Stage 5. Half the group scored at Kohlberg's conventional level (Stages 3, 3/4, and 4), and the other half scored at the postconventional level (Stages 4/5 and 5).

Moral judgment scores are clearly related to subjects' educational attainment in this study, as others have reported (e.g., Colby, Kohlberg, Gibbs, & Lieberman, 1983). All but one of those with advanced degrees scored at the postconventional level, as did the majority of those with college degrees. The remaining college graduates scored at Stage 4. In contrast, no one who did not attend college was scored at the postconventional level, and five scored at Stage 3 or 3/4. (Due to the small size of the sample, statistical analyses were not carried out.)

Among those who had attained college or above, there were no sex differences in moral judgment scores. Men and women were equally likely to be Stage 4 or postconventional. Since there were no men in the sample with less than a college degree, we could not compare men and women at the less educated level.

In surveying published literature reporting scores on the moral judgment measure, we were not able to locate a comparison group matched for education with our sample, primarily because so few studies of moral judgment have been conducted with adults who have less than a college or high school education. For this reason, it is not possible to say definitively whether our moral exemplars show significantly higher scores on the MJI relative to their education than other groups. It does appear, however, that the MJI scores of the exemplars may be somewhat higher than those of groups not selected for outstanding moral behavior. For example, in Kohlberg's 20-year longitudinal study of moral judgment (Colby et al., 1983), only 10% of the college-educated subjects scored at Stage 4/5 or 5 (as compared with over half of those in our study). Fifty percent of the college-educated longitudinal study subjects scored at Stage 4 and 40% at Stage 3/4. None of the college-educated subjects in our study scored below Stage 4. Among the longitudinal subjects with advanced degrees, 46% scored at 4/5 or 5, 46% at Stage 4, and 8% at Stage 3/4. (Recall that all but one of the subjects in our study with advanced degrees [88%] scored at Stage 4/5 or 5.)

Although the exemplars' scores may be higher than those of nonexemplars, it is clear that one need not score at Kohlberg's highest stages in order to exhibit high degrees of moral commitment and exemplary behavior. This was true as well for Hart and Begley's altruistic adolescents, whose MJI scores ranged from 2/3 to 3/4, no higher than scores of the comparison group. These findings are not inconsistent with Kohlberg's theory, however, since there is no reason to believe that sophistication in reasoning about complex moral issues would be necessary in order to carry out many of the altruistic activities that our exemplars engaged in. This contrasts, for example, with the requirements for certain other kinds of roles, such as that of a Supreme Court justice, for example, where careful justifications of moral decisions are needed.

Promoting the development of moral commitment

There is a growing recognition among many scholars of morality and moral development (Kagan and Lamb, 1987; Trevarthen, 1993; Wilson, 1993) that the capacity for morality, including empathy, altruism, and cooperation, is a natural part of the biological endowment of human beings. In contrast with this position, the prevailing culture in contemporary Western society emphasizes a split between personal self-interest and morality such that they are often assumed to be fundamentally in opposition to each other. This cultural tendency to separate morality and self-interest leads many people to think that they can succeed in life by ignoring their moral sense, even that they may *need* to deny morality in order to succeed.

We saw a very different orientation in the moral exemplars that we studied. They were highly motivated and relatively unconflicted primarily because their moral goals were not in opposition to or even fully separate from their personal goals. Their moral goals in large part constituted their very identities. They defined their own welfare and self-interest in moral terms and were, with very few exceptions, extremely happy and fulfilled. Their lives make it clear that one need not see personal goals and responsibility to others as necessarily in opposition. We believe that the intellectual climate of our culture would do better to emphasize the potential for unity in personal and moral goals rather than a seemingly inevitable conflict between them.

We recognize, of course, that human beings' moral capacity is sometimes terribly underdeveloped and is rarely developed to the full extent seen in our moral exemplars. This study provides some clues about how to promote the development of deep moral commitment and sustained altruism. First, we would argue that there is no "critical period" early in life during which children must establish permanent patterns of altruism or exceptional responsibility. On the contrary, people's moral goals and the capacity to pursue them effectively develop across much of life, certainly well into middle adulthood. For this reason, it is important to support positive moral change and deeper moral engagement, not just in children, but throughout life. Many of our exemplars did not even begin their major life work until their 40s.

The concept of transformation of goals implies a need for educational and other intervention programs to engage with the participants' currently most urgent personal goals and needs and to move from there to broaden these goals in an altruistic direction through powerful, interactive social influence. Firsthand experiences working toward important moral goals in collaboration with other people can set the stage for individuals both to be influenced by discovering points of view that may be somewhat different from their own and also to reflect on and change or broaden their own perspectives. Both social influence and individual reflection are important components of development throughout life.

Our exemplars combined a strong certainty about their deepest moral convictions with an open-mindedness about how these play out in real life settings. It is important to support and develop children's and adults' central moral convictions while helping them to consider new information and its implications for them.

In order to make sacrifices or take risks for their moral beliefs and to maintain their commitment in the face of obstacles, people must feel a sense of moral effectiveness and empowerment. One goal, then, of an educational program should be to find ways to help young people gain the experience of effectiveness in their efforts to contribute to others' welfare. They should not be led to believe that they can *solve* major social problems, but they do need to feel that their contributions are valuable and make a difference.

Our study also revealed the role that a positive and optimistic approach to life can play in sustaining altruistic people in the face of the difficulties that they inevitably face. This recognition points to the importance of developing programs that help people to take a joyful approach to their work and to be creative about turning a negative or potentially discouraging situation into a positive one.

The mechanisms we need in order to pursue these leads have yet to be developed. Many of the activities that come to mind as potential mechanisms involve engaging young people and adults with local moral exemplars. In making this suggestion, we are assuming that dedicated people comparable with those in our study can be identified in almost any community. During the nominating phase of our study, in fact throughout the study, new names of exemplars we might add to the study were continually suggested to us. Clearly, this kind of dedicated individual is present in communities all across the country.

Note

1. In this chapter, the interviewees are referred to by the names that they wished to be called in the reporting of their lives. Thus, Virginia Durr is referred to as "Virginia" as a young woman and "Mrs. Durr" as an elder woman. Suzie Valadez is referred to as "Suzie" throughout the chapter because that is the name she uses to refer to herself.

References

Bandura, A. (1982). The psychology of chance encounters and life paths. *American Psychologist, 37,* 747–755.

Blasi, A. (1984). Moral identity: Its role in moral functioning. In W. Kurtines & J. Gewirtz (Eds.), *Morality, moral behavior, and moral development* (pp. 128–140). New York: Wiley.

Colby, A., & Damon, W. (1992). *Some do care: Contemporary lives of moral commitment.* New York: Free Press.

Colby, A. & Kohlberg, L. (1987). *The measurement of moral judgment.* Cambridge: Cambridge University Press.

Colby, A., Kohlberg, L., Gibbs, J., & Lieberman, M. (1983). A longitudinal study of moral judgment. *Monographs of the Society for Research in Child Development. 48* (1–2, Serial No. 200). Chicago: University of Chicago Press.

Damon, W. (1988). *The moral child.* New York: Free Press.

Davidson, P., & Youniss, J. (1991). "Which comes first, morality or identity?" In W. Kurtines & J. L. Gewirtz (Eds.), *Handbook of moral development and behavior* (Vol. 1, pp. 105–121). Hillsdale, NJ: Lawrence Erlbaum.

Gerlach, L. P., & Hine, V. H. (1970). *People, power, change: Movements of social transformation.* Indianapolis: Bobbs-Merrill.

Haste, H., & Locke, D. (1983). *Morality in the making: Action and the social context.* New York: Wiley.

Kagan, J. & Lamb, S. (1987). (Eds.) *The emergence of morality in young children*. Chicago: University of Chicago Press.

Keneally, T. (1982). *Schindler's list*. New York: Simon and Schuster.

Laub, J., & Sampson, R. (1993). Turning points in the life course: Why change matters to the study of crime. *Criminology, 31* (3), 301–325.

Trevarthen, C. (1993). The function of emotions in early infant communication and development. In J. Nadel & L. Camainoi (Eds.), *New perspectives in early communicative development* (pp. 48–81). London: Routledge.

Villafane, E. (1989). *Toward an Hispanic-American pentacostal social ethic with special reference to North Eastern United States*. Unpublished doctoral dissertation, Boston University.

Wilson, J. Q. (1993). *The moral sense*. New York: Free Press.

12 Reasoning about morality and real-life moral problems

Lawrence J. Walker, Russell C. Pitts, Karl H. Hennig, and M. Kyle Matsuba

Morality has been a troublesome, indeed formidable, concept for psychology to handle. The study of its development has been marked by recurrent controversies regarding its definition and appropriate method of investigation (and rightly so). Regardless of the difficulty of these basic definitional and methodological issues, morality is recognized as a fundamental and pervasive aspect of human functioning – because it refers to one's basic values and way of life – and thus it falls squarely within psychology's purview and mandate.

The main argument of this chapter is that contemporary moral psychology has been prodigiously influenced by the significant contributions of Kohlberg's cognitive-developmental paradigm – with its philosophical emphasis on justice and psychological emphasis on reasoning – and this has consequently led to a somewhat restricted view of morality and moral functioning. Our intended contribution here is to prompt interest in some seemingly important aspects of moral functioning that have until now been minimally examined. Our basis for highlighting particular aspects of moral functioning is empirical – based on extensive open-ended interviews with people from across the lifespan. Our belief was that a thorough sampling of laypeople's understandings of morality and experiences in handling moral problems in everyday life might provide a somewhat different focus than what currently dominates the field and would help to redirect both conceptual and empirical attention to some significant aspects of moral functioning. Developmental patterns may also point to factors that contribute to, or

This research was supported by a grant to the senior author from the Social Sciences and Humanities Research Council of Canada (#410-89-0150). I am especially grateful to my typists, Jody Peters and Greg Olson, who competently and cheerfully transcribed many lengthy interviews.

interfere with, the attainment of moral maturity. At this point in the development of the field, moral psychology needs to be more closely based on how people experience morality day by day than on the tight constraints of philosophical conceptualizations (which, of course, do have their role).

Perhaps an appropriate starting point for considering the current state of the field and proposing some new directions would be with a working definition of morality. A problem we readily acknowledge is the historically changing and individually variable boundaries of the moral domain. By proposing a working definition of morality, we intend to make explicit our own assumptions and understandings. We believe our definition to be a very broad one, preferring to be overly inclusive at this point than overly exclusive. It would perhaps have been simpler to omit any definition of morality, but that would not exclude its effect – it would only then be implicit.

In our view, morality refers to voluntary actions that (at least potentially) have social or interpersonal implications and that are governed by some intrapsychic mechanism (cognitive and/or emotive). Thus, we conceptualize morality as a social enterprise, both in its origins and its functions: It prescribes people's activities, regulates their social interactions, and arbitrates conflicts. Our definition of morality does not necessarily exclude social conventions because, despite the somewhat arbitrary nature of their particular expression, they do reflect underlying values and their violation has the potential to harm others, create injustices, and effect other moral consequences. Also, our definition does not preclude the possibility that some aspects of the moral domain are primarily intrapsychic; rather, it is an assertion that these intrapsychic issues (e.g., reflecting basic values and sense of self) do have at least indirect implications for interpersonal interactions.

It is also important to understand the multifaceted nature of moral functioning. Of necessity, it entails the interplay of behavior, thought, and emotion. Unfortunately, the various theoretical traditions in moral psychology have obfuscated the interdependent and interactive nature of behavior, thought, and emotion in moral functioning, in that each approach has regarded different aspects of psychological functioning as central to morality: the identification-internalization approach (derived from psychoanalytic theory) has emphasized emotion, the social-learning approach has emphasized behavior, and the cognitive-developmental approach has emphasized cognition. These differing emphases have created an artificial trichotomy (emotion, behavior, thought) that has imparted the view that these are independent aspects of moral functioning when instead they are necessarily interdependent. Moral emotions cannot occur without having some cognitive content; thoughts always have some emotional tone, be it cold or hot; and it is only involuntary behaviors that do not have an intentional basis. Thus, for a theory in moral psychology to focus solely on one aspect of functioning, ignoring the relevance of the others, is to trivialize what morality is all about. Obviously, a more comprehensive and holistic appreciation of how these different aspects relate to each other is a pressing task for moral psychology. In other domains perhaps a simpler focus may have utility and validity, but in the moral domain it will not suffice.

Clearly, then, a fundamental issue for moral psychology is the definition of the moral domain on which to base theory, research, and practice. The past generation of moral development theory and research has witnessed the ascendance and eventual dominance of the field by Kohlberg's (1969, 1981, 1984) moral stage approach, reflecting the considerable impact of Piagetian cognitive-developmental theory in psychology in general. Kohlberg's approach, explicitly grounded in a Platonic and Kantian tradition or moral philosophy with justice as its basic principle, postulated stages in the development of moral reasoning. Over the past 3 decades, a considerable body of research has been amassed to support the validity of his moral stage model and its explanations for development (Walker, 1988).

The dominance of Kohlberg's cognitive-developmental theory forms the context for contemporary moral psychology. Although the field has been significantly advanced by its many conceptual and empirical contributions, its pervasive influence has given the study of moral development a particular skew, which may now constrain our ability to develop a more holistic understanding of moral functioning and its development, and perhaps it can no longer be considered a progressive research enterprise. Despite the apparent empirical support for Kohlberg's model of moral development, concerns have been expressed that it entails a somewhat restricted notion of morality that is reflected both in the method of assessment (the Moral Judgment Interview, Colby & Kohlberg, 1987), and in theoretical assumptions and stage descriptions (Kohlberg, Levine, & Hewer, 1983). If these concerns have validity, then the inevitable consequence is that we may be ignoring some, or perhaps even much, of what is important in people's moral functioning – in particular, how they understand the moral domain and handle everyday moral issues. This problem with Kohlberg's approach arises because of his reliance on philosophical definitions of morality and the resultant constriction of the moral domain. As Blasi (1990, p. 45) has noted, "Psychologists may risk missing a large portion of . . . people's moral life when they are rigidly guided by definitions constructed within specific philosophical theories." This is not to say that a philosophical basis for moral psychology has no validity, rather it is to claim that philosophical perspectives have the potential to be constraining and thus need to be checked against intuition and the empirical evidence provided by ordinary people's understanding of the domain. Similarly, it would be undesirable, even impossible, for moral psychology to be based entirely on empirical data without the conceptual framework provided by explicit philosophical theories. However, it is the disjunction between theory and evidence that provides the possibility for advances in understanding of these phenomena – that is what is most telling.

Kohlberg (1981, 1984) claimed that his theory had universal validity and applicability. However, the self-admitted intellectual roots of the theory in a Western liberal ideological tradition (Kohlberg, 1981, p. 98) and its empirical roots in a sample of American males (Colby, Kohlberg, Gibbs, & Lieberman, 1983) have led to allegations of ethnocentrism and misogyny by cross-cultural and feminist scholars (e.g., Boyes & Walker, 1988; Gilligan, 1982; Simpson, 1974), who argue that his approach misses or misconstrues some significant aspects of morality expressed by females and people of other cultures. Gilligan has made the well-publicized argument that Kohlberg's model is insensitive to females' ethic of care (cf. Walker, 1991). Boyes and Walker's (1988) review indicated that some significant moral concepts from several cultures (such as filial piety, sorcery, and community harmony) are not well understood by his approach. Although Kohlberg clearly advocated a model of morality with justice as its focus, it is important to note his recent clarification of the model to include more adequately concerns regarding benevolence, care, respect for persons, and so on (Kohlberg, Boyd, & Levine, 1990). Yet, he acknowledged that the approach may still fail "to map the entire moral domain" (Kohlberg, 1986, p. 500) and the authors of the scoring manual admitted that a "subject's ideas, though structurally scorable and fully elaborated, may be original or idiosyncratic, or the particular expression of a stage used by a subject may not be represented in . . . the scoring manuals" (Colby & Kohlberg, 1987, p. 181). These limitations, of course, are partly conceptual and partly methodological. Thus, it is likely that the Kohlbergian approach, because of its a priori definition of morality and focus on cognition, has unnecessarily constricted our view of moral functioning. This is not to fault the Kohlbergian paradigm, but simply to recognize that an inevitable consequence of programmatic research is a restriction of perspective. Kohlberg began with a philosophically based theory and an empirical focus on the aspect of moral functioning that he regarded as fundamental (i.e., reasoning). The field, however, has not yet succeeded in developing a more comprehensive definition of the domain.

Concern has been expressed not only in regards to Kohlberg's definition of morality, but also his assessment of moral development. Critics (e.g.,

Baumrind, 1978; Gilligan, 1982; Haan, 1977; Haan, Aerts, & Cooper, 1985) have alleged that the classic hypothetical dilemmas of the moral judgment interview (MJI) are unfamiliar, irrelevant, constrained, and devoid of contextual information, that they minimize emotional involvement and have limited generalizability. Gilligan argued that these dilemmas, because of their abstracted nature and dearth of contextual information, would tend to elicit justice-type reasoning rather than care-type reasoning (which she believes is more characteristic of females). Also, Boyes and Walker (1988) have suggested that their use may be inappropriate in societies (unlike the Western world) where the ability to reason about hypothetical situations is not frequently required or highly valued.

Kohlberg held that hypothetical dilemmas are optimal for assessing moral reasoning *competence* – for "testing the limits" of individuals' thinking – because most people find them conflictual; they allow reflective thought without interference from preconceived and vested positions, and they allow probing of individuals' moral reasoning ability. Certainly there are empirical advantages to the use of standard stimulus materials: They minimize idiosyncratic responding and yield reliable scores that allow testing of the model and measurement of intervention effects.

As an alternative to the hypothetical dilemmas of the MJI, some researchers have presented actual dilemmas as stimuli. Although responses to such dilemmas may be of considerable interest, the approach remains problematic in some respects. Such actual dilemmas may be factual, more realistic, and perhaps more relevant, but they are always raised by the researcher, not the participants, as moral issues. Thus, many people may not consider them to be moral problems at all, or the moral implications may not be central in their thinking (contemporary examples of such ambiguous issues might include abortion, political protest, environmental issues, and so on). Such dilemmas are not representative of the type or complexity of moral issues typically faced by people; nor does such an approach reveal what kinds of moral problems and issues people confront in everyday living, how they deal with them, and how they conceptualize the moral domain.

One of the inherent problems with the use of standard dilemmas (either classic hypothetical dilemmas or actual ones presented by researchers) is that the conflict has been unambiguously preconstructed (e.g., whether to save a life or obey the law); and the subject is not free to reinterpret the situation or introduce other considerations. Real-life moral problems are rarely as straightforward in their interpretation. The meaning that people attribute to everyday situations would seem pivotal in analyses of their moral reasoning and behavior. It is important to realize that there are at least two major cognitive components involved in moral functioning: first, the *interpretation* of the moral issue; and second, the *resolution* of the problem by choosing the appropriate course of action (Walker, 1986). The use of hypothetical dilemmas – the dominant paradigm in moral psychology – has informed our understanding of the second cognitive component (i.e., the ability to resolve moral dilemmas), but little is as yet known about how people ordinarily conceptualize the moral domain and interpret moral problems. Indeed, there may be considerable individual and developmental differences in understanding morality and in discerning moral features of situations. For example, for some people almost every action has moral implications to be considered, whereas others regard only certain extreme and rare actions as belonging to the moral domain. Thus, the domain may be defined broadly or narrowly by different people. Blasi (1984) has also argued that morality may have differing degrees of centrality in people's lives and that different moral aspects may characterize different individuals' moral identities. Similarly, the first component in Rest's (1983) four-component model of moral behaviors refers to this notion of moral sensitivity: "The person must be able to make some sort of interpretation of the particular situation in terms of what actions were possible, who would be affected by each course of action, and how the interested parties would regard such effects on their welfare" (Rest, 1986a, p. 3). Research with people in the helping professions indicates varying levels of sensitivity to moral issues inherent in their interactions with clients (Rest, 1986a). Obviously, the meaning that individuals attribute to a situation is pivotal in understanding their moral functioning.

One alternative to the use of standard hypothetical or actual dilemmas in assessing moral development is to have subjects recall and discuss real-life moral conflicts from their personal experience. This ensures that the dilemmas are regarded as *moral* issues and are relevant to individuals' lives. Gilligan and her colleagues (Gilligan, 1982; Gilligan & Attanucci, 1988; Lyons, 1983) initiated the use of this paradigm and claimed that it yields evidence of two (sex-related) moral orientations (justice vs. care) in people's thinking. Although Gilligan's theorizing has clearly drawn attention to the need to broaden our conception of the moral domain, the claim that people focus on one orientation or the other and that this phenomenon is related to sex has received, at best, equivocal support (Walker, 1991).

In several of our studies we have similarly asked participants to generate and discuss moral dilemmas from their personal experience. This approach has yielded some heuristic findings. First, content analyses of the moral issues indicated that the dilemmas were wide-ranging and frequently different from the standard dilemmas of the MJI, although levels of moral reasoning were remarkably consistent (Walker, de Vries, & Trevethan, 1987;

Walker & Moran, 1991). This suggests that the prototypic assessment of moral reasoning – Kohlberg's MJI – relies on dilemmas that are not representative of the moral issues typically faced by people.

Second, analyses of reasoning about real-life dilemmas more clearly distinguished individuals and better predicted their behavior than did reasoning regarding less relevant hypothetical dilemmas; for example, Walker and Moran (1991) found that Chinese intellectuals and moral leaders differed in their reasoning about real-life, but not hypothetical, dilemmas, and a similar finding was reported by Trevethan and Walker (1989) with psychopathic delinquents and other young offenders.

Third, the use of hypothetical dilemmas that entail constrained, preinterpreted moral issues also makes it less likely that indigenous moral concepts will be expressed. In a recent study conducted in the People's Republic of China, we (Walker & Moran, 1991) found that eliciting real-life dilemmas revealed a number of concepts, basic to Chinese morality, that were not readily apparent in responses to the MJI. Examples include the collectivistic orientation of the Chinese as evidenced by an emphasis on benevolence and the importance of maintaining "face"; their focus on the traditional Confucian notion of hierarchically structured relationships as central to moral behavior, and their belief that a cultivated moral sense of humanitarianism allows one to intuit what is morally correct in various situations, rather than relying on abstract justifications.

Fourth, we have found that family discussions of children's real-life dilemmas predicted the extent of children's moral reasoning development over a subsequent 2-year longitudinal interval whereas family discussions of hypothetical dilemmas did not (Walker & Taylor, 1991). Hypothetical dilemmas, although cognitively engaging, are of less relevance to the family, minimize emotional involvement, are not particularly focused on the child, and probably are less characteristic of daily interactions. Real-life dilemmas are simply more salient and relevant, and dealing with them has a greater impact than hypothetical dilemmas.

It is now appropriate to summarize the arguments of the previous pages. Contemporary moral psychology has been dominated by Kohlberg's cognitive-developmental mode. This model entails a definition of the moral domain based on a particular philosophical perspective, an emphasis on the cognitive aspects of moral functioning, and a reliance on hypothetical dilemmas to assess moral development. Although one can confidently assert that this model has significantly advanced our understanding of many psychological aspects of morality, it is apparent that the strength of the approach has diminished our view of the moral domain and people's moral functioning. Simply put, our research paradigm for too long has been unnecessarily constrained – subjects have been asked to react to "canned" moral problems within a restricted perspective on morality. It is now time to explore individuals' moral understandings and moral conflicts without imposing such restraints and to base our theory and research more on everyday morality. As Rest (1986b, p. 458) noted, we need a "representative sampling of the moral domain."

The exploratory study reported in this chapter is a beginning attempt to sample laypeople's developing conceptions of morality and definition of the moral domain, as well as their reasoning about real-life moral problems. We believe that this type of research requires a phenomenological approach: "looking at morality from the subject's viewpoint, understanding what the subject is saying in his or her own terms" (Colby & Kohlberg, 1987, pp. 1–2). This necessitates an open-ended semiclinical interview, without standard stimulus materials. Our intent was to explore people's understanding of morality through direct questioning regarding their understanding of morality and moral concepts, as well as by their identification of actual moral dilemmas and their nomination of moral exemplary individuals. Their moral functioning was also assessed by thorough questioning of their handling of real-life moral conflicts. We did not so much expect to discover new aspects of moral functioning, but rather to be able to draw attention to important aspects of morality that have been overlooked in contemporary moral psychology because of these philosophical and methodological blinders. More bluntly, this study represented a bit of "kicking around in the dust."

Method

The sample represented four age groups from across the lifespan, with equal numbers of males and females (total $n = 80$): adolescence (senior high school students, 16–19 years); early adulthood (undergraduate students, 18–25 years); middle adulthood (part-time university students and others drawn from the community, 35–48 years); and late adulthood (attenders of programs for retired people, 65–84 years). Children were not included in the sample because many components of the interview would have been beyond their comprehension. The adults were generally middle class and reasonably well educated. The sample was fairly representative of the Vancouver region in terms of ethnicity (71% Caucasian, 20% Oriental, and 9% other).

These participants were involved in an individual, tape-recorded interview which averaged 90 minutes in length (ranging from 1–2 hours). The interview was later transcribed verbatim and coded. There were no standard stimulus materials (such as dilemmas), but the interview entailed 86 standard questions and frequently many additional probes. The interview was composed of five major sections:

1. The first section explored, in general terms, individuals' conceptions of morality. They were asked about the nature of the moral domain and moral issues, strategies for handling moral problems, important moral values and concepts, and their understanding of the distinction and relation between morality and other related domains (viz., law, religion, and social convention).

2. Next, participants were asked to recall and discuss a recent (and, presumably, typical) real-life moral dilemma from their own experience. They were prompted to describe the moral issues entailed, the relevant considerations and relationships involved, the role of self in the conflict, their feelings and motivations (in addition to their thinking), and their evaluation of the resolution or their action.

3. Then participants were asked to recall and discuss a second real-life dilemma from their own experience, but this time they were asked for the most difficult dilemma they've ever had to face. The line of questioning here was as for the recent dilemma. Having people discuss two dilemmas from their own lives allowed an examination of variability and consistency in their reasoning.

4. Fourth, participants were asked to generate an example of a difficult moral conflict, what we will refer to here as the prototypic moral dilemma. They were asked the same set of questions as for the previous two dilemmas, except those pertaining to self (which would not be relevant). This dilemma was not a report of a personal experience, but it was believed that its formulation would be another indicator of individuals' conceptions of the moral domain.

5. Finally, participants were asked to name two highly moral people and to justify their choices. Nominations were not restricted and thus could be individuals known personally or public, historical figures. This section of the interview was character-, rather than problem-focused, and was an attempt to delineate the major or essential characteristics of moral exemplars that may reveal important, but hitherto ignored, aspects of moral functioning. To conclude the interview, participants were prompted to comment on any aspects of morality they considered important but about which they had not been asked.

Moral reasoning

Several important issues arise from an examination of the content of these 80 interviews, and we will try to address them in turn. Because this project was designed in response to the Kohlbergian dominance of the field, it is perhaps appropriate to begin with a discussion of the adequacy of his approach in handling reasoning about real-life moral conflicts, and then to turn to areas that may provide a broader perspective.

Participants discussed three moral dilemmas: both a recent and a difficult real-life dilemma, as well as a prototypic one. In scoring for moral stage, first, moral judgments were identified – statements that were prescriptive, provided a reason, and were considered valid by the subject. Then, these moral judgments were matched, if possible, to criterion judgments anywhere in the moral stage scoring manual (Colby & Kohlberg, 1987). Since the manual is keyed to particular dilemmas and issues, the scorer relied more on the general stage structure definitions for each criterion judgment than on the particular (and dilemma-specific) critical indicators. Note was also made of moral judgments that were impossible or difficult to score with Kohlberg's system. Such uncodable material speaks to the comprehensiveness of Kohlberg's model. Based on the scored moral judgments, the distribution of reasoning across the moral stages was determined and two summary scores were derived on that basis: a global stage score (GSS, a 9-point scale consisting of pure and mixed stages – 1, 1/2, 2, . . . , 5) and a composite weighted average score (a weighted sum of the percent usage at each stage, with a range of 100–500).

First, we examined age group, sex, and dilemma differences in level of moral reasoning. Relatively few studies of moral reasoning in adulthood have been conducted, but there have been indications of continued moral growth through adulthood (Colby et al., 1983). Regarding sex differences, Gilligan (1982) has argued that Kohlberg's model misconstrues females' moral orientation and downscores their reasoning. And finally, regarding dilemma differences, no previous research, to our knowledge, has elicited reasoning about subject-generated prototypic dilemmas. There is some evidence from previous work, however, that reasoning about real-life dilemmas is frequently at a somewhat lower level than that about hypothetical dilemmas (Walker, 1988). These issues were addressed by a 4(age group) × 2(sex) × 3(dilemma) analysis of variance (ANOVA) with repeated measures on the last factor and using weighted average scores as the dependent variable. Only one significant effect was revealed: For age group, $F(3,72) = 8.00$, $p <.001$. A subsequent Turkey multiple comparison test indicated that the adolescent and young adult groups did not differ ($M = 324$ and 325) and that the middle and older adult groups did not differ ($M = 357$ and 361), but that the two older groups reasoned at a more mature level than the two younger groups, as would be expected. Participants evidenced almost the full range of moral stages in reasoning about these dilemmas (ranging from Stage 2 to 4/5). No sex differences in moral reasoning were revealed, consistent with

Walker's (1991) review and metaanalysis of the available data. Also, no differences across the recent, difficult, and prototypic dilemmas were found (M = 347, 338, and 340, respectively), suggesting a strong consistency in people's ability to reason about moral conflicts, despite the considerable range of moral issues raised (as will become apparent shortly). A stronger test of the consistency across dilemmas would be to examine individual patterns in global stage scores. It was found that 80.0% of the participants evidenced the same or adjacent level of moral reasoning (on the 9-point GSS scale) across all three dilemmas (with separate and blind coding of each dilemma) – strongly supporting the cognitive-developmental notion that stages represent holistic structures.

Obviously, much of individuals' reasoning about real-life dilemmas is "sensible" within the framework of Kohlberg's model – it yields predictable age trends and consistent patterns of reasoning across dilemma contents. We can now turn to the issue of the adequacy or comprehensiveness of his approach. Are there frequently expressed moral judgments, used by people in handling their everyday moral problems, that the model fails to handle adequately? Perhaps, surprisingly, given the idiosyncratic nature of the dilemmas recalled and considerations raised, the vast majority of people's reasoning was readily scorable. However, there were a few themes that posed difficulties. We shall introduce them now and amplify on them later as other relevant data are discussed.

One set of judgments that proved difficult to score was individuals' relatively frequent references, in describing important factors in resolving their conflicts and in evaluating their actions, to practical considerations and outcomes. It is important to note at the outset that the difficult-to-score judgments here were prescriptive ones, not simple descriptions of what people did. These practical considerations and outcomes were ones that people held to be valid factors within a moral framework. They included real costs for taking certain actions (e.g., losing one's job or a major client, getting arrested for shoplifting or expelled from school), as well as anticipated benefits (e.g., one's own pleasure, eventual rewards). In responding to hypothetical dilemmas (i.e., the MJI), such practical considerations and concerns with outcomes are rarely expressed as valid moral judgments by older adolescents and adults; they are more characteristic of young children. Not surprisingly, when they are voiced, Kohlberg's model classifies such reasoning as low stage (i.e., preconventional). But our sample was considerably more sophisticated in the balance of its moral reasoning and this disjunction was troublesome. In the context of hypothetical dilemmas, one has the luxury of ignoring practical considerations and psychological factors. As one male undergraduate (#21) noted, "It's a lot easier to be moral when you have nothing to lose." But in dealing with difficult moral conflicts in everyday life, people did recognize and indeed assert the moral relevance of psychological reality. "It's almost impossible not to accept self-interest as a legitimate part of making decisions. . . . I think the outcome is a major factor whether I was right or wrong. Like you can't separate sort of totally moral principles from reality and sort of practical issues," one high school boy (#60) argued. Similarly, when people evaluated their actions (in response to the question, "How do you know your action was actually right or wrong?"), they frequently appealed to the eventual outcome. Their action was right if no one was hurt or harmed, if relationships were improved or balanced, if confrontation was avoided, if others were supportive or affirming of the decision, if it felt right, and so on; otherwise the action was wrong ("the proof is in the pudding," as a middle-aged man [#87] put it). Bluntly stated, the problem is that participants were expressing moral judgments (prescriptive reasons they considered valid) that, although easily scorable by Kohlberg's system (as low stage), seemed to be misconstrued by a "rational" model of moral philosophy. Interestingly, some moral philosophers and psychologists (Blum, 1990; Darley, 1993; Noddings, 1984; Thomas, 1993) have begun to argue for the legitimacy of self-interest and/or preference for one's own family and friends in moral decision making. As Flanagan (1991) argued, "any moral theory must acknowledge that . . . the projects and commitments of particular persons give each life whatever meaning it has; and that all persons, even very impartial ones, are partial to their own projects. It follows that no ethical conception . . . can reasonably demand a form of impersonality, abstraction, or impartiality which ignores the constraints laid down by the universal psychological features" (pp. 100–101). This does not imply that morality should be reduced to self-interest, but that theories of moral development need to account for its role in everyday functioning. In any case, these data suggest the importance of further examining the psychological factors that people consider relevant in handling real-life moral problems. It seems inappropriate to classify their appreciation of the complex realities of living as simple-minded and morally immature.

A second theme that was difficult for Kohlberg's model to assimilate was the notion of filial piety voiced by many of the ethnic-Chinese participants in the sample. This Confucian notion of respect for and obligation to elders, according to Kohlberg's model, is a relatively immature type of reasoning. Again this seems inconsistent with the relative sophistication of the rest of their reasoning. This misclassification of filial piety by Kohlberg's model has been noted before (Dien, 1982; Walker & Moran, 1991). The problem is a failure to appreciate the rich moral underpinnings of filial piety in the traditional Confucian thought. Unlike the Western conception of the autonomous individual, Confucianism defines the person in terms of relationships with others, relationships that are necessarily structured hierarchically. A key virtue in Confucianism is harmony; thus harmony-within-hierarchy is necessary to maintain order within the sociomoral universe. Moral order is maintained within relationships by having all parties fulfill role interdependencies: Those who are subservient give respect and obedience, whereas those who are in authority give compassion and justice. It is as yet unclear whether Kohlberg's model can assimilate notions such as filial piety or whether an entirely different model is necessary to accommodate such patterns of collectivistic thinking.

A third and very significant theme that Kohlberg's model failed to handle appropriately was many individuals' reliance on notions of religion, faith, and spirituality in resolving real-life moral conflicts. Perhaps the more frequent expression of religious themes in reasoning about real-life dilemmas than is typical in response to hypothetical ones could be attributed to the emphasis on personal morality in most religious traditions, in contrast to the greater emphasis on societal morality in secular moral philosophy. However, the strength of this theme in our sample was surprising given that participants were drawn from the Vancouver area, one of North America's most areligious regions (with regular church attendance at around 5% of the population; Bibby, 1987). Of those expressing a religious conviction, Christianity was most frequent in the sample, but Buddhism, Hinduism, Islam, and Confucianism were also such represented by more than one person. For some people, their religion simply provided a reasonably appropriate system of morality, which they had more or less adopted; but for others their moral framework was firmly *embedded* in their faith. Moral decisions were made on the basis of reading the Bible and discerning the relevance of its standards for the issue at hand, through prayer and meditation, and by trying to "follow Christ's example" and "pleasing God." "My whole thinking should be based on how God would think . . . that's my ideal," claimed an older man (#69). For these people, morality and spirituality were not separate and distinct domains; rather morality was governed by one's faith – the choice of one's values and goals, the resolution of conflicts, and the determination of appropriate social behaviors and relationships were all based on religious experience and belief. Blasi (1990) and Fernhout (1989) have also argued that morality may only acquire meaning for some people within the context of religion. The sophistication of participants' "religious" rationales for moral choices varied, ranging from fear of eternal damnation or anticipation of heavenly rewards, to the importance of church and fellow believers as a community, to rather principled notions of agape love. These understandings do seem to have a stagelike character to them that an appropriate cognitive-developmental analysis could establish, but Kohlberg's coding manual with its 708 criterion judgments is bereft of such notions (with the simplistic exception of Form C, Law Issue, CJ#22, Stage 3, "Stealing is wrong . . . because it's against God's teachings in the Ten Commandments; or because the Bible says you shouldn't steal"). Kohlberg's (1981, pp. 302–305) desire to clearly distinguish morality from religion and to keep moral and religious education separate led him to overlook many people's view that moral actions are primarily based on religious beliefs and motivations.

Dilemma content

Another lens through which to explore individuals' conceptions of the moral domain is by the types of moral dilemmas they recall from personal experience or generate as prototypic examples of moral dilemmas. The identity of people's moral conflicts is also of interest because it reveals the kind of issues they confront in everyday living (and hence ones to which researchers should more closely attend) and indicates the representativeness of the dilemmas used in standard measures, such as the MJI. Age group, sex, and dilemma type (recent, difficult, and prototypic) differences are also of interest.

The first content analysis of these dilemmas was a descriptive one – an attempt to summarize the moral issue or concern that was the focus of each conflict (following Walker et al., 1987). This was not an easy task because, in contrast to the MJI with its simple preconstruction of the issue in conflict, these real-life dilemmas frequently entailed more complex constructions with a variety of subthemes in play. It should also be noted that a few dilemmas, at least in their initial description, were not primarily moral in character according to dominant perspectives in moral philosophy. However, after some probing, invariably moral considerations were voiced and the moral issue became evident. Many of the dilemmas would not be considered difficult by moral philosophers, but they were ones that people confronted in everyday life. Each dilemma was in some sense unique, but 26 categories were derived, each containing more than one dilemma (a 27th category, "miscellaneous," included a small number of single dilemmas that could not be otherwise classified). This typology is provided in Table 12.1, which indicates the frequency of each type of moral issue across the three types of moral dilemmas.

Between the two real-life dilemmas (recent and difficult) there were surprisingly few differences in the frequency of various types of moral

Table 12.1. *Content analysis of the moral issues across types of dilemmas*

Moral issue	Dilemma type		
	Recent	Difficult	Prototypic
1. Relationship with spouse/partner	7	10	8
2. Relationship with children	3	4	1
3. Relationship with parents	5	13	1
4. Relationship with sibling	1	2	–
5. Work performance	5	1	3
6. Work (and social service) relationships	5	6	–
7. Friendship	6	3	4
8. Promises/confidences	4	1	1
9. Apologies/confessions	–	4	1
10. Honesty/cheating/fraud	12	6	1
11. Theft	4	3	1
12. Religious beliefs	1	4	2
13. Racism/discrimination	–	3	2
14. Life preservation	3	2	9
15. Capital punishment	–	–	2
16. Abortion	–	4	21
17. Premarital sex	4	3	2
18. Substance use	6	7	1
19. Abuse (child, sexual)	3	–	1
20. Animal welfare	2	1	1
21. War	2	1	6
22. Altruism	2	–	2
23. Native land claims	–	–	2
24. Political protest/activity	–	1	2
25. Violence to protect family	–	–	2
26. Choosing objects/activities	2	1	–
27. Miscellaneous	3	–	4

issues recalled. Among the most frequent dilemmas were those involving relationships with one's spouse or partner, parents, work colleagues, and friends (Categories 1, 3, 6, and 7). Examples of such conflicts included: whether to have an extramarital affair when his wife was pregnant (#19), whether to live with mother or father following her parents' separation (#63), whether to challenge supervisor's negative evaluation of a teaching colleague (#53), and whether to continue helping a friend with her home-work when she's taking advantage of you (#62). The moral issues inherent in these relational conflicts are minimized by a moral psychology that em-phasizes justice (as has also been argued by Gilligan, 1982, and others). Other common moral issues among the real-life dilemmas were ones con-cerning honesty and substance use (Categories 10 and 18). Examples here included whether to withhold pertinent information in trying to make an insurance sale (#78) and whether to take drugs when pressured by friends (#5). It is only recently that researchers have begun to examine the rele-vance of moral reasoning in understanding the etiology of drug and alcohol abuse (Berkowitz, Guerra, & Nucci, 1991), but it is apparent that for many people such issues are part of the moral struggles in everyday living.

The content analysis of the moral issues in the prototypic dilemma re-vealed a substantially different picture of people's conception of the moral domain. The most frequent dilemma (generated by over one-quarter of the participants) concerned abortion,[1] with the next most frequent category being life preservation (e.g., euthanasia, suicide). These more classic moral dilemmas involving issues of life and death, of conflicting rights and respon-sibilities, were clearly identified as difficult ones to resolve. It should be noted that these abortion and life-preservation dilemmas were also re-ported as real-life dilemmas by several participants, so they are not entirely remote from people's experience. Other frequently generated prototypic dilemmas included relationships with spouse or partner (often pertaining to marital fidelity) and war (e.g., concerning the morality of Canadian involve-ment in the Persian Gulf War in 1991 – many interviews were completed at about that time).

The small number of dilemmas in each category precluded statistical analy-ses, but inspection of the data allows for some observations regarding age group and sex differences. For the real-life dilemmas (recent and difficult), younger participants more frequently reported moral issues involving rela-tionships with parents and with friends and concerning substance abuse, whereas older participants more frequently focused on relationships with spouse, with children, with colleagues, and concerning work performance. These differences, of course, reflect the differing social worlds of younger versus middle-aged and older adults. For the prototypic dilemma, the only notable age group difference concerned abortion, with the young- and middle-aged adults (i.e., those in the prime child-rearing years) more likely to raise the issue than the adolescents and older adults. These findings again illustrate the point that what is identified as a moral conflict varies with the cultural and historical context and with developmental status.

A few sex differences were also apparent in the real-life dilemmas recalled, with females more often reporting moral conflicts involving colleagues and parents and with males often reporting conflicts involving spouse or partner, or pertaining to one's work performance, or to substance use. Regarding the prototypic dilemma, males more frequently identified relationships with spouse or partner as a moral issue, whereas females emphasized abortion and life preservation. It is somewhat surprising that males focused on a relational issue whereas females focused on life-and-death issues (but, of course, abortion is not an issue with equivalent meaning for men and women).

The previous content analysis focused on the moral issue that was at the core of the conflict and it was essentially descriptive. We are going to report two further content analyses of these moral dilemmas that are somewhat more interpretive and may be more clearly reflective of individuals' conceptions of morality. The first of these content analyses examines the domain or nature of the relationships involved in the conflict (and is adapted from Walker et al., 1987). This three-category typology allowed moral dilemmas to be classified as: (1) *personal* – involving a specific person or group of people with whom the subject has a significant relationship, defined generally as one of a continuing nature (e.g., a family member, friend, close neighbor, colleague, associate, partner); (2) *impersonal* – involving a person or group of people whom the subject does not know well (a stranger or acquaintance) or is not specified or is generalized (e.g., students, clients), or as involving institutions (e.g., police); and (3) *intrapsychic* – involving an issue primarily intrinsic to self. This typology was originally developed to examine Gilligan's (1982) notion that the feminine ethic of care entails a concern for maintenance of personal relationships (implying a sex difference in the nature of the relationships involved in the dilemmas people recall). In addition to sex differences, the present study allows an examination of age group and dilemma-type differences in this typology.

Table 12.2a presents the frequency of each category in this content analysis across types of dilemmas. It is apparent that the real-life dilemmas, both the recent and difficult one, are more likely to be conceptualized as entailing personal relationships, whereas the prototypic dilemma is more likely to entail impersonal relationships. The relative frequency of the intrapsychic category should also be noted. For a sizable number of people, the moral issues reported did not directly involve others but were primarily intrinsic to self (e.g., whether or not to plagiarize [#40]). They pertain more to the pursuit of ideals and the maintenance of one's sense of moral self and thus represent a promising avenue of research (in addition to the standard hypothetical dilemmas involving conflicts of rights and/or responsibilities).

Age group and sex differences in this typology of domain of relationships

Table 12.2. *Content analyses of the (a) domain and (b) frame of relationships across types of dilemmas*

	Dilemma type		
Category	Recent	Difficult	Prototypic
a. *Domain of relationships*			
Personal	44	48	34
Impersonal	7	13	23
Intrapsychic	29	19	23
b. *Frame of relationships*			
Attached/detached	25	24	18
Equal/unequal	22	27	33
Both	9	18	15
Neither	24	11	14

in individuals' dilemmas were examined by a series of chi-square analyses.[2] However, no significant differences were revealed. This is particularly surprising given previous evidence that women report more personal dilemmas than men whereas men report more impersonal dilemmas than women (Walker et al., 1987). With the present data, however, there are no indications that women orient more to the personal domain than do men, as Gilligan (1982) has argued.

It is also of interest to examine variability in level of moral reasoning across these domains of relationships in individuals' dilemmas. We (Walker et al., 1987) previously found that impersonal dilemmas elicited a higher level of moral reasoning than did personal dilemmas, suggesting that generalized reasoning is favored in the Kohlbergian approach over the particularized reasoning of personal relationships. To examine this issue, ANOVAs were conducted for each dilemma using the three-category domain of relationship as the independent variable and weighted average scores as the dependent variable. No significant effects were found: Level of moral reasoning did not vary across the domains involved in people's moral dilemmas.

The last content analysis of these moral dilemmas focused on how participants framed the relationships in their conflicts: attached–detached versus equal–unequal. This typology was proposed by Gilligan and her colleagues (Brown, 1987) as part of the interpretive methodology for discerning moral orientations (an ethic of care vs. an ethic of justice). This typology concerns how participants describe themselves in relation to others in their conflict and what they emphasize in the context. The (feminine) care perspective would emphasize themes of attachment or detachment in relationships (i.e., is interdependence, connection, or responsive relations between people emphasized or pertinent to the conflict?). On the other hand, the (masculine) justice perspective would emphasize themes of equality or inequality in relationships (i.e., is relative status, power, or efficacy emphasized or pertinent to the conflict?). This typology, of course, also reflects the familiar dimensions in personality theory of communion and agency (Bakan, 1966). Note that it is the *participant's* framing of the relationship that is important since many relationships can be conceptualized in either terms (e.g., a parent–child relationship). The typology included not only the attached–detached and equal–unequal categories, but also a category for when the relationship was conceptualized in both frameworks and a category for when neither type of framing was relevant.

Table 12.2b displays the frequency of participants' framing of relationships across the three types of dilemmas. There are few notable differences across types of dilemmas with the exception that the prototypic dilemma was more likely to be conceptualized in terms of the equality–inequality dimension, which is not surprising given the tendency for them to be more abstracted and impersonal in nature. Age group and sex differences in this typology of the framing of relationships in individuals' dilemmas were examined by a series of chi-square analyses.[3] However, no significant differences were revealed. The absence of sex differences in this content analysis is particularly surprising given Gilligan's (1982) strong claims regarding the sex-related nature of moral orientations. However, the finding is consistent with reviews of empirical studies of these orientations (e.g., Walker, 1991). Differences in level of moral reasoning across these categories in framing relationships were examined by ANOVAs (using the four categories as the independent variable and weighted average scores as the dependent variable). Again, no differences were revealed for any of the dilemmas, indicating that Kohlberg's model is not apparently biased toward either framework (attachment vs. equality) despite suggestions that it is insensitive to the ethic of care (Gilligan, 1982).

In summary of this section, we have explored people's conceptions of morality through an examination of the content of their real-life and prototypic moral dilemmas. Three different content analyses were used: One focused on the moral issue that was at the heart of the conflict, another focused on the domain or nature of relationships involved in the conflict, and the third focused on participants' framing of relationships. It became apparent that many issues confronting people in their everyday experience (such as relational conflicts with spouse or friends, substance abuse) are not well tapped by standard measures of moral reasoning. It also became apparent that people's experiences of moral conflicts tend to entail the personal domain, but that their conception of prototypic dilemmas focuses more on the impersonal. And, finally, the absence of age group, sex, and moral development differences in people's conceptualization of dilemmas in terms of the domain and frame of relationships was particularly surprising given previous theorizing.

Moral exemplars

In the final section of the interview, participants were asked to name two people whom they regarded as highly moral and to justify their choices. This was an attempt to approach moral functioning without involving problem solving of moral conflicts and, as such, had the potential to be more character- than reasoning-based. It was anticipated that we could delineate some of the major or essential characteristics of moral exemplars, which would point to important, but relatively ignored (at least until now), aspects of moral functioning.

As noted earlier, the dominance of Kohlberg's theory forms the context for contemporary moral psychology,[4] and although this model has significantly advanced our understanding of the cognitive aspects of moral development, it now seems obvious that such a pervasive influence has constricted our view of moral functioning. Despite the considerable empirical base, it has been argued that the model entails a restricted notion of morality (focusing on justice) and an impoverished description of the moral agent (focusing on cognition). The Kohlbergian view characterizes morally exemplary individuals primarily by their principled (high-stage) judgment. Thus, the conception of moral maturity engendered by this approach would perhaps be best exemplified by a Supreme Court justice – someone who uses sophisticated moral reasoning, notably principles. Not to denigrate Supreme Court justices, moral philosophers, and the like, but such a conception is at best incomplete, and more likely rather distorted.[5]

We need a more compelling description of mature moral functioning. Part of what could be included in such an account would be an emphasis on moral commitment, affect, and virtue (which have hitherto been generally ignored in moral psychology and which better represent the Aristotelian tradition in moral philosophy). Two recent works, in particular, have helped to prompt this interest in moral commitment and character: Flanagan's (1991) *Varieties of Moral Personality* presented a persuasive philosophical rationale for a renewed examination of the role of moral virtues. Colby and Damon, in their 1992 book, *Some Do Care,* provided a case-study analysis of the lives of a small sample of Americans who had demonstrated long-standing commitment to moral ideals and an exceptional capacity for moral action (in addition, see Colby & Damon, Chapter 11, this volume). Since Colby and Damon's important but unusual work formed part of the impetus for the present study, a brief analysis follows.

Colby and Damon relied on a number of experts to formulate criteria for moral excellence: "(1) a sustained commitment to moral ideals or principles . . . or a sustained evidence of moral virtue [note that this criterion refers to *both* moral rationality and virtue]; (2) a disposition to act in accord with one's moral ideals or principles; . . . (3) a willingness to risk one's self-interest; . . . (4) a tendency to be inspiring to others and thereby to move them to moral action; (5) a sense of realistic humility" (1992, p. 29). These experts also nominated individuals meeting these criteria, with nominations restricted to living Americans who had demonstrated clear commitment to moral causes over an extended period of time.

Colby and Damon interviewed 23 of the moral exemplars nominated, including 5 who were studied in depth (these five case studies constitute the major portion of their book). Despite the obvious individuality of these exemplars, Colby and Damon inferred four major developmental processes in the acquisition and maintenance of exceptional moral character. One process was the developmental transformation of moral goals, entailing an active receptiveness to progressive social influence (often from followers) and a great capacity for change throughout one's life. Second, these exemplars were marked by certainty about moral principles and values combined (somewhat paradoxically) with persistent truth seeking and open-mindedness (thereby precluding dogmatism). An important observation was that they displayed little evidence of "dilemma-busting" cognitions. Also, they made no claim of moral courage, indeed it was disavowed – risks were considered inevitable consequences of following one's values. Third – surprising, given the dismal circumstances in which they worked – most exemplars displayed great positivity and faith: an enjoyment of life and their work, a sense of optimism, humor, humility (despite great accomplishments and recognition), and capacity to forgive and love. One particularly remarkable finding is that about 80% of the exemplars attributed their moral commitments to religious faith and spirituality (noteworthy since the nominating criteria did not specify anything religious in nature). Finally, it was evident that there was a uniting of self and morality (reflecting the exemplars' identity) – a fusion between personal and moral aspects of life. They saw moral problems in everyday events, saw themselves implicated in these problems and responsible to act.

Table 12.3. *Types of moral exemplars*

Types of moral exemplars	Frequency
1. Family (e.g., wife, father, grandmother)	33
2. Friends	25
3. Religious leaders (e.g., pope, minister, chaplain)	19
4. Humanitarians (e.g., Mother Teresa, Schweitzer, Vanier)	17
5. Revolutionaries (e.g., Gandhi, Mandela, M. L. King)	16
6. Politicians (e.g., Churchill, Trudeau, Lincoln)	9
7. Religious founders (e.g., Jesus, Buddha, Mohammed)	9
8. Activists (e.g., Suzuki, Perry, Sakharov)	6
9. Self	5
10. Professionals (e.g., family physician, teacher)	5
11. Writers/philosophers (e.g., Hesse, Russell)	2
12. Entertainers (e.g., k. d. lang, Bob Barker)	2
13. Journalists (e.g., Moyers)	2
14. Others	3

Our study was intended to provide more systematic, but somewhat different data regarding moral exemplars. Notably, participants' nominations were not restricted to living, public Americans who had evidenced long-term moral commitments (since we, unlike Colby and Damon, did not intend to interview the nominees) and thus nominees could be historical figures or someone known personally. Nor were nominations restricted by experts' criteria; instead, participants were simply asked to justify their choices by describing the exemplar's characteristics.

First, we conducted a content analysis of the types of moral exemplars nominated, of which there was a wide range. This content analysis of responses yielded a 13-category typology (a 14th category, "other," included single exemplars who could not be otherwise classified). Table 12.3 displays this typology as well as the relative frequency of each type (recall that each participant typically nominated two exemplars). This typology included a number of somewhat predictable categories, including humanitarians, revolutionaries, social activists, politicians, and religious leaders and founders; but the most frequent categories were family members and friends. It is significant that many (42%) of the exemplars named were *not* public figures. Many participants expressed an explicit distrust of the public persona of many historical figures, preferring to nominate individuals they knew intimately and were better able to evaluate – including themselves in several cases. The sizable number of religious exemplars nominated echoes our identification of religious themes in participants' reasoning about their moral conflicts and Colby and Damon's (1992) finding of the relevance of faith and spirituality in their case studies of moral exemplars.

The large number of categories in this typology precluded statistical analyses but examination of the data allows for some observations regarding age and sex differences. The only notable age group difference was that the older adults were less likely than people from the younger age groups to name family members and friends as moral exemplars. This could be attributed to the fact that, in this age group, many family members and friends were no longer living. Sex differences were similarly rare; however, there was a tendency for males to name revolutionaries more often than females, and for females to name family members and friends more often than males. In order to examine the relationship between the types of moral exemplars named and level of moral development, a median split was done on weighted average scores and the nominations of those relatively low and high in moral reasoning were compared. This indicated a tendency for those higher in moral reasoning to name social activists and politicians more often; whereas for those lower in moral reasoning, family members and friends were more frequently named. This may, in part, reflect the lower-stage focus, in Kohlberg's model, on the interpersonal sphere and the higher-stage focus on the societal sphere.

The hundreds of characteristics attributed to these exemplars were also content-analyzed into a 40-category typology. Table 12.4 provides these categories along with their relative frequency. Clearly the most common descriptor of moral exemplars was "compassionate/caring," emphasizing virtues such as love and an orientation to others. This theme is also reflected in the "self-sacrificing" category, another frequent descriptor. These aspects of moral functioning are frequently minimized by a model of morality that emphasizes justice and rationality, but they clearly warrant greater attention, particularly in terms of the developmental processes underlying their acquisition.

The significance of compassion and self-sacrifice in the lives of moral exemplars was also noted by Colby and Damon (1992, Chapter 11, this volume). Several other characteristics frequently ascribed to moral exemplars by participants in our study were ones also emphasized by Colby and Damon, including consistency, honesty, and open-mindedness. Integrity – consistency of words and actions – was particularly valued and points to the importance of understanding moral functioning holistically rather than

Table 12.4. *Characteristics of moral exemplars*

Compassionate/caring [87]	Wise [9]
Consistent [48]	Humble [9]
Honest [36]	Sociable [8]
Self-sacrificing [35]	Self-accepting [7]
Open-minded [32]	Patient [6]
Thoughtful/rational [28]	Nonmaterialistic [6]
Socially active [27]	Self-reflective [5]
Just [25]	Forgiving [5]
Courageous [24]	Reserved [5]
Virtuous [21]	Cheerful [4]
Autonomous [19]	Inconsistent [3]
Dedicated [18]	Truth-seeking [3]
Empathic/sensitive [18]	Charitable [2]
Devoutly religious [13]	Temperate [2]
Trustworthy [13]	Nonreligious [2]
Principled [11]	Unpleasant [2]
Charismatic [10]	Dogmatic [2]
Lawful [10]	Humorous [1]
Empowering [10]	Lonely [1]
Nonviolent [10]	Self-righteous [1]

Note: Frequencies are indicated in brackets.

focusing on disparate aspects. It was apparent that most exemplars were chosen more for their character, virtues, and behavior than their principled judgments; although it should be noted that references to the cognitive aspects of morality were not entirely lacking (cf. the thoughtful-rational, autonomous, and principled catagories). Among the low-frequency categories were some characteristics that could be considered negative (e.g., inconsistent, unpleasant, dogmatic, lonely, self-righteous). One explanation for these rather idiosyncratic characteristics is that they were descriptive of specific persons, not of highly moral people in general; but perhaps it is inevitable that socially active individuals with clear moral values are bound to give offense at some point. It should also be acknowledged that a focus on moral character may be no more adequate than a focus on moral reasoning in yielding a clear and uncontroversial account of moral excellence (Flanagan, 1991). This is the case for at least two reasons: First, no

Table 12.5. *Characteristics associated with major types of moral exemplars*

Types of moral exemplars	Characteristics
Family	Compassionate-caring and open-minded
Friends	Compassionate-caring and consistent
Religious leaders	Compassionate-caring and consistent
Humanitarians	Compassionate-caring and self-sacrificing
Revolutionaries	Socially active and nonviolent
Politicians	Socially active and just
Religious founders	Compassionate-caring and self-sacrificing
Activists	Socially active and consistent

one person could embody the full range of desirable moral virtues, nor are all of these characteristics equally desirable in all contexts; and second, most of these virtues seem to entail some maladaptive (perhaps even morally questionable) aspects to their expression.

The large number of categories precluded a statistical analysis of sex differences in the characteristics ascribed to moral exemplars, but an examination of the data revealed a remarkably similar pattern. For example, the largest sex difference was for the "compassionate-caring" category (17% of females' descriptors vs. 13% of males').

Finally, it is of interest to examine what characteristics are associated with the major types of moral exemplars. It might be expected that different moral exemplars were nominated for different reasons – they are hardly a homogeneous group. The two most frequent categories of characteristics for each of the more common types of moral exemplars are provided in Table 12.5. Not surprising given its overall frequency, the compassionate-caring category is associated with most types of moral exemplars, with the exception of politicians, revolutionaries, and activists who were identified more for their social activism than for their compassion. The importance of open-mindedness, flexibility, and tolerance within the family context is noteworthy. Religious founders and humanitarians shared the same pattern of characteristics (compassionate-caring and self-sacrificing) which could be explained by many humanitarians' basing of their values and actions on faith or religion. Friends and religious leaders also shared the same pattern of characteristics (compassionate-caring and consistent), which is understandable since many of the religious leaders were well known to participants (e.g., as their minister). In any case, this points to the importance of integrity in close relationships.

In summary of this section, we have explored people's conceptions of moral functioning by examining the types of highly moral people they identify and the characteristics by which they justified their choices. This process helped to identify several components of the moral domain that have received insufficient conceptual and empirical attention.

Feelings and motivations

As has been argued before, moral psychology has pervasively focused on cognition and has failed to acknowledge adequately the role of affect in moral functioning (also see Kagan, 1993). In our own previous research, the data have helped us to appreciate the significance of the affective domain. For example, Walker and Taylor (1991) found that the affective quality of parents' interactions with their child (e.g., support, hostility) was predictive of the child's subsequent moral development; and Matsuba and Walker (1993) found that children's level of moral reasoning was strongly associated with their ego functioning.

The role of affect in moral functioning is multifarious. Affect may help to sensitize us to the moral implications of situations and to instigate action (e.g., empathy). The recognition of moral default or failure (i.e., inconsistency with one's own or others' standards) also elicits emotions such as guilt and shame (Tangney, 1991). It is important to recognize, as well, that affect may serve to "corrupt" reasoning. Bandura's (1991) notion of moral disengagement illustrates such emotive self-regulatory mechanisms in moral functioning.

In the present study, we attempted to tap the affective domain in moral functioning by asking participants to recall their emotions and motivations in handling real-life conflicts (in addition to their reasoning). There are, of course, some significant limitations here: It is not always easy to verbalize emotions; there are presentation biases in reporting one's own motivations; and, in describing the solution of moral conflicts, moral triumphs were understandably more common than moral failures. Nevertheless, some interesting patterns were apparent in our content analysis of the feelings and motivations people reported.

Particularly striking in interviews with many people was the genuine expression of *angst* in struggling through truly difficult conflicts. As one middle-aged woman (#7) remarked, "There was just no bottom to the agony." These moral conflicts left people feeling torn apart, drained, and shaken – between the proverbial rock and a hard place. Real-life moral conflicts are hardly experienced in the same way as the idle intellectual exercises of the MJI's dilemmas. Other participants, while not experiencing the deep angst just mentioned, did report considerable *confusion* in deciding between alternatives, struggling with temptation, responding to pressure, and simply not knowing what to do. The action choices in real-life conflicts, unlike most hypothetical dilemmas, are frequently not readily apparent and often there is a Gordian knot of interrelated issues with which to contend.

Other frequently expressed emotions included *anger* (e.g., about a double standard or not being trusted); *pain* (e.g., from being isolated, rejected, misunderstood, betrayed, vulnerable); *sadness* or *sorrow* (e.g., for victims or others harmed); *guilt* (e.g., for letting down personal standards); and *shame* (e.g., being embarrassed by others' reactions). Also verbalized were feelings of *satisfaction* (e.g., for having done the right thing) and *power* or *confidence* (e.g., for being able to resolve the conflict and act appropriately). Although many people accorded considerable significance to their emotions ("My heart would carry more moral weight than my mind," a middle-aged man [#19] claimed, others indicated some distrust of the affective domain and described their feelings as those of *detachment* or *objectivity*. One retired naval officer (#82) remarked that he had been trained to suppress his feelings and to remain objective. Here it should be noted that being just, principled, rational, and so on, does not necessarily imply that the moral agent is affectively detached as some have implied; rather, emotional engagement in the particulars of the context should make one more sensitive to the moral implications involved (Boyd, 1989).

In the context of discussing the affective domain in moral functioning, it is appropriate to mention many participants' reliance on *intuition* in resolving moral issues and in evaluating their actions. Many people reported that simply feeling good about a decision – having a gut reaction – was important, if not often sufficient, in justifying their behavior. Although many readily conceded that intuition (particularly that of others) was unreliable as a moral indicator, they could rarely proffer viable alternatives and remained confident regarding the role of "the little voice within." Research earlier in the century examined the developmental precursors for "conscience," but it now seems appropriate to revisit both the conceptualizations and empirical evidence regarding moral intuition. (Shweder & Haidt, 1993, articulated similar arguments regarding the role of intuition in moral functioning.) The role of automaticity or habitual responding also needs to be examined better in moral psychology, in contrast to the contemporary emphasis of reflectivity. Confucianism, for example, emphasizes the cultivation of a moral sense, which allows one to intuit, automatically, what is correct, without real reflection, even in unusual circumstances.

This discussion of the affective domain and moral intuition perhaps can be profitably focused by examining the role of the "self" in moral functioning. Several theorists have noted the motivational power of the self in real-life moral conflicts (e.g., Gilligan, 1982; Linn, 1987). Blasi (1983, 1984), in particular, proposed a self-model in moral functioning, a model that has three major aspects. The first component, the *moral self,* focuses on the role of morality in one's self-definition and identity. Certainly, it was readily apparent in our interviews that morality had differing degrees of centrality in people's identities: For some, moral considerations and issues were pervasive in their experience because morality was rooted in the heart of their being; for others, moral issues seemed remote and the maintenance of moral values and standards was not basic to their self-concept and self-esteem. As well, it is possible that different aspects of morality may be foundational to different people's self-definition. In this context, it is important to recall that one of the major processes noted by Colby and Damon (1992) in the development of exceptional moral character and action was the uniting of self and morality. In the lives of moral exemplars, personal goals and moral goals were seemingly fused – morality was evidently fundamental to their identity.

The second component in Blasi's self-model focuses on one's sense of *responsibility* for moral action: Is what is morally good also strictly necessary to do? Perhaps this component could be better understood as a process of moral engagement (Haste, 1990). Kohlberg and Candee (1984) have more extensively explicated this aspect of moral functioning. They distinguished between a deontic judgment (a judgment regarding what is the right thing to do) and a judgment of responsibility (a judgment regarding one's obligation to perform the action). This motivation to action may have its developmental roots in a process of moral attachment, the formation of specific relationships to other people which contributes to the sense of responsibility and commitment (Kohlberg & Diessner, 1991). For Kohlberg, this sense of responsibility is a major connector between cognition and action. (The frequent disjunction between cognition and action is one of the major conundrums facing moral psychology.) Kohlberg and Candee argued that a judgment of responsibility entailed implicating self in action, considering others' welfare and needs, and valuing both social relationships and one's sense of personal moral worth (thereby connecting the judgment of responsibility to one's self-definition, the moral self). Thus, it might be expected that the strength of this sense of responsibility would vary developmentally and from person to person.

The third component in Blasi's self-model focuses on *self- consistency* or, in more common terms, integrity. This aspect addresses the consistency between one's judgment regarding what is right to do and one's action. Blasi believes that the dynamism of self-consistency is a basic tendency in personality organization, a motive that can only be satisfied by a congruence of action with what one has judged to be right and good. Thus, it is the sense of the self's integrity that is at stake in moral action. Recall that such consistency was one of the most frequently named characteristics of the moral exemplars identified in our study. In our interviews, although we did question people regarding the relation between their reasoning and action in real-life moral conflicts, it was found that reported inconsistency was exceedingly rare. As noted before, we were concerned, of course, about presentation biases in such self-reports of what is clearly value-laden activity; and Bandura (1991) has cogently demonstrated the corrupting power of rationalizations in the preservation of one's sense of the moral self. Haan et al. (1985) have also noted people's strong need to regard themselves as good and moral, even in the face of overwhelming evidence to the contrary (e.g., even heinous criminals claim to be good). Obviously, moral psychology requires a systematic empirical examination of the role of self in moral functioning. Such an enterprise presents considerable methodological challenges, but it has the potential to link the cognitive and emotive aspects of moral functioning to behavior.

Conceptions of morality

The final issue addressed by this project concerned individuals' conceptualization of the moral domain, in general, and their differentiation of morality from related domains. Of course, people's conceptions of morality have already been indirectly explored through an examination of dilemma content and reasoning, identification of moral exemplars, and so forth; but in the initial portion of the interview, participants were explicitly questioned regarding basic moral values and concepts, appropriate strategies for handling moral problems, and how they knew whether a particular action was moral. We then content-analyzed their responses in order to discern common themes.

First, we explored the basic moral values and concepts identified by the participants in this initial portion of the interview. Our content analysis yielded an 18-category typology with the most frequently identified value being *honesty* or *truth* (19% of responses). Many people believed that the maintenance of appropriate social relationships precluded deception. Two other concepts were also frequently mentioned (each with 14% of responses): *compassion* or *love* (including values such as kindness and sharing) and *respect for others* (including not harming others). These concepts emphasize the caring activity that forms the basis of many relationships. Other frequently identified moral values and concepts include *integrity* (8%), *open-mindedness* (8%), *religion* (7%), and the *Golden Rule* (7%). (Each of the remaining categories of moral values and concepts had frequencies less than 5%.) In many respects, these commonly named moral values and concepts resemble those identified, in another portion of the interview, as characteristics of moral exemplars. Thus, with different types of prompting, people stress the moral significance of compassion, integrity, honesty, open-mindedness, and faith. It is surprising, perhaps, that religion was so frequently mentioned given that moral values were being elicited, but this again reinforces the point that, for many people, faith and spirituality provide the grounding for their moral understandings.

Second, we explored the strategies people advocated for handling moral problems. A 10-category typology was devised to capture the notions expressed. The most frequent strategy advocated was a *rational approach* in which one weighs pros and cons and applies standards (31% of responses). Clearly, people believe that a reasoned approach to moral problems is desirable, but note that this characteristic was not among the most frequently named for moral exemplars. Of course, the question prompted participants to propose strategies for resolving moral problems (which is somewhat different than for living the virtuous life). Other people advocated the importance of *dialogue,* of talking through problems and issues with others (18%). This, again emphasizes the relational component of moral functioning. Other proposed strategies included considering how it *affects others* (14%), *intuition* or *conscience* (11%), *being true to self* (8%), and *open-mindedness* (7%). (The other four categories were each mentioned in less than 5% of the responses.) Note that, although many participants relied on gut reactions in handling their own real-life problems, relatively few advocated that as a general strategy. Perhaps it is the complexity or the immediacy of actual conflicts that forces people to rely more frequently on intuition.

Third, we explored how participants would know, in general, if a particular action was moral. Here we find an interesting pattern, one that contrasts with the strategies discussed in the previous paragraph. Clearly more than any other category (in the eight-category typology), participants relied on *intuition* or *conscience* (44% of responses) when evaluating moral actions. As noted in previous sections, many people consider one's gut feelings to be a reliable indicator of the morality of potential actions. Although rarely mentioned as a strategy for resolving moral problems, intuition is frequently regarded as a means for evaluating the morality of the outcome. Also mentioned as ways to evaluate actions were *societal standards and others' opinions* (16%), *balancing perspectives* (11%), *personal standards* (9%), *consideration of harm* (7%), *weighing alternatives* (7%), and *faith and religion* (e.g., reading the Bible, praying) (7%). Note, again, the religious references in people's understanding of moral functioning.

Finally, we addressed people's differentiation of morality and related domains (viz., legality, religion, and social convention). We asked people to explain any differences among these domains and to judge what one should do when they were in conflict (e.g., "What should you do when your moral judgment tells you to do something that is against your religion?"). Turiel (1983) has argued for the validity of distinguishing among domains of social cognition – for example, the moral, social (conventional), and psychological (personal) domains. Turiel and his colleagues have been able to demonstrate that people do make distinctions across domains (e.g., in the extent to which a rule is alterable by authorities), but most scenarios used in their research have been simplistic. There is now a beginning recognition that these distinctions vary across individuals and cultures and that many situations are multifaceted and ambiguous, with their domain classification dependent not only on the objective features of events but also on informational assumptions and construal (Haidt, Koller, & Dias, 1993; Miller & Luthar, 1989; Turiel, Hildebrandt, & Wainryb, 1991; Turiel, Killen, & Helwig, 1987). In other words, it is difficult to limit the domain of morality if people believe that injustice or harm will follow from an action (even a violation of a seemingly trivial social convention). Further, Haidt et al. (1993) have demonstrated that even actions with no harmful consequences are considered moral violations in some cultural contexts, implying that the domain of morality is frequently broader in other cultures.

Our interest was in the possibility that domains may not be mutually exclusive, but embedded or hierarchical. As suggested before, it may be that morality may only acquire meaning within the broader context of faith or religion (or some system greater than oneself). As well, for some people, the moral domain may be largely defined by legal considerations. Our findings indicated that when the moral and social conventional domains were put in conflict, that the vast majority of individuals (96%) believed that morality should take precedence. This is consistent with the findings of numerous studies of Turiel and his colleagues. When morality and legality were put in conflict, the majority of individuals (77.6%) held that one should follow their moral judgment rather than the law, but a sizable proportion (18.4%) argued that the law should take precedence. Their rationales included the clarity of the law versus the ambiguity of morality and the significant practical considerations involved in violating legal constraints. (Recall that in handling real-life moral conflicts, people frequently stressed the relevance of outcomes and costs in engaging in particular actions.)

When the demands of morality and religion were put in conflict, again a majority (76.7%) believed that morality should take precedence, but a sizable minority (11.0%) held that religious beliefs were more important to follow or that the domains were of equal importance (12.3%). These findings are fairly consistent with those of Nucci and Turiel (1993) in their study of the relation between moral and religious understandings with a sample of Christian (Amish Mennonite and Dutch Reform Calvinist) and Jewish (Conservative and Orthodox) children and adolescents. They found that moral rules were regarded as nonalterable by religious authorities and were generalizable to people outside the religion, whereas many nonmoral religious rules were alterable by authorities and were not generalizable to others. One of the difficulties here, which we anecdotally noted in our interviews, was that many people who argued for the priority of morality over religion did so because of their rejection of the dictates of *institutional* religious authority, not necessarily a rejection of spiritual values and beliefs. Unfortunately, our line of questioning did not allow a distinction between the rules of institutional religion and the more personal aspects of religious faith and spirituality. Further research is warranted to explicate the potentially complex relationships between morality and religion or spirituality. For example, in what ways are these separate domains and what determines the extent to which moral or religious considerations might be embedded in the other domain?

Concluding thoughts

The aims of this exploratory project were modest – simply to point to aspects of moral functioning that have been overlooked or minimized by contemporary moral psychology. We did not aspire to present confirmatory evidence regarding the role of these facets of morality and their development, but rather to suggest that further research could profitably be focused in certain areas. We would be content if some colleagues in the field merely found something here with which to react.

As argued earlier, the theoretical and empirical context for contemporary moral psychology has been overwhelmingly influenced by the Kohlbergian paradigm, a model that has contributed significantly to our understanding of moral reasoning development but which may have obscured our vision of some other important aspects of moral functioning. The major complaints regarding the Kohlbergian approach concern its a priori (and consequently narrow) definition of the moral domain with a focus on justice and its restricted conception of the psychological aspects of moral functioning with a focus on cognition. Hence, the approach emphasizes the ability to reason about conflicting rights and responsibilities within the context of hypothetical moral dilemmas.

Our project probed individuals' conceptions of the moral domain and handling of real-life moral conflicts in a preliminary attempt, using a phenomenological approach, to expand the boundaries and chart the landscape of moral functioning. Our intent was to balance currently dominant philosophical perspectives on morality with ordinary people's experiences of moral functioning in everyday life, and to explore similarities and differences in these experiences across the lifespan.

The real-life dilemmas that people recalled from their own lives frequently focused on relationships – relationships with spouse, parents, children, colleagues, and friends. The moral issues inherent in our significant relationships are frequently overlooked by a model of morality that focuses on justice, rights, and duties. Other dilemmas focused on the intrapsychic domain (in contrast to the personal and impersonal domains) and reflect the fact that many crucial moral issues concern conflicts that are primarily intrinsic to self. These relational and intrapsychic issues have not been well tapped by the standard dilemmas of the MJI and other such measures, thus suggesting new content areas for measures of moral functioning.

Surprisingly, most individuals' reasoning regarding these real-life dilemmas was sensible within Kohlberg's coding system, despite the idiosyncratic and varying nature of the dilemmas recalled. Nevertheless, there was a couple of significant themes that could not be adequately handled by his approach. One was individuals' frequent focus on the moral relevance of psychological factors, practical considerations, and outcomes in handling moral problems. These arise in the context of real-life issues but are ignored or downscored in the context of hypothetical dilemmas. Any adequate theory of moral psychology must account for the complexity of real-life concerns in resolving moral conflicts. The other theme that was difficult for the Kohlbergian model to assimilate was individuals' reference to notions of religion, faith, and spirituality in dealing with real-life moral issues and conflicts. For many people, their moral framework and understanding is to some extent, if not entirely, embedded in their religion and faith. Our questioning of people regarding their domain classifications similarly revealed the complexity of understandings in this area – clearly calling for a more comprehensive examination of the various factors entailed in this relationship.

We were not only interested in people's reasoning about real-life moral conflicts, but also their feelings and motivations. The affective domain has been minimized by the cognitive-developmental tradition, but there is an increasing body of evidence pointing to its significance and to the need to understand its role in relation to cognition. Particularly noteworthy were the expressions of angst, confusion, anger, and pain in dealing with real-life conflicts. Actual dilemmas do not resemble the somewhat intellectual gaming of hypothetical dilemmas since real-life conflicts entail complex considerations in their interpretation and frequently there are no alternatives that are acceptable. Not surprisingly, then, many people stressed the validity of intuition in resolving these conflicts, despite acknowledging its fallibility. Obviously, in considering everyday morality, it is necessary to understand the role of the self – for it is the individual's sense of self that is at risk in moral action. Important factors for future research to consider in examining the role of the self in moral functioning include the centrality of morality in people's identity, the acquisition of a sense of responsibility to act, and the dynamism of integrity (the consistency of judgment and action) in personality organization. A better understanding of such factors would considerably further attempts to develop a more holistic conception of moral functioning.

Finally, we focused on people's conceptions of the moral domain through their identification of moral exemplars. In the cognitive-developmental approach, morally exemplary individuals are primarily identified by their complex and principled moral judgment. We believe that this represents a narrow description of moral maturity and that a renewed examination of moral character and virtue, affect and action, may help to provide a more full-bodied account of moral functioning – to put some flesh on bare bones. The moral exemplars identified by participants in our project were wide-ranging, including humanitarians and activists, but also (and quite frequently) family members and friends. It is noteworthy that so many of the exemplars named were not public figures, but rather individuals known personally, whose moral character and actions could be judged directly. Rarely were moral exemplars identified for their sophisticated moral reasoning; instead, their valued characteristics were more likely virtues such as compassion and self-sacrifice, integrity, and open-mindedness. These findings hold the promise of new vistas in our attempt to survey the moral landscape.

Notes

1. It is perhaps noteworthy that since 1988 Canada has had no legislation regulating abortion.
2. Because of low expected frequencies in some cells, the "impersonal" and "intrapsychic" categories were collapsed for a few analyses.
3. Because of low expected frequencies in some cells, the "both" and "neither" categories were collapsed for a few analyses.
4. It is noteworthy that the main challenger to Kohlberg's domination of the field, Gilligan, similarly emphasizes the ability to reason about moral conflicts.
5. In fairness to Kohlberg, it should be noted that the moral exemplars he most typically identified were not Supreme Court justices and moral philosophers, but rather people such as Martin Luther King, Mother Teresa, Mahatma Gandhi, and Socrates. However, what he emphasized about these moral exemplars was their principled moral judgment, not their virtues, character, emotions, and action.

References

Bakan, D. (1966). *The duality of human existence: An essay on psychology and religion.* Chicago: Rand McNally.

Bandura, A. (1991). Social cognitive theory of moral thought and action. In W. M. Kurtines & J. L. Gewirtz (Eds.), *Handbook of moral behavior and development* (Vol. 1, pp. 45–103). Hillsdale, NJ: Lawrence Erlbaum.

Baumrind, D. (1978). A dialectical materialist's perspective on knowing social reality. In W. Damon (Ed.), *New directions for child development: Moral development* (No. 2, pp. 61–82). San Francisco: Jossey-Bass.

Berkowitz, M. W., Guerra, N., & Nucci, L. (1991). Sociomoral development and drug and alcohol abuse. In W. M. Kurtines & J. L. Gewirtz (Eds.), *Handbook of moral behavior and development* (Vol. 3, pp. 35–53). Hillsdale, NJ: Lawrence Erlbaum.

Bibby, R. (1987). *Fragmented gods: The poverty and potential of religion in Canada.* Toronto: Irwin.

Blasi, A. (1983). Moral cognition and moral action: A theoretical perspective. *Developmental Review, 3,* 178–210.

Blasi, A. (1984). Moral identity: Its role in moral functioning. In W. M. Kurtines & J. L. Gewirtz (Eds.), *Morality, moral behavior, and moral development* (pp. 128–139). New York: Wiley.

Blasi, A. (1990). How should psychologists define morality? Or, the negative side effects of philosophy's influence on psychology. In T. Wren (Ed.), *The moral domain: Essays in the ongoing discussion between philosophy and the social sciences* (pp. 38–70). Cambridge, MA: MIT Press.

Blum, L. (1990). Universality and particularity. In D. Schrader (Ed.), *New directions for child development* (No. 47, pp. 59–69). San Francisco: Jossey-Bass.

Boyd, D. (1989). The character of moral education. In L. P. Nucci (Ed.), *Moral development and character education* (pp. 95–123). Berkeley, CA: McCutchan.

Boyes, M. C., & Walker, L. J. (1988). Implications of cultural diversity for the universality claims of Kohlberg's theory of moral reasoning. *Human Development, 31,* 44–59.

Brown, L. M. (Ed.). (1987). *A guide to reading narratives of moral conflict and choice for self and moral voice.* Unpublished manuscript, Harvard University Graduate School of Education GEHD Study Center, Cambridge, MA.

Colby, A., & Damon. W. (1992). *Some do care: Contemporary lives of moral commitment.* New York: Free Press.

Colby, A., & Kohlberg, L. (1987). *The measurement of moral judgment* (Vols. 1–2). Cambridge: Cambridge University Press.

Colby, A., Kohlberg, L., Gibbs, J., & Lieberman, M. (1983). A longitudinal study of moral judgment. *Monographs of the Society for Research in Child Development, 48* (1–2, Serial No. 200). Chicago: University of Chicago Press.

Darley, J. M. (1993). Research on morality: Possible approaches, actual approaches [Review of the *Handbook of Moral Behavior and Development*]. *Psychological Science, 4,* 353–357.

Dien, D. S. (1982). A Chinese perspective on Kohlberg's theory of moral development. *Developmental Review, 2,* 331–341.

Fernhout, H. (1989). Moral education as grounded in faith. *Journal of Moral Education, 18,* 186–198.

Flanagan, O. (1991). *Varieties of moral personality: Ethics and psychological realism.* Cambridge, MA: Harvard University Press.

Gilligan, C. (1982). *In a different voice: Psychological theory and women's development.* Cambridge, MA: Harvard University Press.

Gilligan, C., & Attanucci, J. (1988). Two moral orientations: Gender differences and similarities. *Merrill-Palmer Quarterly, 34,* 223–237.

Haan, N. (1977). *Coping and defending: Processes of self-environment organization.* New York: Academic Press.

Haan, N. Aerts, E., & Cooper, B. A. B. (1985). *On moral grounds: The search for practical morality.* New York: New York University Press.

Haidt, J., Koller, S. H., & Dias, M. G. (1993). Affect, culture, and morality, or is it wrong to eat your dog? *Journal of Personality and Social Psychology, 65,* 613–628.

Haste, H. (1990). Moral responsibility and moral commitment: The integration of affect and cognition. In T. Wren (Ed.), *The moral domain: Essays in the ongoing discussion between philosophy and the social sciences* (pp. 315–359). Cambridge, MA: MIT Press.

Kagan, J. (1993). The meanings of morality [Review of the *Handbook of Moral Behavior and Development*]. *Psychological Science, 4,* 353, 357–360.

Kohlberg. L. (1969). Stage and sequence: The cognitive-developmental approach to socialization. In D. A. Goslin (Ed.), *Handbook of socialization theory and research* (pp. 347–480). Chicago: Rand McNally.

Kohlberg. L. (1981). *Essays on moral development: Vol. 1. The philosophy of moral development.* San Francisco: Harper and Row.

Kohlberg. L. (1984). *Essays on moral development: Vol 2. The psychology of moral development.* San Francisco: Harper and Row.

Kohlberg, L. (1986). A current statement on some theoretical issues. In S. Modgil & C. Modgil (Eds.), *Lawrence Kohlberg: Consensus and controversy* (pp. 485–546). Philadelphia: Falmer.

Kohlberg, L., Boyd, D. R., & Levine, C. (1990). The return of Stage 6: Its principle and moral point of view. In T. Wren (Ed.), *The moral domain: Essays in the ongoing discussion between philosophy and the social sciences* (pp. 151–181). Cambridge, MA: MIT Press.

Kohlberg, L., & Candee, D. (1984). The relationship of moral judgment to moral action. In L. Kohlberg, *Essays on moral development: Vol. 2. The psychology of moral development* (pp. 498–581). San Francisco: Harper and Row.

Kohlberg, L., & Diessner, R. (1991). A cognitive-developmental approach to moral attachment. In J. L. Gewirtz & W. M. Kurtines (Eds.), *Intersections with attachment* (pp. 229–246). Hillsdale, NJ: Lawrence Erlbaum.

Kohlberg, L., Levine, C., & Hewer, A. (1983). *Moral stages: A current formulation and a response to critics.* Basel: Karger.

Linn, R. (1987). Moral disobedience during the Lebanon war: What can the cognitive-developmental approach learn from the experience of the Israeli soldiers? *Social Cognition, 5,* 383–402.

Lyons, N. P. (1983). Two perspectives: On self, relationships, and morality. *Harvard Educational Review, 53,* 125–145.

Matsuba, M. K., & Walker, L. J. (1993, November). *Understanding children's moral reasoning from adaptational styles.* Paper presented at the meeting of the Association for Moral Education, Tallahassee, FL.

Miller, J. G., & Luthar, S. (1989). Issues of interpersonal responsibility and accountability: A comparison of Indians' and Americans' moral judgments. *Social Cognition, 7,* 237–261.

Noddings, N. (1984). *Caring: A feminine approach to ethics and moral education.* Berkeley: University of California Press.

Nucci, L., & Turiel, E. (1993). God's word, religious rules, and their relation to Christian and Jewish children's concepts of morality. *Child Development, 64,* 1475–1491.

Rest, J. R. (1983). Morality. In J. H. Flavell & E. M. Markman (Eds.), *Handbook of child psychology: Cognitive development* (4th ed., Vol. 3, pp. 556–629). New York: Wiley.

Rest, J. R. (1986a). *Moral development: Advances in research and theory.* Westport, CT: Praeger.

Rest, J. R. (1986b). Moral research methodology. In S. Modgil & C. Modgil (Eds.), *Lawrence Kohlberg: Consensus and controversy* (pp. 455–469). Philadelphia: Falmer.

Shweder, R. A., & Haidt, J. (1993). The future of moral psychology: Truth, intuition, and the pluralist way [Review of the *Handbook of Moral Behavior and Development*]. *Psychological Science, 4,* 353, 360–365.

Simpson, E. L. (1974). Moral development research: A case study of scientific cultural bias. *Human Development, 17,* 81–106.

Tangney, J. P. (1991). Moral affect: The good, the bad, and the ugly. *Journal of Personality and Social Psychology, 61,* 598–607.

Thomas, L. (1993). Moral flourishing in an unjust world. *Journal of Moral Education, 22,* 83–96.

Trevethan, S. D., & Walker, L. J. (1989). Hypothetical versus real-life moral reasoning among psychopathic and delinquent youth. *Development and Psychopathology, 1,* 91–103.

Turiel, E. (1983). *The development of social knowledge: Morality and convention.* Cambridge: Cambridge University Press.

Turiel, E., Hildebrandt, C., & Wainryb, C. (1991). Judging social issues: Difficulties, inconsistencies, and consistencies. *Monographs of the Society for Research in Child Development, 56* (2, Serial No. 224). Chicago: University of Chicago Press.

Turiel, E., Killen, M., & Helwig, C. C. (1987). Morality: Its structure, functions, and vagaries. In J. Kagan & S. Lamb (Eds.), *The emergence of morality in young children* (pp. 155–243). Chicago: University of Chicago Press.

Walker, L. J. (1986). Cognitive processes in moral development. In G. L. Sapp (Ed.), *Handbook of moral development: Models, processes, techniques, and research* (pp. 109–145). Birmingham, AL: Religious Education Press.

Walker, L. J. (1988). The development of moral reasoning. *Annals of Child Development, 5,* 33–78.

Walker, L. J. (1991). Sex differences in moral reasoning. In W. M. Kurtines & J. L. Gewirtz (Eds.), *Handbook of moral behavior and development* (Vol. 2, pp. 333–364). Hillsdale, NJ: Lawrence Erlbaum.

Walker, L. J., de Vries, B., & Trevethan, S. D. (1987). Moral stages and moral orientations in real-life and hypothetical dilemmas. *Child Development, 58,* 842–858.

Walker, L. J., & Moran, T. J. (1991). Moral reasoning in a communist Chinese society. *Journal of Moral Education, 20,* 139–155.

Walker, L. J., & Taylor, J. H. (1991). Family interactions and the development of moral reasoning. *Child Development, 62,* 264–283.

Author index

409

Subject index

417